HARCOURT
·TROPHIES·

A HARCOURT READING/LANGUAGE ARTS PROGRAM

TIMELESS TREASURES

SENIOR AUTHORS
Isabel L. Beck ◆ Roger C. Farr ◆ Dorothy S. Strickland

AUTHORS
Alma Flor Ada ◆ Marcia Brechtel ◆ Margaret McKeown
Nancy Roser ◆ Hallie Kay Yopp

SENIOR CONSULTANT
Asa G. Hilliard III

CONSULTANTS
F. Isabel Campoy ◆ David A. Monti

Harcourt

Orlando   Boston   Dallas   Chicago   San Diego

Visit *The Learning Site!*

www.harcourtschool.com

Acknowledgments appear in the back of this book.

Printed in the United States of America

ISBN 0-15-339789-6

4 5 6 7 8 9 10   048   10 09 08 07 06 05

HARCOURT

· T R O P H I E S ·

A HARCOURT READING/LANGUAGE ARTS PROGRAM

TIMELESS TREASURES

Dear Reader,

You will find many kinds of treasures in this book. Some are ancient, like the artworks and artifacts found in the pharaohs' tombs. Some are modern, such as the iron gates sculpted by blacksmith Philip Simmons. Some are personal treasures, such as author Jerry Spinelli's trophy for winning a race. Others are living treasures, such as those found in the ocean depths by diver Sylvia Earle. Finally, there are the treasures of the heart. When a Danish family saves a Jewish friend during World War II, readers realize what a priceless treasure friendship is.

Books, stories, and poems themselves can be treasures, because they give meaning and enjoyment to our lives. We hope that **Timeless Treasures** will provide you with many types of reading experiences to treasure for years to come.

Sincerely,

The Authors

The Authors

PERSONAL BEST

CONTENTS

Using Reading Strategies...16

Theme Opener..18

Realistic Fiction/Social Studies 🌐
The Best School Year Ever...20
by Barbara Robinson • illustrated by Tom Newson

Focus Skill Narrative Elements

Realistic Fiction/Music 🎵
Yang the Eldest and His Odd Jobs...........................40
by Lensey Namioka • illustrated by Kees de Kiefte

Biography/Visual Arts
Pint-Size Picasso..56
by Kirsty Murray

Focus Skill Prefixes, Suffixes, and Roots

Autobiography/Physical Education ⚽
Knots in My Yo-yo String..64
by Jerry Spinelli • illustrated by Gary Davis and Kathy Lengyel

Poetry/Physical Education
From the Autograph Album...78
Anonymous

Good Sportsmanship...79
by Richard Armour • illustrated by Mike Gardner

Focus Skill Make Judgments

Reading
**Across
Texts**

Reading
**Across
Texts**

Short Story/Physical Education
The Marble Champ.. 84
by Gary Soto • illustrated by David Diaz

Magazine Article/Physical Education
It's Tiger Time!...100
from *Children's Digest*

Focus Skill Narrative Elements

Reading **Across** Texts

Realistic Fiction/Social Studies
Darnell Rock Reporting.....................................106
by Walter Dean Myers • illustrated by James Ransome

Poetry/Social Studies
Courage...124
by Naomi Shihab Nye • illustrated by Dan Yaccarino

Direction..125
by Alonzo Lopez • illustrated by Michael Luke

Focus Skill Prefixes, Suffixes, and Roots

Reading **Across** Texts

5

FRIENDS TO THE RESCUE

CONTENTS

Theme Opener...130

Historical Fiction/Social Studies
Number the Stars..132
by Lois Lowry • illustrated by Russ Wilson

Focus Skill Narrative Elements

Realistic Fiction/Social Studies
The Summer of the Swans...160
by Betsy Byars • illustrated by Lori Lohstoeter

Focus Skill Literary Devices

Realistic Fiction/Social Studies
Old Yeller..184
by Fred Gipson • illustrated by David Moreno

Reading
Across
Texts

Magazine Article/Social Studies
Puppies with a Purpose 200
from *National Geographic World*

Focus Skill Summarize and Paraphrase

Nonfiction/Science
Trapped by the Ice!..206
written and illustrated by Michael McCurdy

Reading Across Texts

Expository Nonfiction/Science
Antarctica..230
by Joyce Pope

Focus Skill Literary Devices

Expository Nonfiction/Science
Flood: Wrestling with the Mississippi..236
by Patricia Lauber

Focus Skill Summarize and Paraphrase

UNLOCKING THE PAST

CONTENTS

Theme Opener...258

Informational Text/Social Studies 🌐
The Stone Age News..260
by Fiona Macdonald

   Focus Skill Text Structure: Main Idea and Details

Expository Nonfiction/Social Studies 🌐
Ancient China..282
by Robert Nicholson and Claire Watts

Magazine Article/Social Studies
The Chinese Dynasties...298
from *Kids Discover*

   Focus Skill Graphic Aids

Reading Across Texts

Expository Nonfiction/Social Studies 🌐
Pyramids..304
from *Kids Discover*

   Focus Skill Graphic Aids

Expository Nonfiction/Social Studies

Look Into the Past: The Greeks 326

by A. Susan Williams

Look Into the Past: The Romans

by Peter Hicks

Focus Skill   Text Structure: Main Idea and Details

Play/Social Studies

The Skill of Pericles 350

by Paul T. Nolan • illustrated by David Scott Meier

Fables/Social Studies

Aesop's Fables 366

retold by Margaret Clark • illustrated by Charlotte Voake

Focus Skill   Prefixes, Suffixes, and Roots

Creative Solutions

CONTENTS

Theme Opener..372

Realistic Fiction/Science

My Side of the Mountain 374
by Jean Craighead George • illustrated by Allen Garns

Focus Skill Literary Devices

Reading
Across
Texts

Realistic Fiction/Performing Arts

Fall Secrets 392
by Candy Dawson Boyd • illustrated by Floyd Cooper

Magazine Article/Social Studies

Kids Did It! 408
from *National Geographic World*

Focus Skill Word Relationships

Nonfiction/Science

Girls Think of Everything.....................................414
by Catherine Thimmesh • illustrated by Melissa Sweet

Focus Skill Text Structure: Compare and Contrast

Realistic Fiction/Science

A Do-It-Yourself Project 438
by Anilú Bernardo • illustrated by Karen Blessen

Poem

Preface to *The Other Side* 456
by Angela Johnson • illustrated by Cornelius Von Wright

Focus Skill Text Structure: Compare and Contrast

Biography/Social Studies

Catching the Fire: Philip Simmons, Blacksmith 462
by Mary E. Lyons

Poem

The Road Not Taken 478
by Robert Frost

Focus Skill Word Relationships

Reading
Across
Texts

Reading
Across
Texts

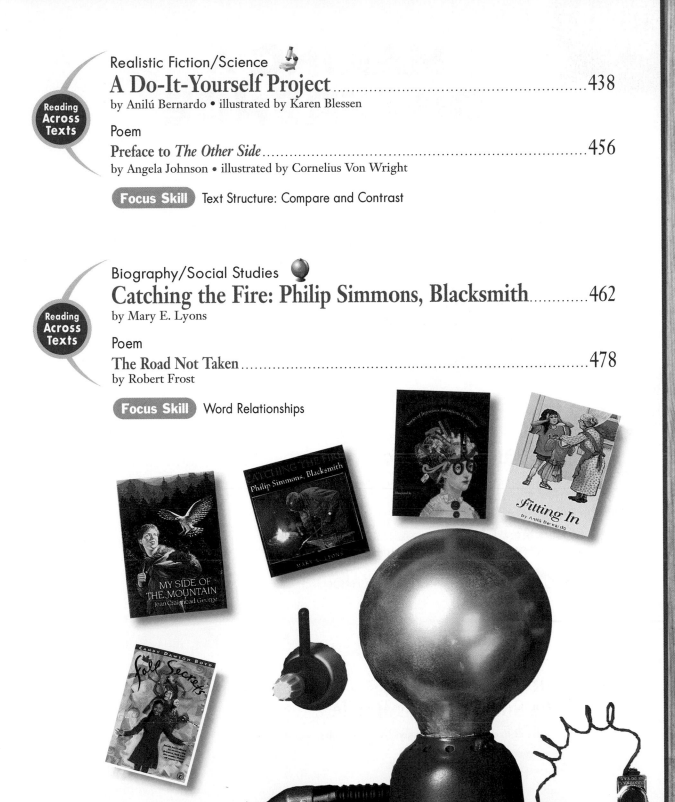

MAKING A DIFFERENCE

CONTENTS

Theme Opener..484

Short Story/Social Studies 🌐
Seventh Grade...486
by Gary Soto • illustrated by Stephanie Garcia

Focus Skill Draw Conclusions

Reading
Across
Texts

Realistic Fiction/Social Studies 🌐
My Name Is San Ho..506
by Jayne Pettit • illustrated by Amy Ning

Nonfiction/Social Studies
Dia's Story Cloth...522
by Dia Cha • stitched by Chue and Nhia Thao Cha

Focus Skill Author's Purpose and Perspective

Biography/Social Studies 🌐
Out of Darkness:
The Story of Louis Braille...530
by Russell Freedman • illustrated by Glenn Harrington

Focus Skill Draw Conclusions

Reading Across Texts

Play/Social Studies
Anne of Green Gables.................................548
by Lucy Maud Montgomery • adapted by Jamie Turner • illustrated by Mitchell Heinze

Recipe/Math
Tea Biscuits...570
by Carolyn Strom Collins and Christina Wyss Eriksson

Focus Skill Word Relationships

Reading Across Texts

Nonfiction/Social Studies
Cowboys: Roundup on an American Ranch.................576
by Joan Anderson • photographs by George Ancona

Poem
This Big Sky..592
by Pat Mora • illustrated by Steve Jenkins

Focus Skill Author's Purpose and Perspective

EXPANDING WORLDS

CONTENTS

Theme Opener 598

Reading Across Texts

Expository Nonfiction/Science
Atlas in the Round 600
by Keith Lye and Alastair Campbell

Myth/Science
A Strange Sled Race 618
retold by Vivian L. Thompson • illustrated by Leslie Wu

Focus Skill Text Structure: Cause and Effect

Reading Across Texts

Nonfiction/Science
Dive! My Adventures in the Deep Frontier 626
by Sylvia A. Earle

Magazine Article/Science
Some Like It Wet 638
from *Contact Kids*

Focus Skill Fact and Opinion

Reading Across Texts

Expository Nonfiction/Science
I Want to Be an Astronaut 644
by Stephanie Maze and Catherine O'Neill Grace

Magazine Article/Science
What It's Like Up There 658
by Karen Romano Young

Focus Skill Text Structure: Cause and Effect

Expository Nonfiction/Social Studies

CyberSurfer......666
by Nyla Ahmad • illustrated by Martha Newbigging

Nonfiction/Social Studies

In the Next Three Seconds 684
by Rowland Morgan • illustrated by Rod and Kira Josey

Focus Skill Fact and Opinion

Short Story/Science

The Case of the Shining Blue Planet......692
by Seymour Simon • illustrated by Leo Espinosa

Focus Skill Draw Conclusions

Writer's Handbook 711
Glossary 734
Index......746

Using Reading Strategies

A strategy is a plan for doing something well.

You probably already use some strategies as you read. For example, you may **look at the title and illustrations before you begin reading** a story. You may **think about what you want to find out while reading.** Using strategies like these can help you become a better reader.

Look at the list of strategies on page 17. You will learn about and use these strategies as you read the selections in this book. As you read, look back at the list to remind yourself of the **strategies good readers use.**

- Use Decoding/Phonics
- Make and Confirm Predictions
- Create Mental Images
- Self-Question
- Summarize

- Read Ahead
- Reread to Clarify
- Use Context to Confirm Meaning
- Use Text Structure and Format
- Adjust Reading Rate

Here are some ways to check your own comprehension:

✔ Make a copy of this list on a piece of construction paper shaped like a bookmark.

✔ Have it handy as you read.

✔ After reading, talk with a classmate about which strategies you used and why.

CONTENTS

The Best School Year Ever............... 20
by Barbara Robinson

Focus Skill Narrative Elements

**Yang the Eldest
and His Odd Jobs**....................40
by Lensey Namioka

Pint-Size Picasso......................56
by Kirsty Murray

Focus Skill Prefixes, Suffixes, and Roots

Knots in My Yo-yo String..................64
by Jerry Spinelli

From the Autograph Album...............78
Anonymous

Good Sportsmanship......................79
by Richard Armour

Focus Skill Make Judgments

The Marble Champ...................84
by Gary Soto

It's Tiger Time!...............................100
from *Children's Digest*

Focus Skill Narrative Elements

Darnell Rock Reporting..................106
by Walter Dean Myers

Courage......................124
by Naomi Shihab Nye

Direction......................125
by Alonzo Lopez

Focus Skill Prefixes, Suffixes, and Roots

▲ The Best School Year Ever

quality

compliment

inventive

resourceful

shrewd

enterprising

embarrassment

Vocabulary Power

In "The Best School Year Ever," the students in one sixth-grade class study an unusual topic. They study themselves.

What do you think is your best **quality**? What makes you the kind of person you are? Suppose you had to give yourself a **compliment**, or say something nice about yourself. What words could you use?

Are you **inventive**, or good at thinking of ways to solve problems? An inventive person might invent a new kind of sandwich or a better way to organize homework assignments.

Are you **resourceful**, or able to handle unexpected situations? Maybe you have helped someone out of a jam by your quick thinking.

Are you **shrewd**, or clever at understanding people and situations? Maybe you have shrewdly persuaded a family member to lend you something.

Are you **enterprising**, or creative and willing to take on challenges? Maybe you have ideas for projects or take the lead in school activities. Do you like to stand up before an audience, or does the spotlight make you turn red with **embarrassment**?

Vocabulary–Writing CONNECTION

Think about a special friend or relative. Write a paragraph describing what you feel is his or her best **quality**.

Genre

Realistic Fiction

Realistic fiction tells about characters and events that are like people and events in real life.

In this selection, look for

- **Characters that have feelings that real people have**

- **A setting that is familiar to most readers**

The Best School Year Ever

by **Barbara Robinson**

illustrated by **Tom Newson**

The students in Miss Kemp's sixth-grade class have had a year-long assignment: to think of at least one compliment for each of their classmates. Now they have each drawn a name, and on the last day of school, they must shower that person with compliments. Unfortunately, Beth draws the name of Imogene Herdman, a member of the rowdiest family of kids in town. How can Beth find anything positive to say about Imogene?

This year there was no big surprise about what we would do on the last day. It was up on the blackboard—Compliments for Classmates—and we had each drawn a name from a hat and had to think of more compliments for that one person.

"We've been thinking about this all year," Miss Kemp said. She probably knew that some kids had but most kids hadn't—but now everybody would think about it in a hurry. "And on the last day of school," she went on, "we're going to find out what we've learned about ourselves and each other."

courage

I had finally thought of a word for Albert. Once you get past thinking *fat* you can see that Albert's special quality is optimism, because Albert actually believes he will be thin someday, and says so. Another word could be *determination,* or even *courage.* There were lots of good words for Albert, so I really hoped I would draw his name.

I didn't. The name I drew was Imogene Herdman, and I had used up the one and only compliment I finally thought of for Imogene—*patriotic.*

"Patriotic?" my mother said. "What makes you think Imogene is especially patriotic?"

"When we do the Pledge of Allegiance," I said, "she always stands up."

"Everybody stands up," Charlie said. "If everybody sat down and *only* Imogene stood up, that would be patriotic."

"That would be brave," I said.

"Well, she would do that," Charlie said. "I mean, she would do whatever everybody else didn't do."

Would that make Imogene brave? I didn't really think so, but I had to have some more compliments, so I wrote it down—*patriotic, brave.*

Two days later I still had just *patriotic* and *brave* while other people had big long lists. I saw the bottom of Joanne Turner's list, sticking out of her notebook: "Cheerful, good sport, graceful, fair to everybody." I wondered who *that* was.

Maxine Cooper asked me how to spell *cooperative* and *enthusiastic,* so obviously she had a terrific list. Boomer must have drawn a boy's name, because all his compliments came right out of the Boy Scout Rules—*thrifty, clean, loyal.*

I kept my eye on Imogene as much as possible so if she did something good I wouldn't miss it, but it was so hard to tell, with her, what was good.

I thought it was good that she got Boyd Liggett's head out of the bike rack, but Mrs. Liggett didn't think so.

Mrs. Liggett said it was all the Herdmans' fault in the first place. "Ollie Herdman told Boyd to do it," she said, "and then that Gladys got him so scared and nervous that he couldn't get out, and then along came Imogene . . ."

I could understand how Boyd got his head *into* the bike rack—he's only in the first grade, plus he has a skinny head—but at first I didn't know why he couldn't get it *out.*

Then I saw why. It was his ears. Boyd's ears stuck right straight out from his head like handles, so his head and his ears were on one side of the bike rack and the rest of him was on the other side, and kids were hollering at him and telling him what to do. "Turn your head upside down!" somebody said, and somebody else told him to squint his eyes and squeeze his face together.

Boyd's sister Jolene tried to fold his ears and push them through but that didn't work, even one at a time. Then she wanted half of us to get in front of him and push and the other half to get in back and pull. "He got his head through there," she said. "There must be some way to get it back out."

I didn't think pushing and pulling was the way but Boyd looked ready to try anything.

Then Gladys Herdman really cheered him up. "Going to have to cut off your ears, Boyd," she said. "But maybe just one ear. Do you have a favorite one? That you like to hear out of?"

You could tell that he believed her. If you're in the first grade with your head stuck through the bike rack, this is the very thing you think will happen.

Several teachers heard Boyd yelling, "Don't cut my ears off!" and they went to tell Mr. Crabtree. Mr. Crabtree called

the fire department, and while he was doing that the kindergarten teacher stuck her head out the window and called to Boyd, "Don't you worry, they're coming to cut you loose."

But she didn't say who, or how, and Gladys told him they would probably leave a little bit of ear in case he ever had to wear glasses, so Boyd was a total wreck when Imogene came along.

She wanted to know how he got in there—in case she ever wanted to shove somebody else in the bike rack, probably—but Boyd was too hysterical to tell her, and nobody else knew for sure, so I guess she decided to get him loose first and find out later.

Imogene Scotch-taped his ears down and buttered his whole head with soft margarine from the lunchroom, and then she just pushed on his head—first one side and then the other—and it slid through.

Of course Boyd was a mess, with butter all over his eyes and ears and up his nose, so Jolene had to take him home. She made him walk way away from her and she told him, "As soon as you see Mother, you yell, 'I'm all right. I'm all right.'" She looked at him again. "You better tell her who you are, too."

Even so, Mrs. Liggett took one look and screamed and would have fainted, Jolene said, except she heard Boyd telling her that he was all right.

"What do you think of that?" Mother asked my father that night. "She buttered his head!"

"I think it was resourceful," my father said. "Messy, but resourceful."

"That's like a compliment, isn't it?" I asked my father. "It's good to be resourceful?"

"Certainly," he said. So I wrote that down, along with *patriotic* and *brave*.

I thought we would just hand in our compliment papers on the last day of school, but Alice thought Miss Kemp would read three or four out loud—"Some of the best ones," Alice said, meaning, of course, her own—and Boomer thought she would read the different compliments and we would have to guess the person. So when Miss Kemp said, "Now we're going to share these papers," it was no big surprise.

brave

28

But then she said, "I think we'll start with Boomer. LaVerne Morgan drew your name, Boomer. I want you to sit down in front of LaVerne and listen to what she says about you."

LaVerne squealed and Boomer turned two or three different shades of red and all over the room kids began to check their papers in case they would have to read out loud some big lie or, worse, some really personal compliment.

LaVerne said that Boomer was smart and good at sports—but not stuck up about it—and friendly, and two or three other normal things. "And I liked when you took the gerbil back to the kindergarten that time," she said, "in case they wanted to bury it. That was nice."

It *was* nice, I thought, and not everybody would have done it, either. To begin with, not everybody would have *picked up* the gerbil by what was left of its tail, let alone carry it all the way down the hall and down the stairs to the kindergarten room.

"Good, Boomer," I said when he came back to his seat—glad to get there, I guess, because he was all sweaty with embarrassment from being told nice things about himself face to face and in front of everybody.

Next came Eloise Albright and then Louella and then Junior Jacobs and then Miss Kemp said, "Let's hear about you, Beth. Joanne Turner drew your name."

I remembered Joanne Turner's paper—"Cheerful, good sport, graceful, fair to everybody." I had wondered who that was.

It was me.

"I know we weren't supposed to say things about how you look," Joanne said, "but I put down graceful anyway because I always notice how you stand up very straight and walk like some kind of dancer. I don't know if you can keep it up, but if you can I think people will always admire the way you stand and walk."

It was really hard, walking back to my seat now that I was famous for it—but I knew if I did it now, with everybody watching, I *could* probably keep it up for the rest of my life and, if Joanne was right, be admired forever. This made me feel strange and loose and light, like when you press your hands hard against the sides of a door, and

when you walk away your hands float up in the air all by themselves.

I was still feeling that way three people later when Miss Kemp said it was Imogene's turn.

"To do what?" Imogene said.

"To hear what Beth has to say about you. She drew your name."

Imogene gave me this dark, suspicious look. "No, I don't want to."

"You're going to hear *good* things, you know, Imogene," Miss Kemp said, but you could tell Miss Kemp wasn't too sure about that, and Imogene probably never *heard* any good things about herself, so she wasn't too sure, either.

"That's okay," I said. "I mean, if Imogene doesn't want to, I don't care."

This didn't work. I guess Miss Kemp was curious like everybody else. "Imogene Herdman!" Louella had just whispered. "That's whose name you drew? How could you think of compliments for Imogene Herdman?"

"Well, you had to think of *one*," I said. "We had to think of one compliment for everybody."

Louella rolled her eyes. "I said she was healthy. I didn't know anything else to say."

Louella wasn't the only one who wanted to hear my Imogene words. The whole room got very quiet and I was glad, now, that at the last minute I had looked up *resourceful* in the dictionary.

"I put down that you're patriotic," I told Imogene, "and brave and resourceful . . . and cunning and shrewd and creative, and enterprising and sharp and inventive. . ."

"Wait!" she yelled. "Wait a minute! Start over!"

Inventive

"Oh, honestly!" Alice put in. "You just copied that out of the dictionary! They're all the same thing!"

"And," I went on, ignoring Alice, "I think it was good that you got Boyd's head out of the bike rack."

"Oh, honestly!" Alice said again, but Miss Kemp shut her up.

Of course she didn't say, "Shut up, Alice"—she just said that no one could really comment on what anybody else said because it was very personal and individual. "That's how Beth sees Imogene," she said.

Actually, it wasn't. Alice was right about the words. I did copy them out of the dictionary so I wouldn't be the only person with three dumb compliments, and I didn't exactly connect them with Imogene, except *sharp* because of her knees and elbows which she used like weapons to leave you black and blue.

But now, suddenly, they all turned out to fit. Imogene *was* cunning and shrewd. She *was* inventive. Nobody else thought of buttering

Cunning

Boyd's head or washing their cat at the Laundromat. She was creative, if you count drawing pictures on Howard . . . and enterprising, if you count charging money to look at him. She was also powerful enough to keep everybody away from the teachers' room forever, and human enough to give Howard her blanket.

Imogene *was* all the things I said she was, and more, and they were good things to be—depending on who it was doing the inventing or the creating or the enterprising. If Imogene could keep it up, I thought, till she got to be civilized, if that ever happened, she could be almost anything she wanted to be in life.

She could be Imogene Herdman, President . . . or, of course, Imogene Herdman, Jailbird. It would be up to her.

At the end of the day Miss Kemp said, "Which was harder—to give compliments or to receive them?" and everyone agreed that it

Resourceful

was really uncomfortable to have somebody tell you, in public, about the best hidden parts of you. Alice, however, made this long, big-word speech about how it was harder for her to *give* compliments because she wanted to be very accurate and truthful, "and not make things up," she said, looking at me.

"I didn't make things up," I told her later, "except, maybe, brave. I don't know whether Imogene is brave."

"You made her sound like some wonderful person," Alice said, "and if that's not making things up, what is?"

When the bell rang everybody whooped out to get started on summer, but Imogene grabbed me in the hall, shoved a Magic Marker in my face, and told me to write the words on her arm.

"On your arm?" I said.

"That's where I keep notes," she said, and I could believe it because I could still see the remains of several messages—something pizza . . . big rat . . . get Gladys . . .

Get Gladys something? I wondered. No, probably just get Gladys.

There was only room for one word on her skinny arm, so Imogene picked *resourceful.* "It's the best one," she said. "I looked it up and I like it. It's way better than graceful, no offense." She turned her arm around, admiring the word. "I like it a lot."

Think and Respond

1 What does Beth learn about giving and receiving **compliments**?

2 How does the author use humor to tell the story? Support your answer with an example that you think is especially effective.

3 Beth and Alice disagree about whether Beth's compliments to Imogene are truthful. Which character do you agree with and why?

4 Would you like to hear compliments about yourself in front of your class? Why or why not?

5 What strategy helped you as you read the selection? Explain.

MEET THE AUTHOR

Barbara Robinson

Barbara Robinson introduced readers to the rowdy Herdman kids in her book *The Best Christmas Pageant Ever*. This popular novel was later made into a TV special and a play.

What if your teacher told you to think of compliments for Barbara Robinson? You might come up with these:

✓ **hardworking**—She has written many books and short stories for young readers.

✓ **funny**—Her books make people laugh.

✓ **interested in kids**—She often visits schools to meet with young people.

Now let's think of compliments for *The Best School Year Ever:*

✓ **zany**—The characters get themselves into outrageous situations.

✓ **original**—The Herdman kids are unusual and interesting characters.

✓ **realistic**—Beth's feelings about school and her relationships with her classmates are like those of real students.

Visit *The Learning Site!*
www.harcourtschool.com

Making Connections

Compare Texts

1 Why is this selection included in a theme called Personal Best?

2 Contrast Beth's feelings toward Imogene at the beginning of the selection with her feelings at the end.

3 Think about the way the illustrator shows Imogene Herdman. Do you picture her differently? Explain your answer.

4 Compare this selection with another fiction selection you have read that has a school setting.

5 Would you like to read the rest of the novel from which this selection was taken? Why or why not?

Write a Paragraph That Explains

Write a paragraph in which you give yourself one or more compliments. You may use words like those in "The Best School Year Ever," or you may tell about things that you do well. Use a web to plan your paragraph.

Writing CONNECTION

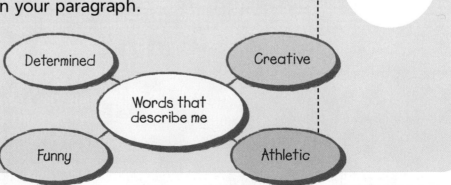

Perform a Dramatic Skit

Work with two or three classmates to present a skit in class. Choose a scene from "The Best School Year Ever." Decide which character each of you will be. You can make up your own dialogue for the characters in addition to using dialogue from the story.

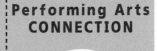

Develop a Chart

Use your social studies textbook or a biography to research a famous person in history. Make a two-column chart to list the person's traits. In the left column, write adjectives that describe him or her. On the right, provide evidence for each adjective you choose.

Julius Caesar	
Powerful	Dictator of Rome
Sympathetic	Made laws to help the poor

Narrative Elements (Focus Skill)

A story's **theme** is the main message that the author wants you to take away from the reading. Often, it relates to real life in some way. What do you think is the theme of "The Best School Year Ever"? You should consider all that you know about a story to identify its theme.

Setting (time and place)	The last day of school in Miss Kemp's sixth-grade classroom
Problem	Beth is assigned to find compliments for the rowdiest student in the class.
Characters' Actions	Miss Kemp—asks students to think of compliments for each other Imogene—behaves in a way that makes it hard for students to find compliments for her Beth—uses creative ways to find compliments for Imogene

The author may give other clues to help you identify the theme. For example, why do you think Imogene is the focus of the selection? The author probably chose Imogene to show that Beth could find compliments even for a classmate she didn't particularly like. If you apply the author's idea to real life, you will have identified the theme of the story: Everyone has positive traits.

Visit *The Learning Site!*
www.harcourtschool.com

See *Skills* and *Activities*

Test Prep
Narrative Elements

▶ **Read the passage. Then answer the questions.**

> Maria looked nervously around the classroom. It was her first day in a new school. Her teacher had been very helpful, but Maria wasn't sure how to make friends with the other students. All of her classmates seemed to have known each other for years. Suddenly, another student tapped Maria on the shoulder. "My name is Laurie," she said. "You can share my history book. I know how it feels to be the new student."

1. **What problem does Maria face?**

   A She lost her history book.

   B She doesn't know how to make friends.

   C None of the students like her.

   D She is nervous about meeting her teacher.

Eliminate the choices that cannot be supported by the passage. For example, did it say that none of the students liked Maria?

2. **The theme of this passage is that—**

   F it's fun to be a new student

   G you must always be prepared for class

   H you must never be late for class

   J other people can understand your feelings

What message about real life does the writer want you to take from this passage?

▲ Yang the Eldest and His Odd Jobs

novelty

arcade

vendors

unaccompanied

flourish

sulkiness

hilarious

Vocabulary Power

In the next selection, a musician needs money for a new violin. Saving enough money to buy something can be a big problem. Sometimes the solution is just outside your window.

Market Fair Opens

The jugglers at the Market Fair are a real **novelty**. It's the first time anyone has performed here. The jugglers help to attract buyers to the outdoor shops in the nearby **arcade**. All the **vendors** there are trying to sell products to the people in the audience.

Music Students Perform

The voice students from the Washington Avenue School sang **unaccompanied** by a pianist during their outdoor performance on Saturday. They ended their song with a real **flourish** when they held a long high note without taking a breath. When they finished, dance students from the school performed for the crowd.

Village Street Fair a Success!

If you were in a bad mood, your **sulkiness** would have disappeared at the Village Street Fair. The clowns were so funny, children and adults laughed at their **hilarious** performance. They will certainly be invited back to perform at next year's fair.

Vocabulary-Writing CONNECTION

There are many new and interesting ways to earn money. Think of a job you consider to be a **novelty**. Create a list with reasons why you feel it is interesting.

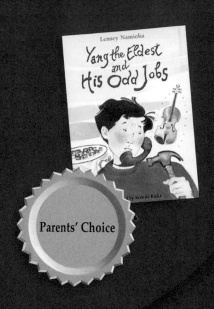

Genre

Realistic Fiction

Realistic fiction tells about characters and events that are like people and events in real life.

In this selection, look for

- A plot with a beginning, a middle, and an ending
- A main character who overcomes a challenge
- Descriptive language

Eldest Brother, of the musical Yang family, hopes to become a famous violinist someday, but first he needs a new violin to replace the one he brought with him from China. He has his eye on a beautiful, handcrafted violin, but it is expensive. Eldest Brother, who has never worked before, sets out to make the money to buy it. Fortunately for him, Fourth Brother and Third Sister are eager to help out.

Yang the Eldest and His Odd Jobs

by Lensey Namioka

illustrated by Kees de Kiefte

I had always admired Eldest Brother for his strength. I had seen him fearlessly climb a tall tree to rescue our cat, Rita. He could play a fiendishly hard piece of music for hours, repeating it over and over again until he got it absolutely perfect. There seemed to be nothing he couldn't do. But an evening of baby-sitting the Schultzes had drained his strength and aged him. His shoulders drooped, and he plodded upstairs like an old man. In real time it might take him three years to earn enough for a decent violin, but it would feel like fifty years.

"I've got the perfect job for Eldest Brother!" said Fourth Brother the next day. "Mrs. Conner took me and Matthew to Pike Place Market, and we saw some musicians playing on the sidewalk. They were making good money!"

I had been to Pike Place Market before. It's popular with both Seattle people and tourists. In the covered arcade of the market, there are colorful stalls where farmers sell vegetables, fruit, and flowers. There are also shops selling fish, sausages, and other fresh meats. In addition, artists come to the market to sell pictures, sculptures, and other things they made themselves. The stalls and the cheerful chatter of the vendors reminded me of the open-air markets in China.

"I don't remember musicians at Pike Place Market," I said. "I only saw an organ grinder with a monkey. You don't expect Eldest Brother to play a hand organ, do you? Besides, where would we get a monkey?"

"I can always hop up and down, and pass a tin cup around," laughed Fourth Brother. "But seriously, Matthew and I saw a violinist and a flutist playing duets. They had their instrument cases open on the ground, and people were throwing money in."

Somehow I didn't like the idea of Eldest Brother playing in the street, with people throwing coins into his violin case. "It sounds almost like begging."

"It's not begging!" protested Fourth Brother. "He'd be earning

money by playing music for people to enjoy. It's no different from playing in a concert that people buy tickets to hear."

He had a point. "And you think Eldest Brother might make real money this way?" I asked.

"The two kids we saw got a whole bunch of dollar bills, and maybe a few fives," said Fourth Brother. "And they weren't even very good. I bet Eldest Brother could make a lot more."

Maybe it was worth a try. When I mentioned playing at Pike Place Market to Eldest Brother, he reacted the way I had at first. "It's like begging!" he said, looking offended. "I need money, but not that badly!"

I used Fourth Brother's argument. "It's not begging. It's more like an outdoor concert, since you'll be performing, not passing a hat around. People who like your playing should be glad to pay."

As Eldest Brother still hesitated, I added, "Instead of changing diapers and heating bottles, you'll be doing something you love: playing the violin!"

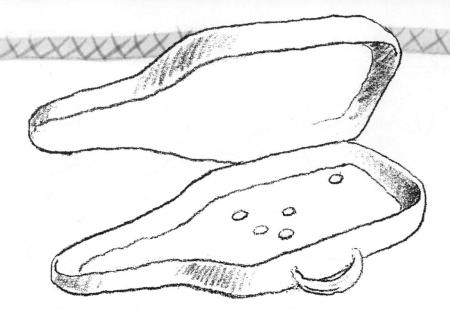

Eldest Brother finally came around. "All right, all right, I'll give it a try. What have I got to lose, except my dignity?"

Next day, Eldest Brother and I took the bus to Pike Place Market. It was a weekday, and there weren't as many tourists as there are on weekends. We saw a man twisting a couple of long balloons into the shape of a dog, and after making barking sounds, he managed to sell the balloon dog to a little boy.

Eldest Brother frowned. "Does this mean I have to bark like a dog to attract an audience?"

I tried to put him in a good mood, and music was the thing that always worked best. "Why don't you just start playing?"

Eldest Brother opened his violin case and took out his instrument. As I had expected, once he started playing his sulkiness disappeared. He had chosen a Telemann unaccompanied sonata, a very hard piece that needed all his concentration. For him, the other people on the sidewalk became completely invisible.

I looked around. It seemed that Eldest Brother was invisible to the other people, as well. They walked past us and went about their business of buying fruit, vegetables, flowers, and embroidered aprons.

True, one young girl stopped and listened for a bit and put a quarter in Eldest Brother's violin case, but then she ran off. The balloon seller was attracting more attention.

I decided to investigate the rest of the market. I had to walk almost the length of the arcade before I saw any musicians. First I heard some piping sounds. Then I saw them: two recorder players doing "Stars and Stripes Forever."

This piece is usually played by a big, brassy marching band, and hearing it played on these delicate wooden instruments was hilarious. That must have been what the players intended. A small crowd had gathered, and at the end, everyone laughed and clapped. The two teenage players, a boy and a girl, grinned broadly and made elaborate bows to the audience. The secret, it seemed, was to put on a funny act.

I put some money in a little box the players had, and I took a quick peek. There wasn't much in it, just a few coins. This didn't look like a promising way to make serious money.

I went back to Eldest Brother. He had finally attracted an audience: a couple of tourists with their arms full of flowers and Seattle souvenirs. They listened to the end of the sonata and applauded as well as they could. As the husband held the flowers, the wife opened her purse. After a struggle, she managed to fish out a dollar bill. It turned out to be the biggest piece of money Eldest Brother received that day.

But Eldest Brother looked cheerful enough. After putting away his violin, he went over to listen to the two recorder players. He burst out laughing when they launched into the opening movement of Beethoven's Fifth Symphony. Afterwards he chatted with them. I don't often see him talk with other people his age. We had always assumed he was too wrapped up in his music to care about making friends. For the first time, I began to wonder whether he was ever lonely.

When we returned from our visit to Pike Place Market, Fourth Brother asked how we did. I told him that we'd have to think of something else. "There weren't enough people there, so it would take a long time to make much money."

"Those two recorder players suggested playing at a street fair where there are mobs of people," Eldest Brother said. "They were able to make a lot more at some of those."

"Is there a street fair coming up soon?" I asked.

"Hey, there's one next weekend in Fremont!" said Fourth Brother.

On Saturday we set off for the Fremont street fair. We were lucky with the weather. In Seattle, summer is the driest season, but that doesn't mean we can always count on the sun. On the day of the street fair, however, the sky was cloudless.

Fourth Brother and I went with Eldest Brother to the fair, to give him moral support. By the time we got to the Fremont area of town, it was getting warm, and the crowd was thick.

On both sides of the street I saw colorful booths where artists were selling their paintings, drawings, photographs, ceramics, jewelry, embroidered shirts, stuffed animals, candles. . . . Wonderful smells floated up from the food stalls: shish kebab, stir-fried noodles, garlic sausages. . . .

I was so fascinated that I almost forgot why we had come. A beautiful string of beads tempted me, and I started to reach for my wallet. The thought of money reminded me that our purpose here was to *make* money, not *spend* it. It was time for Eldest Brother to start playing and earning.

We had trouble finding a space for him to set up his music stand. Even elbow room was limited ("elbow room" is one of my favorite American expressions). We finally found a small open area near the canal, where the crowd was thinner and a nice breeze came from the water.

"With all this noise, I don't know if anyone can hear a note," muttered Eldest Brother, as he unfolded his stand and placed his sheet music on it. The music promptly blew away.

Fourth Brother was fast, and he caught the music before it could fly into the canal. He was also prepared for the wind. He brought out two clothespins from his pocket and pinned the music back on the stand. We were ready for business.

Eldest Brother tuned his fiddle and grimaced when he heard the buzzing sound. But there was plenty of buzzing from the crowd all around us, anyway. He chose one of his favorite pieces—an unaccompanied sonata by Bach—and began to play. It was so beautiful that I closed my eyes in order to absorb the music. All the distracting noises around us seemed to retreat into the distance.

"Nobody is paying any attention," whispered Fourth Brother.

I opened my eyes and looked. He was right: The crowd pretty much ignored us. A few people glanced briefly at Eldest Brother, but most of them just went by without even turning their heads.

A little distance away, a juggler was throwing around three lit torches. His face was dead white, except for his bright-red lips and the two-inch black lashes painted around his eyes. As he juggled, he cracked jokes, but I found his dead-white face and red lips a little scary. His audience seemed to find him funny, though. Maybe Eldest Brother should try wearing makeup?

"Eldest Brother," I hissed, "I think you'll have to play something faster and louder!"

It took a few moments for Eldest Brother to cut himself off from Bach. He finally blinked and looked at me. "What was that you said?"

I pointed to the juggler and the crowd around him. "To attract people's attention, you'll have to play something a lot more showy."

He understood. In his school orchestra, the conductor knew which pieces would jar the audience awake. Looking through his music, Eldest Brother took out a fast and furious Irish jig.

"Make it nice and loud," I said to him.

Eldest Brother nodded. He threw himself into the piece, and he swayed and stomped to the music. This time he managed to stop some passersby in their tracks. Of course it helped that the juggler had stopped and gone to a booth to get himself a drink.

Eldest Brother ended the piece with a flourish of his bow in the air. Fourth Brother and I led the applause, and quite a few people joined us. A little girl toddled up unsteadily with a dollar bill that her mother had handed her. Very slowly and carefully, she placed it in Eldest Brother's violin case. Then she turned around and gave him a brilliant smile. Everybody laughed. Several other people came up and added more money.

As Eldest Brother tuned his fiddle and rubbed rosin in his bow, I took a peek at our take: several ones and a five, and some quarters. There was even a penny. Whoever threw that in was either pretty hard up, or hated Irish jigs. You can't win every time.

Now that he knew what sort of music attracted the crowd, Eldest Brother lost no time launching into a couple of other fast and furious pieces. The crowd grew, and so did the pile of money in the violin case. This was a lot better than Pike Place Market.

For a change of pace, Eldest Brother also played some lively Chinese folk tunes. When he started "The Flower Drum Song," I found an empty plastic ice-cream bucket, turned it upside down, and pounded on it like a drum as accompaniment. The audience liked that, and more money poured in.

We had to take a break after two more pieces. The day was getting pretty hot, and Fourth Brother offered to get us some drinks. He didn't come back for a long time, so Eldest Brother decided to start playing again. But strangely enough, he could no longer attract a good crowd. Even a dazzling capriccio by Paganini drew only four listeners.

Fourth Brother came back finally with three lemonades. "Where were you?" I asked him. "We're dying of thirst!"

"I was listening to our competition," he said. "Do you hear that?"

The sound of a violin floated toward us along the canal. I listened to a few measures of Mozart. It wasn't the most exciting performance I'd ever heard, but at least all the notes were there. "That doesn't sound like much competition," I said.

"She's got a big crowd, though," said Fourth Brother. "I think you'd better take a look."

I followed him toward the sound of the music. As we got closer, the crowd got thicker. Then I saw the performer and knew why we couldn't compete. The violinist was a little girl around four years old. She had a huge mop of golden curls and wore a pink dress trimmed all over with lace.

"We've got problems," I muttered. Eldest Brother didn't stand a chance against a competitor like that.

"You know, she's not too bad," said Eldest Brother, who had come up with his fiddle in his hands. "I rather like her phrasing."

I listened more closely, and decided he was right. The girl was too timid to put much expression into her playing, but she seemed to know what Mozart was about.

She did have trouble with one passage, though. She couldn't seem to manage the ornament—the little twiddly bit. Suddenly I heard the phrase played behind me. Eldest Brother couldn't resist showing the girl how the passage should sound.

The girl whipped around and stared. Then she picked up her bow and played the passage again. "Like this?" she asked.

"Not quite," said Eldest Brother. He played the same phrase, more slowly.

The girl nodded and tried again, and this time she got it right. She continued with the piece, and Eldest Brother joined her by playing an upper part that he made up on the spot. The girl's father, who was standing nearby, frowned at us. Apparently he felt that Eldest Brother was trying to force himself into the act.

But the crowd liked the duet. At the end of the piece, there was clapping and even some whistling. Money poured into the girl's little violin case. Her father beamed and came up to us. "Hey, Lisa's got herself a free violin lesson here."

"She's not bad," Eldest Brother said, and smiled at the girl.

The father looked thoughtfully at the heap of money in his

daughter's violin case. His eyes narrowed as he calculated. "Say, maybe the two of you could do a joint act. We could split the take fifty-fifty, and we'd still wind up ahead."

Eldest Brother looked startled. "Well . . ."

"Why don't you join her?" I said to him.

"Yeah, that's a good idea," said Fourth Brother.

So Eldest Brother joined the little girl in pink, and they played several more duets. He stopped a few times to point out how she could improve some passage or another. The crowd seemed to like that.

The father was delighted with their success. "It must be the novelty. People never saw a public music lesson before."

Personally, I'd pay money to *avoid* having to listen to a music lesson. But I saw his point. Lisa, the little girl, was genuinely musical, and it was very satisfying to hear her getting even better.

"You know, I've taken Lisa to several street fairs," continued the father, "but this is the most we've ever made."

Eldest Brother wasn't doing badly either, I thought.

Think and Respond

1. How does Eldest Brother's family try to help him solve his problem?

2. What does the author do to bring to life the market **arcade** and the street fair?

3. How would this story be different if it were told by Eldest Brother rather than his sister?

4. Eldest Brother is worried about losing his dignity if he plays for money. Do you think he does lose his dignity? Explain your answer.

5. Tell how a reading strategy, such as the strategy of creating mental images, helped you understand what you read.

♫

Meet the Author
Lensey Namioka

When she was only eight years old, Lensey Namioka wrote her first book, *Princess with the Bamboo Sword.* "I wrote my book on pieces of scratch paper and sewed them together with thread," she recalls. As an adult, Namioka has written more than 20 books, many of them award-winning.

Before moving to the United States at age nine, Namioka lived in Beijing, China, with her parents. Her father made up her first name, Lensey, based on a Chinese phonetic system he helped to create. She might be the only one in the world with her first name, thanks to her inventive father.

Namioka's personal experiences in adjusting to life as a Chinese American have influenced her writings about the Yangs, a fictional family that emigrated from China to the United States. "I have written stories about what it's like to move to a new country and learn a new language," she said.

Like the Yang family, Namioka lives in Seattle, Washington, with her family. When she's not writing, she keeps herself busy with music.

Lensey Namioka

**Visit *The Learning Site!*
www.harcourtschool.com**

Pint-Size Picasso

by Kirsty Murray

Alexandra was bored. She lay on the sofa in the living room and picked at a loose thread on one of the cushions. Her mom looked in around the door and frowned at the sight of her miserable four-year-old daughter.

"Alexandra, why don't you go outside and play? It's such a nice sunny day out there—why do you have to lie there and sulk?"

"I want my coloring books back," said Alexandra, pushing her blond hair out of her eyes and glaring at her mother.

"Alexandra, I told you before, I'm not buying any more coloring books for you. You spend too much time with them. You need to learn to do other things, too."

"I want my crayons," she shouted.

"Go out and play, darling," replied her mother.

"I don't want to play, Mama. I want to draw."

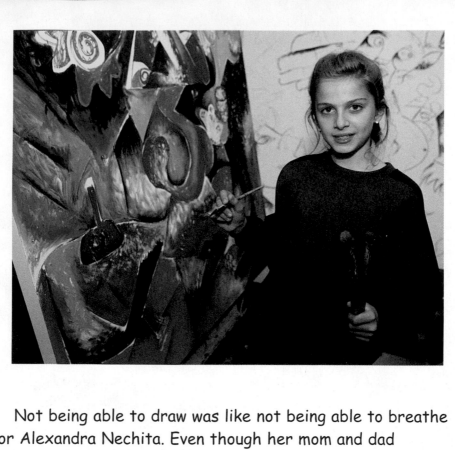

Not being able to draw was like not being able to breathe for Alexandra Nechita. Even though her mom and dad stopped buying her coloring books, Alexandra wasn't going to give up her passion. When she finally got the crayons back, she took to drawing her own pictures on the back of computer paper that her mom brought home from work.

Alexandra Nechita was destined to be a painting prodigy. She was born in Romania on August 27, 1985, but when she was one year old her parents immigrated to America. They settled in a little bungalow in Los Angeles, California.

When Alexandra was two, her parents bought her first set of crayons. She was using watercolor paints by the time she was five. Alexandra could draw and paint for hours without stopping. At seven, she moved on to painting in oils and acrylics on real canvas. Her parents bought her what she needed, but sometimes they wished she wouldn't use quite as much color in the lively pictures she produced—she was costing them a fortune in materials. They set aside a little area for her to use as a studio, but the bungalow began to fill up with her work.

When she was eight, they enrolled her in art classes, but, after looking at her work, the teacher realized Alexandra had a unique talent that she was better off developing by herself, and sent her home again.

The bungalow was getting so crowded that her parents decided to exhibit Alexandra's work in local libraries. Soon her first picture sold for $50.

Eventually, an artist's agent spotted one of her paintings and was impressed. When he was told that the painter was only eight years old, he thought it was a hoax and refused to believe it. He tracked down the Nechita family and asked if he could watch Alexandra at work. After watching her paint for a couple of hours he realized Alexandra's gift was both genuine and unique. He decided to promote the young prodigy.

On April 1, 1994—the day she became an American citizen—Alexandra had her first commercial exhibition. She was still only eight years old.

By the time she was 11, Alexandra had earned more than $5 million from the sale of her artwork. She was dubbed a "Pint-Size Picasso" by some of her fans, and art collectors around the world competed to buy up her work. Some of her paintings now sell for more than $100,000!

Alexandra has produced hundreds of paintings, and her work is in demand all over the world. She says she'd still spend all her time painting, even if people only paid her $1 for what she does. She does it because she loves to paint—she has to paint. That's what being a superstar means—absolute dedication to what you do.

THINK AND RESPOND

Why do you think the agent at first did not believe Alexandra's age?

Making Connections

Compare Texts

1 What does Eldest Brother discover about himself in this selection?

2 Compare how Eldest Brother feels about earning money at the beginning of the selection with how he feels at the end.

3 How was your purpose for reading the fiction story "Yang the Eldest and His Odd Jobs" different from your purpose for reading the article "Pint-Size Picasso"?

4 Compare Eldest Brother's and Alexandra's feelings about their artistic gifts.

5 If you could choose to be a musician or a painter, which would you choose? Why?

Write a Diary Entry

Eldest Brother is changing through his experiences at the market and the street fair. Write a diary entry in which Eldest Brother expresses his feelings about becoming a street musician to make the money for a new violin. Use time order to organize your ideas.

Writing CONNECTION

Make a Chart

Social Studies/Math
CONNECTION

The outdoor market reminds Third Sister of open-air markets in China, where merchants still use the abacus. The abacus is a counting device invented in ancient China. Research the history of the abacus. Record your information on a K-W-L chart.

K	W	L
What I Know	What I Want to Know	What I Learned

Listen to Violin Music

Language Arts/Music
CONNECTION

Eldest Brother plays music written for the violin by Bach, Mozart, Telemann, and Paganini. Listen to a cassette or CD recording of violin music by one of these composers. With a partner, talk about how listening to the music adds to your understanding of the selection.

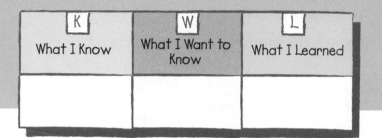

Prefixes, Suffixes, and Roots

Focus Skill

You can figure out the meaning of many words by understanding the meaning of the word parts. **Prefixes**, **suffixes**, and **roots** are word parts that carry meaning. One root, the basic part of a word, can unlock the meaning of many words. Look at how prefixes and suffixes can be added to the root *struct*. Knowing that *struct* means "build" can help you define other words.

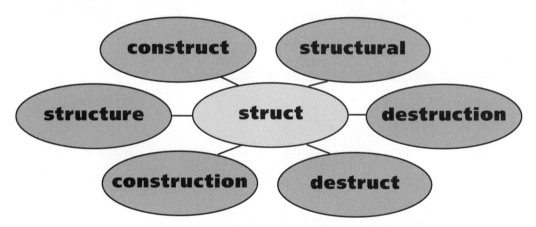

construct   structural
structure   **struct**   destruction
construction   destruct

Many English words have roots that were borrowed from the Greek and Latin languages. The chart below shows some common roots. Notice that a word may have more than one root.

Example Word	Root	Meaning of Root	Language of Origin
biology	bio ology	life study of	Greek Greek
geography	geo graph	earth write	Greek Greek
attract	trac/tract	pull	Latin
mission	miss/mit	send	Latin

Visit *The Learning Site!*
www.harcourtschool.com

See *Skills* and *Activities*

Test Prep

Prefixes, Suffixes, and Roots

▶ **Read the passage. Then answer the questions.**

> As soon as Josh comes home from school each day, he practices the piano for an hour. His music is so important to him that nothing can distract him. Even his baby brother's crying doesn't bother him. Josh's piano teacher, Mr. Gomez, is also a professor at the university, where he teaches musicology. Sometimes Mr. Gomez tells Josh about the history of the piano music that he is learning to play.

1. **In this passage, what does the word *distract* mean?**

   A without pulling

   B the opposite of *pull*

   C draw attention toward something

   D pull attention from something

Tip

Combine what you know about the prefix *dis-* and the root *tract*. Be sure your answer makes sense in the sentence.

2. **What is the meaning of the word *musicology* in this passage?**

   F modern music

   G musical instrument

   H study of music

   J famous musicians

Tip

You know what the word *music* means. Use the root *ology* to figure out what *musicology* means.

▲ Knots in My
Yo-yo String

Vocabulary Power

When he was a child, author Jerry Spinelli loved sports. Playing shortstop in Little League or running in a big race gave him the greatest feeling in the world. It also taught him that sports can be about a lot more than winning or losing.

favored

immune

peak

glare

trotted

console

memento

STARS WIN CHAMPIONSHIP

The Stars won the Little League championship last night, 10–0. The Stars were **favored** to win the game because of their great hitting. They have seemed **immune** to failure all year, winning ten out of ten games! During last night's game, the Stars seemed to be at the **peak**, or high point, of their skills. Their opponents, the Braves, could only **glare** at each other in angry silence as the score went up and up.

WILLIAMS FIRST IN 100-YARD DASH

Kevin Williams, a student at Moorestown School, **trotted** to the starting line as if he were about to jog slowly around the track. Then the whistle blew and the race began. Williams sprinted into the lead in the 100-yard dash and never looked back. Afterward, the other runners had to **console** themselves with talk of "next time" while Williams

received his trophy. He lifted the trophy high and then took it home as a **memento** of his day of triumph.

Vocabulary–Writing CONNECTION

A memento can be anything from a trophy sitting on a shelf to a card in a scrapbook. Describe a memento you have saved. Tell what special time or event it reminds you of.

Knots
in My
Yo-yo
String

The Autobiography of a Kid

Spinelli

Award-Winning
Author

Genre

Autobiography

An autobiography is a person's story of his or her own life.

In this selection, look for

- The author's personal thoughts and feelings

- First-person point of view

As a kid growing up in the 1950s, Jerry Spinelli explored the neighborhoods, fields, and salamander-filled creek of Norristown, Pennsylvania. He played games with his friends all summer long. One particular summer, he discovered that although he knew all about sports, he still had a lot to learn.

ERNIE BAN

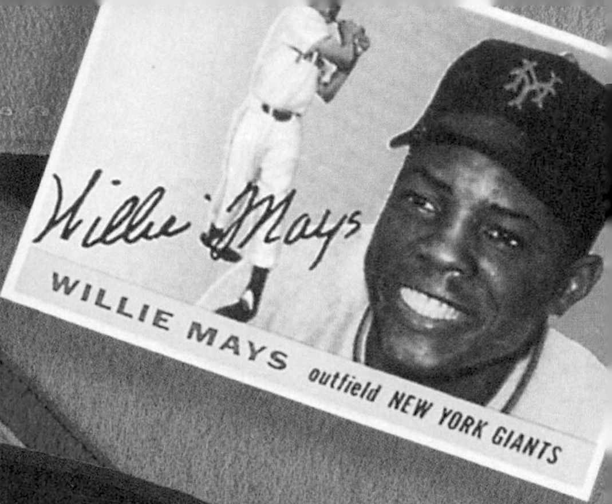

KNOTS IN MY Yo-yo String

by Jerry Spinelli

illustrated by
Gary Davis
and **Kathy Lengyel**

In a green metal box in a bedroom closet, tucked into a fuzzy gray cotton pouch, lies the most cherished memento of my grade-school days. It is a gold-plated medal no bigger than a postage stamp. Inscribed on the back are the words "50-YARD DASH—CHAMPION."

The medal came from the only official race I ever participated in. There were many unofficial ones . . .

"Race you to the store!"

"Last one in's a monkey!"

"Ready . . . Set . . . Go!"

Like kids the world over, we raced to determine the fastest. In the early 1950s on the 800 block of George Street in the West End of Norristown, Pennsylvania, that was me. I was usually the winner, and never the monkey.

I reached my peak at the age of twelve. That summer I led the Norristown Little League in stolen bases. In an all-star playoff game I did something practically unheard of: I was safe at first base on a ground ball to the pitcher.

Some days I pulled my sneaker laces extra tight and went down to the railroad tracks. The cinders there had the feel of a running track. I measured off fifty or a hundred yards and sprinted the distance, timing myself with my father's stopwatch. Sometimes, heading back to the starting line, I tried to see how fast I could run on the railroad ties. Sometimes I ran on the rail.

It was during that year that I won my medal. I represented Hartranft in the fifty-yard dash at the annual track-and-field meet for the Norristown grade schools. The meet was held at Roosevelt Field, where the high school track and football teams played.

Favored to win the race was Laverne Dixon of Gotwals Elementary. "Froggy," as he was known to everyone but his teachers, had won the fifty-yard dash the year before

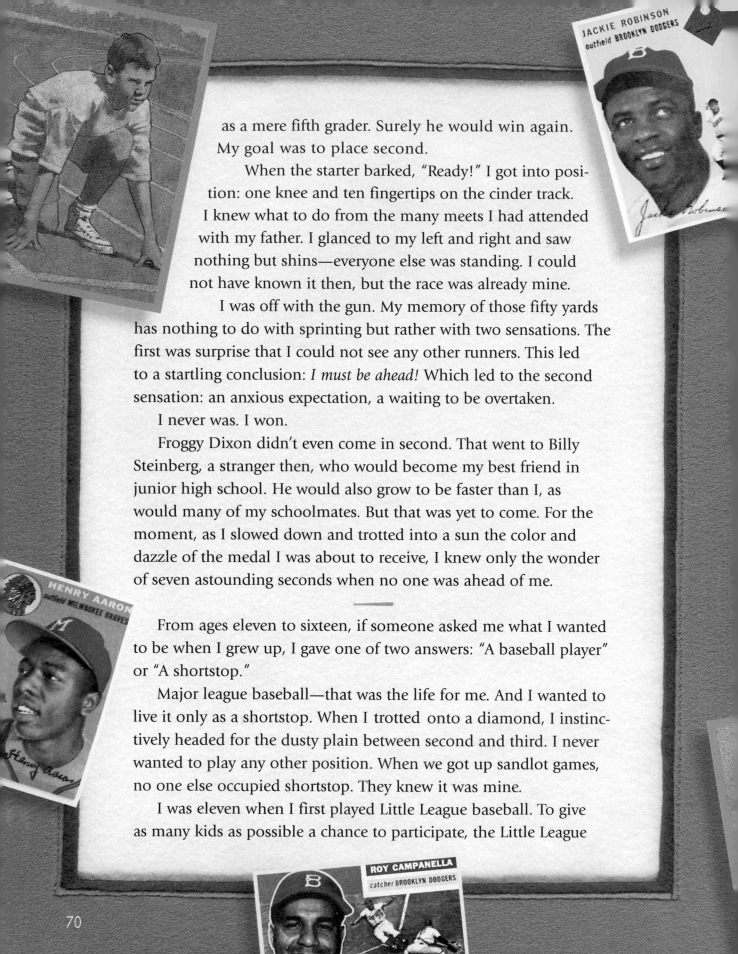

as a mere fifth grader. Surely he would win again. My goal was to place second.

When the starter barked, "Ready!" I got into position: one knee and ten fingertips on the cinder track. I knew what to do from the many meets I had attended with my father. I glanced to my left and right and saw nothing but shins—everyone else was standing. I could not have known it then, but the race was already mine.

I was off with the gun. My memory of those fifty yards has nothing to do with sprinting but rather with two sensations. The first was surprise that I could not see any other runners. This led to a startling conclusion: *I must be ahead!* Which led to the second sensation: an anxious expectation, a waiting to be overtaken.

I never was. I won.

Froggy Dixon didn't even come in second. That went to Billy Steinberg, a stranger then, who would become my best friend in junior high school. He would also grow to be faster than I, as would many of my schoolmates. But that was yet to come. For the moment, as I slowed down and trotted into a sun the color and dazzle of the medal I was about to receive, I knew only the wonder of seven astounding seconds when no one was ahead of me.

———

From ages eleven to sixteen, if someone asked me what I wanted to be when I grew up, I gave one of two answers: "A baseball player" or "A shortstop."

Major league baseball—that was the life for me. And I wanted to live it only as a shortstop. When I trotted onto a diamond, I instinctively headed for the dusty plain between second and third. I never wanted to play any other position. When we got up sandlot games, no one else occupied shortstop. They knew it was mine.

I was eleven when I first played Little League baseball. To give as many kids as possible a chance to participate, the Little League

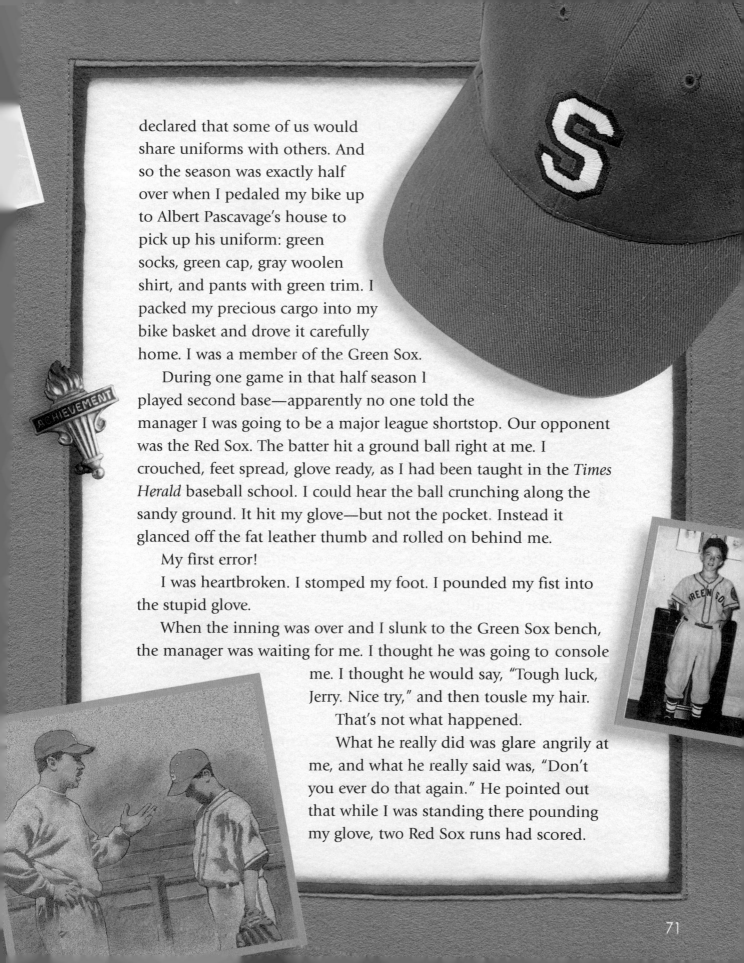

declared that some of us would share uniforms with others. And so the season was exactly half over when I pedaled my bike up to Albert Pascavage's house to pick up his uniform: green socks, green cap, gray woolen shirt, and pants with green trim. I packed my precious cargo into my bike basket and drove it carefully home. I was a member of the Green Sox.

During one game in that half season I played second base—apparently no one told the manager I was going to be a major league shortstop. Our opponent was the Red Sox. The batter hit a ground ball right at me. I crouched, feet spread, glove ready, as I had been taught in the *Times Herald* baseball school. I could hear the ball crunching along the sandy ground. It hit my glove—but not the pocket. Instead it glanced off the fat leather thumb and rolled on behind me.

My first error!

I was heartbroken. I stomped my foot. I pounded my fist into the stupid glove.

When the inning was over and I slunk to the Green Sox bench, the manager was waiting for me. I thought he was going to console me. I thought he would say, "Tough luck, Jerry. Nice try," and then tousle my hair.

That's not what happened.

What he really did was glare angrily at me, and what he really said was, "Don't you ever do that again." He pointed out that while I was standing there pounding my glove, two Red Sox runs had scored.

"Next time you miss the ball, you turn around and chase it down. You don't just stand there feeling sorry for yourself. Understand?"

I nodded. And I never forgot.

———

Like most of the kids in my class, I got better at sports simply by growing older. I went from being one of the worst players in Little League as an eleven-year-old to making the all-star team as a twelve-year-old. The following year I was the only seventh grader to start on the Stewart Junior High School team—at shortstop, of course. It mattered little that I was not very good at hitting a curve ball, since most pitchers threw only fastballs.

During the summer of junior high school I played in a baseball league called Connie Mack Knee-Hi, for thirteen- to fifteen-year-olds. Before each game, one team would line up along the first-base line, the other team along third base. The umpire stood on the pitcher's mound, took off his cap, and read aloud the Sportsmanship Pledge, pausing after each line so the rest of us could repeat it in chorus. We pledged ourselves to be loyal to, among other things, "clean living and clean speech." In the final line we promised to be "a generous victor and a gracious loser."

In the Knee-Hi summer of 1955, I had little chance to be a gracious loser. My team, Norristown Brick Company, swept through the local league undefeated, winning our games by an average score of 12–1. One score was 24–0. One team simply refused to show up. Our pitchers threw four no-hitters, three by Lee Holmes. Opposing batters could no more hit Bill Bryzgornia's fastball than spell his name. We were a powerhouse.

We beat Conshohocken two out of three to gain the state playoffs. Three wins there put us into the title game. On a bright Saturday afternoon at War Memorial Field in Doylestown,

GENUINE   016

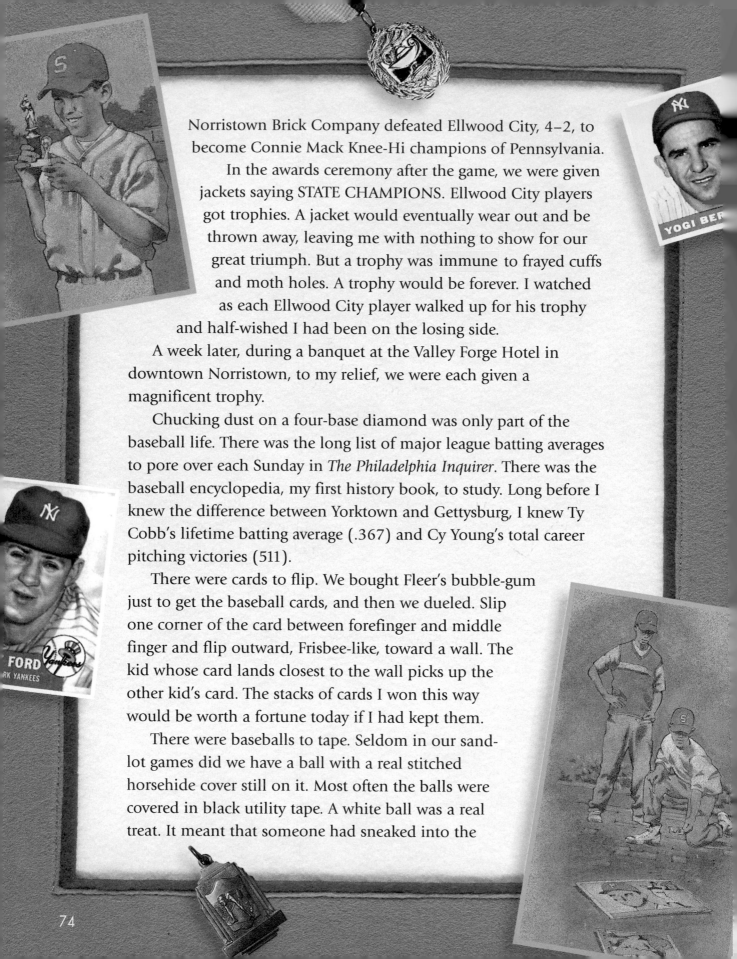

Norristown Brick Company defeated Ellwood City, 4–2, to become Connie Mack Knee-Hi champions of Pennsylvania. In the awards ceremony after the game, we were given jackets saying STATE CHAMPIONS. Ellwood City players got trophies. A jacket would eventually wear out and be thrown away, leaving me with nothing to show for our great triumph. But a trophy was immune to frayed cuffs and moth holes. A trophy would be forever. I watched as each Ellwood City player walked up for his trophy and half-wished I had been on the losing side.

A week later, during a banquet at the Valley Forge Hotel in downtown Norristown, to my relief, we were each given a magnificent trophy.

Chucking dust on a four-base diamond was only part of the baseball life. There was the long list of major league batting averages to pore over each Sunday in *The Philadelphia Inquirer*. There was the baseball encyclopedia, my first history book, to study. Long before I knew the difference between Yorktown and Gettysburg, I knew Ty Cobb's lifetime batting average (.367) and Cy Young's total career pitching victories (511).

There were cards to flip. We bought Fleer's bubble-gum just to get the baseball cards, and then we dueled. Slip one corner of the card between forefinger and middle finger and flip outward, Frisbee-like, toward a wall. The kid whose card lands closest to the wall picks up the other kid's card. The stacks of cards I won this way would be worth a fortune today if I had kept them.

There were baseballs to tape. Seldom in our sand-lot games did we have a ball with a real stitched horsehide cover still on it. Most often the balls were covered in black utility tape. A white ball was a real treat. It meant that someone had sneaked into the

medicine chest at home and used up half a roll of first-aid tape.

There were hours to spend bouncing tennis balls off neighbors' brick walls, any wall but that of the mysterious barber across the street. For hours each week I scooped up the rebounding grounders, practicing to be a great shortstop. Considering the thumping I gave those houses, it's a wonder I was never chased off. Maybe the people behind the walls understood that in my mind I was not really standing on George Street but in the brown dust of Connie Mack Stadium, out at shortstop, fielding hot shots off the bat of Willie Mays.

And there was the glove. My glove bore the signature of Marty Marion, slick-fielding shortstop of the St. Louis Cardinals.

Each year at the end of summer vacation, I rubbed my glove with olive oil from the kitchen cabinet. Then I pressed a baseball deep into the pocket of the glove, curled the leather fingers about the ball, and squeezed the whole thing into a shoebox. Standing on a chair, I set the box high on a closet shelf. Baseball season was officially over.

For the next six months we would hibernate, shortstop and glove, dreaming of the Chiclets-white bases at Connie Mack Stadium, feeling in the palm the hard, round punch of a grounder well caught.

Think and Respond

1 How did Jerry Spinelli prepare for his sports activities, and what happened as a result?

2 Why is the author's most prized **memento** of his grade-school days a medal for winning the 50-yard dash?

3 Why do you think the author tells about his first fielding error at second base?

4 What lessons have you learned by playing or watching sports?

5 What strategy helped you read this selection? When did you use it?

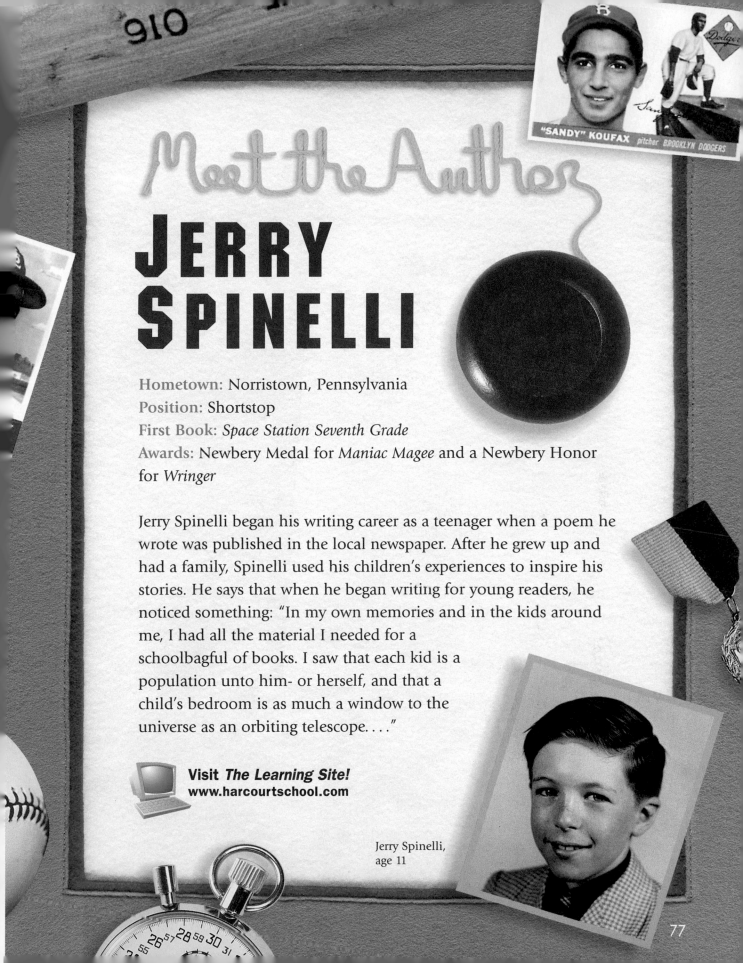

"SANDY" KOUFAX pitcher BROOKLYN DODGERS

Meet the Author
JERRY SPINELLI

Hometown: Norristown, Pennsylvania
Position: Shortstop
First Book: *Space Station Seventh Grade*
Awards: Newbery Medal for *Maniac Magee* and a Newbery Honor for *Wringer*

Jerry Spinelli began his writing career as a teenager when a poem he wrote was published in the local newspaper. After he grew up and had a family, Spinelli used his children's experiences to inspire his stories. He says that when he began writing for young readers, he noticed something: "In my own memories and in the kids around me, I had all the material I needed for a schoolbagful of books. I saw that each kid is a population unto him- or herself, and that a child's bedroom is as much a window to the universe as an orbiting telescope...."

Visit *The Learning Site!*
www.harcourtschool.com

Jerry Spinelli,
age 11

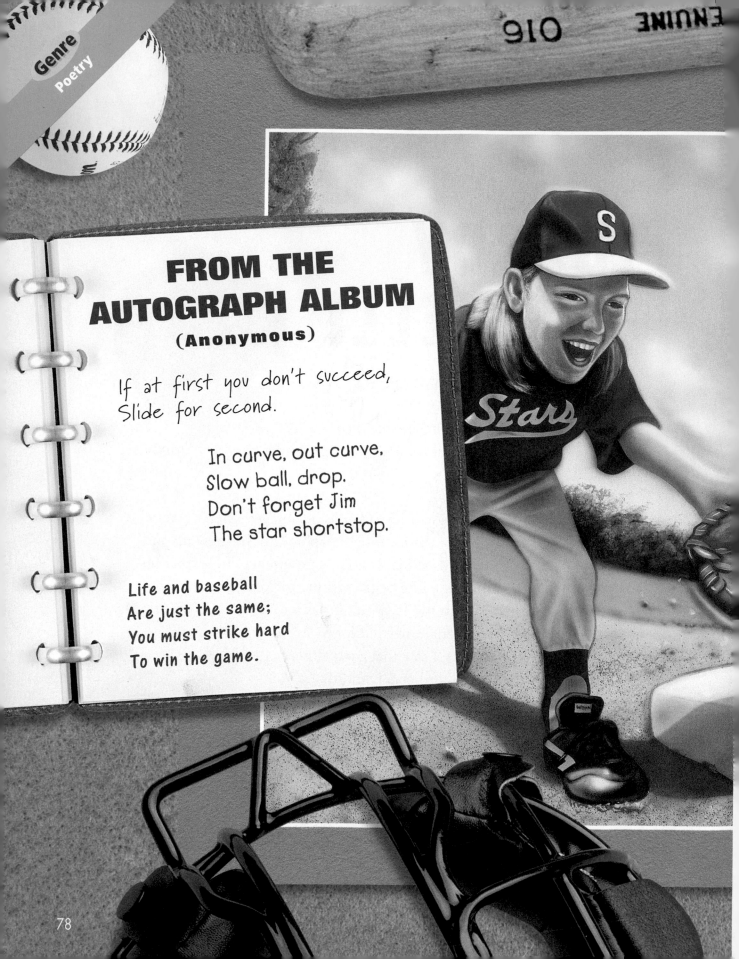

FROM THE AUTOGRAPH ALBUM

(Anonymous)

If at first you don't succeed,
Slide for second.

In curve, out curve,
Slow ball, drop.
Don't forget Jim
The star shortstop.

Life and baseball
Are just the same;
You must strike hard
To win the game.

Good Sportsmanship

—Richard Armour

Good sportsmanship we hail, we sing,
    It's always pleasant when you spot it.
There's only one unhappy thing:
    You have to lose to prove you've got it.

illustrated by Mike Gardner

79

▲ Knots in My
Yo-yo String

Making Connections

Compare Texts

1 What is the connection between Jerry Spinelli's experiences and the theme Personal Best?

2 Do you think Jerry Spinelli would appreciate the poems "From the Autograph Album" and "Good Sportsmanship"? Explain your answer.

3 Compare "Knots in My Yo-yo String" with the poems that follow it. Do the autobiography and the poems provide similar or different ideas about what it's like to be an athlete? Explain your answer.

4 How would "Knots in My Yo-yo String" be different if it were written about Jerry Spinelli by someone else?

5 Would you like to read other books by Jerry Spinelli? Why or why not?

Write a News Story

In this selection, the author describes his own experiences as a young athlete. Write a news story for a student newspaper about one of the athletic events described in "Knots in My Yo-yo String." Use a web diagram to organize your main idea and supporting details.

Writing CONNECTION

Supporting Detail

Main Idea

80

Make a Chart

Jerry Spinelli describes running the 50-yard dash. Track-and-field competition is part of the modern Olympic Games. Research the history of the Olympic Games. Make a chart that compares and contrasts the ancient and the modern Olympic Games. You might include facts answering the questions *where? when? who? what?* and *how?*

Ancient Games	Modern Games

Social Studies CONNECTION

Role-Play an Interview

Work with a partner to research information about an athlete you both admire. Write questions you would like to ask the athlete. Then role-play an interview between the athlete and a television sports reporter. Present your interview to the class.

Language Arts CONNECTION

Make Judgments (Focus Skill)

Being an informed reader of nonfiction involves **making judgments** about the way the author presents information. You can examine the evidence that the author uses to support opinions and conclusions. Does what the author tells you make sense? Are his or her conclusions supported with details and reasons? Is the information accurate? You may need to check, or confirm, the information with another reliable source, especially if the author is trying to convince you of something.

What judgments might you make about "Knots in My Yo-yo String"? Examine the evidence. Do you find the author's presentation of himself believable and realistic? Can you confirm any of the information with another source?

Jerry Spinelli's portrayal of himself is believable and realistic.	He shares personal events and feelings. He experienced disappointment as well as success. He lived in a town like my own or one that I have learned about.
Jerry Spinelli presents factual information accurately.	I can confirm in an almanac information such as Ty Cobb's lifetime batting average. I can research Norristown, Pennsylvania, to find out if Connie Mack Stadium really existed in the 1950s.

Visit *The Learning Site!*
www.harcourtschool.com

See *Skills* and *Activities*

Test Prep
Make Judgments

▶ **Read the passage. Then answer the questions.**

> Everyone loves to be part of a winning team. That's why baseball teams across the country have been choosing Home Run to supply them with the baseballs that deliver results. Each ball is assembled with the finest materials available and inspected to be sure it meets the needs of professional athletes. For only $1.99 per ball, you can experience what it's like to hit a home run, whether you are a beginner or a baseball star.

1. **Why might you question the information in the passage?**

   A because baseball players don't care about baseballs

   B because it tells how the balls are assembled

   C because the price seems unreasonably low

   D because the passage is written for both professionals and beginners

Tip

Make a judgment about the author's purpose for writing. Does the information seem realistic?

2. **The passage tries to interest you in Home Run baseballs by—**

   F reducing the price

   G saying you'll hit home runs

   H explaining the inspection process

   J telling what's wrong with other baseballs

Tip

Eliminate any choices that cannot be supported by evidence in the passage. Then think about a baseball player's main purpose for playing.

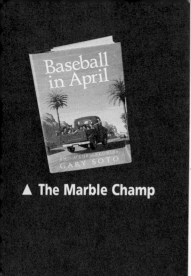

▲ **The Marble Champ**

Vocabulary Power

instinct

reluctantly

flexed

exhaustion

fumed

rummaged

"The Marble Champ" is about a girl who's a terrific student but not good at sports. Does that sound familiar? It seems that everybody is good at something, but nobody is good at everything. Read what three students have to say about their abilities.

I think some people, like my best friend, Lee, have a natural ability for sports. It's an **instinct**, something they're born with and never outgrow. Unfortunately, I'm not one of them. I was finally picked for the basketball team in gym class, but the captain chose me **reluctantly**. I knew he didn't really want me.

Every weekend I take swimming lessons at our community pool. My teacher is terrific, and I try to do everything he says. Today when I practiced, I kicked hard and **flexed** my leg muscles to make them stronger. I swam for two hours. Maybe that was a mistake. My legs were so sore, I could barely walk. I was weak with **exhaustion**.

I **fumed** with irritation when I realized I would never be a great runner. Then I decided to find a new interest. I **rummaged** through some boxes of books in our attic and found one about dog training. Two months later I entered our dog, Max, in his first show. We both turned out to be winners!

Vocabulary-Writing CONNECTION

Have you ever **reluctantly** participated in an activity? Write a few sentences describing how you felt when your heart wasn't completely in what you were doing.

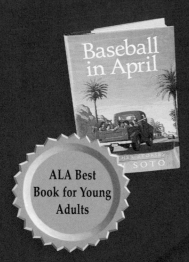

ALA Best
Book for Young
Adults

Genre

Short Story

A short story is a fictional narrative that is not part of a novel.

In this selection, look for

- The qualities of the main character

- A focus on one problem or main event

The Marble Champ

by Gary Soto

illustrated by David Diaz

Lupe Medrano, a shy girl who spoke in whispers, was the school's spelling bee champion, winner of the reading contest at the public library three summers in a row, blue ribbon awardee in the science fair, the top student at her piano recital, and the playground grand champion in chess. She was a straight-A student and—not counting kindergarten, when she had been stung by a wasp—had never missed one day of elementary school. She had received a small trophy for this honor and had been congratulated by the mayor.

But though Lupe had a razor-sharp mind, she could not make her body, no matter how much she tried, run as fast as the other girls'. She begged her body to move faster, but could never beat anyone in the fifty-yard dash.

The truth was that Lupe was no good in sports. She could not catch a pop-up or figure out in which direction to kick the soccer ball. One time she kicked the ball at her own goal and scored a point for the other team. She was no good at baseball or basketball either, and even had a hard time making a hula hoop stay on her hips.

It wasn't until last year, when she was eleven years old, that she learned how to ride a bike. And even then she had to use training wheels. She could walk in the swimming pool but couldn't swim, and chanced roller skating only when her father held her hand.

"I'll never be good at sports," she fumed one rainy day as she lay on her bed gazing at the shelf her father had made to hold her awards. "I wish I could win something, anything, even marbles."

At the word "marbles," she sat up. "That's it. Maybe I could be good at playing marbles." She hopped out of bed and rummaged through the closet until she found a can full of her brother's marbles. She poured the rich glass treasure on her bed and picked five of the most beautiful marbles.

She smoothed her bedspread and practiced shooting, softly at first so that her aim would be accurate. The marble rolled from her thumb and clicked against the targeted marble. But the target wouldn't budge. She tried again and again. Her aim became accurate, but the power from her thumb made the marble move only an inch or

two. Then she realized that the bedspread was slowing the marbles. She also had to admit that her thumb was weaker than the neck of a newborn chick.

She looked out the window. The rain was letting up, but the ground was too muddy to play. She sat cross-legged on the bed, rolling her five marbles between her palms. Yes, she thought, I could play marbles, and marbles is a sport. At that moment she realized that she had only two weeks to practice. The playground championship, the same one her brother had entered the previous year, was coming up. She had a lot to do.

To strengthen her wrists, she decided to do twenty push-ups on her fingertips, five at a time. "One, two, three..." she groaned. By the end of the first set she was breathing hard, and her muscles burned from exhaustion. She did one more set and decided that was enough push-ups for the first day.

She squeezed a rubber eraser one hundred times, hoping it would strengthen her thumb. This seemed to work because the next day her thumb was sore. She could hardly hold a marble in her hand, let alone send it flying with power. So Lupe rested that day and listened to her brother, who gave her tips on how to shoot: get low, aim with one eye, and place one knuckle on the ground.

"Think 'eye and thumb'—and let it rip!" he said.

After school the next day she left her homework in her backpack and practiced three hours straight, taking time only to eat a candy bar for energy. With a popsicle stick, she drew an odd-shaped circle and tossed in four marbles. She used her shooter, a milky agate with hypnotic swirls, to blast them. Her thumb *had* become stronger.

After practice, she squeezed the eraser for an hour. She ate dinner with her left hand to spare her shooting hand and said nothing to her parents about her dreams of athletic glory.

Practice, practice, practice. Squeeze, squeeze, squeeze. Lupe got better and beat her brother and Alfonso, a neighbor kid who was supposed to be a champ.

"Man, she's bad!" Alfonso said. "She can beat the other girls for sure. I think."

The weeks passed quickly. Lupe worked so hard that one day, while she was drying dishes, her mother asked why her thumb was swollen.

"It's muscle," Lupe explained. "I've been practicing for the marbles championship."

"You, honey?" Her mother knew Lupe was no good at sports.

"Yeah. I beat Alfonso, and he's pretty good."

That night, over dinner, Mrs. Medrano said, "Honey, you should see Lupe's thumb."

"Huh?" Mr. Medrano said, wiping his mouth and looking at his daughter.

"Show your father."

"Do I have to?" an embarrassed Lupe asked.

"Go on, show your father."

Reluctantly, Lupe raised her hand and flexed her thumb. You could see the muscle.

The father put down his fork and asked, "What happened?"

"Dad, I've been working out. I've been squeezing an eraser."

"Why?"

"I'm going to enter the marbles championship."

Her father looked at her mother and then back at his daughter. "When is it, honey?"

"This Saturday. Can you come?"

The father had been planning to play racquetball with a friend Saturday, but he said he would be there. He knew his daughter thought she was no good at sports and he wanted to encourage her. He even rigged some lights in the backyard so she could practice after dark. He squatted with one knee on the ground, entranced by the sight of his daughter easily beating her brother.

The day of the championship began with a cold blustery sky. The sun was a silvery light behind slate clouds.

"I hope it clears up," her father said, rubbing his hands together as he returned from getting the newspaper. They ate breakfast, paced nervously around the house waiting for 10:00 to arrive, and walked the two blocks to the playground (though Mr. Medrano wanted to drive so Lupe wouldn't get tired). She signed up and was assigned her first match on baseball diamond number three.

Lupe, walking between her brother and her father, shook from the cold, not nerves. She took off her mittens, and everyone stared at her thumb. Someone asked, "How can you play with a broken thumb?" Lupe smiled and said nothing.

She beat her first opponent easily, and felt sorry for the girl because she didn't have anyone to cheer for her. Except for her sack of marbles, she was all alone. Lupe invited the girl, whose name was Rachel, to stay with them. She smiled and said, "OK." The four of them walked to a card table in the middle of the outfield, where Lupe was assigned another opponent.

She also beat this girl, a fifth-grader named Yolanda, and asked her to join their group. They proceeded to more matches and more wins, and soon there was a crowd of people following Lupe to the finals to play a girl in a baseball cap. This girl seemed dead serious. She never even looked at Lupe.

"I don't know, Dad, she looks tough."

Rachel hugged Lupe and said, "Go get her."

"You can do it," her father encouraged. "Just think of the marbles, not the girl, and let your thumb do the work."

The other girl broke first and earned one marble. She missed her next shot, and Lupe, one eye closed, her thumb quivering with energy, blasted two marbles out of the circle but missed her next shot. Her opponent earned two more before missing. She stamped her foot and said "Shoot!" The score was three to two in favor of Miss Baseball Cap.

The referee stopped the game. "Back up, please, give them room," he shouted. Onlookers had gathered too tightly around the players.

Lupe then earned three marbles and was set to get her fourth when a gust of wind blew dust in her eyes and she missed badly. Her opponent quickly scored two marbles, tying the game, and moved ahead six to five on a lucky shot. Then she missed, and Lupe, whose eyes felt scratchy when she blinked, relied on instinct and thumb muscle to score the tying point. It was now six to six, with only three marbles left. Lupe blew her nose and studied the angles. She dropped to one knee, steadied her hand, and shot so hard she cracked two marbles from the circle. She was the winner!

"I did it!" Lupe said under her breath. She rose from her knees, which hurt from bending all day, and hugged her father. He hugged her back and smiled.

Everyone clapped, except Miss Baseball Cap, who made a face and stared at the ground. Lupe told her she was a great player, and they shook hands. A newspaper photographer took pictures of the two girls standing shoulder-to-shoulder, with Lupe holding the bigger trophy.

Lupe then played the winner of the boys' division, and after a poor start beat him eleven to four. She blasted the marbles, shattering one into sparkling slivers of glass. Her opponent looked on glumly as Lupe did what she did best—win!

The head referee and the President of the Fresno Marble Association stood with Lupe as she displayed her trophies for the newspaper photographer. Lupe shook hands with everyone, including a dog who had come over to see what the commotion was all about.

That night, the family went out for pizza and set the two trophies on the table for everyone in the restaurant to see. People came up to congratulate Lupe, and she felt a little embarrassed, but her father said the trophies belonged there.

Back home, in the privacy of her bedroom, she placed the trophies on her shelf and was happy. She had always earned honors because of her brains, but winning in sports was a new experience. She thanked her tired thumb. "You did it, thumb. You made me champion." As its reward, Lupe went to the bathroom, filled the bathroom sink with warm water, and let her thumb swim and splash as it pleased. Then she climbed into bed and drifted into a hard-won sleep.

Think and Respond

1 What problem does Lupe want to solve, and how does she solve it?

2 What do Lupe's hours of practice, in spite of her **exhaustion**, show about her character?

3 How is Lupe's father important to the story?

4 Would you like to play against Lupe in a sports contest? Why or why not?

5 What reading strategies did you use to help you understand the selection? When did you use them?

GARY SOTO

Gary Soto has won many awards for his writing. Although Lupe in "The Marble Champ" is not based on a real person, the character and the author share a competitive spirit. An interviewer asked Gary Soto these questions about his life and his writings.

What were you like as a child?

I was a playground kid. I jumped at every chance to play—the game didn't matter. It could be kickball or baseball, or chess or Chinese checkers—anything that allowed me to compete.

Where do you get your ideas for writing?

I write about the small events of day-to-day life that reveal big themes: love and friendship, or success and failure. I draw on my childhood experiences growing up in a Mexican *barrio* as I shape my stories. In fact, I grew up in the neighborhood I wrote about in "The Marble Champ."

How do you feel about your success as a writer?

I am happy that the characters of my stories and poems are living in the hearts of young readers!

Visit *The Learning Site!*
www.harcourtschool.com

DAVID DIAZ

Like Lupe, David Diaz is no stranger to competition. His high school art teacher encouraged his students to enter art competitions. Diaz soon realized that he could be successful *and* make a living doing something he loved. Over the years, he experimented with different techniques until he developed his own unique style. David Diaz's hard work and competitive spirit have helped him become an award-winning illustrator.

It's Tiger

from *Children's Digest*

Golfing sensation Tiger Woods thinks all kids should get a chance to give golf a try. That's why he is hitting the links with kids from all kinds of backgrounds, to show that the game that has been great to him can be great to them, too.

"So many kids across the country have been told no, they can't play; they're not good enough to play," Tiger said in Indianapolis. "I know how it feels; I was one of those kids."

Tiger has put together a special organization to encourage kids to take up the game of golf. "I've had tremendous support from my parents, great friends, and mentors growing up that took time out of their lives to participate in mine," Tiger said. Now he wants to do the same thing for kids today, so that "They can go out and not only participate in golf if they choose, but make an impact on our society."

Tiger is targeting kids who might not otherwise get a chance to play golf, like inner-city children. "No matter what culture, what race, what religious choice you may have, you should have access to establish a game of golf."

Excelling at golf can give kids the ticket to making their own lives better, as well as improving the lives of others in their community. "So many times kids are influenced by others because they don't have the self-esteem to stand up," Tiger said. "We're here to say, no, you do have the choice; you can stand up but it has to come from within."

Tiger gets to work with lots of kids on their golf skills. Steven Hamer, sixteen, of Indiana,

Time!

Steven Hamer and Brianda White enjoyed chatting with and learning from Tiger.

benefited from tips from Tiger. "It's just incredible that such a big celebrity would do this for kids," said Steven. "It's a great game, but if you can make a couple of kids happy and give them the thrill of a lifetime, then more power to Tiger, I guess. It's just great that he's doing it."

Steven especially enjoyed his time with Tiger, because he is engaged in the biggest battle of his life: he's fighting bone cancer.

Watching Tiger's success has sparked big ideas for lots of kids. Brianda White, eight, of Indianapolis, sees Tiger as a real role model. "I like playing golf because I look on TV and I see all these people play and I want to be like him," said Brianda, who usually plays golf with her grandfather.

Tiger's organization will choose several cities every year for a visit, where local kids can learn from Tiger about choosing to do the best they can, in golf and in ordinary life.

"Let them make the choice," said Tiger. "It's up to all of us to make golf available to them at whatever age, but it's up to these kids here whether they want to play the game or not; our job is to provide the opportunity."

Think and Respond

What words would you use to describe Tiger Woods? Why would you use those words?

▲ The Marble Champ

Making Connections

Compare Texts

1 How does "The Marble Champ" relate to the theme of being one's personal best?

2 How do Lupe's feelings about her sports ability change from the first to the last scenes of the story?

3 Compare and contrast "The Marble Champ" and "It's Tiger Time!" What does each selection suggest about the importance to young people of learning to play a sport?

4 Why is "The Marble Champ" an example of realistic fiction? Explain your answer.

5 Would you like to read other short stories about young athletes? Why or why not?

Write a Journal Entry

Imagine that you are Lupe, keeping a journal as you prepare for the marble championship. Write three short entries that describe your feelings. Write the first entry when you begin to practice. Write the second entry just before the championship. Write the last entry after the championship. Use a chart to organize your ideas.

Writing CONNECTION

Beginning	Middle	End
	nervous, excited	

Create an Experiment

Make a marble track. Tape two yardsticks parallel to each other on a tabletop. Place two marbles at opposite ends of the yardsticks. Then shoot one marble at the other. In your notebook, describe what happens.

Science CONNECTION

Create an Ad

Find out how people of long ago played with marbles. Then write an ad inviting people to attend a marble championship in ancient times. The ad should include some of the facts from your research. Use a graphic organizer to arrange your facts.

Social Studies CONNECTION

Marbles

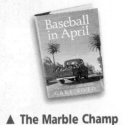

Narrative Elements

Focus Skill

As you were reading "The Marble Champ," you wanted to find out whether Lupe would reach her goal of becoming a champion. You probably predicted that she would, because she practiced for long hours and was determined to be the best.

In many stories, the main character's qualities help move the plot, or sequence of events, along. The plot has a **conflict**, or problem, and a **resolution**, or outcome. How would the resolution of "The Marble Champ" have been different if Lupe had been someone who became discouraged easily?

This chart shows how you can analyze the plot of a story.

Main Character(s)	Conflict/ Problem	Resolution	Character Traits That Affect Resolution
Lupe	She wants to prove that she can win at a sport.	She wins the marble championship.	willingness to work hard, determination, dedication

Visit *The Learning Site!*
www.harcourtschool.com

See *Skills* and *Activities*

Test Prep

Narrative Elements

▶ **Read the passage. Then answer the questions.**

> With homework and a part-time job, Jeremy was always busy. He needed to work in order to earn money for a two-week computer camp in July. Since Jeremy loved computers, he knew he would have a great time there. Two months ago Jeremy had started his own pet care business. Every week, he walked, fed, and bathed fifteen dogs in his neighborhood. He felt proud of himself when he had finally saved the money he needed. It would be a great summer after all.

1. **How does Jeremy resolve his problem?**

   A He skips his homework.

   B He buys a new computer.

   C He starts a pet care business.

   D He takes care of his own dog.

Tip

Identify the story conflict before you find the resolution in the passage.

2. **How do Jeremy's qualities affect the resolution of the plot? Use details and information from the passage in your answer.**

Tip

Think about Jeremy's actions to help you decide what his special qualities are.

▲ Darnell Rock
Reporting

Vocabulary Power

issue

funding

agenda

postpone

ordinance

violations

effective

In "Darnell Rock Reporting," a boy becomes a reporter on the school paper. Here are some articles written by student writers.

Student Council Takes a Stand
by Marilyn Iglesias

Thursday, November 8

At the most recent student council meeting, members discussed an important subject. The **issue** was whether to continue our after-school creative writing and art programs. The **funding** that provided the money for these programs ended last month. The student council president said, "This is the most important topic on the **agenda** for today's meeting. Many students feel that these programs must continue." The council members agreed. They decided to **postpone** talking about the other topics on the schedule until next month's meeting.

Mayor Richards Visits Our School

by Carol Lin

Thursday, November 15

Last Monday our school held a special assembly about working together to improve our community. The guest speaker was Mayor Lenore Richards. She talked about a new city **ordinance** that will require dog owners to keep their dogs on a leash in city parks. "Right now, there are too many **violations** of park rules," Mayor Richards said. "We need an **effective** program to stop park visitors from breaking the law. Your help can make the difference."

Vocabulary-Writing CONNECTION

There are many ways to help the community. Whether you help clean the sidewalks or tutor a classmate, your efforts can be very **effective**. Write a paragraph that describes ways you can help your community.

Darnell

Genre

Realistic Fiction

Realistic fiction tells about characters and events that are like people and events in real life.

In this selection, look for

- **Challenges and problems that might happen in real life.**

- **A plot with a beginning, a middle, and an ending.**

- **A main character who demonstrates a willingness to help others.**

Rock Reporting

by Walter Dean Myers
illustrated by James Ransome

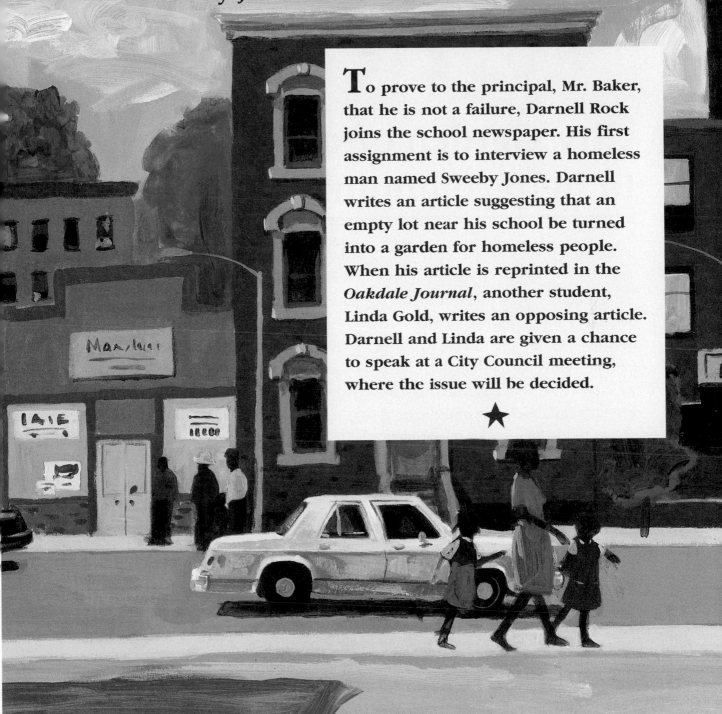

To prove to the principal, Mr. Baker, that he is not a failure, Darnell Rock joins the school newspaper. His first assignment is to interview a homeless man named Sweeby Jones. Darnell writes an article suggesting that an empty lot near his school be turned into a garden for homeless people. When his article is reprinted in the *Oakdale Journal*, another student, Linda Gold, writes an opposing article. Darnell and Linda are given a chance to speak at a City Council meeting, where the issue will be decided.

★

City Garden offers a chance to help community

by Darnell Rock

"Nobody wants to be homeless," Sweeby Jones said. He is a homeless man who lives in our city of Oakdale. It is for him and people like him that I think we should build a garden where the basketball courts were, near the school. That way the homeless people can help themselves by raising food.

"You see a man or woman that's hungry and you don't feed them, or help them feed themselves, then you got to say you don't mind people being hungry," Mr. Jones said. "And if you don't mind people being hungry, then there is something wrong with you."

This is what Mr. Sweeby Jones said when I spoke to him. I don't want to be the kind of person who says it's all right for some people to be hungry. I want to do something about it. But I think there is another reason to have the garden. Things can happen to people that they don't plan. You can get sick, and not know why, or even homeless. But sometimes there are things you can do to change your life or make it good. If you don't do anything to make your life good, it will probably not be good.

"I was born poor and will probably be poor all my life," Mr. Sweeby Jones said.

I think maybe it is not how you were born that makes the most difference, but what you do with your life. The garden is a chance for some people to help their own lives.

Empty lot should benefit local teachers

by Linda Gold

Teaching is a difficult profession. Teachers need as much support as they can possibly get. After all, we are dependent on them for our future. Education is the key to a good and secure future, and teachers help us to get that education. We must give them all the support we can. This is why I am supporting the idea of building a parking lot near the school.

There are some people in our school who think it is a good idea to build a garden so that the homeless can use it. Use it for what? Homeless people don't have experience farming and could not use the land anyway. This is just a bad idea that will help nobody and will hurt the teachers. The teachers give us good examples on how we should live and how we should conduct ourselves. The homeless people, even though it is no fault of theirs, don't give us good examples.

On Friday evening, at 7:00 p.m., the City Council will meet to make a final decision. I urge them to support the teachers, support education, and support the students at South Oakdale.

"You see anybody from the school?" Larry looked over the large crowd at the Oakdale Court building.

"There goes Mr. Derby *and* Mr. Baker." Tamika pointed toward the front of the building.

Darnell felt a lump in the pit of his stomach. There were at least a hundred people at the City Council meeting.

Tamika led them through the crowd to where she had spotted Mr. Derby and South Oakdale's principal. The large, high-ceilinged room had rows of benches that faced the low platform for the City Council. Linda Gold was already sitting in the front row. Darnell saw that her parents were with her.

He had brought a copy of the *Journal* with him and saw that a few other people, grown-ups, also had copies of the paper.

The nine members of the City Council arrived, and the meeting was called to order. The city clerk said that there were five items on the agenda, and read them off. The first three items were about Building Code violations. Then came something about funding the city's library.

"The last item will be the use of the basketball courts as a parking lot at South Oakdale Middle School," the clerk said. "We have three speakers scheduled."

Linda turned and smiled at Darnell.

"You want me to run up there and punch her out?" Tamika whispered to Darnell.

Darnell didn't know what Building Code violations were but watched as building owners showed diagrams explaining why there were violations. The first two weren't that interesting, but the third one was. A company had built a five-story building that was supposed to be a minimum of twenty feet from the curb, but it was only fifteen feet.

"You mean to tell me that your engineers only had fifteen-foot rulers?" one councilman asked.

"Well, er, we measured it right the first time"—the builder shifted from one foot to the other—"but then we made some changes in the design and somehow we sort of forgot about the er . . . you know . . . the other five feet."

To Darnell the builder sounded like a kid in his homeroom trying to make an excuse for not having his homework.

"Can you just slide the building back five or six feet?" the councilman asked.

Everybody laughed and the builder smiled, but Darnell could tell he didn't think it was funny.

Somebody touched Darnell on the shoulder, and he turned and saw his parents.

"We have this ordinance for a reason," a woman on the Council was saying. "I don't think we should lightly dismiss this violation. An exception granted here is just going to encourage others to break the law."

"This is going to ruin me," the builder said. "I've been in Oakdale all of my life and I think I've made a contribution."

"Let's have a vote." The head of the Council spoke sharply.

"Let's have a vote to postpone a decision," the woman who had spoken before said. "We'll give Mr. Miller an opportunity to show his good faith."

"What do you want me to do?" the builder asked.

"That's up to you," the woman said.

"Next time you'd better get it right!" Tamika called out.

"She's right," the councilwoman said.

There was a vote, and the decision was postponed. The builder gave Tamika a dirty look as he pushed his papers into his briefcase.

The city library funding was next, and eight people, including Miss Seldes, spoke for the library, but the Council said it didn't have any more money. There was some booing, including some from Tamika and Larry. Darnell knew that if he didn't have to speak he would have enjoyed the meeting.

"The issue at South Oakdale is should the old basketball courts be used as a parking lot, or should they be used as a community garden?"

"Who's going to pay for paving the lot?" a councilman asked. "Does it have to be paved?"

"It's my understanding that it doesn't have to be paved," the head of the Council answered. "Am I right on that?"

"Yes, you are," Miss Joyner spoke up from the audience.

"We have two young people from the school to speak," the councilwoman said. "The first is a Miss Gold."

Linda went into the middle aisle, where there was a microphone. She began reading her article in the snootiest voice that Darnell had ever heard. He felt a knot in his stomach. He turned to look at his mother, and she was smiling. On the stage some of the councilmen were looking at some papers.

"I hope I don't mess up," he whispered to Tamika.

"You won't," Tamika said.

Linda finished reading her article and then turned toward Darnell.

"Although everybody would like to help the homeless," she said, "schools are supposed to be for kids, and for those who teach kids! Thank you."

There was applause for Linda, and Miss Joyner stood up and nodded toward her. Darnell felt his hands shaking.

Darnell's name was called, and he made the long trip to the microphone.

"When I first thought about having a garden instead of a parking lot, I thought it was just a good idea," Darnell said. "Then, when the *Journal* asked me to send them a copy of my interview with Mr. Jones, I was thinking that it was mainly a good idea to have a garden to help out the homeless people. But now I think it might be a good idea to have the garden to help out the kids— some of the kids—in the school.

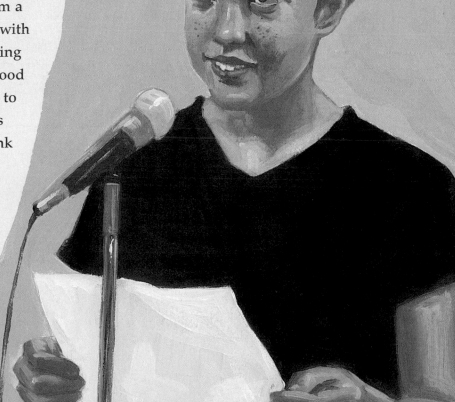

"Sometimes, when people go through their life they don't do the things that can make them a good life. I don't know why they don't do the right thing, or maybe even if they know what the right thing is sometimes.

"But I see the same thing in my school, South Oakdale. Some of the kids always do okay, but some of us don't. Maybe their parents are telling them something, or maybe they know something special. But if you're a kid who isn't doing so good, people start off telling you what you should be doing, and you know it, but sometimes you still don't get it done and mess up some more. Then people start expecting you to mess up, and then *you* start expecting you to mess up. Teachers get mad at you, or the principal, or your parents, and they act like you're messing up on purpose. Like you want to get bad marks and stuff like that. Then you don't want people getting on your case all the time so you don't do much because the less you do the less they're going to be on your case. Only that doesn't help anything, and everybody knows it, but that's the way it goes."

"You seem to be doing all right, young man," the head of the City Council said.

"I wasn't doing too hot before," Darnell said, taking a quick look over to where Mr. Baker sat. "But when I got on the paper and the *Journal* printed my article, then everybody started treating me different. People came up to me and started explaining their points of view instead of just telling me what to do. And you people are listening to me. The kids I hung out with, they called us the Corner Crew, are mostly good kids but you wouldn't listen to them unless they got into trouble.

"In South Oakdale some kids have bad things happen to them— like they get sick—and I don't know why that happens, but all they can do is to go to the hospital. And some kids just get left out of the good things and can't find a way of getting back into them. People get mad at them the same way they get mad at the homeless people or people who beg on the street. Maybe the garden will be a way for

the homeless people to get back into some good things, and maybe seeing the homeless people getting back into a better life will be a way for some of the kids to think about what's happening to them. Thank you."

There was some applause as Darnell turned to go back to his seat.

"Just a minute, young man," one of the councilmen called to him. "The girl said that these people don't know anything about raising a garden. Is that true?"

"It doesn't matter," someone said from the audience. "I'm from the college, and we can help with technical advice."

"I didn't ask you," the councilman said.

"I'm telling you anyway," the man said.

"I don't know how effective a community garden would be," the councilman said. "You can't feed people from a garden."

"You could sell what you grow," Darnell heard himself saying.

"I think bringing people who are . . . nonschool people into that close a contact with children might not be that good an idea," the councilman said. "Who's the last speaker?"

"A Mr. Jones," the clerk said.

Sweeby came into the middle aisle, and a lot of people began to talk among themselves. There were a lot of things they were interested in, and most of them were not interested in the school parking lot.

"I just want to ask you why you don't want to listen to this boy," Sweeby asked.

"You have four minutes to speak," the councilman said. He seemed angry. "We don't have to answer your questions."

"You don't have to answer my questions," Sweeby said. "And you don't have to have the garden. You don't have to think about us—what you call us?—nonschool people?

"But it's a shame you don't want to listen to this boy. I wish he had been my friend when I was his age. Maybe I would be sitting in one of your seats instead of being over here."

"Is there anything more?" the councilman asked.

"No, you can just forget about the whole thing now," Sweeby said. "Go on back to your papers."

"I think we can vote on this issue now," the councilman said.

"I think Mr."—the councilman looked at the agenda to find Darnell's name—"Mr. Darnell Rock had some good points, but it's still a tough issue. Let's get on with the vote."

The vote went quickly. Three councilpeople decided not to vote, five voted against the garden, and only one voted for it.

Darnell took a deep breath and let it out slowly. Tamika patted him on his hand. When he looked at her she had tears in her eyes.

Darnell felt he had let Sweeby down. His father patted him on his back, and Miss Seldes came over.

"You did a good job," she said. "Really good."

"I lost," Darnell said.

"Sometimes you lose," Miss Seldes said. "But you still did a good job."

Sweeby and some of his friends were waiting outside the Council meeting, and they shook hands with Darnell. Sweeby was telling him how the members of the Council didn't really care about people when Darnell saw Linda through the crowd. She waved and he waved back. She was smiling.

Larry's mother came over and asked his father for a lift home, and they were waiting for Larry when Peter Miller from the *Journal* came over.

"Hey, you want to write another article for the paper?" he said. "There's a guy who wants to donate a couple of lots for a garden in another location. My boss wants to run it as a human interest piece."

"Yeah, sure," Darnell said. "You want a long article or a short one?"

"I don't know. Call the paper tomorrow and ask for the city desk," the reporter said. "My editor will give you the word count."

"Okay," Darnell said. "But first I have to check with my editor to see what she wants."

Darnell was disappointed that the Jackson Avenue garden was as small as it was, but as Sweeby said, it was a start. It was located between two abandoned buildings and was fifty feet deep by thirty-five feet wide. A flatbed truck was parked in front of it and was being used as a platform for the mayor as he made his speech about how some kids from South Oakdale had "made things happen."

"And as long as I'm mayor, I'll always listen to the kids, for they are the future!" he said. Then he got down from the truck, got into a limousine, and was gone.

"They should have named it after you!" Larry said.

"When they name stuff after you it means you're dead!" Darnell said.

"Darnell!" It was Linda Gold.

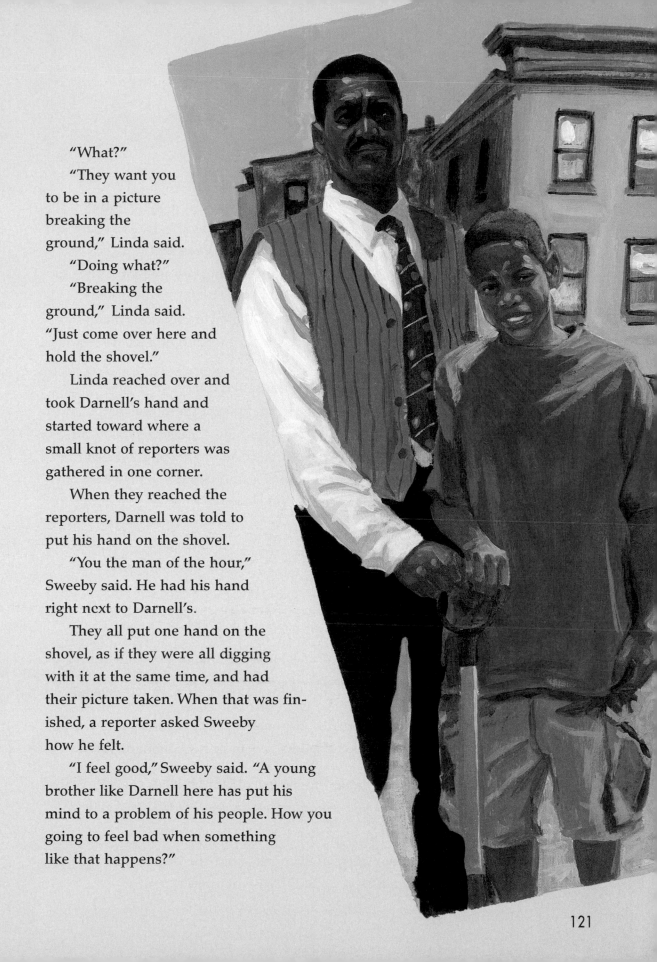

"What?"

"They want you to be in a picture breaking the ground," Linda said.

"Doing what?"

"Breaking the ground," Linda said. "Just come over here and hold the shovel."

Linda reached over and took Darnell's hand and started toward where a small knot of reporters was gathered in one corner.

When they reached the reporters, Darnell was told to put his hand on the shovel.

"You the man of the hour," Sweeby said. He had his hand right next to Darnell's.

They all put one hand on the shovel, as if they were all digging with it at the same time, and had their picture taken. When that was finished, a reporter asked Sweeby how he felt.

"I feel good," Sweeby said. "A young brother like Darnell here has put his mind to a problem of his people. How you going to feel bad when something like that happens?"

"Do you really think this garden is going to make a difference?" the reporter asked.

"It's going to make a big difference," Sweeby said. "Because every time somebody walks by this place they're going to remember that there are people who need some help, and there are some people who are willing to help. You can't see that?"

"Yeah, I guess so," the reporter said, closing his notebook. He shook Sweeby's hand before walking away.

"Looka that," Sweeby said to Darnell after the reporter had left. "When's the last time you think he shook the hand of a used-to-be homeless man?"

"You got a place to stay now?" Darnell asked.

"You got me so excited about being down at the City Council and in the newspapers that I had to do something," Sweeby said. "And me being in the newspapers helped because the hospital offered me a job. Like this garden, it's small, but it's a start. Now, you take care of yourself. I got about a half hour to get to work."

Think and Respond

1. How does Darnell make a difference in his community?

2. What positive result followed the City Council debate?

3. How does Darnell's personal experience affect the way he feels about the homeless people in his community?

4. The City Council was persuaded by Linda's speech. Whose speech did you find more *effective*, Darnell's or Linda's? Explain.

5. Were your early predictions about the outcome of the story confirmed as you read? Tell why or why not.

Meet the Author
Walter Dean Myers

NEW YORK, N.Y. — Like his fictional character, Darnell Rock, award-winning author Walter Dean Myers has discovered the good in himself through writing. He says, "I wrote fiction on a regular basis from the time I was ten or eleven, filling up notebooks." However, he "never knew writing was a job." He worked at several jobs after leaving the army at age twenty, but none was as rewarding to him as writing.

In the late 1960s Walter Dean Myers won a writing contest. He started writing novels for and about teenagers a few years later. His best-known books are about African American teenagers who live in Harlem, a neighborhood of New York City. He has also written science fiction, nonfiction, and mystery adventure stories.

I wrote fiction on a regular basis from the time I was ten or eleven, filling up notebooks.
—Walter Dean Myers

Meet the Illustrator
James Ransome

POUGHKEEPSIE, N.Y. — James Ransome describes himself as a "visual story-teller." He believes that "the pictures should tell the story that the writer has written." Ransome became interested in art at a very early age when he began watching television and reading comic books. By the time he was a teenager, he was writing and illus-trating his own stories. Ransome feels that his work is successful when readers feel as if they are part of the story.

Visit *The Learning Site!*
www.harcourtschool.com

123

Genre
Poetry

COURAGE

by NAOMI SHIHAB NYE illustrated by DAN YACCARINO

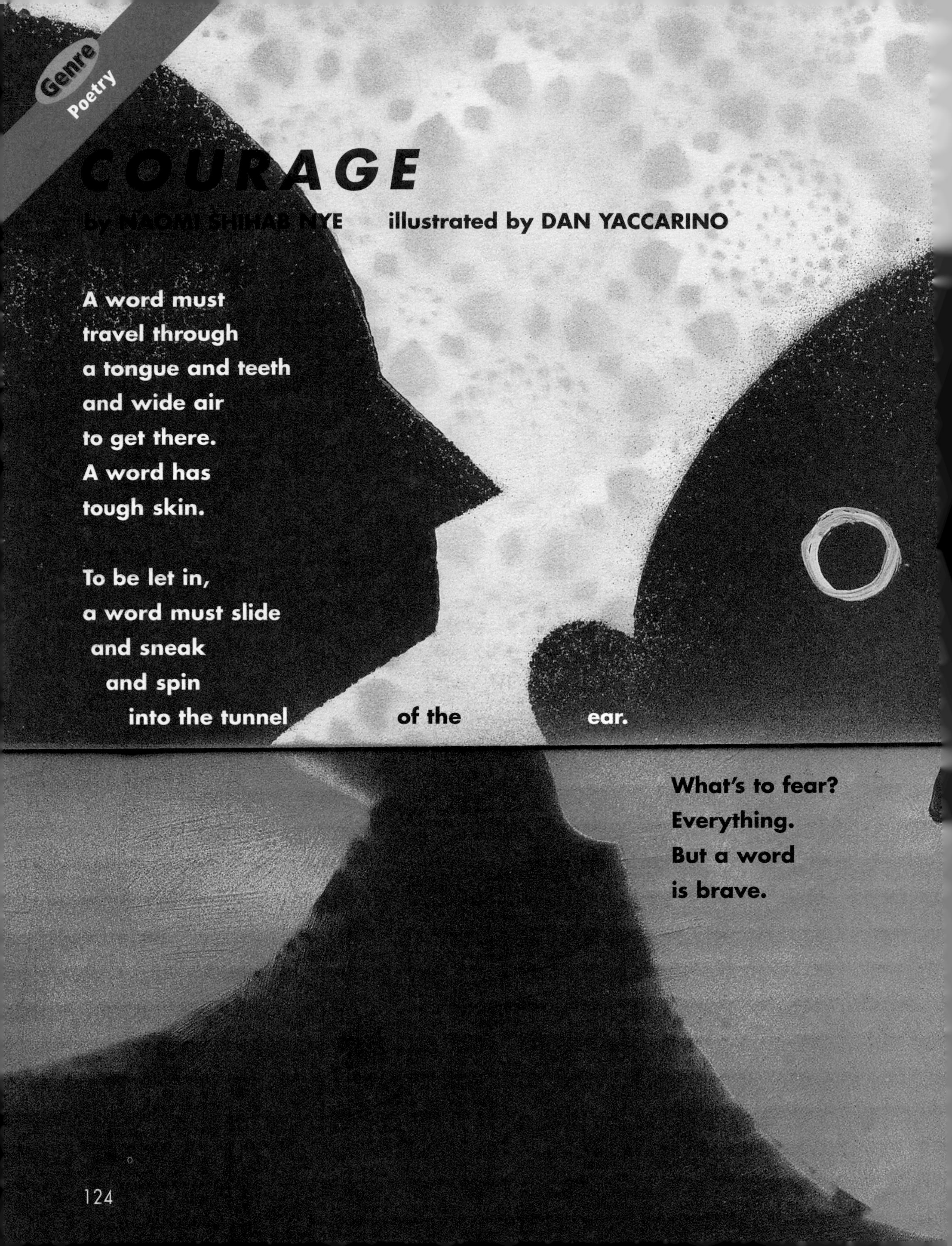

A word must
travel through
a tongue and teeth
and wide air
to get there.
A word has
tough skin.

To be let in,
a word must slide
and sneak
and spin
into the tunnel of the ear.

What's to fear?
Everything.
But a word
is brave.

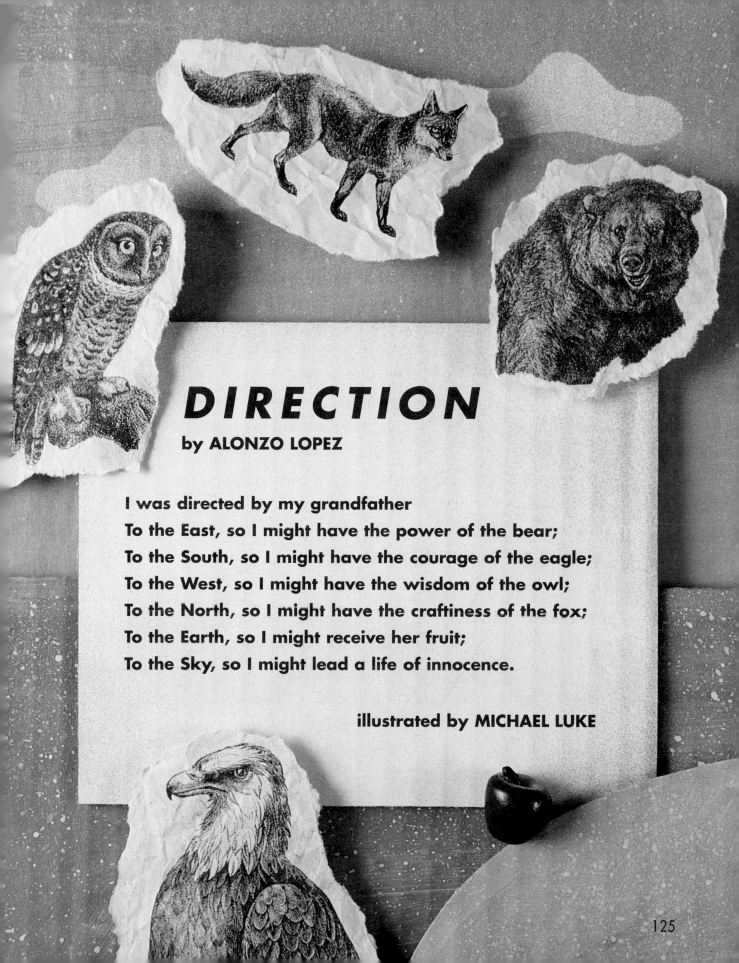

DIRECTION

by ALONZO LOPEZ

I was directed by my grandfather
To the East, so I might have the power of the bear;
To the South, so I might have the courage of the eagle;
To the West, so I might have the wisdom of the owl;
To the North, so I might have the craftiness of the fox;
To the Earth, so I might receive her fruit;
To the Sky, so I might lead a life of innocence.

illustrated by MICHAEL LUKE

▲ Darnell Rock Reporting

Making Connections

Compare Texts

1. How does "Darnell Rock Reporting" express the theme of bringing out the best in ourselves and others?

2. Compare the viewpoints expressed in the articles written by Darnell and Linda.

3. Compare and contrast what "Darnell Rock Reporting" and the poems say about the importance of inner strength.

4. How is Darnell similar to or different from another fictional character you've read about who wanted to make a difference?

5. How could you find out if you could build a community garden in your neighborhood?

Write a Persuasive Essay

Darnell writes an article explaining why the basketball courts should be made into a community garden. Write a persuasive essay in which you take a stand on an issue that affects your school or your community. State your opinion and provide details that will persuade other people to agree with you. Use a chart to organize your ideas.

Writing CONNECTION

The issue I will write about: _____
My opinion: _____

Details that support my opinion: _____
_____
_____

Make a Map

Where would you build a garden in your community? Draw a map of your neighborhood that includes a community garden in a convenient location. Your map should include a compass rose, map symbols, and a key that explains what each symbol stands for.

Trees
Plants
Houses
Stores

Community Garden

Plan a Garden

Darnell proposes creating a garden for homeless people in the community. Research the materials and natural resources you would need to plant and care for a garden in your community. List them in a chart. Identify each natural resource as renewable or nonrenewable.

Materials	Natural Resources	Renewable	Nonrenewable
shovels	dirt	✔	

Prefixes, Suffixes, and Roots

Focus Skill

Prefixes and suffixes are word parts that are added to a root or a root word. Recognizing prefixes and suffixes can help you figure out the meanings of words.

- A **prefix** is added to the beginning of a word to change the meaning.

- A **suffix** is added to the end of a word to change the meaning.

Look at how adding a prefix to the word *courage* changes the meaning. **courage** *n.* Bravery; fearlessness

Prefix	Meaning of Prefix	New Word	Meaning of New Word	Sample Sentence
en-	"cause to"	encourage	*v.* To give courage to	As team captain, I *encourage* my teammates during the game.
dis-	"not, opposite of"	discourage	*v.* To cause to lose courage	Darnell let no one *discourage* him.

Try adding each prefix and suffix in this chart to a root or a root word.

Prefix	Meaning	Suffix	Meaning
de-	opposite	-en	cause to be, become
fore-	before	-ful	filled with, able
inter-	between	-less	without
non-	not	-ment	act, action, state of
re-	again	-y	consisting of, inclined to

Test Prep
Prefixes, Suffixes, and Roots

▶ **Read the passage. Then answer the questions.**

> On Saturday afternoon, Linda and her younger brother, Lee, went to the park. If they could have <u>foreseen</u> the afternoon's events, however, Linda and Lee would have stayed home. As they were eating a picnic lunch, a passing dog noticed their food. Lee's efforts to distract the dog were <u>useless</u>. The dog ate most of the food before his owner could stop him.

1. **What is the meaning of the word** *foreseen* **in this passage?**

   A seen again

   B never seen

   C opposite of *seen*

   D seen beforehand

2. **The word** *useless* **means —**

   F never used

   G used again

   H without use

   J effective

Tip

If you can't remember the meaning of the prefix, think of another word you know with the same prefix. Do you know the meaning of *forecast*?

Tip

The answer you choose will make sense in the context of the passage. Try each answer before you select one.

FRIENDS TO THE RESCUE

CONTENTS

Number the Stars......................132
by Lois Lowry

Focus Skill   Narrative Elements

The Summer of the Swans.....................160
by Betsy Byars

Focus Skill   Literary Devices

Old Yeller......................184
by Fred Gipson

Puppies with a Purpose.....................200
from *National Geographic World*

Focus Skill   Summarize and Paraphrase

Trapped by the Ice!.....................206
by Michael McCurdy

Antarctica......................230
by Joyce Pope

Focus Skill   Literary Devices

Flood: Wrestling with the Mississippi.....................236
by Patricia Lauber

Focus Skill   Summarize and Paraphrase

▲ **Number the Stars**

occupation

disdainfully

belligerently

soothingly

exasperated

unwavering

Vocabulary Power

"Number the Stars" is set in Denmark during World War II. During this time, from 1939 to 1945, much of the world was at war. The war affected the lives of many children.

During the **occupation**, hundreds of enemy soldiers remained in our village after they captured it. We tried to follow our normal daily routine, but life was very hard. Our people did not like the soldiers. The soldiers spoke **disdainfully** about our country. I think they looked down on us because they had defeated our army. Sometimes they even threatened us **belligerently**, as if they wanted to fight.

I picked this flower in the field near the market square during the last year of the war. I saw a soldier and became frightened, but my mother spoke **soothingly** to calm me. I was **exasperated** because I wasn't able to gather more flowers. My sister told me not to get annoyed about something that was so unimportant.

This is from the first birthday party we had after the war ended. Our country was free again. Although many people doubted our army would win, my parents disagreed. They were **unwavering** in their belief that we would defeat the enemy.

Vocabulary-Writing CONNECTION

Recall someone who spoke **soothingly** to you during a rough time in your life. Write a thank-you note to that person for helping.

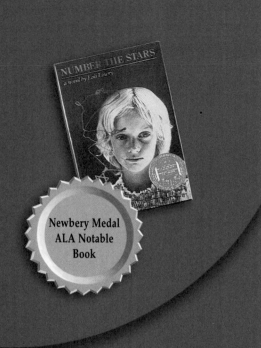

Genre

Historical Fiction

Historical fiction is a story that is set in the past and portrays people, places, and events that did or could have happened.

In this selection, look for

- A real time and place in the past

- Some made-up events

NUMBER

BY LOIS LOWRY
ILLUSTRATED BY
RUSS WILSON

In 1943, German troops had occupied Denmark for about a year. Annemarie Johansen; her little sister, Kirsti; and her best friend, Ellen, could remember when the tall German soldier, "the Giraffe," and his partner didn't stand watch on the street corner near the school. When the Germans began to "relocate" all the Jews in Denmark, the Johansens acted heroically to help their Jewish friends.

Alone in the apartment while Mama was out shopping with Kirsti, Annemarie and Ellen were sprawled on the living room floor playing with paper dolls. They had cut the dolls from Mama's magazines, old ones she had saved from past years. The paper ladies had old-fashioned hair styles and clothes, and the girls had given them names from Mama's very favorite book. Mama had told Annemarie and Ellen the entire story of *Gone With the Wind*, and the girls thought it much more interesting and romantic than the king-and-queen tales that Kirsti loved.

"Come, Melanie," Annemarie said, walking her doll across the edge of the rug. "Let's dress for the ball."

"All right, Scarlett, I'm coming," Ellen replied in a sophisticated voice. She was a talented performer; she often played the leading roles in school dramatics. Games of the imagination were always fun when Ellen played.

The door opened and Kirsti stomped in, her face tear-stained and glowering. Mama followed her with an exasperated look and set a package down on the table.

"I won't!" Kirsti sputtered. "I won't ever, *ever* wear them! Not if you chain me in a prison and beat me with sticks!"

Annemarie giggled and looked questioningly at her mother. Mrs. Johansen sighed. "I bought Kirsti some

new shoes," she explained. "She's outgrown her old ones."

"Goodness, Kirsti," Ellen said, "I wish my mother would get *me* some new shoes. I love new things, and it's so hard to find them in the stores."

"Not if you go to a *fish* store!" Kirsti bellowed. "But most mothers wouldn't make their daughters wear ugly *fish* shoes!"

"Kirsten," Mama said soothingly, "you know it wasn't a fish store. And we were lucky to find shoes at all."

Kirsti sniffed. "Show them," she commanded. "Show Annemarie and Ellen how ugly they are."

Mama opened the package and took out a pair of little girl's shoes. She held them up, and Kirsti looked away in disgust.

"You know there's no leather anymore," Mama explained. "But they've found a way to make shoes out of fish skin. I don't think these are too ugly."

Annemarie and Ellen looked at the fish skin shoes. Annemarie took one in her hand and examined it. It was odd-looking; the fish scales were visible. But it was a shoe, and her sister needed shoes.

"It's not so bad, Kirsti," she said, lying a little.

Ellen turned the other one over in her hand. "You know," she said, "it's only the color that's ugly."

"Green!" Kirsti wailed. "I will never, *ever* wear green shoes!"

"In our apartment," Ellen told her, "my father has a jar of black, black ink. Would you like these shoes better if they were black?"

Kirsti frowned. "Maybe I would," she said, finally.

"Well, then," Ellen told her, "tonight, if your mama doesn't mind, I'll take the shoes home and ask my father to make them black for you, with his ink."

Mama laughed. "I think that would be a fine improvement. What do you think, Kirsti?"

Kirsti pondered. "Could he make them shiny?" she asked. "I want them shiny."

Ellen nodded. "I think he could. I think they'll be quite pretty, black and shiny."

Kirsti nodded. "All right, then," she said. "But you mustn't tell anyone that they're *fish*. I don't want anyone to know." She took her new shoes, holding them disdainfully, and put them on a chair. Then she looked with interest at the paper dolls.

"Can I play, too?" Kirsti asked. "Can I have a doll?" She squatted beside Annemarie and Ellen on the floor.

Sometimes, Annemarie thought, Kirsti was such a pest, always butting in. But the apartment was small. There was no other place for Kirsti to play. And if they told her to go away, Mama would scold.

"Here," Annemarie said, and handed her sister a cut-out little girl doll. "We're playing *Gone With the Wind*. Melanie and Scarlett are going to a ball. You can be Bonnie. She's Scarlett's daughter."

Kirsti danced her doll up and down happily. "I'm going to the ball!" she announced in a high, pretend voice.

Ellen giggled. "A little girl wouldn't go to a ball. Let's make them go someplace else. Let's make them go to Tivoli!"

"Tivoli!" Annemarie began to laugh. "That's in Copenhagen! *Gone With the Wind* is in America!"

"Tivoli, Tivoli, Tivoli," little Kirsti sang, twirling her doll in a circle.

"It doesn't matter, because it's only a game anyway," Ellen pointed out. "Tivoli can be over there, by that chair. 'Come, Scarlett,'" she said, using her doll voice, "'we shall go to Tivoli to dance and watch the fireworks, and maybe there will be some handsome men there! Bring your silly daughter Bonnie, and she can ride on the carousel.'"

Annemarie grinned and walked her Scarlett toward the chair that Ellen had designated as Tivoli. She loved Tivoli Gardens, in the heart of Copenhagen; her parents had taken her there, often, when she was a little girl. She remembered the music and the brightly colored lights, the carousel and ice cream and especially the magnificent fireworks in the evenings: the huge colored splashes and bursts of lights in the evening sky.

"I remember the fireworks best of all," she commented to Ellen.

"Me too," Kirsti said. "I remember the fireworks."

"Silly," Annemarie scoffed. "You never saw the fireworks." Tivoli Gardens was closed now. The German occupation forces had burned part of it, perhaps as a way of punishing the fun-loving Danes for their lighthearted pleasures.

Kirsti drew herself up, her small shoulders stiff. "I did too," she said belligerently. "It was my birthday. I woke up in the night and I could hear

the booms. And there were lights in the sky. Mama said it was fireworks
for my birthday!"

Then Annemarie remembered. Kirsti's birthday was late in August. And that
night, only a month before, she, too, had been awakened and frightened by
the sound of explosions. Kirsti was right— the sky in the southeast had been
ablaze, and Mama had comforted her by calling it a birthday celebration.
"Imagine, such fireworks for a little girl five years old!" Mama had said, sitting
on their bed, holding the dark curtain aside to look through the window at the
lighted sky.

The next evening's newspaper had told the sad truth. The Danes had
destroyed their own naval fleet, blowing up the vessels one by one, as the
Germans approached to take over the ships for their own use.

"How sad the king must be," Annemarie had heard Mama say to Papa
when they read the news.

"How proud," Papa had replied.

It had made Annemarie feel sad and proud, too, to picture the tall, aging
king, perhaps with tears in his blue eyes, as he looked at the remains of his
small navy, which now lay submerged and broken in the harbor.

"I don't want to play anymore, Ellen," she said suddenly, and put her
paper doll on the table.

"I have to go home, anyway," Ellen said. "I have to help Mama with the
housecleaning. Thursday is our New Year. Did you know that?"

"Why is it yours?" asked Kirsti. "Isn't it our New Year, too?"

"No. It's the Jewish New Year. That's just for us. But if you want, Kirsti, you
can come that night and watch Mama light the candles."

Annemarie and Kirsti had often been invited to watch Mrs. Rosen light the
Sabbath candles on Friday evenings. She covered her head with a cloth and
said a special prayer in Hebrew as she did so. Annemarie always stood very
quietly, awed, to watch; even Kirsti, usually such a chatterbox, was always still
at that time. They didn't understand the words or the meaning, but they could
feel what a special time it was for the Rosens.

"Yes," Kirsti agreed happily. "I'll come and watch your mama light the
candles, and I'll wear my new black shoes."

But this time was to be different. Leaving for school on Thursday with her sister, Annemarie saw the Rosens walking to the synagogue early in the morning, dressed in their best clothes. She waved to Ellen, who waved happily back.

"Lucky Ellen," Annemarie said to Kirsti. "She doesn't have to go to school today."

"But she probably has to sit very, very still, like we do in church," Kirsti pointed out. "*That's* no fun."

That afternoon, Mrs. Rosen knocked at their door but didn't come inside. Instead, she spoke for a long time in a hurried, tense voice to Annemarie's mother in the hall. When Mama returned, her face was worried, but her voice was cheerful.

"Girls," she said, "we have a nice surprise. Tonight Ellen will be coming to stay overnight and to be our guest for a few days! It isn't often we have a visitor."

Kirsti clapped her hands in delight.

"But, Mama," Annemarie said, in dismay, "it's their New Year. They were going to have a celebration at home! Ellen told me that her mother managed to get a chicken someplace, and she was going to roast it—their first roast chicken in a year or more!"

"Their plans have changed," Mama said briskly. "Mr. and Mrs. Rosen have been called away to visit some

141

relatives. So Ellen will stay with us. Now, let's get busy and put clean sheets on your bed. Kirsti, you may sleep with Mama and Papa tonight, and we'll let the big girls giggle together by themselves."

Kirsti pouted, and it was clear that she was about to argue. "Mama will tell you a special story tonight," her mother said. "One just for you."

"About a king?" Kirsti asked dubiously.

"About a king, if you wish," Mama replied.

"All right, then. But there must be a queen, too," Kirsti said.

Though Mrs. Rosen had sent her chicken to the Johansens, and Mama made a lovely dinner large enough for second helpings all around, it was not an evening of laughter and talk. Ellen was silent at dinner. She looked frightened. Mama and Papa tried to speak of cheerful things, but it was clear that they were worried, and it made Annemarie worry, too. Only Kirsti was unaware of the quiet tension in the room. Swinging her feet in their newly blackened and shiny shoes, she chattered and giggled during dinner.

"Early bedtime tonight, little one," Mama announced after the dishes were washed. "We need extra time for the long story I promised, about the king and queen." She disappeared with Kirsti into the bedroom.

"What's happening?" Annemarie asked when she and Ellen were alone with Papa in the living room. "Something's wrong. What is it?"

Papa's face was troubled. "I wish that I could protect you children from this knowledge," he said quietly. "Ellen, you already know. Now we must tell Annemarie."

He turned to her and stroked her hair with his gentle hand. "This morning, at the synagogue, the rabbi told his congregation that the Nazis have taken the synagogue lists of all the Jews. Where they live, what their names are. Of course the Rosens were on that list, along with many others."

"Why? Why did they want those names?"

"They plan to arrest all the Danish Jews. They plan to take them away. And we have been told that they may come tonight."

"I don't understand! Take them where?"

Her father shook his head. "We don't know where, and we don't really know why. They call it 'relocation.' We don't even know what that means. We only know that it is wrong, and it is dangerous, and we must help."

Annemarie was stunned. She looked at Ellen and saw that her best friend was crying silently.

"Where are Ellen's parents? We must help them, too!"

"We couldn't take all three of them. If the Germans came to search our apartment, it would be clear that the Rosens were here. One person we can hide. Not three. So Peter has helped Ellen's parents to go elsewhere. We don't know where. Ellen doesn't know either. But they are safe."

Ellen sobbed aloud, and put her face in her hands. Papa put his arm around her. "They are safe, Ellen. I promise you that. You will see them again quite soon. Can you try hard to believe my promise?"

Ellen hesitated, nodded, and wiped her eyes with her hand.

"But, Papa," Annemarie said, looking around the small apartment, with its few pieces of furniture: the fat stuffed sofa, the table and chairs, the small bookcase against the wall. "You said that we would hide her. How can we do that? Where can she hide?"

Papa smiled. "That part is easy. It will be as your mama said: you two will sleep together in your bed, and you may giggle and talk and tell secrets to each other. And if anyone comes—"

Ellen interrupted him. "Who might come? Will it be soldiers? Like the

143

ones on the corners?" Annemarie remembered how terrified Ellen had looked the day when the soldier had questioned them on the corner.

"I really don't think anyone will. But it never hurts to be prepared. If anyone should come, even soldiers, you two will be sisters. You are together so much, it will be easy for you to pretend that you are sisters."

He rose and walked to the window. He pulled the lace curtain aside and looked down into the street. Outside, it was beginning to grow dark. Soon they would have to draw the black curtains that all Danes had on their windows; the entire city had to be completely darkened at night. In a nearby tree, a bird was singing; otherwise it was quiet. It was the last night of September.

"Go, now, and get into your nightgowns. It will be a long night."

Annemarie and Ellen got to their feet. Papa suddenly crossed the room and put his arms around them both. He kissed the top of each head: Annemarie's blond one, which reached to his shoulder, and Ellen's dark hair, the thick curls braided as always into pigtails.

"Don't be frightened," he said to them softly. "Once I had three daughters. Tonight I am proud to have three daughters again."

• • •

"Do you really think anyone will come?" Ellen asked nervously, turning to Annemarie in the bedroom. "Your father doesn't think so."

"Of course not. They're always threatening stuff. They just like to scare people." Annemarie took her nightgown from a hook in the closet.

"Anyway, if they did, it would give me a chance to practice acting. I'd just pretend to be Lise. I wish I were taller, though." Ellen stood on tiptoe, trying to make herself tall. She laughed at herself, and her voice was more relaxed.

"You were great as the Dark Queen in the school play last year," Annemarie told her. "You should be an actress when you grow up."

"My father wants me to be a teacher. He wants *everyone* to be a teacher, like him. But maybe I could convince him that I should go to acting school." Ellen stood on tiptoe again, and made an imperious gesture with her arm. "I am the Dark Queen," she intoned dramatically. "I have come to command the night!"

"You should try saying, 'I am Lise Johansen!'" Annemarie said, grinning. "If you told the Nazis that you were the Dark Queen, they'd haul you off to a mental institution."

Ellen dropped her actress pose and sat down, with her legs curled under her, on the bed. "They won't really come here, do you think?" she asked again.

Annemarie shook her head. "Not in a million years." She picked up her hairbrush.

The girls found themselves whispering as they got ready for bed. There was no need, really, to whisper; they were, after all, supposed to be normal sisters, and Papa had said they could giggle and talk. The bedroom door was closed.

But the night did seem, somehow, different from a normal night. And so they whispered.

"How did your sister die, Annemarie?" Ellen asked suddenly. "I remember when it happened. And I remember the funeral — it was the only time I have ever been in a Lutheran church. But I never knew just what happened."

"I don't know *exactly*," Annemarie confessed. "She and Peter were out somewhere together, and then there was a telephone call, that there had been an accident. Mama and Papa rushed to the hospital — remember, your mother came and stayed with me and Kirsti? Kirsti was already asleep and she slept right through everything, she was so little then. But I stayed up, and I was with your mother in the living room when my parents came home in the middle of the night. And they told me Lise had died."

"I remember it was raining," Ellen said sadly. "It was still raining the next morning when Mama told me. Mama was crying, and the rain made it seem as if the whole *world* was crying."

Annemarie finished brushing her long hair and handed her hairbrush to her best friend. Ellen undid her braids, lifted her dark hair away from the thin gold chain she wore around her neck — the chain that held the Star of David—and began to brush her thick curls.

"I think it was partly because of the rain. They said she was hit by a car. I suppose the streets were slippery, and it was getting dark, and maybe the driver just couldn't see," Annemarie went on, remembering. "Papa looked so angry. He made one hand into a fist, and he kept pounding it into the other hand. I remember the noise of it: slam, slam, slam."

146

Together they got into the wide bed and pulled up the covers. Annemarie blew out the candle and drew the dark curtains aside so that the open window near the bed let in some air. "See that blue trunk in the corner?" she said, pointing through the darkness. "Lots of Lise's things are in there. Even her wedding dress. Mama and Papa have never looked at those things, not since the day they packed them away."

Ellen sighed. "She would have looked so beautiful in her wedding dress. She had such a pretty smile. I used to pretend that she was *my* sister, too."

"She would have liked that," Annemarie told her. "She loved you."

"That's the worst thing in the world," Ellen whispered. "To be dead so young. I wouldn't want the Germans to take my family away — to make us live someplace else. But still, it wouldn't be as bad as being dead."

Annemarie leaned over and hugged her. "They won't take you away," she said. "Not your parents, either. Papa promised that they were safe, and he always keeps his promises. And you are quite safe, here with us."

For a while they continued to murmur in the dark, but the murmurs were interrupted by yawns. Then Ellen's voice stopped, she turned over, and in a minute her breathing was quiet and slow.

Annemarie stared at the window where the sky was outlined and a tree branch moved slightly in the breeze. Everything seemed very familiar, very comforting. Dangers were no more than odd imaginings, like ghost stories that children made up to frighten one another: things that couldn't possibly happen. Annemarie felt completely safe here in her own home, with her parents in the next room and her best friend asleep beside her. She yawned contentedly and closed her eyes.

It was hours later, but still dark, when she was awakened abruptly by the pounding on the apartment door.

Annemarie eased the bedroom door open quietly, only a crack, and peeked out. Behind her, Ellen was sitting up, her eyes wide.

She could see Mama and Papa in their nightclothes, moving about. Mama held a lighted candle, but as Annemarie watched, she went to a lamp and switched it on. It was so long a time since they had dared to use the strictly rationed electricity after dark that the light in the room seemed startling to Annemarie, watching through the slightly opened bedroom door. She saw her mother look automatically to the blackout curtains, making certain that they were tightly drawn.

Papa opened the front door to the soldiers.

"This is the Johansen apartment?"

A deep voice asked the question loudly, in the terribly accented Danish.

"Our name is on the door, and I see you have a flashlight," Papa answered. "What do you want? Is something wrong?"

"I understand you are a friend of your neighbors the Rosens, Mrs. Johansen," the soldier said angrily.

"Sophy Rosen is my friend, that is true," Mama said quietly. "Please, could you speak more softly? My children are asleep."

"Then you will be so kind as to tell me where the Rosens are." He made no effort to lower his voice.

"I assume they are at home, sleeping. It is four in the morning, after all," Mama said.

Annemarie heard the soldier stalk across the living room toward the kitchen. From her hiding place in the narrow sliver of open doorway, she could see the heavy uniformed man, a holstered pistol at his waist, in the entrance to the kitchen, peering in toward the sink.

Another German voice said, "The Rosens' apartment is empty. We are wondering if they might be visiting their good friends the Johansens."

"Well," said Papa, moving slightly so that he was standing in front of Annemarie's bedroom door, and she could see nothing except the dark blur of his back, "as you see, you are mistaken. There is no one here but my family."

"You will not object if we look around." The voice was harsh, and it was not a question.

"It seems we have no choice," Papa replied.

"Please don't wake my children," Mama requested again. "There is no need to frighten little ones."

The heavy, booted feet moved across the floor again and into the other bedroom. A closet door opened and closed with a bang.

Annemarie eased her bedroom door closed silently. She stumbled through the darkness to the bed.

"Ellen," she whispered urgently, "take your necklace off!"

Ellen's hands flew to her neck. Desperately she began trying to unhook the tiny clasp. Outside the bedroom door, the harsh voices and heavy footsteps continued.

"I can't get it open!" Ellen said frantically. "I never take it off—I can't even remember how to open it!"

Annemarie heard a voice just outside the door. "What is here?"

"Shhh," her mother replied. "My daughters' bedroom. They are sound asleep."

"Hold still," Annemarie commanded. "This will hurt." She grabbed the little gold chain, yanked with all her strength, and broke it. As the door opened and light flooded into the bedroom, she crumpled it into her hand and closed her fingers tightly.

Terrified, both girls looked up at the three Nazi officers who entered the room.

One of the men aimed a flashlight around the bedroom. He went to the closet and looked inside. Then with a sweep of his gloved hand he pushed to the floor several coats and a bathrobe that hung from pegs on the wall.

There was nothing else in the room except a chest of drawers, the blue decorated trunk in the corner, and a heap of Kirsti's dolls piled in a small rocking chair. The flashlight beam touched each thing in turn. Angrily the officer turned toward the bed.

"Get up!" he ordered. "Come out here!"

Trembling, the two girls rose from the bed and followed him, brushing past the two remaining officers in the doorway, to the living room.

Annemarie looked around. These three uniformed men were different from the ones on the street corners. The street soldiers were often young, sometimes ill at ease, and Annemarie remembered how the Giraffe had, for a moment, let his harsh pose slip and had smiled at Kirsti.

But these men were older and their faces were set with anger.

Her parents were standing beside each other, their faces tense, but Kirsti was nowhere in sight. Thank goodness that Kirsti slept through almost everything. If they had wakened her, she would be wailing—or worse, she would be angry, and her fists would fly.

"Your names?" the officer barked.

"Annemarie Johansen. And this is my sister—"

"Quiet! Let her speak for herself. Your name?" He was glaring at Ellen.

Ellen swallowed. "Lise," she said, and cleared her throat. "Lise Johansen."

The officer stared at them grimly.

"Now," Mama said in a strong voice, "you have seen that we are not hiding anything. May my children go back to bed?"

The officer ignored her. Suddenly he grabbed a handful of Ellen's hair. Ellen winced.

He laughed scornfully. "You have a blond child sleeping in the other room. And you have this blond daughter—" He gestured toward Annemarie with his head. "Where did you get the dark-haired one?" He twisted the lock of Ellen's hair. "From a different father? From the milkman?"

Papa stepped forward. "Don't speak to my wife in such a way. Let go of my daughter or I will report you for such treatment."

"Or maybe you got her someplace else?" the officer continued with a sneer. "From the Rosens?"

For a moment no one spoke. Then Annemarie, watching in panic, saw her father move swiftly to the small bookcase and take out a book. She saw that he was holding the family photograph album. Very quickly he searched through its pages, found what he was looking for, and tore out three pictures from three separate pages.

He handed them to the German officer, who released Ellen's hair.

"You will see each of my daughters, each with her name written on the photograph," Papa said.

Annemarie knew instantly which photographs he had chosen. The album had many snapshots—all the poorly focused pictures of school events and birthday parties. But it also contained a portrait, taken by a photographer, of each girl as a tiny infant. Mama had written, in her delicate handwriting, the name of each baby daughter across the bottom of those photographs.

She realized too, with an icy feeling, why Papa had torn them from the book. At the bottom of each page, below the photograph itself, was written the date. And the real Lise Johansen had been born twenty-one years earlier.

"Kirsten Elisabeth," the officer read, looking at Kirsti's baby picture. He let the photograph fall to the floor.

"Annemarie," he read next, glanced at her, and dropped the second photograph.

"Lise Margrete," he read finally, and stared at Ellen for a long, unwavering

moment. In her mind, Annemarie pictured the photograph that he held: the baby, wide-eyed, propped against a pillow, her tiny hand holding a silver teething ring, her bare feet visible below the hem of an embroidered dress. The wispy curls. Dark.

The officer tore the photograph in half and dropped the pieces on the floor. Then he turned, the heels of his shiny boots grinding into the pictures, and left the apartment. Without a word, the other two officers followed. Papa stepped forward and closed the door behind him.

Annemarie relaxed the clenched fingers of her right hand, which still clutched Ellen's necklace. She looked down, and saw that she had imprinted the Star of David into her palm.

 Think and Respond

1. How does Annemarie's family work together to help save Ellen from the German soldiers during the **occupation** of Denmark?

2. How does the author use dialogue and actions to make the German soldiers seem powerful and threatening?

3. In what way is Annemarie the real hero of the story?

4. Do you think the Johansens were right to have hidden Ellen? Explain why you feel as you do.

5. How did creating mental images help you understand the selection? When did you use this strategy?

Meet the Author

Lois Lowry

Lois Lowry has written many award-winning books for young readers. Here, Lowry talks about her Newbery Award-winning *Number the Stars*.

Q: What inspired you to write *Number the Stars*?

A: I went on vacation with a Danish friend of mine. We talked about her childhood. As we talked, I began to get an idea of what it was like for her during World War II. Although the incident in the story did not happen to her, she was able to tell me what it felt like when the Jewish families in her neighborhood started disappearing.

Q: Did you do any special research while writing the book?

A: After I started writing, I saw that I would need to do a great deal of research for the story, and I eventually went to Denmark. I spoke to people who lived through the war, and I went to the Holocaust Museum, which is dedicated to the role Denmark played. That was where I saw the shoes of fish skin that I used in the story.

Q: The Danes were very good about protecting Jewish people from the Nazis.

A: Yes. Like all Danes, my friend is proud of her country and its role in the war. For example, Danish doctors put Jewish people in hospitals, pretending they were patients, in order to save them. Of course, the doctors had to fill out medical papers for them, and as a sort of bitter joke, they put down German measles as a diagnosis. As my friend told me these stories, I began to see that they would make a wonderful children's book.

Visit *The Learning Site!*
www.harcourtschool.com

Lois Lowry

Making Connections

Compare Texts

1 How does "Number the Stars" relate to the theme of reaching out to help others?

2 How are the soldiers who come to the door different from the soldiers Annemarie is used to seeing on the streets?

3 Compare the mood of "Number the Stars" with the mood of "Yang the Eldest and His Odd Jobs." Why did the author of "Number the Stars" create the mood she did?

4 Nonfiction accounts of rescues during the Holocaust have also been written. How can you tell that "Number the Stars" is fiction rather than nonfiction?

5 What questions do you have about World War II after reading "Number the Stars"?

Write a Response to Literature

The characters in "Number the Stars" experience many emotions while Ellen stays with the Johansens. Choose a character, and write a paragraph describing at least three emotions that your character experienced. Use a web to organize your ideas. Support your ideas with evidence from the selection.

Writing CONNECTION

character's name

Collect Research Facts

Social Studies CONNECTION

Ellen's Star of David is a symbol of her Jewish religion. Research the origin of the Star of David and its importance to the ancient Hebrews. Share your findings with the class. Use a web diagram to collect your facts.

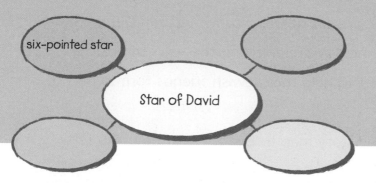

six-pointed star

Star of David

Present a Skit

Drama CONNECTION

Choose a favorite scene from "Number the Stars." Then work with a partner or a small group to present the scene to your classmates as a short dramatic skit. Use dialogue from the story. Think about the characters' feelings and their relationships with each other, and write additional dialogue for your scene.

Narrative Elements

Focus Skill

The **setting** of a story often has an important effect on the **plot**. This is especially true in a piece of historical fiction, such as "Number the Stars." The conflict between the Johansens and the German soldiers is a result of the circumstances in Denmark during World War II. The Nazis were arresting the Jews there. The Johansens' attempt to help their Jewish friends forms the plot of the story.

As you read the story map below, think of how the setting influences the feelings and actions of the characters.

Setting
Denmark in 1943 during World War II

↓

Conflict
Ellen Rosen and the Johansen family
vs.
the Nazi soldiers who come to the Johansens' house, looking for Ellen Rosen

↓

Resolution
Ellen pretends to be Annemarie's sister Lise. Papa saves Ellen by tearing Lise's photograph from an album to "prove" her identity to the soldiers.

Visit *The Learning Site!*
www.harcourtschool.com

See *Skills* and *Activities*

Test Prep
Narrative Elements

▶ **Read the passage. Then answer the questions.**

> The smell of smoke drifted across the summer camp. From inside their cabins, the campers could hear forest animals racing through the tall grass. The camp counselors wanted the group to leave the area immediately. As the campers walked down the hiking trail to safety, flames crackled in the distance. Suddenly, claps of thunder and dark storm clouds filled the sky. A thunderstorm soaked the forest. The campers celebrated when they realized the fire was out and they could go back to their cabins.

1. **What is the conflict in this story?**

   A A forest fire is a danger to the campers.

   B The campers get lost on a hike.

   C There is a fire near the campers' van.

   D Forest animals come into the camp.

   Tip
   Think about what disturbs the campers. You know choice C is wrong because there is nothing in the passage about a van.

2. **What effect does the storm have on the campers?**

   F It floods their camp.

   G It forces them to leave their cabins.

   H It attracts animals to their camp.

   J It allows them to return to their cabins.

   Tip
   This question asks you to identify how the event influences the characters' actions. Choose the answer that is supported by facts in the passage.

▲ The Summer of
the Swans

Vocabulary Power

expanse

engulf

compulsion

anguish

waver

disbelief

wailed

Have you ever searched for someone who was lost? Have you ever been lost yourself? The authors of these journal entries have. They write about both sides of being lost.

Friday, December 3

We organized a search party for the missing hikers this afternoon. The area we are searching is a great **expanse** of land that includes high mountains and deep valleys. If the soft snow did **engulf** and cover the hikers, I'm not sure we can save them in time. None of the volunteers will give up. They all feel a **compulsion** to try to save the lost hikers.

Tuesday, May 19

Today our dog got lost. "Mom, will I ever see Max again?" Chris asked, with tears of **anguish** in his eyes. I knew I had to find Max. I drove all around the neighborhood. Then I walked down to the lake behind the houses. As I called Max, I heard a faint sound **waver** in my ears. I followed the unsteady sound to the drainage ditch that connected to the lake. There was Max! His whining turned to excited yelps when he saw me. Chris was overjoyed when I brought Max home.

Sunday, July 20

The flood had destroyed the roads and bridges of our small village, turning it into a prison. When a small plane finally landed, we stared at the pilot in **disbelief**. We had almost given up hope that anyone would rescue us. Some of my neighbors **wailed** and sobbed as they told the pilot about the floodwaters' destructiveness. They were so grateful for her help.

Vocabulary–Writing CONNECTION

Imagine that you are in a high place, such as the top of a hill or a tower. Tell where you are, and describe the **expanse** that you see below. Use details that show how you feel.

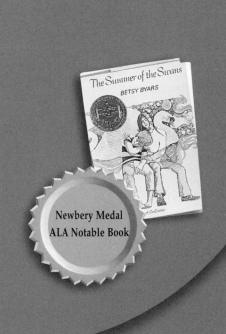

The Summer of the Swans
BETSY BYARS

Genre

Realistic Fiction

Realistic fiction tells about characters and events that are like people and events in real life.

In this selection, look for

- **The effect of the characters' actions on the plot**
- **Third-person point of view**

The Summer of the Swans

by Betsy Byars
illustrated by Lori Lohstoeter

Charlie is a ten-year-old boy who is developmentally disabled and unable to speak. He leaves his house one night, looking for the swans he has seen that day. He soon becomes lost in the nearby woods and is very frightened.

The next day, when his older sister, Sara, discovers he is missing, she and her classmate Joe search for him. After searching for hours, though, all they have found is Charlie's slipper.

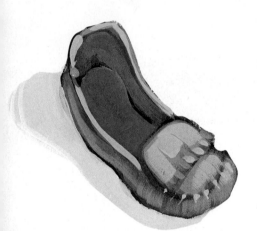

There was a ravine in the forest, a deep cut in the earth, and Charlie had made his way into it through an early morning fog. By chance, blindly stepping through the fog with his arms outstretched, he had managed to pick the one path that led into the ravine, and when the sun came out and the fog burned away, he could not find the way out.

All the ravine looked the same in the daylight, the high walls, the masses of weeds and wild berry bushes, the trees. He had wandered around for a while, following the little paths made by dirt washed down from the hillside, but finally he sat down on a log and stared straight ahead without seeing.

After a while he roused enough to wipe his hands over his cheeks where the tears and dirt had dried together and to rub his puffed eyelids. Then he looked down, saw his bare foot, put it on top of his slipper, and sat with his feet overlapped.

There was a dullness about him now. He had had so many scares, heard so many frightening noises, started at so many shadows, been hurt so often that all his senses were worn to a flat hopelessness. He would just sit here forever.

It was not the first time Charlie had been lost, but never before had there been this finality. He had become separated from Aunt Willie once at the county fair and had not even known he was lost until she had come bursting out of the crowd screaming, "Charlie, Charlie," and enveloped him. He had been lost in school once in the hall and could not find his way back to his room, and he had walked up and down the halls, frightened by all the strange children looking out of every door, until one of the boys was sent out to lead him to his room. But in all his life there had never been an experience like this one.

He bent over and looked down at his watch, his eyes on the tiny red hand. For the first time he noticed it was no longer moving. Holding his breath in his concern, he brought the watch closer to his face. The hand was still. For a moment he could not believe it. He watched it closely, waiting. Still the hand did not move. He shook his hand back and forth, as if he were trying to shake the watch off his wrist. He had seen Sara do this to her watch.

Then he held the watch to his ear. It was silent. He had had the watch for five months and never before had it failed him. He had not even known it could fail. And now it was silent and still.

He put his hand over the watch, covering it completely. He waited. His breathing had begun to quicken again. His hand on the watch was almost clammy. He waited, then slowly, cautiously, he removed his hand and looked at the tiny red hand on the dial. It was motionless. The trick had not worked.

Bending over the watch, he looked closely at the stem. Aunt Willie always wound the watch for him every morning after breakfast, but he did not know how she did this. He took the stem in his fingers, pulled at it clumsily, then harder, and it came off. He looked at it. Then, as he attempted to put it back on the watch, it fell to the ground and was lost in the leaves.

A chipmunk ran in front of him and scurried up the bank. Distracted for a moment, Charlie got up and walked toward it. The chipmunk paused and then darted into a hole, leaving Charlie standing in the shadows trying to see where it had gone. He went closer to the bank and pulled at the leaves, but he could not even find the place among the roots where the chipmunk had disappeared.

Suddenly something seemed to explode within Charlie, and he began to cry noisily. He threw himself on the bank and began kicking, flailing at the ground, at the invisible chipmunk, at the silent watch. He wailed, yielding in helplessness to his anguish, and his piercing screams, uttered again and again, seemed to hang in the air so that they overlapped. His fingers tore at the tree roots and dug beneath the leaves and scratched, animal-like, at the dark earth.

His body sagged and he rolled down the bank and was silent. He looked up at the trees, his chest still heaving with sobs, his face strangely still. After a moment, his eyelids drooped and he fell asleep.

"Charlie! Charlie!"

The only answer was the call of a bird in the branches overhead, one long tremulous whistle.

"He's not even within hearing distance," Sara said.

For the past hour she and Joe Melby had been walking deeper and deeper into the forest without pause, and now the trees were so thick that only small spots of sunlight found their way through the heavy foliage.

"Charlie, oh, Charlie!"

She waited, looking down at the ground.

Joe said, "You want to rest for a while?"

Sara shook her head. She suddenly wanted to see her brother so badly that her throat began to close. It was a tight feeling she got sometimes when she wanted something, like the time she had

had the measles and had wanted to see her father so much she couldn't even swallow. Now she thought that if she had a whole glass of ice water—and she was thirsty— she probably would not be able to drink a single drop.

"If you can make it a little farther, there's a place at the top of the hill where the strip mining is, and you can see the whole valley from there."

"I can make it."

"Well, we can rest first if— "

"I can make it."

She suddenly felt a little better. She thought that if she could stand up there on top of the hill and look down and see, somewhere in that huge green valley, a small plump figure in blue pajamas, she would ask for nothing more in life. She thought of the valley as a relief map where everything would be shiny and smooth, and her brother would be right where she could spot him at once. Her cry, "There he is!" would ring like a bell over the valley and everyone would hear her and know that Charlie had been found.

She paused, leaned against a tree for a moment, and then continued. Her legs had begun to tremble.

It was the time of afternoon when she usually sat down in front of the television and watched game shows, the shows where the married couples tried to guess things about each other and where girls had to pick out dates they couldn't see. She would sit in the doorway to the hall where she always sat and Charlie would come in and watch with her, and the living room would be dark and smell of the pine-scented cleaner Aunt Willie used.

Then "The Early Show" would come on, and she would sit through the old movie, leaning forward in the doorway, making fun, saying things like, "Now, Charlie, we'll have the old Convict Turning Honest scene," and Charlie, sitting on the stool closer to the television, would nod without understanding.

She was good, too, at joining in the dialogue with the actors. When the cowboy would say something like, "Things are quiet around here tonight," she would join in with, "Yeah, *too* quiet," right on cue. It seemed strange to be out here in the woods with Joe Melby instead of in the living room with Charlie, watching *Flame of Araby*, which was the early movie for that afternoon.

Her progress up the hill seemed slower and slower. It was like the time she had won the slow bicycle race, a race in which she had to go as slow as possible without letting a foot touch the ground, and she had gone slower and slower, all the while feeling a strong compulsion to speed ahead and cross the finish line first. At the end of the race it had been she and T.R. Peters, and they had paused just before the finish line, balancing motionless on their bicycles. The time had seemed endless, and then T.R. lost his balance and his foot touched the ground and Sara was the winner.

She slipped on some dry leaves, went down on her knees, straightened, and paused to catch her breath.

"Are you all right?"

"Yes, I just slipped."

She waited for a moment, bent over her knees, then she called, "Charlie! Charlie," without lifting her head.

"Oh, Charleeeeee," Joe shouted above her.

Sara knew Charlie would shout back if he heard her, the long wailing cry he gave sometimes when he was frightened during the night. It was such a familiar cry that for a moment she thought she heard it.

She waited, still touching the ground with one hand, until she was sure there was no answer.

"Come on," Joe said, holding out his hand.

He pulled her to her feet and she stood looking up at the top of the hill. Machines had cut away the earth there to get at the veins of coal, and the earth had been pushed down the hill to form a huge bank.

"I'll never get up that," she said. She leaned against a tree whose leaves were covered with the pale fine dirt which had filtered down when the machines had cut away the hill.

"Sure you will. I've been up it a dozen times."

He took her hand and she started after him, moving sideways up the steep bank. The dirt crumbled beneath her feet and she slid, skinned one knee, and then slipped again. When she had regained her balance she laughed wryly and said, "What's going to happen is that I'll end up pulling you all the way down the hill."

"No, I've got you. Keep coming."

She started again, putting one foot carefully above the other, picking her way over the stones. When she paused, he said, "Keep coming. We're almost there."

"I think it's a trick, like at the dentist's when he says, 'I'm almost through drilling.' Then he drills for another hour and says, 'Now, I'm really almost through drilling,' and he keeps on and then says, 'There's just one more spot and then I'll be practically really through.' "

"We must go to the same dentist."

"I don't think I can make it. There's no skin at all left on the sides of my legs."

"Well, we're really almost practically there now, in the words of your dentist."

She fell across the top of the dirt bank on her stomach, rested for a moment, and then turned and looked down the valley.

She could not speak for a moment. There lay the whole valley in a way she had never imagined it, a tiny finger of civilization set in a sweeping expanse of dark forest. The black treetops seemed to crowd against the yards, the houses, the roads, giving the impression that at any moment the trees would close over the houses like waves and leave nothing but an unbroken line of black-green leaves waving in the sunlight.

Up the valley she could see the intersection where they shopped, the drugstore, the gas station where her mother had once won a set of twenty-four stemmed glasses which Aunt Willie would not allow them to use, the grocery store, the lot where the yellow school buses were parked for the summer. She could look over the valley and see another hill where white cows were all grouped together by a fence and beyond that another hill and then another.

She looked back at the valley and she saw the lake and for the first time since she had stood up on the hill she remembered Charlie.

Raising her hand to her mouth, she called, "Charlie! Charlie! Charlie!" There was a faint echo that seemed to waver in her ears.

"Charlie, oh, Charlie!" Her voice was so loud it seemed to ram into the valley.

Sara waited. She looked down at the forest, and everything was so quiet it seemed to her that the whole valley, the whole world was waiting with her.

"Charlie, hey, Charlie!" Joe shouted.

"Charleeeeee!" She made the sound of it last a long time. "Can you hear meeeeee?"

With her eyes she followed the trail she knew he must have taken— the house, the Akers' vacant lot, the old pasture, the forest. The forest that seemed powerful enough to engulf a whole valley, she thought with a sinking feeling, could certainly swallow up a young boy.

"Charlie! Charlie! Charlie!" There was a waver in the last syllable that betrayed how near she was to tears. She looked down at the Indian slipper she was still holding.

"Charlie, oh, Charlie."

She waited. There was not a sound anywhere. "Charlie, where are you?"

"Hey, Charlie!" Joe shouted.

They waited in the same dense silence. A cloud passed in front of the sun and a breeze began to blow through the trees. Then there was silence again.

"Charlie, Charlie, Charlie, Charlie, Charlie."

She paused, listened, then bent abruptly and put Charlie's slipper to her eyes. She waited for the hot tears that had come so often this summer, the tears that had seemed so close only a moment before. Now her eyes remained dry.

I have cried over myself a hundred times this summer, she thought, I have wept over my big feet and my skinny legs and my nose, I have even cried over my stupid shoes, and now when I have a true sadness there are no tears left.

She held the felt side of the slipper against her eyes like a blindfold and stood there, feeling the hot sun on her head and the wind wrapping around her legs, conscious of the height and the valley sweeping down from her feet.

"Listen, just because you can't hear him doesn't mean anything. He could be— "

"Wait a minute." She lowered the slipper and looked down the valley. A sudden wind blew dust into her face and she lifted her hand to shield her eyes.

"I thought I heard something. Charlie! Answer me right this minute."

She waited with the slipper held against her breasts, one hand to her eyes, her whole body motionless, concentrating on her brother. Then she stiffened. She thought again she had heard something— Charlie's long high wail. Charlie could sound sadder than anyone when he cried.

In her anxiety she took the slipper and twisted it again and again as if she were wringing water out. She called, then stopped abruptly and listened. She looked at Joe and he shook his head slowly.

She looked away. A bird rose from the trees below and flew toward the hills in the distance. She waited until she could see it no longer and then slowly, still listening for the call that didn't come, she sank to the ground and sat with her head bent over her knees.

Beside her, Joe scuffed his foot in the dust and sent a cascade of rocks and dirt down the bank. When the sound of it faded, he began to call, "Charlie, hey, Charlie," again and again.

Charlie awoke, but he lay for a moment without opening his eyes. He did not remember where he was, but he had a certain dread of seeing it.

There were great parts of his life that were lost to Charlie, blank spaces that he could never fill in. He would find himself in a strange place and not know how he had got there. Like the time Sara had been hit in the nose with a baseball at the Dairy Queen, and the blood and the sight of Sara kneeling on the ground in helpless pain had frightened him so much that he had turned and run without direction, in a frenzy, dashing headlong up the street, blind to cars and people.

By chance Mr. Weicek had seen him, put him in the car, and driven him home, and Aunt Willie had put him to bed, but later he remembered none of this. He had only awakened in bed and looked at the crumpled bit of ice-cream cone still clenched in his hand and wondered about it.

His whole life had been built on a strict routine, and as long as this routine was kept up, he felt safe and well. The same foods, the same bed, the same furniture in the same place, the same seat on the school bus, the same class procedure were all important to him. But always there could be the unexpected, the dreadful surprise that would topple his carefully constructed life in an instant.

The first thing he became aware of was the twigs pressing into his face, and he put his hand under his cheek. Still he did not open his eyes. Pictures began to drift into his mind; he saw Aunt Willie's cigar box which was filled with old jewelry and buttons and knickknacks, and he found that he could remember every item in that box—the string of white beads without a clasp, the old earrings, the tiny book with souvenir fold-out pictures of New York, the plastic decorations from cakes, the turtle made of sea shells. Every item was so real that he opened his eyes and was surprised to see, instead of the glittering contents of the box, the dull and unfamiliar forest.

He raised his head and immediately felt the aching of his body. Slowly he sat up and looked down at his hands. His fingernails were black with earth, two of them broken below the quick, and he got up slowly and sat on the log behind him and inspected his fingers more closely.

Then he sat up straight. His hands dropped to his lap. His head cocked to the side like a bird listening. Slowly he straightened until he was standing. At his side his fingers twitched at the empty air as if to grasp something. He took a step forward, still with his head to the side. He remained absolutely still.

Then he began to cry out in a hoarse excited voice, again and again, screaming now, because he had just heard someone far away calling his name.

At the top of the hill Sara got slowly to her feet and stood looking down at the forest. She pushed the hair back from her forehead and moistened her lips. The wind dried them as she waited.

Joe started to say something but she reached out one hand and took his arm to stop him. Scarcely daring to believe her ears, she stepped closer to the edge of the bank. Now she heard it unmistakably—the sharp repeated cry—and she knew it was Charlie.

"Charlie!" she shouted with all her might.

She paused and listened, and his cries were louder and she knew he was not far away after all, just down the slope, in the direction of the ravine.

"It's Charlie, it's Charlie!"

A wild joy overtook her and she jumped up and down on the bare earth and she felt that she could crush the whole hill just by jumping if she wanted.

She sat and scooted down the bank, sending earth and pebbles in a cascade before her. She landed on the soft ground, ran a few steps, lost her balance, caught hold of the first tree trunk she could find, and swung around till she stopped.

She let out another whoop of pure joy, turned and ran down the hill in great strides, the puce tennis shoes slapping the ground like rubber paddles, the wind in her face, her hands grabbing one tree trunk after another for support. She felt like a wild creature who had traveled through the forest this way for a lifetime. Nothing could stop her now.

At the edge of the ravine she paused and stood gasping for breath. Her heart was beating so fast it pounded in her ears, and her throat was dry. She leaned against a tree, resting her cheek against the rough bark.

She thought for a minute she was going to faint, a thing she had never done before, not even when she broke her nose. She hadn't even believed people really did faint until this minute when she clung to the tree because her legs were as useless as rubber bands.

There was a ringing in her ears and another sound, a wailing siren-like cry that was painfully familiar.

"Charlie?"

Charlie's crying, like the sound of a cricket, seemed everywhere and nowhere.

She walked along the edge of the ravine, circling the large boulders and trees. Then she looked down into the ravine where the shadows lay, and she felt as if something had turned over inside her because she saw Charlie.

He was standing in his torn pajamas, face turned upward, hands raised, shouting with all his might. His eyes were shut tight. His face was streaked with dirt and tears. His pajama jacket hung in shreds about his scratched chest.

He opened his eyes and as he saw Sara a strange expression came over his face, an expression of wonder and joy and disbelief, and Sara knew that if she lived to be a hundred no one would ever look at her quite that way again.

She paused, looked down at him, and then, sliding on the seat of her pants, went down the bank and took him in her arms.

"Oh, Charlie."

His arms gripped her like steel.

"Oh, Charlie."

She could feel his fingers digging into her back as he clutched her shirt. "It's all right now, Charlie, I'm here and we're going home." His face was buried in her shirt and she patted his head, said again, "It's all right now. Everything's fine."

She held him against her for a moment and now the hot tears were in her eyes and on her cheeks and she didn't even notice.

"I know how you feel," she said. "I know. One time when I had the measles and my fever was real high, I got lost on my way back from the bathroom, right in our house, and it was a terrible feeling, terrible, because I wanted to get back to my bed and I couldn't find it, and finally Aunt Willie heard me and came and you know where I was? In the kitchen. In our kitchen and I couldn't have been more lost if I'd been out in the middle of the wilderness."

She patted the back of his head again and said, "Look, I even brought your bedroom slipper. Isn't that service, huh?"

She tried to show it to him, but he was still clutching her, and she held him against her, patting him. After a moment she said again, "Look, here's your slipper. Let's put it on." She knelt, put his foot into the shoe, and said, "Now, isn't that better?"

He nodded slowly, his chest still heaving with unspent sobs.

"Can you walk home?"

He nodded. She took her shirttail and wiped his tears and smiled at him. "Come on, we'll find a way out of here and go home."

"Hey, over this way," Joe called from the bank of the ravine. Sara had forgotten about him in the excitement of finding Charlie, and she looked up at him for a moment.

"Over this way, around the big tree," Joe called. "That's probably how he got in. The rest of the ravine is a mass of brier bushes."

She put one arm around Charlie and led him around the tree. "Everybody in town's looking for you, you know that?" she said. "Everybody. The police came and all the neighbors are out—there must be a hundred people looking for you. You were on the radio. It's like you were the President of the United States or something. Everybody was saying, 'Where's Charlie?' and 'We got to find Charlie.' "

Suddenly Charlie stopped and held up his hand and Sara looked down. "What is it?"

He pointed to the silent watch.

She smiled. "Charlie, you are something, you know that? Here we are racing down the hill to tell everyone in great triumph that you are found, *found*, and we have to stop and wind your watch first."

She looked at the watch, saw that the stem was missing, and shook her head. "It's broken, Charlie, see, the stem's gone. It's broken."

He held it out again.

"It's *broken*, Charlie. We'll have to take it to the jeweler and have it fixed."

He continued to hold out his arm.

"Hey, Charlie, you want to wear my watch till you get yours fixed?" Joe asked. He slid down the bank and put his watch on Charlie's arm. "There."

Charlie bent his face close and listened.

"Now can we go home?" Sara asked, jamming her hands into her back pockets.

Charlie nodded.

Think and Respond

1. What does Sara learn about herself as she searches for Charlie?

2. How does the author reveal Charlie's and Sara's **anguish**? Why is her technique effective?

3. How do you think the experience described in the story will change Sara's relationship with Charlie?

4. Would you recommend this selection to a friend who wanted to read a story about brothers and sisters? Explain why or why not.

5. Which focus strategy did you use while reading this selection? Why did you use it?

Betsy Byars

Award-winning author Betsy Byars's novels have been made into TV movies, and her books have been translated into nine languages. She is so popular with young readers that she receives about 200 fan letters a week.

Byars got the story idea for *The Summer of the Swans* while volunteering to teach children with learning disabilities. The children she met sparked ideas for the book. "Although the character Charlie is not one of the children I tutored—he is purely a fictitious character—he was an outgrowth of the experience," she says.

Byars's children helped her learn how to write for young readers. "Living with my own teenagers taught me that not only must I not write down to my readers, I must write up to them," Byars says. She also learns from students. "When I visit classrooms and talk with students, I am always impressed to find how many of them are writing stories and how knowledgeable they are about writing."

Visit *The Learning Site!*
www.harcourtschool.com

Making Connections

Compare Texts

1 How does "The Summer of the Swans" express the theme Friends to the Rescue?

2 Compare Sara's and Charlie's feelings during the search.

3 How do you know that Charlie's watch is an important part of his daily routine?

4 Compare "The Summer of the Swans" to the historical fiction selection "Number the Stars." Describe one similarity and one difference.

5 Would you like to read the rest of the novel from which this selection was taken? Why or why not?

Write a Description

The author of "The Summer of the Swans" describes various outdoor settings, including a forest and a valley. Imagine that you are lost in an outdoor place. Write a paragraph describing what you see, hear, smell, and touch. Use a chart to organize your ideas before you write.

**Writing
CONNECTION**

Outdoor Place	
What I see:	_____
What I hear:	_____
What I smell:	_____
What I touch:	_____

Read a Map

Social Studies
CONNECTION

Sara thinks of the valley as a relief map. Study a relief map of your state. Then list six facts about your state's geography that you can learn from the map. Use a chart to record the information.

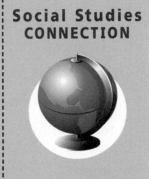

Map of _____
1. A mountain range borders the northern part of the state.
2. _____
3. _____
4. _____
5. _____
6. _____

Draw and Label a Forest

Art/Science
CONNECTION

Research the way plants and animals live together in a forest ecosystem. Then draw a picture of a forest and label the different kinds of plants and animals. Under each label, explain briefly how each living thing affects the environment.

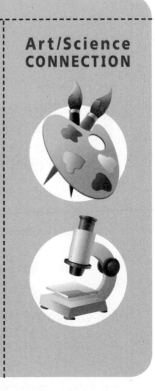

Literary Devices

**Focus
Skill**

To write a story, an author must choose a **point of view**. Will the author, or one of the characters, be the narrator? Which characters' thoughts and feelings will be shown?

First Person One of the story characters tells the story in his or her own voice, using the first-person pronoun *I*.
Third-Person Limited The narrator tells what one person in the story knows and thinks, using third-person pronouns (*he, she, they*).
Third-Person Omniscient The narrator is an all-knowing observer who may tell what all the characters know and think.

Betsy Byars chose the third-person omniscient point of view for "The Summer of the Swans" so that she could show what both Sara and Charlie experience. What does each passage below tell you about the character's thoughts and feelings?

> There were great parts of his life that were lost to Charlie, blank spaces that he could never fill in. He would find himself in a strange place and not know how he had got there.

> Sara shook her head. She suddenly wanted to see her brother so badly that her throat began to close. It was a tight feeling she got sometimes when she wanted something, like the time she had had the measles and had wanted to see her father so much she couldn't even swallow.

What would the story be like if the author had shown only Sara's thoughts and feelings?

Visit *The Learning Site!*
www.harcourtschool.com

See *Skills* and *Activities*

Test Prep
Literary Devices

▶ **Read the passage. Then answer the questions.**

> Jose and his twin sister, Clara, felt tired and upset after searching in the park for their dog, Sam, for almost an hour. Sam had wandered away while they were playing softball with their friends. "He's just a puppy," Jose said. "I don't think he'll know how to get home." Jose and Clara's friends spread out across the park to help them look for Sam. They knew there would be a better chance of locating Sam if everyone helped. Suddenly, everyone heard a loud barking in the distance. Jose and Clara smiled and ran in the direction of the sound.

1. **Which point of view did the author of this passage choose?**

   A first person

   B third-person limited

   C third-person omniscient

   D first and third person

Tip

Don't let the word *I* in the dialogue confuse you. Ask yourself which of the characters' thoughts and feelings the author reveals.

2. **How can you tell that Clara is worried about Sam?**

   F by what she says

   G by her thoughts and actions

   H by what Jose says about her

   J by her tone of voice

Tip

Review the passage again to eliminate the wrong answers. You know F and J are wrong because Clara does not speak in the passage.

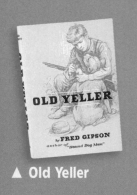

Vocabulary Power

yarns

charging

romping

frantic

lunging

pounced

In the next selection, a boy named Travis faces dangers as a Texas pioneer. Look at this review of a book featuring some difficult times for the pioneers.

All the stories in this book about pioneer life are true. There are no **yarns**, or tall tales, here. In one chapter, a bull escaped from a barn and came **charging** across a field.

The animal rushed toward a young child who had been **romping**, or running and playing, in the grass. His older sister heard his **frantic** screams and pulled the boy over the fence to safety.

Another story describes a bobcat suddenly **lunging** forward from its hiding place near a pioneer cabin. It **pounced** on a wild rabbit, quickly seizing the animal with its strong jaws. The pioneer woman frightened the bobcat away with a stick.

**Vocabulary–Writing
CONNECTION**

Imagine living as a pioneer. What would you do if a wild animal came **charging** toward you? Write a few sentences describing how you would handle the situation.

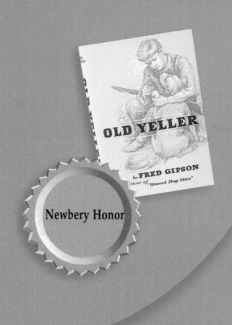

OLD YELLER

by FRED GIPSON
author of "Hound Dog Man"

Newbery Honor

Genre

Realistic Fiction

Realistic fiction tells about characters and events that are like people and events in real life.

In this selection, look for

- **Details that help the reader picture the setting**

- **A narrator who describes his feelings about the events**

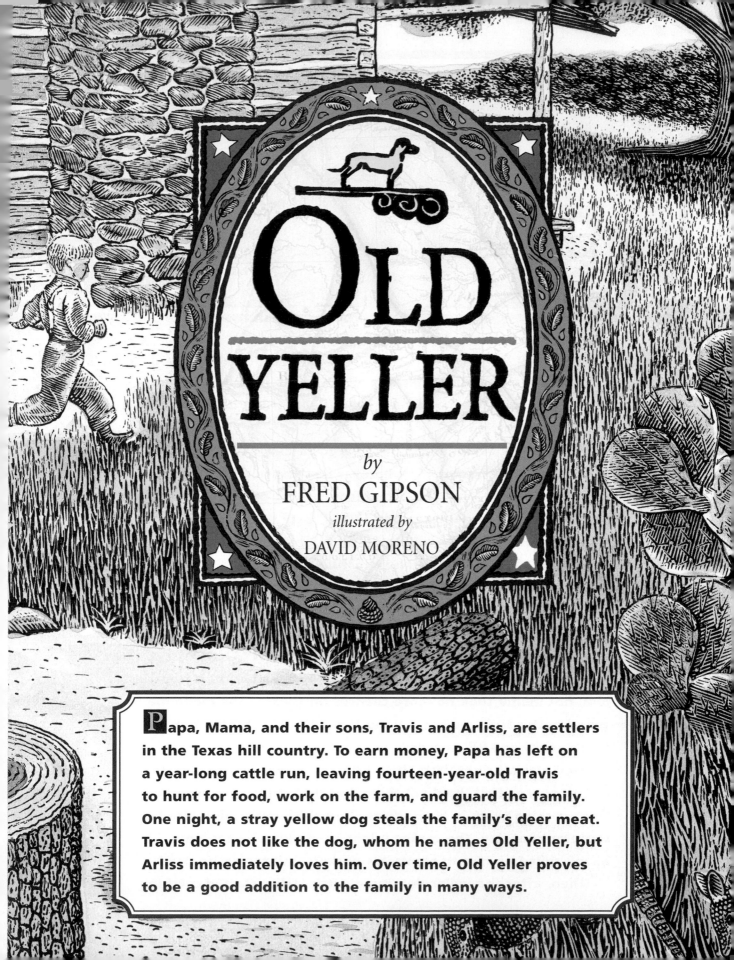

OLD YELLER

by

FRED GIPSON

illustrated by

DAVID MORENO

Papa, Mama, and their sons, Travis and Arliss, are settlers in the Texas hill country. To earn money, Papa has left on a year-long cattle run, leaving fourteen-year-old Travis to hunt for food, work on the farm, and guard the family. One night, a stray yellow dog steals the family's deer meat. Travis does not like the dog, whom he names Old Yeller, but Arliss immediately loves him. Over time, Old Yeller proves to be a good addition to the family in many ways.

That Little Arliss! If he wasn't a mess! From the time he'd grown up big enough to get out of the cabin, he'd made a practice of trying to catch and keep every living thing that ran, flew, jumped, or crawled.

Every night before Mama let him go to bed, she'd make Arliss empty his pockets of whatever he'd captured during the day. Generally, it would be a tangled-up mess of grasshoppers and worms and praying bugs and little rusty tree lizards. One time he brought in a horned toad that got so mad he swelled out round and flat as a Mexican *tortilla* and bled at the eyes. Sometimes it was stuff like a young bird that had fallen out of its nest before it could fly, or a green-speckled spring frog or a striped water snake. And once he turned out of his pocket a wadded-up baby copperhead that nearly threw Mama into spasms. We never did figure out why the snake hadn't bitten him, but Mama took no more chances on snakes. She made me spend better than a week, taking him out and teaching him to throw rocks and kill snakes.

That was all right with Little Arliss. If Mama wanted him to kill his snakes first, he'd kill them. But that still didn't keep him from sticking them in his pockets along with everything else he'd captured that day. The snakes might be stinking by the time Mama called on him to empty his pockets, but they'd be dead.

Then, after the yeller dog came, Little Arliss started catching

188

even bigger game. Like cottontail rabbits and chaparral birds
and a baby possum that sulked and lay like dead for the first
several hours until he finally decided that Arliss wasn't going to
hurt him.

Of course, it was Old Yeller that was doing the catching.
He'd run the game down and turn it over to Little Arliss. Then
Little Arliss could come in and tell Mama a big fib about how he
caught it himself.

I watched them one day when they caught a blue catfish out
of Birdsong Creek. The fish had fed out into water so shallow
that his top fin was sticking out. About the time I saw it, Old
Yeller and Little Arliss did, too. They made a run at it. The fish
went scooting away toward deeper water, only Yeller was too
fast for him. He pounced on the fish and shut his big mouth
down over it and went romping to the bank, where he dropped
it down on the grass and let it flop. And here came Little Arliss
to fall on it like I guess he'd been doing everything else. The
minute he got his hands on it, the fish finned him and he went
to crying.

But he wouldn't turn the fish loose. He just grabbed it up and
went running and squawling toward the house, where he gave
the fish to Mama. His hands were all bloody by then, where the
fish had finned him. They swelled up and got mighty sore; not
even a mesquite thorn hurts as bad as a sharp fish fin when it's

run deep into your hand.

But as soon as Mama had wrapped his hands in a poultice of mashed-up prickly-pear root to draw out the poison, Little Arliss forgot all about his hurt. And that night when we ate the fish for supper, he told the biggest windy I ever heard about how he'd dived 'way down into a deep hole under the rocks and dragged that fish out and nearly got drowned before he could swim to the bank with it.

But when I tried to tell Mama what really happened, she wouldn't let me. "Now, this is Arliss's story," she said. "You let him tell it the way he wants to."

I told Mama then, I said: "Mama, that old yeller dog is going to make the biggest liar in Texas out of Little Arliss."

But Mama just laughed at me, like she always laughed at Little Arliss's big windies after she'd gotten off where he couldn't hear her. She said for me to let Little Arliss alone. She said that if he ever told a bigger whopper than the ones I used to tell, she had yet to hear it.

Well, I hushed then. If Mama wanted Little Arliss to grow up to be the biggest liar in Texas, I guessed it wasn't any of my business.

All of which, I figure, is what led up to Little Arliss's catching the bear. I think Mama had let him tell so many big yarns about his catching live game that he'd begun to believe them himself.

When it happened, I was down the creek a ways, splitting rails to fix up the yard fence where the bulls had torn it down. I'd been down there since dinner, working in a stand of tall slim post oaks. I'd chop down a tree, trim off the branches as far up as I wanted, then cut away the rest of the top. After that I'd start splitting the log.

I'd split the log by driving steel wedges into the wood. I'd start at the big end and hammer in a wedge with the back side of my axe. This would start a little split running lengthways of the log. Then I'd take a second wedge and drive it into this split. This would split the log further along and, at the same time, loosen the first wedge. I'd then knock the first wedge loose and move it up in front of the second one.

Driving one wedge ahead of the other like that, I could finally split a log in two halves. Then I'd go to work on the halves, splitting them apart. That way, from each log, I'd come out with four rails.

Swinging that chopping axe was sure hard work. The sweat poured off me. My back muscles ached. The axe got so heavy I

could hardly swing it. My breath got harder and harder to breathe.

An hour before sundown, I was worn down to a nub. It seemed like I couldn't hit another lick. Papa could have lasted till past sundown, but I didn't see how I could. I shouldered my axe and started toward the cabin, trying to think up some excuse to tell Mama to keep her from knowing I was played clear out.

That's when I heard Little Arliss scream.

Well, Little Arliss was a screamer by nature. He'd scream when he was happy and scream when he was mad and a lot of times he'd scream just to hear himself make a noise. Generally, we paid no more mind to his screaming than we did to the gobble of a wild turkey.

But this time was different. The second I heard his screaming, I felt my heart flop clear over. This time I knew Little Arliss was in real trouble.

I tore out up the trail leading toward the cabin. A minute before, I'd been so tired out with my rail splitting that I couldn't have struck a trot. But now I raced through the tall trees in that creek bottom, covering ground like a scared wolf.

Little Arliss's second scream, when it came, was louder and shriller and more frantic-sounding than the first. Mixed with it was a whimpering crying sound that I knew didn't come from him. It was a sound I'd heard before and seemed like I ought to know what it was, but right then I couldn't place it.

Then, from way off to one side came a sound that I would have recognized anywhere. It was the coughing roar of a charging bear. I'd just heard it once in my life. That was the time Mama had shot and wounded a hog-killing bear and Papa had had to finish it off with a knife to keep it from getting her.

My heart went to pushing up into my throat, nearly choking off my wind. I strained for every lick of speed I could get out of my running legs. I didn't know what sort of fix Little Arliss had got himself into, but I knew that it had to do with a mad bear, which was enough.

The way the late sun slanted through the trees had the trail all cross-banded with streaks of bright light and dark shade. I ran through these bright and dark patches so fast that the changing light nearly blinded me. Then suddenly, I raced out into the open where I could see ahead. And what I saw sent a chill clear through to the marrow of my bones.

There was Little Arliss, down in that spring hole again. He was lying half in and half out of the water, holding onto the hind leg of a little black bear cub no bigger than a small coon. The bear cub was out on the bank, whimpering and crying and clawing the rocks with all three of his other feet, trying to pull away. But Little Arliss was holding on for all he was worth, scared now and screaming his head off. Too scared to let go.

How come the bear cub ever to prowl close enough for Little Arliss to grab him, I don't know. And why he didn't turn on him and bite loose, I couldn't figure out, either. Unless he was like Little Arliss, too scared to think.

But all of that didn't matter now. What mattered was the bear cub's mama. She'd heard the cries of her baby and was coming to save him. She was coming so fast that she had the brush popping and breaking as she crashed through and over it. I could see her black heavy figure piling off down the slant on the far side of Birdsong Creek. She was roaring mad and ready to kill.

And worst of all, I could see that I'd never get there in time!

Mama couldn't either. She'd heard Arliss, too, and here she came from the cabin, running down the slant toward the spring, screaming at Arliss, telling him to turn the bear cub loose. But Little Arliss wouldn't do it. All he'd do was hang with that hind leg and let out one shrill shriek after another as fast as he could suck in a breath.

Now the she-bear was charging across the shallows in the creek. She was knocking sheets of water high in the bright sun, charging with her fur up and her long teeth bared, filling the canyon with that awful coughing roar. And no matter how fast Mama ran or how fast I ran, the she-bear was going to get there first!

I think I nearly went blind then, picturing what was going to happen to Little Arliss. I know that I opened my mouth to scream and not any sound came out.

Then, just as the bear went lunging up the creek bank toward Little Arliss and her cub, a flash of yellow came streaking out of the brush.

It was that big yeller dog. He was roaring like a mad bull. He wasn't one-third as big and heavy as the she-bear, but when he piled into her from one side, he rolled her clear off her feet. They went down in a wild, roaring tangle of twisting bodies and scrambling feet and slashing fangs.

As I raced past them, I saw the bear lunge up to stand on her hind feet like a man while she clawed at the body of the yeller dog hanging to her throat. I didn't wait to see more. Without ever checking my stride, I ran in and jerked Little Arliss loose from the cub. I grabbed him by the wrist and yanked him up out of that water and slung him toward Mama like he was a half-empty sack of corn. I screamed at Mama. "Grab him, Mama! Grab him and run!" Then I swung my chopping axe high and wheeled, aiming to cave in the she-bear's head with the first lick.

But I never did strike. I didn't need to. Old Yeller hadn't let the bear get close enough. He couldn't handle her; she was too big and strong for that. She'd stand there on her hind feet,

hunched over, and take a roaring swing at him with one of those big front claws. She'd slap him head over heels. She'd knock him so far that it didn't look like he could possibly get back there before she charged again, but he always did. He'd hit the ground rolling, yelling his head off with the pain of the blow; but somehow he'd always roll to his feet. And here he'd come again, ready to tie into her for another round.

I stood there with my axe raised, watching them for a long moment. Then from up toward the house, I heard Mama calling: "Come away from there, Travis. Hurry, son! Run!"

That spooked me. Up till then, I'd been ready to tie into that bear myself. Now, suddenly, I was scared out of my wits again. I ran toward the cabin.

But like it was, Old Yeller nearly beat me there. I didn't see it, of course; but Mama said that the minute Old Yeller saw we were all in the clear and out of danger, he threw the fight to that she-bear and lit out for the house. The bear chased him for a little piece, but at the rate Old Yeller was leaving her behind, Mama said it looked like the bear was backing up.

But if the big yeller dog was scared or hurt in any way when he came dashing into the house, he didn't show it. He sure didn't show it like we all did. Little Arliss had hushed his screaming, but he was trembling all over and clinging to Mama like he'd never let her go. And Mama was sitting in the middle of the floor, holding him up close and crying like she'd never stop. And me, I was close to crying, myself.

Old Yeller, though, all he did was come bounding in to jump on us and lick us in the face and bark so loud that there, inside the cabin, the noise nearly made us deaf.

The way he acted, you might have thought that bear fight hadn't been anything more than a rowdy romp that we'd all taken part in for the fun of it.

Till Little Arliss got us mixed up in that bear fight, I guess I'd been looking on him about like most boys look on their little brothers. I liked him, all right, but I didn't have a lot of use for him. What with his always playing in our drinking water and getting in the way of my chopping axe and howling his head off and chunking me with rocks when he got mad, it didn't seem to me like he was hardly worth the bother of putting up with.

But that day when I saw him in the spring, so helpless against the angry she–bear, I learned different. I knew then that I loved him as much as I did Mama and Papa, maybe in some ways even a little bit more.

So it was only natural for me to come to love the dog that saved him.

Think and Respond

1 How do Travis's feelings about Old Yeller change? What causes this change?

2 How does the author help you picture the bear *lunging* at Little Arliss on the creek bed?

3 Why does the author tell this story from Travis's point of view instead of using a third-person narrator?

4 What would you like or dislike about being a pioneer living near Birdsong Creek?

5 What strategies did you use while reading this selection?

About the Author
FRED GIPSON

As a young boy, Fred Gipson (1908–1973) worked on his family's farm in Mason, Texas. Back then, Fred's father used to entertain the family by telling stories. When Fred grew up, he found work as a reporter. When he started writing fiction, he used his Texas background to inspire his stories.

Fred Gipson's most popular book was *Old Yeller*. He later wrote the screenplay for the movie based on the story. In an interview, he explained why he enjoyed creating exciting, realistic stories. "I've always liked true adventure tales and have always felt that I learned more about the history of my country from these tales than I ever did from the history books."

Meet the Illustrator
DAVID MORENO

David Moreno lives in Central Texas, the setting of *Old Yeller*. In fact, the story takes place near his hometown. This made it very easy for Moreno to research the area and take photographs. When he is not at work photographing, designing, or illustrating, Moreno relaxes by biking, windsurfing, or riding horses.

Visit *The Learning Site!*
www.harcourtschool.com

Puppies with a Purpose

from *National Geographic World*

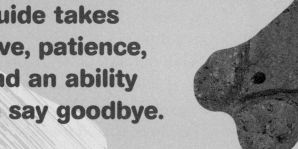

**Training a Dog
Guide takes
love, patience,
and an ability
to say goodbye.**

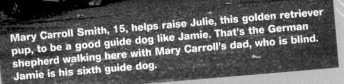

Mary Carroll Smith, 15, helps raise Julie, this golden retriever pup, to be a good guide dog like Jamie. That's the German shepherd walking here with Mary Carroll's dad, who is blind. Jamie is his sixth guide dog.

Julie seems like any other lively puppy. She romps and wrestles with other dogs. But unlike most pups, Julie has an important job ahead of her. One day she will serve as substitute eyes for a blind person.

For the first 16 months of her life, Julie is living with Mary Carroll Smith, 15, of Nutley, New Jersey. Mary Carroll is in The Seeing Eye Puppy-Raising Program/4-H Project. The program places future guide dogs with volunteer puppy raisers who start preparing the puppies for the job ahead. Mary Carroll wanted to raise puppies so she could help other people have the same freedom that her blind father has with his guide dog.

Getting Julie used to strangers and new places is Mary Carroll's most important task. She takes Julie to soccer and softball games, into stores and restaurants, and sometimes to school. "At first she was nervous," said Mary Carroll. "But the more I took her out, the better she got. Now she's mellow!"

Playing with Julie is part of Mary Carroll's job, too. Playing helps Julie become a friendly, loving dog. Mary Carroll also teaches her to obey simple commands such as "sit" and "come." "I praise her by talking to her and petting her," explains Mary Carroll. "I correct her by telling her 'no' firmly."

Julie will eventually leave Mary Carroll and return to Seeing Eye headquarters for more guide dog training. Raising a puppy and then giving it up isn't easy. Even so, Mary Carroll says, "It's a good feeling to know you're helping someone else."

Class Act
Every two weeks, Mary Carroll joins other 4-H puppy raisers for talk and training. Here she learns a signal that tells Julie to "rest."

Good Doggies
When the puppy raisers go for an after-class snack, their guide-dogs-in-training are allowed to follow. They learn to stay under the table and not beg.

Think and Respond
Which of Mary's responsibilities seems most difficult to you?

A Nose for Snooze
Julie waits patiently for Mary Carroll's Latin class to end. Like any good guide dog, she lies still until Mary Carroll signals that it's time to get going.

Making Connections

Compare Texts

1 Why is "Old Yeller" included in the theme Friends to the Rescue?

2 Compare Travis's feelings about Arliss at the beginning and at the end of "Old Yeller."

3 Which selection do you think provides a more effective picture of a special relationship between dog and owner, "Old Yeller" or "Puppies with a Purpose"? Explain.

4 How is the description of pioneer life in "Old Yeller" different from a description you might find in a history textbook?

5 Where could you find more information about animals that help people with special needs?

Write a Letter That Explains

Write a letter in which Travis explains to his father what happened to Arliss. Use a sequence chart to organize the events in time order.

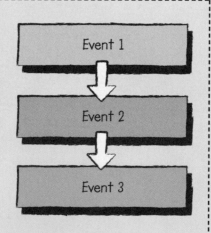

Event 1

Event 2

Event 3

Writing
CONNECTION

Make a Chart

"Old Yeller" is about the relationship between a dog and a family. Dogs and people have lived and worked together for at least 10,000 years. Using an encyclopedia, research the roles of dogs in ancient times. Record your findings in a chart.

Dogs in Ancient Times
1. hunters
2. _____
3. _____

Make a Food Chain

In "Old Yeller," you read about the wild creatures Travis saw in the Texas hill country. What kinds of wild animals are common in your state? Create and illustrate a food chain that includes several of these animals. Label each illustration with the plant's or animal's name and one fact about it.

▲ Old Yeller

Summarize and Paraphrase

As you read a story, it is often helpful to stop several times to summarize what you have read. When you **summarize**, you tell in one or two sentences the most important information.

To **paraphrase** a passage, you retell it, in detail, in your own words. The length of the text often stays the same.

Read this paragraph from "Old Yeller." Then look at the chart below to see how summarizing and paraphrasing are different.

> There was Little Arliss, down in that spring hole again. He was lying half in and half out of the water, holding onto the hind leg of a little black bear cub no bigger than a small coon. The bear cub was out on the bank, whimpering and crying and clawing the rocks with all three of his other feet, trying to pull away. But Little Arliss was holding on for all he was worth, scared now and screaming his head off. Too scared to let go.

Summarize Tell only the most important information.	Little Arliss grabbed a bear cub's leg and refused to let go.
Paraphrase Tell main ideas and details in your own words.	While in a spring hole, Little Arliss grabbed the back leg of a small bear cub. Although the bear cub cried and tried to get away, Little Arliss continued to hold the animal tightly. The boy screamed because he was scared to let go.

Test Prep
Summarize and Paraphrase

▶ **Read the passage. Then answer the questions.**

> Leo and his dog, Skipper, had been swimming in Mill Creek all afternoon. "We'd better go home now," Leo said. "We can take a short-cut by using the old hiking trail. It's not far from the creek." Halfway down the trail, Leo slipped and fell. When he tried to get up, he realized that his ankle was badly sprained. "Run home to get help," Leo said to Skipper. "Hurry!" Before long, Leo spotted his parents coming up the trail in the distance. Skipper was directly in front of them, leading the way.

1. **Which is the *best* summary for this passage?**

   A Leo and Skipper swam all afternoon in Mill Creek.

   B Leo and Skipper found an old hiking trail close to the creek.

   C Leo fell on a hiking trail and badly sprained his ankle.

   D Leo's dog got help for him after he fell on the way home from Mill Creek.

Tip

Each of these things happens in the passage. You must decide which one includes the most important information.

2. **Retell the passage in your own words.**

Tip

As you paraphrase, don't forget to include the information in the dialogue. Leo's words help you know what is happening.

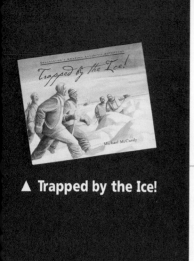

▲ **Trapped by the Ice!**

Vocabulary Power

perilous

dehydration

bailed

grueling

impassable

rancid

For centuries, explorers have risked their lives to discover new lands. They set off in many different directions, but they all faced one common challenge—nature!

In 1492 Christopher Columbus set sail on a **perilous** trip across the Atlantic Ocean. The journey was dangerous because it was so long. If the water supply ran out, the sailors would die of **dehydration**. When a storm filled their ships with water, they **bailed** with all their strength so they wouldn't sink. At the end of this **grueling** and difficult journey, Columbus and his crew reached North America.

Lewis and Clark set out to explore the western part of the United States in 1804. At first their boats were in danger of capsizing, or turning over, in the Missouri River. Then they had to cross the Rocky Mountains, which were so large, they seemed **impassable**. Fortunately, a Native American guide helped them find the best route to follow, and they reached their goal.

In the early 1800s, a group called the Mountain Men discovered an easy way to cross the Rocky Mountains in Wyoming. These adventurers wanted to get furs to sell. When their food became **rancid**, or spoiled, they trapped wild animals to get fresh meat.

Vocabulary-Writing CONNECTION

Early explorers often faced **perilous** conditions. Imagine that you are an explorer trying to cross an icy river. Write a journal entry describing your adventure.

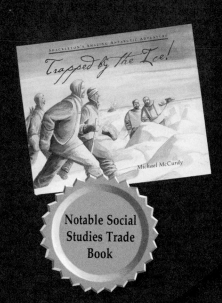

TRAP

Genre

Nonfiction

Nonfiction tells about people, things, events, or places that are real.

In this selection, look for

- An interesting historical event

- The presentation of events in time order

- People who help one another

PED by the ICE!

by Michael McCurdy

Foreword

In 1914, Sir Ernest Shackleton (1874-1922) sailed from England on his third Antarctic expedition. Since Roald Amundsen had reached the pole in 1911, Shackleton had longed to be the first to cross the polar ice cap.

Soon after leaving South Georgia Island in the South Atlantic Ocean, Shackleton's ship, the *Endurance*, entered the ice pack of the Weddell Sea. When the ship had almost reached land, it became trapped in the ice and was carried northward by the current, away from land. The adventure, lasting two years, is one of the most remarkable true-life survival stories on record.

October 27, 1915

The *Endurance* was trapped. Giant blocks of ice were slowly crushing her sides. From the deck, Sir Ernest Shackleton looked at the snow and ice that spread to the horizon. Ten months before, all he had wanted was to be the first person to cross the South Pole's ice cap. Now his only concern was for his men. What would happen to them—and how much longer did the ship have before it broke apart? The *Endurance* was leaking badly. Shack could not delay.

Shack ordered his crew off the *Endurance* and camp was set up on the frozen Weddell Sea. Tools, tents, scrap lumber for firewood, sleeping bags, and what little food rations and clothing the men had left were saved from their ship, along with three lifeboats in case they ever reached open water. The *Endurance* was a sad sight now, a useless hulk lying on its side. For months she had been the crew's home. Now they would have to get used to life on the ice—stranded hundreds of miles from the nearest land.

November 21, 1915

Almost one month later, the sound of crushing wood startled the men. It was what they had feared. Turning toward the ship's wreckage, they saw her stern rise slowly in the air, tremble, and slip quickly beneath the ice. Minutes later, the hole had frozen up over the ship. She was gone forever, swallowed by the Weddell Sea. Shack talked with the ship's skipper, Frank Worsley, and his next-in-command, Frankie Wild. Among them, they would have to decide what to do next.

December 23, 1915

Executing their plan would be difficult. By pulling the lifeboats, loaded with supplies, they would try to cross the barren ice to open water. If they made it, they would use the three boats to reach the nearest land. Shack studied the unending snow and ice ahead of him. Was it possible? Each boat was mounted on a sledge. Harnessed like horses, the men pulled, one boat at a time. Pulling 2,000-pound loads was hard work. Soon everybody was so tired and sore that no one could pull anymore. The crew would have to wait for the ice, moved by the sea's current, to carry them north to open water.

Over the next few months, food was always a concern, and it was Tom Orde-Lees's job to find it. Penguins and seals were growing scarce. To find meat to eat, hunters had to go farther away. This was dangerous. Once, when Tom was skiing back to camp, a monstrous head burst from the ice. A giant sea leopard lunged at Tom, only to slip quickly back into the dark water, stalking Tom from below, as sea leopards do when they hunt penguins. Tom tripped and fell. The huge animal lunged again, this time springing out of the water and right onto the ice. Back on his feet, Tom tried to get away. He cried for help, and Frankie Wild rushed over from camp carrying a rifle. The sea leopard now charged Frankie, who dropped calmly to one knee, took careful aim, and fired three shots. The sea leopard fell dead. There was plenty to eat for days afterward!

April 8, 1916

The men smelled terrible. During their five and a half months on the ice they hadn't had a bath. Clothes were greasy and worn thin, and they rubbed against the men's skin, causing painful sores. Hands were cracked from the cold and wind, and hunger sapped everyone's strength. By now, the ice floes were breaking up into smaller and smaller pieces all around the men as they drifted closer to the edge of the polar sea. Shack thought it was a good time to launch the lifeboats, rigged with small canvas sails. He knew his men could not all survive the grueling 700-mile open-boat journey to the whaling station on South Georgia Island. So he decided to try to reach Elephant Island first.

Steering around the blocks of ice was hard. The boats bumped into ice floes—or crashed into icebergs. As night fell, the boats were pulled up onto a big floe and the tents were raised. But sleeping was difficult with damp bags and blankets, and with noisy killer whales circling around.

One night, Shack suddenly felt something was wrong. He shook Frankie, and they crawled out of their tent for a look. A huge wave smacked headlong into the floe with a great thud, and the floe began to split into two pieces. The crack was headed straight toward Tent Number 4! Then Shack heard a splash. Looking into the crevasse, he saw a wriggling shape below in the dark water. It was a sleeping bag—with Ernie Holness inside! Shack acted quickly. Reaching down, he pulled the soggy bag out of the water with one mighty jerk. And just in time, too—within seconds the two great blocks of ice crashed back together.

April 13, 1916

Finally, the men reached open water. The savage sea slammed furiously into the three little boats—called the *James Caird*, the *Dudley Docker*, and the *Stancomb Wills*. Tall waves lifted them up and down like a roller coaster. Blinding sea spray blew into the men's faces. Most of them became seasick. Worst of all, they were very thirsty, because seawater had spoiled the freshwater. The men's tongues had swelled so much from dehydration they could hardly swallow. Shack had his men suck on frozen seal meat to quench their thirst. They *had* to make land. They had to get to Elephant Island!

April 15, 1916

After an exhausting week battling the sea, the men nearly lost all hope. Big Tom Crean tried to cheer the men with a song, but nothing worked. Finally, something appeared in the distance. Shack called across to Frank Worsley in the *Dudley Docker*, "There she is, Skipper!" It was land. It was Elephant Island at last. It looked terribly barren, with jagged 3,500-foot peaks rising right up out of the sea, yet it was the only choice the men had.

April 24, 1916

Elephant Island was nothing but rock, ice, snow—and wind. Tents were pitched but quickly blew away. Without resting, Shack planned his departure for South Georgia Island. There he would try to get help. Twenty-two men would stay behind while Shack and a crew braved the 700-mile journey in the worst winter seas on earth. The five ablest men were picked: Frank Worsley; Big Tom Crean; the carpenter, Chippy McNeish; and two seamen, Tim McCarthy and John Vincent. With frozen fingers and a few tools, Chippy prepared the *Caird* for the rough journey ahead. Only nine days after the men had first sighted the deserted island, Shack and his crew of five were on open water once again.

For the men who stayed behind, permanent shelter was now needed or they would freeze to death. Frankie Wild had the men turn the two remaining boats upside down, side by side. Then the boats were covered with canvas and a cookstove was put inside. The hut was dark and cramped, lit only by a burning wick. And something happened that the men had not expected: heat from their bodies and the stove melted the ice under them as well as piles of frozen bird droppings left for years by the frigate birds and penguins. The smell was terrible! Day after day the men looked toward the sea, wondering if Shack would make it back to rescue them. How long would they be left here? Was Shack all right?

May 5, 1916

The *Caird* made her way through the storm-tossed seas, while Shack and his men drank rancid seal oil to prevent seasickness. The ocean swelled and hissed and broke over the small boat as the men worried about the terrible graybeards found in these waters. Graybeards are monstrous waves that come quietly and quickly, threatening everything in their path. The men had to battle to keep the boat free of ice, because any added weight might sink the *Caird*. Suddenly, Shack screamed from the tiller. The men turned around to face the biggest wave they had ever seen. It was a graybeard! The boat shuddered on impact as the mountain of water spun it around like a top. Water filled the *Caird* while the men bailed furiously. Jagged rocks in her hull, which Chippy had used to keep the boat from capsizing, saved the day.

May 10, 1916

Finally, after seventeen grueling days at sea, young McCarthy shouted, "Land ho!" South Georgia Island lay dimly ahead. The whaling station was on the other side of the island, but the men had to land *now* or die. Their freshwater was gone, and they were too weak to battle the sea to the other side of the island. While the men planned their landing attempt, they were hit by the worst hurricane they had ever encountered. For nine terrible hours they fought to keep afloat. Miraculously, just as things looked hopeless, the sea calmed enough to allow the *Caird* to land safely on the rocky beach of Haakon Bay.

The men landed near a small cave with a freshwater spring nearby. The cave would become a temporary home for John Vincent and Chippy McNeish. Both had suffered too much on the voyage and could not survive the long hike across the island to the whaling station. Tim McCarthy stayed behind to take care of the two sick men. Fortunately, water for drinking, wood from old shipwrecks for fire, and albatross eggs and seals to eat meant those who stayed behind would be all right while waiting for their rescue. But Shack, Big Tom, and Skipper Worsley would have to climb over a series of jagged ridges that cut the island in half like a saw blade. All they could carry was a little Primus stove, fuel for six meals, fifty feet of rope, and an ice ax. Their only food consisted of biscuits and light rations that hung in socks around their necks. On their eighth day ashore, May 18, it was time to set off on the most dangerous climb they had ever attempted.

May 19, 1916

Three times the men struggled up mountains, only to find that the terrain was impassable on the other side. The men stopped only to eat a soup called "hoosh," to nibble on stale biscuits, or to nap five minutes, with each man taking a turn awake so that there would be someone to wake the others. On and on the exhausted men hiked. From one mountain summit they saw that night was coming fast. Being caught on a peak at night meant certain death. They had to make a dangerous gamble. Shack assembled a makeshift toboggan from the coiled-up rope and the men slid 1,500 feet down the mountain in one big slide. Despite the perilous landing, they couldn't help but laugh with relief after they had crashed, unhurt, into a large snowbank.

The men had survived the long slide, but danger still lay ahead. They had been hiking for more than thirty hours now without sleep. Finally, all three heard the sound of a far-off whistle. Was it the whaling station? They climbed a ridge and looked down. Yes, there it was! Two whale-catchers were docked at the pier. From this distance, the men at the station were the size of insects. Shack fought against being too reckless. The three still had to lower themselves down a thirty-foot waterfall by hanging on to their rope and swinging through the icy torrents. At last, the ragged explorers stumbled toward the station. They had done it!

4 p.m. May 20, 1916

Thoralf Sørlle [sû(r)´lə], the manager of the whaling station, heard a knock outside his office and opened the door. He looked hard at the ragged clothes and blackened faces of the men who stood before him. "Do I know you?" he asked.

"I'm Shackleton," came the reply. Tears welled up in Sørlle's eyes as he recognized his old friend's voice.

The three explorers received a hero's welcome from the whaling crew. The whalers knew that no one had ever done what Shack had accomplished. The next day, Skipper Worsley took a boat and picked up McCarthy, Vincent, and McNeish while Shack began preparations for the Elephant Island rescue. It would take more than three months—and four attempts—to break through the winter pack ice and save the stranded men. But Shack finally did it—and without any loss of life. The men were glad to have a ship's deck once again under their feet. Finally, they were going home!

227

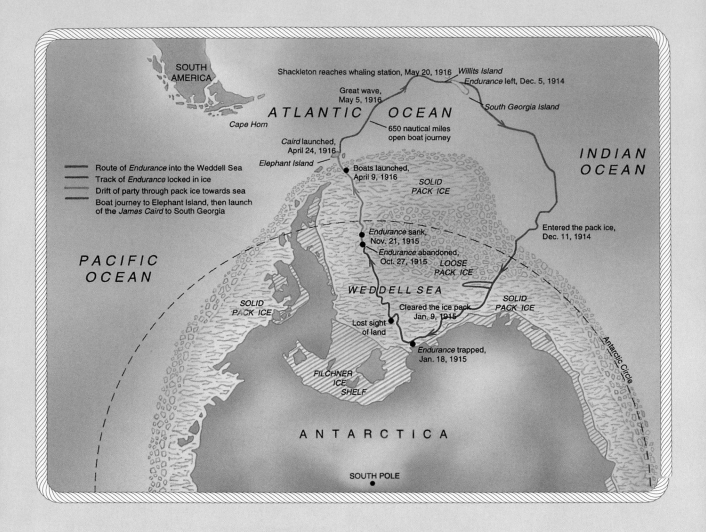

Think and Respond

1 What do you learn about Sir Ernest Shackleton's character from his actions?

2 Why do you think the author included dates at the top of some of the pages in this selection?

3 What do you think was the author's purpose for writing this selection?

4 Would you have wanted to be a member of the crew on this **grueling** adventure?

5 Which strategy did you use while reading the selection? Why?

Meet the Author
Michael McCurdy

Michael McCurdy was an artist at a young age. "When I was in junior high and senior high in Marblehead, Massachusetts, I was always drawing," he recalls. In the classroom, he would often doodle on scrap paper.

McCurdy lived in a household that appreciated the works of authors and artists. His father was an illustrator, and his mother liked to read. "I got the feeling that creative people like these were the most interesting people on earth," he says. In 1960, when he was eighteen, McCurdy enrolled at the School of the Museum of Fine Arts in Boston. There he became fascinated with book illustration.

McCurdy has since illustrated more than 170 titles. He lives in the Berkshire Hills of Massachusetts with his wife and children. He says, "I have a good life, a creative life, of solitary work time in my old barn studio."

Michael McCurdy

Visit *The Learning Site!*
www.harcourtschool.com

229

ANTAR

THE CHILDREN'S
ATLAS
OF
NATURAL WONDERS

Outstanding Science Trade Book

I CY ANTARCTICA, the southernmost continent, has not always been so cold. Geologists have found there fossils of reptiles that lived in warmer times. They have also seen seams of coal exposed on cliff faces. Coal is formed from trees that once grew in warm climates. These coal seams must have been formed when Antarctica occupied another part of the Earth, before it drifted to its present chilly position.

Antarctica floats on one plate. It consists of old rocks that form high lands. Beneath the ice rocky plateaus rise to 13,000 feet (3,950 meters) above sea level, and mountain ranges rise almost to 17,000 feet (5,200 meters).

The Antarctic plate is a part of Gondwana, the great southern continent that once also contained the continents of South America, Africa, and Australia. About 100 million years ago, Antarctica broke away and began to drift southward.

Now, an icecap up to 1 1/4 miles (2 kilometers) thick covers the continent. It extends over the sea, forming an ice shelf that covers 1,540,000 square miles (4 million square kilometers).

◄ Emperor penguins are flightless birds found only in Antarctica.

CTICA

by Joyce Pope

◀ Mount Erebus, overlooking McMurdo Sound, is one of several active volcanoes on Antarctica. They are the most southerly part of the "ring of fire," the ring of volcanoes encircling the Pacific Ocean.

▲
Antarctica is the only continent that is uninhabited by humans. Scientists often pass the winter there, but there are no permanent residents.

Think and Respond

What evidence tells scientists that Antarctica was once a warmer place?

Making Connections

Compare Texts

1 Explain why "Trapped by the Ice!" belongs in the theme Friends to the Rescue.

2 How do the text and the illustrations work together to show the dangerous situations the *Endurance* crew faced?

3 "Trapped by the Ice!" and "Antarctica" represent different types of nonfiction. Explain how the authors' purposes are different in the two selections.

4 Compare "Trapped by the Ice!" to another true adventure story you have read. How does the author of each use suspense to make the story exciting?

5 What additional questions do you have about Shackleton's journey?

Write a Story

Writing CONNECTION

"**T**rapped by the Ice!" is a story about a true adventure. Write a story about an adventure that you would like to have. Create a problem or conflict, and decide how it will be resolved. Use a story map to organize your ideas.

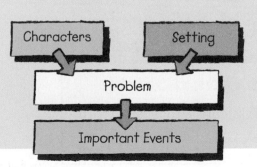

232

Construct a Time Line

The events in "Trapped by the Ice!" take place over a seven-month period as the men struggle to reach safety. Identify the most important events in Shackleton's journey by creating a time line. Label each date on your time line with a brief description of what happened on that day.

Social Studies CONNECTION

October 27, 1915 ———————————— May 20, 1916

Create a Diagram

Millions of years ago, Antarctica was part of a larger continent. Research the geological history of Antarctica. Find out when it broke free and how it has moved over time. Then create a labeled diagram that shows what you learned.

Science CONNECTION

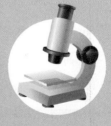

▲ Trapped by the Ice!

Literary Devices

Focus Skill

The author of "Trapped by the Ice!" uses many vivid details to help you imagine what the explorers experience. Look at this description of their boat's encounter with a huge wave:

> **The boat shuddered on impact as the mountain of water spun it around like a top.**

The words *mountain of water* and *like a top* add vividness to the description. There is no actual mountain in the scene; instead, the water is compared to a mountain. There is no top in the scene; the boat is compared to a top. These comparisons between unlike things are examples of **figurative language.**

The opposite of figurative language is **literal language**, or words in their usual meanings. The author might have written, *The huge wave spun the boat around and around.* However, this literal description does not make the wave seem so large or the boat so small.

Here are some of the main kinds of figurative language.

Simile	Metaphor	Personification
A comparison between two unlike things that uses the word *like* or *as*. "Tall waves lifted them up and down <u>like a roller coaster</u>." (p. 218)	A direct comparison between two unlike things that does not use the word *like* or *as*. The wave was a <u>mountain</u>.	A comparison in which something non-human is given human qualities. The sea <u>swallowed</u> the ship.

Visit *The Learning Site!*
www.harcourtschool.com

See *Skills* and *Activities*

Test Prep
Literary Devices

▶ **Read the passage. Then answer the questions.**

> To the children, the falling snow looked like pieces of cotton candy, and they tried to catch it on their tongues. Soon the ground was a soft, white blanket that stretched for miles. The children pulled their sleds through the deep snow drifts toward the hill. The wind roared fiercely through the trees, but the children did not mind. Again and again, they coasted down the steep hill.

1. **What is the meaning of the phrase** *falling snow looked like pieces of cotton candy*?

   A The snow had a sugary taste.

   B The snow looked good enough to eat.

   C The snow melted as it fell.

   D The snow looked fluffy.

Tip

The word *like* tells you the description may be a simile. What picture does the author want you to imagine in this phrase?

2. **According to the passage, which of the following is** *true*?

   F The children used white blankets to cover the ground.

   G The children used white blankets to keep warm.

   H The white snow was so smooth that it looked like a blanket.

   J White snow covered each child's blanket.

Tip

Look in the passage to find the information the question is asking about. Decide if the language is figurative or literal.

▲ Flood: Wrestling with the Mississippi

levees

seeping

reservoirs

crested

floodplain

awed

yearned

Vocabulary Power

People need water to live. They use it in their work and play. There are times, however, when water becomes a deadly danger. What can people do then?

People often try to protect their land from floods by building **levees**. These are raised banks along a river that are made from earth. When water starts **seeping** through a levee, or passing slowly through small openings in it, volunteers rush into action. They use sandbags to fill in the damaged sections.

Reservoirs , or human-made lakes, might have prevented this flood by holding the extra water. Instead, when the river **crested** , or reached its highest point, it flooded the nearby farms. These farms were built on a **floodplain**, which is flat land along a river.

These people watched the rising floodwaters in fear and wonder. They were **awed** by nature's great power. They **yearned** , or longed, for the time when they would be able to return to their homes.

Vocabulary–Writing CONNECTION

Think back to a storm you experienced that **awed** you with its power. Write a poem about that storm.

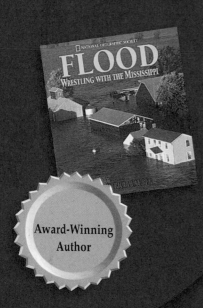

Genre

Expository Nonfiction

Expository nonfiction presents and explains information or ideas.

In this selection, look for

● **Illustrations with captions**

● **A text structure that is organized by main ideas and details**

F L
WRESTLING
WITH
THE
MISSISSIPPI

BY PATRICIA LAUBER

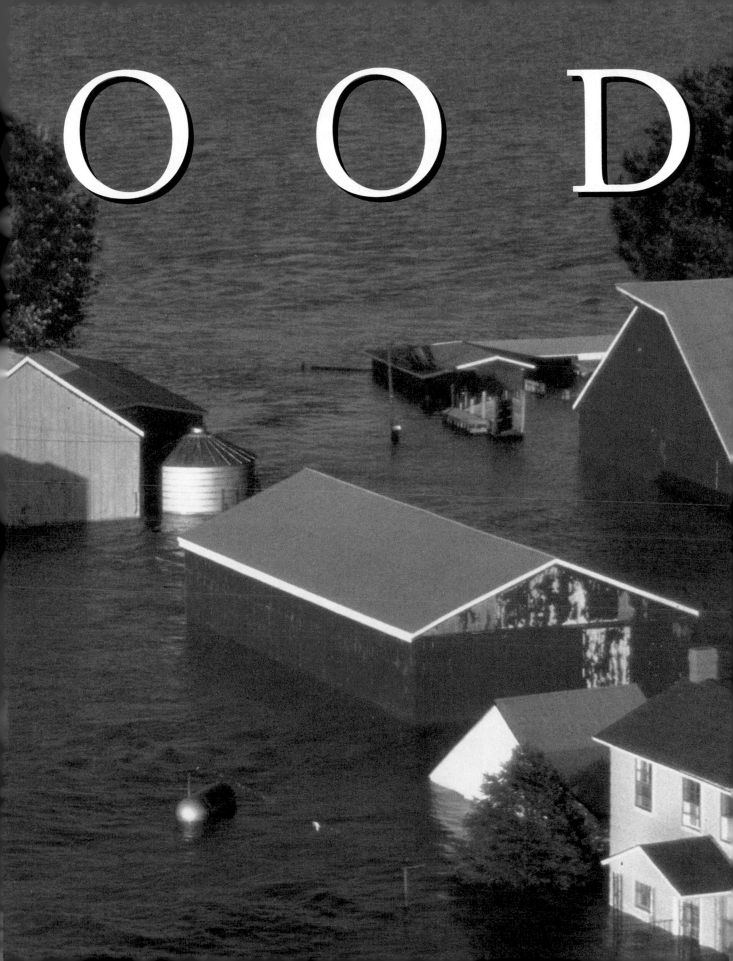

O O D

From its beginnings as a small stream in Minnesota, the Mississippi River travels more than 2,000 miles to the Gulf of Mexico. Along the way, the river deposits tons of rich soil and creates thousands of acres of valuable farmland. Farmers all along the way have built levees to try to control the great river. In the summer of 1993, however, the levees were not strong or tall enough to control the Mississippi's raging waters.

Above: St. Louis, with its Gateway Arch, was one of the cities with a floodwall. The 11-mile-long concrete wall was built by the Corps of Engineers.

Right: A levee on the Illinois River near St. Louis forms an arch in this photograph. The barrier stretching across the arch was placed there in case the levee was overtopped during the 1993 flood.

240

ENDLESS RAIN

Spring of 1992 brought drought. Across Iowa and other states of the upper Middle West, farmland dried into a crumbly crust. In early July, the skies finally darkened and rain began to fall. People rejoiced.

But once started, the rains didn't stop. All summer long, it rained and rained and rained. Summer was also cooler than usual. High above the earth there was haze in the atmosphere, caused by a volcanic eruption in the Philippines. The haze cut off some of the sun's rays. Less water was drawn back into the atmosphere. More stayed on the land, soaking it through and through.

Autumn was rainy.

Winter of 1992–93 brought heavy rains.

Spring brought storms.

As the rain-filled spring crept by, people began to worry. Rivers were rising steadily between their levees. The mighty Mississippi was swollen and rushing. So were its tributaries, the many rivers and streams that added their waters to the big river.

In June worry changed to alarm. The ground had long since soaked up all the water it could hold. The only place rainwater could go was into the rapidly rising creeks, streams, and rivers.

There had been floods before, times when main streets filled with water and farmland turned into lakes. Each time people cleaned up, rebuilt, and went on with their lives. Some flooding, they felt, was a price they had to pay for farming the rich soil of a floodplain.

Over the years defenses had been strengthened. Cities had concrete floodwalls and levees armored with concrete, built by the Corps of Engineers. Earthen levees built by local groups were higher and longer.

Below: A typical Mississippi River Valley levee system

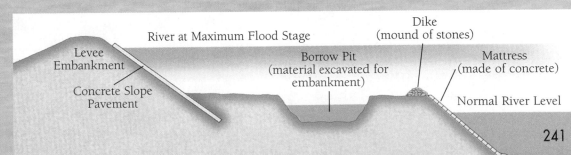

To hold back water, the Corps had built dams and reservoirs on some tributaries of the Mississippi. All this work had one aim: to keep the river in its channel so that people could safely live and work on the floodplain.

Would the defenses hold? In early summer of 1993, people could only wonder—and worry. No one could remember seeing the river rise so high. Nor had anyone ever seen such rain. Even if a day started fair, by afternoon storm clouds were building up again. Nights were shattered by bolts of lightning, claps of thunder, and the drumming of rain on roofs.

Weather scientists could explain what was happening, but they could not offer much hope. Winds high in the atmosphere were steering hot, moist air into the upper Midwest. There the air collided with cold air from Canada. The cold caused moisture to condense out of the warm air and fall as rain. Usually, storms broke up and moved east. In 1993 they could not. They were blocked by a mass of hot, dry air over the East Coast. Until that mass of air moved out to sea, rain would go on falling and falling on the Midwest. Sometimes 5 to 12 inches fell in a single day.

By the middle of July, rain had fallen on the Midwest for 49 straight days. And by then rivers had been bursting through levees, spreading over farms and towns. A satellite picture showed much of Iowa colored blue, as if it were one of the Great Lakes. In eight states, rivers had taken back 15 million acres of farmland and driven 36,000 people from their homes.

Along the Mississippi the worst flooding took place between Davenport, Iowa, and the area south of St. Louis, Missouri. Here there were no reservoirs or lakes to hold back water. And here the Mississippi received the waters of several large tributaries—the Iowa, the Des Moines, the Illinois, and the Missouri. On July 19, there were floods along 464 miles of the Mississippi, from McGregor, Iowa, to St. Louis.

Below: Satellite images show the difference between normal summer water levels of the Mississippi and Missouri rivers (left) and those of the 1993 flood (right). The Mississippi and Illinois rivers are at the top of the images, the Missouri at the left.

NORMAL

ILLINOIS RIVER

MISSISSIPPI RIVER

MISSOURI RIVER

1993

ILLINOIS RIVER

MISSISSIPPI RIVER

MISSOURI RIVER

Above: Pigs, rescued from the roof of a barn, are lifted into a boat at Kaskaskia, Illinois. On the Mississippi itself, the worst flooding took place between Davenport, Iowa, and the area south of St. Louis.

THE SNY ISLAND LEVEE

As the Mississippi twists and turns out of Iowa and into Missouri and Illinois, it is fairly narrow—only 1,500 feet wide at some points. Nearing Quincy, Illinois, it can carry 250,000 cubic feet of water a second without flooding. In the summer of 1993, it was carrying more than twice that amount.

The town of Quincy stands on bluffs, high above the Mississippi. It looks out over 110,000 acres of fertile farmlands, up and down the river. All are part of a levee district named Sny Island.

In late spring of 1993, farm buildings and fields of corn and soybeans lay snug behind a 54-mile-long levee. But the men and women who worked and lived there were watching the river. Since April it had been high, as it often was after winter snow had melted. But the water had always gone down as summer arrived. This year it

Above: When this levee gave way, Valmeyer, Illinois, was swamped.

didn't. Instead, it began to rise, slowly but steadily. In late June one of Quincy's two bridges to Missouri was closed. The Missouri end, which had no levees, was underwater.

A thunderstorm raged during the night of Wednesday, June 30. It dumped six inches of rain on Quincy and more to the north. The river rose two feet. People began to wonder whether the levee would hold. In 120 years, it had had only one serious break. But it had never faced a test like this one.

By Thursday morning small creeks had flooded roads, and the river was rising steadily. The Sny levee stood 28 feet above the river channel. The normal height of the river was 11 feet. On the morning of July 1, it was about a foot below the top of the levee and rising an inch an hour. Water was seeping through the base of the levee. And the National Weather Service was predicting that a crest of water 30 feet high would pass Quincy on Saturday, July 3.

People of the floodplain loaded cars

and trucks with their belongings—sofas, TV sets, refrigerators, rugs, desks—to be stored with friends or relatives on higher ground. Farm animals were trucked away to be boarded or sent to market.

A call went out for helpers, trucks, bulldozers, and sandbags. The levee had to be raised and strengthened.

One section was a weak link. During the 1960s most of the Sny was rebuilt, using large amounts of sand. When a levee needs to be raised, wet sand can be bulldozed from its base up the side and will stay in place. Wet earth does not. Bulldozed toward the top, it slides back to the base. For some reason, one mile-long section had not been rebuilt. It was still made of earth. There was only one way to raise it: build a wall of wooden boards along its top and support the wall with beams and sandbags.

Farmers began arriving, some from high ground miles away. Most were strangers, but help was needed and so they came, driving bulldozers and trucks. Over the next three weeks, hundreds of other strangers would also volunteer to help raise the Sny levee and work on the weak link.

All day long that first day, men and women hauled wood, sawed it, and hammered it. They worked in 95° heat, high humidity, swarms of mosquitoes, and never-ending mud. By evening stretches of board were rising on top of the weak link. Work went on into the night, and by 3 a.m. the first section of boards and beams was in place. Now it had to be backed by thousands of sandbags. Each one needed to be filled, moved along the levee, and put in place by hand.

Below: At the Sny, as at other levees, sandbags had to be filled before they could be used.

Above: Kaskaskia is an island that, for a time, appeared as part of the Mississippi.

The river was only inches below the top of the old levee. With no time to waste, everyone was up early and back at work.

Work continued into the night. Somewhere upstream a levee gave way and water poured off the river onto the floodplain. At Sny Island the pressure eased, and the river seemed to be holding steady at just under 28 feet. When work stopped, 42,000 sandbags, each weighing 30 to 40 pounds, had been put in place.

Sunday, July 4, brought heavy rain to the Midwest. The Weather Service forecast that a crest of 31.5 feet would pass Quincy on July 11. That meant the mile-long board fence had to be raised. The governor of Illinois called in the National Guard to help.

Late on the afternoon of July 9, another levee gave way upstream and water rushed over 10,000 acres. At Sny Island the river began to drop, but heavy rains were still falling over Iowa and other parts of the Midwest, draining off the land, swelling rivers, and rushing toward the Mississippi. The Weather Service now forecast a crest of 32.5 feet at Quincy on Wednesday, July 14. The board fence had to be raised again.

By Tuesday morning the fence had been raised. Workers in human chains were passing and placing sandbags—adding to the half million already in place. They felt sure of finishing before the crest arrived. Then the sky turned black, the wind rose, and bolts of lightning streaked the sky. For safety's sake, all workers were pulled off the levee. The river was five inches below the top of the boards.

The battle seemed to be lost, but that night two more levees gave way upstream. The river dropped 2 feet. The Weather Service now forecast that the 32.5-foot crest would pass Quincy on Thursday.

On Thursday night the crest came, 32 feet high. The Sny levee held. The river stayed as high on Friday. The Sny held. Work on the levee now slowed. Workers patrolled, watching for signs of weakness or small leaks. Bulldozers pushed up sand. The river was still pressing against the levee, which was now soggy and weakening.

A week later the river was still at 30 feet. Day and night, farmers watched the Sny. Farmhouses and barns were empty. Corn and soybeans still stretched as far as the eye could see, but it was too early to tell if there would ever be a harvest.

That weekend the rains began again. Slowly the river began to rise. It was one time too many. Part of the Sny levee gave way, not the weak link with the board fence but another part. By evening on Sunday, July 25, 44,000 acres of corn and soybeans lay under 15 feet of water. Only the roofs of houses and barns showed that Sny Island was not a lake. People had done all they could, but it was not enough.

Below: During the summer of 1993, farmers of the floodplain watched anxiously as the Mississippi rose ever higher behind its levees.

UP AND DOWN THE VALLEY

In the upper valley of the Mississippi and along its tributaries, town after town suffered in the summer of 1993. The small river town of Alexandria, Missouri, saw the river rise in spring—and go on rising. On July 8, the levee broke and the town went under for the rest of the summer.

Niota, Illinois, was one of several towns helped by prisoners—young, fit, first offenders sentenced for non-violent crimes. They were city men, most of whom had never seen the Mississippi or a farm. At first, Niota seemed strange to them. But working shoulder-to-shoulder with local people, they soon came to feel that Niota was their town, too, and they worked with a will. For nine straight days, they threw sandbags from 8 a.m. until dark, in rain, sun, heat, humidity, and mud. The townspeople were awed by how hard they worked. The young prisoners were awed by how nice the townspeople were, thanking them, supplying cold drinks, and feeding them roast beef, chicken, catfish, meatloaf, apple pie, and peach cobbler.

At 6 p.m. on July 10, the levee broke. Some of the prisoners cried, as did men and women of Niota. They had done their best, yet the river had won. That last night, the prisoners refused to eat because they had not saved the town.

Davenport, Iowa, had no levees. The city had missed its chance to have the federal government build levees and floodwalls. Later, its citizens decided

Below: Cairo lies on a point of land where the big Ohio River (right) flows in from the east to join the Mississippi.

Above: A family photo and a banjo clock were among the few items saved from a flooded house.

they could not afford to pay for the work themselves. Besides, they did not want to wall off the river and lose their view. The city suffered widespread flooding.

There were also places where defenses did hold. One was Hannibal, Missouri, boyhood home of Mark Twain. The town had built a levee that stood 31 feet higher than the river bottom. As the water rose, townspeople raised the levee 3 feet with sandbags. The river crested at 32 feet, and Hannibal was safe.

Above: Volunteers also helped with the clean-up. This one is shoveling out a house in Hull, Illinois.

The Missouri joins the Mississippi about 20 miles north of St. Louis. St. Louis was the largest city in harm's way. It was also the first to face the floodwaters of both the Missouri and the Mississippi. At one time more than 480 million gallons of water a minute churned past the city. But most of the city stayed dry behind its 11-mile-long concrete floodwall. Damage came chiefly from a small tributary that backed up when forced to take water from the Mississippi.

Downriver from St. Louis was Ste. Genevieve, Missouri, which called itself the first settlement west of the Mississippi. It had stood there for 250 years, but in late July its future did not look bright. Its levee rose 36 to 38 feet above the river bottom; the river was expected to crest at 45 feet. If Ste. Genevieve flooded, it would lose what it most prized: houses made of logs stuck together with clay, animal hair, and straw—the country's best examples of what the French settlers built.

The town's problems began to attract attention on television and in newspapers. From miles away—Colorado, Minnesota, Tennessee, Florida—people decided to help. They piled into buses, cars, and trucks and drove to the small town. All told, some 1,200 volunteers arrived to help. They filled and set in place 1,100,000 sandbags, raising the levee by ten feet. To strengthen it they dumped 100,000 tons of rock behind the sandbags. The old buildings were saved.

Once the floodwaters reached Cape Girardeau and Cairo, they were no longer a problem. The giant lower Mississippi easily swallowed the vast tide that was sweeping south. Its own tributaries were low in the summer of 1993.

AS THE WATERS FELL

There was no one day when the flood of 1993 ended, no one day when people knew they were safe from the river. But in August the weather pattern began slowly to change. People sensed that the worst was over. Those who had been flooded out yearned to go home. Most were living nearby, crammed in with friends or relatives or in mobile homes that the federal government had brought in. But no one could go home until the water drained back into the river. Rain still fell. Some towns went under a second, or even a third, time. In places, farms still lay under muddy water 11 miles wide and 20 feet deep.

Days were spent making the rounds from one government agency to another, applying for loans, grants, and other kinds of help. In early evening, families might

Below: A father and daughter from Taos, Missouri, used a boat to reach their trailer and swam in through the door to save what little they could.

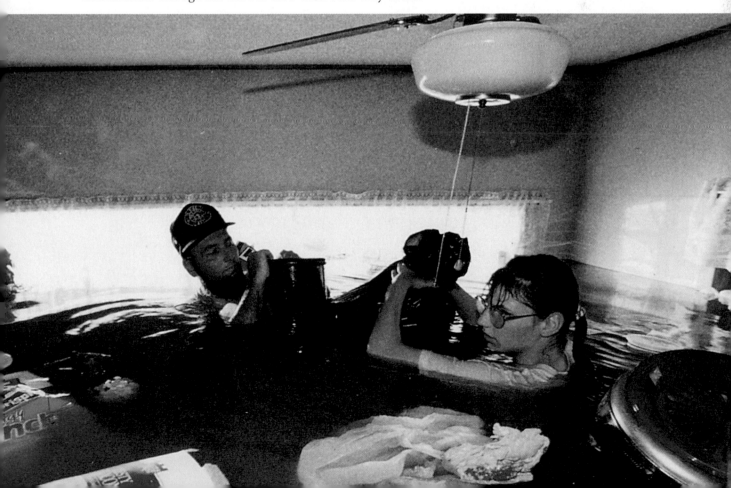

drive to the edge of the water, park, and talk to neighbors. Ahead was the road that used to lead to home; now it dipped under the water and disappeared. Sometimes people would boat into their towns and float down Main Street. At first there was little to see except a chimney, a TV antenna, the top of a telephone pole. As the water dropped, they began to see the remains of houses—windows blown out, porches sagging.

Finally the time came when they could get into their houses. What many found were mud-caked ruins: eight inches of thick dark mud on the floors, mud on the walls, mud on the ceiling, mud on the furniture. They found mildew, mold, and dead fish. But these were people who had sandbagged for days on end, women who had cooked for hundreds of volunteers and washed their muddy clothes. They were workers. They were people raised to believe that life is good but hard, people raised to believe that you work for what you get. And so they set to work hauling out soggy rugs and couches, ruined refrigerators and TVs, and piling them on lawns covered with slime. With shovels, brooms, and buckets of water and bleach, they attacked the houses that could be repaired. They might still be cleaning up when the first frost came, but they never doubted. They would be back.

Think and Respond

1. How did people work together to save their communities from flooding? Why weren't they always successful?

2. Why do you think the author uses chronological order to tell the story? How does it help you follow what is happening?

3. How was it useful to compare the information in the satellite images of the Mississippi and Missouri Rivers?

4. Think about the description of the floodwater when it **crested.** How does the selection make you feel about the power of nature?

5. What reading strategies did you use to help you understand the selection?

Meet the Author

Patricia Lauber

Patricia Lauber has written more than 90 nonfiction and fiction books. She has won many awards, including the Newbery Honor for *Volcano: The Eruption and Healing of Mount St. Helens*. We talked with the author about her writing and asked what inspired her to write about the floods of 1993.

Q: What do you like to write about?
A: I write about the many things that interest me. All of my books are based on what I see around me. I like to stand and stare at things, to talk with people, and to read a lot. By doing these things, I always learn something new.

Q: Where do you get your ideas?
A: My ideas come from everywhere—from things I read and from things people tell me. The things that interest me the most are the things I want to share with others.

Q: Why did you write about the Mississippi floods?
A: The story of the Mississippi, and of the people who use its waters, tugged at my imagination. The river often seemed to have a mind of its own. The floods of 1993 moved me to write a book exploring the river and the human lives it impacted.

Visit *The Learning Site!*
www.harcourtschool.com

Making Connections

Compare Texts

1 Why is "Flood" included in the theme Friends to the Rescue?

2 How is the diagram of a Mississippi Valley levee on page 241 different from the photographs of levees in the selection?

3 How is "Flood" similar to and different from "Trapped by the Ice!"?

4 How would this selection be different if it were written as journal entries by someone who lived along the Mississippi River?

5 What questions do you still have about the flood of 1993?

Write a News Story

"**F**lood" describes an emergency faced by people who lived near the Mississippi River in 1993. Write a news story about an event discussed in this selection. Be sure to answer the questions *who, what, where, when,* and *how*. Use a chart to organize your ideas.

Writing CONNECTION

1. Who is the story about?

2. What happens?

3. Where does it take place?

4. When does it take place?

5. How does it happen?

Make an Ecology Chart

Think about the ways the flood of 1993 affected plants and animals—including insects, birds, and fish—that lived in and beside the river. With a partner, find information about plant and animal life along a part of the Mississippi River. Then create a chart showing how that plant and animal life changed after 1993.

Science CONNECTION

Plant and Animal Life Before 1993	Plant and Animal Life After 1993

Create a Poster

Many ancient civilizations were established along the banks of great rivers because the rivers provided the resources the people needed. Use the Internet or an encyclopedia to find information about the major river systems of Egypt, China, or India. Find out how one of the rivers affected the civilization in the area. Record your information on a poster that includes pictures and facts.

Social Studies CONNECTION

Summarize and Paraphrase

Summarizing and paraphrasing nonfiction will help you gain a better understanding of the main points and remember what you read. A **summary** is a brief statement that includes the most important information of a passage or selection. Summaries are shorter than the original text and do not include details. **Paraphrasing** is restating information in your own words. When you summarize, you usually paraphrase, too.

To summarize a section of text, consider the main points in each paragraph. Here's one way to summarize the information under the heading "As the Waters Fell" from "Flood."

Main Idea
Although the weather pattern began to improve in August of 1993, rainfall continued to worry residents.

Main Idea
People applied for different kinds of government help, and they examined the flood damage.

Main Idea
When the water dropped and people could return to their homes, the cleanup process began.

Summary
In August a change in the weather pattern eventually allowed the water to drop. Then residents returned to their homes to begin cleaning up.

Visit *The Learning Site!*
www.harcourtschool.com

See *Skills* and *Activities*

Test Prep
Summarize and Paraphrase

▶ **Read the passage. Then answer the questions.**

> In September of 1999, Florida residents got ready for one of the strongest hurricanes in history. For days, weather forecasters had predicted that Hurricane Floyd would be a possible danger to cities throughout the state. Hardware stores and grocery stores quickly sold out of essential items such as batteries, water, and candles. People who lived along Florida's east coast had to leave their homes for shelters in safer areas. Surprisingly, Floyd weakened before reaching land. The hurricane was far less damaging to Florida's coastline than most people had expected.

1. **Which would not belong in a summary of the passage?**

   A Hurricane Floyd threatened Florida's coast.

   B Stores sold out of batteries.

   C Floyd's strength weakened as it reached the coast.

   D Floyd caused little damage in Florida.

Tip

The important word here is *not*. Remember that summaries include the most important information.

2. **Retell the passage in your own words.**

Tip

Your paraphrase should not include any extra information. Synonyms for key words will make your writing original.

UNLOCKING THE PAST

CONTENTS

The Stone Age News.................... 260
by Fiona Macdonald

   Focus Skill   Text Structure: Main Idea and Details

Ancient China.................... 282
by Robert Nicholson and Claire Watts

The Chinese Dynasties 298
from *Kids Discover*

   Focus Skill   Graphic Aids

Pyramids 304
from *Kids Discover*

   Focus Skill   Graphic Aids

Look Into the Past: The Greeks 326
by A. Susan Williams

Look Into the Past: The Romans
by Peter Hicks

   Focus Skill   Text Structure: Main Idea and Details

The Skill of Pericles.................... 350
by Paul T. Nolan

Aesop's Fables.................... 366
retold by Margaret Clark

   Focus Skill   Prefixes, Suffixes, and Roots

▲ The Stone Age News

Vocabulary Power

I magine reading a newspaper that was written 100, 200, or even 300 years ago. If you think people back then didn't do things to make headlines—think again.

astounded

sociable

scouring

reliable

newfangled

specialty

skewer

flourished

The Plymouth News

Winter Brings Heavy Snow

Many of our Pilgrim colonists were **astounded** by the cold weather and amazed by the heavy snow this winter. We are usually **sociable** people who enjoy each other's company. Unfortunately, we now spend most of our time looking for food, carefully **scouring** the land for even the smallest berry to eat.

Next Year's Harvest

Native American friends taught us to plant corn for next year's harvest. They also showed us a **reliable** way to trap animals, so we can be certain of having warm fur for the winter. These are **newfangled** ways to us, but we must learn new methods to survive.

A Day for Giving Thanks

Today we celebrated our first harvest with a day of thanksgiving. Each family prepared a **specialty** from a favorite family recipe. One cook decided to **skewer** the meat, or run a rod through it, to turn it slowly over the fire. We **flourished** in England. Now we will prosper in America, too.

Vocabulary–Writing CONNECTION

Historians have learned amazing things about our past. Take a few minutes to write about something from history that has **astounded** you.

Award-Winning Author

Informational Text

Informational text gives information, but the people and events themselves might not be real.

In this selection, look for

- Elements of nonfiction and fiction
- Newspaper format used to present information in an entertaining way

The AGE

BY FIONA MACDONALD

STONE NEWS

Newspapers did not exist in the Stone Age, but newsworthy events were happening all the time. The Stone Age people's search for a better way of life, their survival during the Ice Age, and the invention of farming are just a few of the stories that would have made headlines.

ICE CREEPS CLOSER

TIME TO GO: As the weather worsens, people in central Russia head south.

Lee Montgomery

WE ALL MOAN about today's weather, but we've got it easy. There can be nothing worse than living at the peak of an ice age, as this report from 16,000 B.C. shows!

IN ALL MY years as *The Stone Age News*'s weather reporter, I've never known cold quite like this.

The large icecaps that stretch out from the North and South Poles are slowly but surely growing bigger. And there seem to be hardly any regions where the winters aren't getting longer, and the summers, cooler!

Take northeast Europe, for example. No one can remember a time when it wasn't just a barren and icy wasteland. It's hard to believe that all sorts of plants and animals once flourished there.

And now the icecaps are creeping even farther south, over the plains of central Russia.

Recently, I traveled to the Russian plains to find out how people were coping with the ever-worsening climate. It was only late summer, but harsh winter storms were already beginning to beat down upon the land, and there were few living creatures to be seen.

THE WINTER IS COMING

When at last I found a family group, they were packing up and preparing to move south. Looking thin and drawn, they told me that winter in their lands now lasts for nine months of the year and that even in summer the hunting is barely good enough to keep them alive.

But this is not a new story. The same thing is happening in Germany, Belgium, Britain, and northern France, too—and people are flocking south toward the coast of the Mediterranean.

And the reports from other parts of the globe are just as grim. Icecaps from the South Pole have spread nearly as far as Tasmania. Most of Australia is so cold, dry, and windswept that people have been forced toward the coasts—the only places in Australia where it still rains.

Where will it all end? I wonder. I can't help thinking that if this terrible weather continues, the whole world will turn into a solid block of ice!

Maxine Hamil

ICE AGES: THE COLD FACTS

During an ice age, temperatures around the world are much lower than normal, and even the hottest countries cool down.

❄

As the earth gets colder, vast sheets of ice, up to 10,000 feet thick, spread outward from the icecaps at the North and South Poles, blanketing both land and sea.

❄

Much of the earth's water turns into ice. The oceans shrink and new areas of coastland appear, since large parts of the seabed become uncovered.

❄

Lands not covered by icecaps suffer from drought, as water is absorbed into the icecaps and little rain falls to replace it.

Very few animals can survive in the regions closest to the icecaps and most move on to warmer areas.

❄

Human groups can survive near the icecaps by using clothing and shelters to keep themselves warm. But when the animals that they hunt for food move on, they are forced to follow them.

❄

Ice ages vary in length from several thousand years to just a few hundred. They tend to start very slowly but end rapidly.

❄

No one is certain why ice ages happen, but experts believe they are caused by changes in the way that the earth moves around the sun.

NEWFANGLED FARMING

THIS SPECIAL REPORT, first printed in 8400 B.C., broke the hottest news story of recent times. In it, our Middle East reporter describes a new way of gathering food that was developed there—called farming.

I'D HEARD a rumor that some people in Syria were experimenting with a new way of producing food, and that instead of following the herds like the rest of us, they were living in one place; I just had to go and investigate this strange behavior.

When I arrived, one of the women offered to show me around. She took me to an area where hundreds of tall plants were growing in clusters. I recognized them as wheat, rye, and barley, but I'd never seen so many growing this close together before. Usually, you find just one or two small clumps at a time. I asked my guide to tell me how these big clusters of plants had come about.

SEEDS OF SUCCESS

Apparently, some years ago, the climate in this region became extremely dry. Reliable sources of water were harder and harder to find, so people couldn't roam as widely as they once had. Instead, they were forced to remain close to rivers.

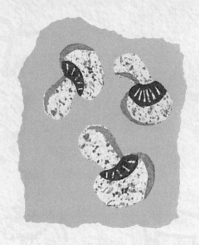

Because they could no longer go far in search of food, they started to build up a store of grains and nuts to last them through the winter months. Then one spring, they noticed how grains that had been dropped on the ground had sprouted.

As an experiment, they tried spilling more seeds, this time on land they had cleared by gathering wild grain the previous year. It took several attempts, but at last they managed to grow their own plants. Now they scatter grain each spring.

When the seed heads become ripe, they are cut off using curved flint-bladed knives. The grain is then separated from the husks and spread out to dry in the sun, before being stored in baskets.

I was astounded by all that I had seen. The more I thought about it, the more this "farming" idea made sense. It could change everything—just think, we could settle in one place and grow our own food plants, as the people here do. Then we wouldn't have to spend all those long fall days scouring the land for enough wild food to last through the winter. And whenever animals are scarce and the hunting is poor, there will still be a supply of food at home.

REAPING THE BENEFITS: Harvesting a field of grain is hard but rewarding work.

Sharif Tarabay

Stone Age people can be set in their ways, but you have to move with the times. And I, for one, hope that this newfangled farming catches on!

BURNING ISSUES

COOKS THESE DAYS have more ways of preparing food than ever before. But can you really beat a good old-fashioned roast? *The Stone Age News* asked a traditional cook and one who prefers to experiment with new recipes to explain their views.

THE FAMILY ROAST: A tradition to be proud of.

Chris Molan

THE TRADITIONALIST

"I'm a firm believer that the old ways are the best. Roasting is a tried and trusted method. Why waste any precious food trying out new ways of cooking that might not even work?

You can roast a piece of meat anywhere. All you need do is skewer it on a wooden spit and find a couple of supports to raise it above a fire.

It's a sociable way of cooking, too. My family group likes nothing better than to gather around the fire for a chat while waiting for the hot, juicy strips of roast meat to be sliced off the joint.

And while the meat is roasting, you can watch to make sure it cooks to perfection. With this new style of cooking, I've heard you put all the food in a bag. It must be nerve-racking not being able to tell if the food inside is raw or cooked."

THE EXPERIMENTER

"It's true that traditional roasting produces good results, but I get bored with cooking the same dish every day. I like to try out new ideas. My favorite at the moment is the 'boil-in-the-bag' approach. It's really easy.

First you need to make a cooking pit by digging a hole in the ground. Then lay a thick piece of hide over the hole and push it down so that it forms a water-proof liner.

Next, carefully clean out an animal stomach, pack it with food, and tie it up very tightly so that nothing can leak out.

Fill up the hole with water and bring it to a boil by dropping in red-hot stones that have been heated in a fire. When the water is boiling, you simply add the parcel of food and let it cook.

The meat boils in its own

Chris Molan

BOIL-IN-THE-BAG: A new way of cooking that's really stirring things up!

juices and makes a lovely, rich stew. And you can vary the taste by putting herbs and spices, or even vegetables and fruit, in the parcel, too. Try reindeer and beans, or water bird with berries and garlic!

My family group really looks forward to mealtimes now—everyone loves trying to guess what's in each new dish.

You know what they say, 'Vari-ety is the spice of life.' Well, that's always true with a boil-in-the-bag stew!"

HOME SWEET HOME: Caves provide ideal shelter.

Chris Molan

A CAVE OF MY OWN

SOME PEOPLE SEEM to have a knack for making a cozy home out of even the humblest hovel! *The Stone Age News* sent a reporter to the south of France to find out how one woman copes with cave living.

"OUR FAMILY GROUP discovered this cave in late summer and we've spent the entire winter here. The cave's size and location are just perfect.

It has plenty of room for all of us. There's a stream just outside, and as you can see, the trees on the hillside not only supply us with wood for burning and for making tools, but they also shelter the cave from the worst of the wind and snow. Best of all, there's plenty of food—animals to hunt and masses of berries and nuts to pick.

Let me show you around. Watch

your head, the entrance is low, but that makes it easier to defend, especially against fierce animals.

We always keep a fire burning in the entrance, too. I like to have a hot fire handy for heating up food. And I find that if you throw on a handful or two of pine needles and fan the smoke into the cave, it freshens the air and also helps to drive out sickness.

Here, you'd better take one of these lamps. It gets quite dark as you go deeper into the cave. I make these lamps myself—they're very simple, just a hollow stone filled with burning fat, with a small thread of moss to act as a wick.

Like most caves, this one is a mixture of large chambers and passages. It stretches back a very long way and has a lot more space than we need to use.

There are a number of passages leading off this main chamber, which in turn lead to more rooms.

HOME COMFORTS

Over here I've built a sleeping shelter—well out of the way of any drafts. It's basically just a wooden frame that I've covered with some dried grass and propped against the wall. You can use turf or dried moss instead, but grass is the best for keeping the warmth in.

Inside the shelter I've put thick hides on the floor—well greased to keep out the damp—as well as a few lighter furs for sleeping under. Most of us don't need shelters, but old people feel the cold more and like the extra warmth and comfort they give.

I've also organized some storage space. I use all the ledges for fragile items, such as baskets of dried berries and various herbs.

I've been so happy here this winter. But, of course, now that spring is coming, we'll all be moving on soon, just as we always do. I'll miss this place, though. It's not always easy turning a cave into a home, but this one has certainly made my task much simpler. We'll definitely be coming back here next winter!"

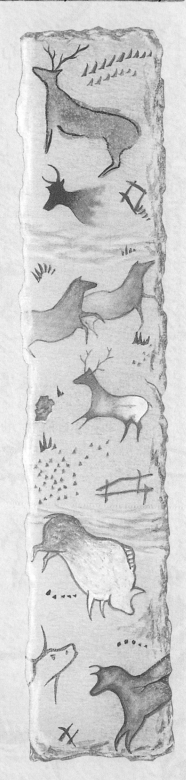

PERFECT PITCH

SADLY, ONLY THOSE of us who travel through hilly or mountainous lands can live in caves. But don't forget that tents can be almost as cozy—especially if you follow *The Stone Age News*'s tips for placing and pitching them.

⌇ Choose a sheltered, well-drained site with a good source of water within easy reach.

⌇ For a tepee-shaped tent, arrange wooden stakes in a circle and tie them together at the top. This construction is very stable, and if your poles are properly tied, there will be little chance of your tent collapsing on your head.

⌇ Wind is your greatest enemy—a strong gust can easily leave you homeless! It's a good idea to place your tents side by side in a semi-circle to make an effective windbreak.

⌇ Keep out wind and rain by using thick skins, such as bison hides, to cover the tent poles. The weight of the skins will also steady your tent during a gale.

⌇ So the skins won't flap in the wind, put large stones around the bottom.

⌇ Waterproof the skins by rubbing them with animal fat, and coat the seams with pine resin.

⌇ As a quick alternative to a tent, make a lean-to by propping branches against a cliff face or boulder and cover it with hides.

A DOG'S LIFE

TODAY IN 8000 B.C., many of us keep hunting dogs. But how many readers know that our friendly pets are related to that ferocious animal, the wolf? This article, from 2,500 years ago, tells how it all began.

IT'S AMAZING, but it's true—humans and wolves, two completely different species, are living side by side!

Hunters in northern Europe have now reared litters of wolves that enjoy human company and even obey their owners' commands.

PUPPY LOVE

The idea of taming wolves happened by chance, when children found some abandoned wolf cubs while out playing. They took the cubs home, fed them scraps, and cuddled and fussed over them.

We're so used to being terrified of wolves that we can't think of them as pets. And yet contact with humans tamed these wild cubs.

Instead of running away as soon as they were old enough to hunt for themselves, these wolves seemed to look upon the children as their "family." They joined in the children's games and even tried to copy some human expressions by curling their lips into a smile. Now, no wild wolf would do that!

When the children grew older and joined in the hunting, their pet wolves went along too.

Naturally, the wolves had very good hunting instincts. Not only did they enjoy the chase, but they could sniff out animals hiding in trees or bushes and then hold them prisoner there for their owners to kill.

Once other hunters had seen how useful these tame wolves were, they got wolf cubs of their own. People and dogs—could this be the beginning of a beautiful friendship?

Maxine Hamil

BEST OF FRIENDS: Children play with their pet wolf cub.

MADE IN JAPAN

WE PRIDE OURSELVES on being the first newspaper with the big stories, and here we reprint one of our greatest "scoops." This sensational article appeared back in 9000 B.C., when it broke the news of a brilliant Japanese invention—pottery!

JUST WHEN YOU think life can't get any more exciting, along comes a brand new way of using a familiar old material.

I'm talking about clay. You know the stuff—it's the soft sticky earth that gets stuck between your

Christian Hook

ALL FIRED UP: These new Japanese pots are the best thing since stone knives.

toes when it rains!

Clay is what bakes into a hard crust beneath your cooking fire. Some artists have made statues

and beads out of it, but no one has ever thought up any other use for it.

Not until now, that is! We have

just received news of an amazing invention—pottery, the art of making useful cooking vessels, called pots, out of clay.

The Jomon people of Japan have proved that it's possible to turn lumps of clay into containers that are heatproof, watertight, and strong!

These fantastic Jomon pots are cone-shaped and usually a reddish brown in color. Often they're decorated with scratched patterns.

To cook with them, the Japanese simply fill them with food and water and place them in a fire.

And I'm told that the Jomon specialty—baked fish with herbs and a local vegetable called bamboo shoots—is delicious!

TRADE SECRETS

But I'm not just going to describe this wonderful invention. I can also reveal how the pots are made.

Jomon potters start by kneading a lump of clay until it softens. Then, with the palms of their hands, they shape small balls from the clay.

PERFECT POT: Not just pretty, but practical, too!

Some of these are molded into a cup-shaped base. Others are rolled back and forth to form long sausagelike shapes, which are wound around the base to build up the sides of the pot.

After smoothing the pot's surface by rubbing their fingers across the clay, the potters may decorate it by pressing a pattern into it with a stick or their fingers.

The pots are left for several days, until the clay is completely dry. Then comes the final, most exciting stage—baking the pots in a big bonfire until they are rock hard.

The pots are carefully arranged on the hot ashes of an earlier fire. Then wood is piled over them and set aflame.

Building the fire and keeping it going takes great skill, as any sudden change in temperature will crack the pots.

Finally, after around five hours, the piping-hot pots are pulled out of the glowing embers with a long stick and placed in rows to cool.

So there you have it. There's only one question left unanswered—will this exciting new Japanese idea catch on and spread to other lands? Only time will tell!

THINK AND RESPOND

1 How did the Ice Age affect Stone Age people?

2 How does the newspaper format make the selection more interesting to read?

3 Based on the information in this selection, what qualities do you think people needed to survive during the Stone Age?

4 Do you think the information in this selection is **reliable**? Explain your answer.

5 What reading strategies did you use to help you understand the selection? When did you use them?

Meet the Author
Fiona Macdonald

History has always appealed strongly to award—winning author Fiona Macdonald. Her interest in the history and culture of ancient peoples is reflected in "The Stone Age News." Before she became a full—time writer, she taught history to both children and adults. Macdonald continues to educate through her writing. She has written some 70 books for young readers, mostly on historical subjects.

Fiona Macdonald

Visit *The Learning Site!*
www.harcourtschool.com

Making Connections

Compare Texts

1. Why do you think this selection is included in the theme Unlocking the Past?

2. Notice the headings, such as *World Events* and *Cookery Pages*, at the tops of the pages. Why are they included?

3. Which article uses a comparison-and-contrast organization? Explain.

4. Compare the format of this selection with that of a modern daily newspaper.

5. What further questions about the Stone Age would you like to ask the author?

Write a Persuasive Letter

Imagine that your local museum is planning an exhibit about life in another time. Write a letter to the director of the museum telling why you think the museum should choose the Stone Age or another time in the past. Use a graphic organizer to arrange your ideas.

Writing CONNECTION

| My Opinion | ⇨ | Reasons/Explanations | ⇨ | Conclusion |

Create a Chart

Research ways in which Stone Age people had to adapt to their environments to survive. Make a problem/solution chart to record some of your findings. In a column titled *Problem*, write at least five challenges Stone Age people faced. In another column titled *Solution*, explain what they did to solve each problem.

Problem	Solution
1. Extreme cold during Ice Age	1. People moved to warmer areas.

Make a Map

A map of the world during the Ice Age would have looked different from the maps we use today. Use an encyclopedia (in print or online) to find out how the world may have looked at that time. Make a map of an area of your choice, showing how much of it was covered with ice. Be sure to include a compass rose and a map legend.

Making Connections

Text Structure:
Main Idea and Details

Focus Skill

Informational text is often organized by main ideas and supporting details.

- The **main idea** is the broadest or most general idea in a paragraph or section. Often it is stated directly at the beginning of the paragraph or section, but sometimes it may come in the middle or at the end.

- The **details** are the specific facts, reasons, or examples that explain or support the main idea.

Identifying main ideas helps you make connections between the parts of a selection. It also helps you make connections to ideas in other selections you have read. For example, as you read "The Stone Age News," you may have thought of facts you had read in your social studies textbook.

Sometimes the main idea in a paragraph or passage is implied rather than stated. Can you identify the main idea of this paragraph from "The Stone Age News"?

> **We always keep a fire burning in the entrance, too. I like to have a hot fire handy for heating up food. And I find that if you throw on a handful or two of pine needles and fan the smoke into the cave, it freshens the air and also helps to drive out sickness.**

Supporting Detail	**Supporting Detail**	**Supporting Detail**
It heats up food.	It freshens the air.	It drives out sickness.

Main Idea
A fire burning in the entrance has several uses.

Visit *The Learning Site!*
www.harcourtschool.com

See *Skills* and *Activities*

Test Prep

Text Structure: Main Idea and Details

▶ **Read the passage. Then answer the questions.**

> Wolves were first tamed by Stone Age children in 8,000 B.C. The hungry wolf cubs happily ate the food scraps the children fed them. Later the young wolves joined in the children's games. When the children grew older, the wolves started hunting with their new masters. Soon these wolves became used to their human friends.

1. **What is the main idea of this passage?**

   A   The hungry wolf cubs happily ate the food scraps the children fed them.

   B   Later the young wolves joined in the children's games.

   C   Wolves were first tamed by Stone Age children in 8,000 B.C.

   D   The wolves started hunting with their new masters.

Choose the answer that is a broad statement about the topic. The others are details that support the main idea.

2. **Which of these would not belong in this passage?**

   F   During hunting, wolves sniffed out their prey.

   G   Eventually, the wolves obeyed human commands.

   H   Cats became pets some time later.

   J   At first, it was hard to think of wolves as pets.

Try inserting each sentence in the passage. If you can find a place for it, you can eliminate it as an answer choice.

▲ Ancient China

civilization

inhabitants

terraces

famine

administrative

elaborate

Vocabulary Power

Every time you look at a clock or write on paper, you are using an invention from ancient China. Look at these scenes of Chinese life from thousands of years ago.

Do you know where Chinese **civilization** began? This amazing culture was started by the people who lived near the Yellow River. The **inhabitants** of this river valley grew crops in the rich yellow soil there.

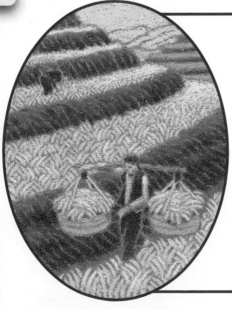

How did people in ancient China farm as much land as possible? They cut **terraces**, or steps made out of earth, into the hillside. However, they still faced times of **famine**, when there wasn't enough to eat.

282

How did the ancient Chinese leaders rule such a large country? They set up an **administrative** system of officials to manage the government. There were many departments in this very **elaborate**, detailed system.

Vocabulary–Writing CONNECTION

Imagine that you are a student 1,000 years from now. Write a short article describing how the **civilization** of the United States has changed.

ANCIENT

by **Robert Nicholson**

and **Claire Watts**

CHINA

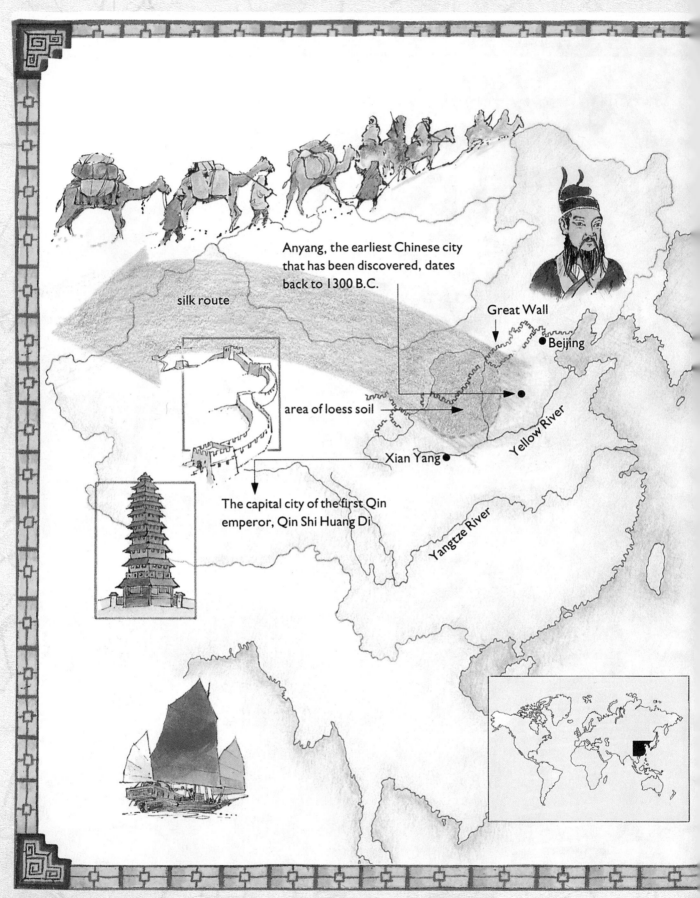

silk route

Anyang, the earliest Chinese city that has been discovered, dates back to 1300 B.C.

Great Wall

Beijing

area of loess soil

Xian Yang

Yellow River

The capital city of the first Qin emperor, Qin Shi Huang Di

Yangtze River

China is one of the world's oldest known civilizations. Beginning thousands of years ago, powerful families took control and ruled this enormous region. A family that ruled for a long period of time became known as a dynasty. Influences from many of these great dynasties have survived to this day.

CHINESE LANDS

China is a huge country, stretching over 1,800 miles from the mountains and ice of Tibet in the west through forests and deserts to the tropical coastline of the east.

Chinese civilization first began around the Yellow River in the center of the country, where the soil is a rich yellow earth called loess. This fertile earth has been blown onto the land by the wind over thousands of years.

The ancient Chinese discovered that they could grow good crops on this loess only if it was kept well watered. They developed a system of terraces cut into the hillsides to make the most of the land. In the north, wheat was the main crop, and in the south, where there was more water, rice was grown in flooded fields called paddies.

Peasant farmers provided food for the entire Chinese empire but usually had scarcely enough to eat themselves. Crops often failed, causing periods of great famine. Sometimes the starving peasants rebelled against the rich landlords.

▶ *Complex irrigation systems were set up to water the fields.*

▲ *Terraces were cut into the hillsides to make the most of every bit of land.*

THE GREAT WALL

The Great Wall of China was built to protect China's northern border from invading tribes. In 221 B.C. the new emperor, Qin Shi Huang Di, (CHIN SHEE HWAHNG·DEE) sent 30,000 men to start building the wall. From then on emperor after emperor extended and rebuilt it right up to this century. The wall was made of pounded earth covered with stones. It was wide at the bottom and narrowed at the top, where there was a walkway for guards. The length of the wall was broken at intervals by watchtowers.

▶ *Traders used to travel along China's northern border, taking their silk to India, the Middle East, and Europe.*

GREAT WALL FACTS
- The wall is between 16 feet and 32 feet high.
- The walkway along the top is 16 feet wide.
- Watchtowers are located every 290 feet to 585 feet along the wall.
- The wall originally stretched for 3,700 miles along China's border.

Cross section of the Great Wall. ▲

THE FORBIDDEN CITY

China was one of the first countries in the world to have large numbers of people living close to one another in cities. Chinese cities were built with walls all around them to protect them from enemies. Inside the most important city, the emperor had a palace which also had high walls, creating a city within a city.

For example, during the Ming dynasty, the emperor Yongle (YUHNG·LEH) rebuilt China's main city, Beijing. By this time Beijing had a million inhabitants. Inside the city walls was a walled imperial city where the important government officials lived and worked. Inside this area was a palace known as the Forbidden City—also surrounded by a high wall—where the emperor lived. At night no man other than the emperor was allowed inside the walls.

▶ *Coins were introduced during the Qin dynasty. The coins were round with holes in the middle.*

GOVERNMENT

The first Chinese emperors gave huge estates all over China to their friends and relatives and enlisted their support to help govern the country. However, these lords often became too powerful for the emperor to control and civil war would break out. In the Qin dynasty, the emperors set up a form of civil service to govern the country instead. People who wanted to join the civil service had to take very difficult exams to prove that they could do the job.

▲ *People walking along the long, straight road to the Forbidden City could be seen long before they arrived at the gates.*

CITY LIFE

The Chinese believed that the world was square, so they built their cities to reflect this, laid out in regular patterns, with straight streets crossing each other at right angles. This divided the town into squares, known as *wards*. Usually the houses of the rich would be found at one end, near the palace, and those of the poor at the other end.

The poor people had houses built from mud and thatch. To keep out drafts in winter, the houses were built with floors below ground level, and blankets were hung over the windows and doors. In the center of the house was a sunken pit containing the fire, but there was no chimney to let out the smoke.

Rich people's houses were built around huge courtyards. They were made of painted wood, and roofed with pottery tiles. They contained little furniture—straw mattresses which were rolled up during the day, cushions rather than chairs, and big chests and cupboards.

FESTIVALS

Most Chinese people worked very hard and had no weekends or other days off. Instead there were festivals throughout the year, which were celebrated with processions and dancing in the street. Fireworks would be let off, kites flown, and people would dress up in dragon costumes, because dragons were supposed to represent fun and excitement.

INVENTIONS

Chinese scientists discovered many things that have made great changes to civilization throughout the world. They were interested in medicine, navigation, chemistry and, of course, they were always trying to improve agriculture to feed the enormous population.

THE WHEELBARROW

The Chinese invented all sorts of lifting apparatus, including the wheelbarrow, which they called a wooden ox.

COMPASS

The Chinese discovered magnetism and made compasses by floating magnets in bowls of water. They were used for navigation, and to check that a new building faced in a direction that would bring good fortune.

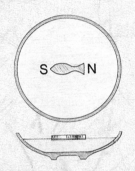

CLOCKS

Clocks were another Chinese invention. Giant water clocks were invented that rang every 15 minutes to record the passing of the day for the royal officials. The records of this invention were kept so carefully that modern clock makers have been able to use them to reconstruct the clocks.

▲ *This huge waterwheel powered the giant water clock.*

PAPER

Perhaps the greatest Chinese invention of all was paper and, with it, printing.

The earliest Chinese writing has been found carved on animal bones. After this, the Chinese began to paint on bamboo strips and silk. In about A.D. 100 paper was invented. Wood pulp, hemp and other waste materials were mashed up, mixed with water, rolled, stretched and dried in the sun to form paper. Paper was the cheapest writing material, and it was much quicker and easier to write on than anything people had used before.

Within a few hundred years the Chinese had developed a form of printing. Wooden blocks carved with lines of text were rubbed with ink and then paper was smoothed over them. This was much quicker than writing books by hand and copies could be made very easily.

CHINESE WRITING

Chinese letters are different from ours. Each of our letters represents a sound, and for them to mean anything we have to combine them to make up a word. Chinese letters are called *characters*. They do not represent sounds but meanings. At first some characters were pictures that could very easily be understood, but gradually the signs became simpler, to make them quicker and easier to write.

EARLY CHARACTERS	MODERN	ENGLISH
𣲗	山	mountain
⊖	日	sun
☾	月	moon
𢒉	馬	horse

1. Cutting reeds and soaking them

2. Mashing the pulp

MAKE YOUR OWN PRINTING BLOCK

The ancient Chinese carved their printing blocks out of wood, but here's an easier way to do it! Draw a design and trace it. Cut several copies of the design out of lightweight cardboard and glue them, one on top of another, to a piece of heavy cardboard, so that the design is raised above the surface. Cover your printing block with ink or paint and press onto a sheet of paper.

Always ask a grown-up to help you when you use sharp scissors.

4. Heating the pulp

5. Stretching and drying the paper

3. Pounding the pulp

CRAFTS

The Chinese were experts in many crafts. They produced beautiful objects in metal, stone, and pottery.

JADE

Jade is a hard, green stone that was considered very valuable by the Chinese. They believed it represented five essential virtues: charity, trustworthiness, courage, wisdom, and fairness. This funeral suit is made from 2,000 pieces of jade threaded together with gold-covered wire.

CHINA

The Chinese invented porcelain, a fine-grained type of ceramic, which we still call *china*. They decorated it with delicate patterns and colors.

SILK

The Chinese kept the secret of silk making to themselves for many years. Silk thread comes from the cocoon of a type of caterpillar, which has to be carefully cared for and fed on mulberry leaves. The cloth made from this thread was the source of China's trade with other countries.

GARDENS

Gardening was regarded as a great art. Chinese cities were designed to include peaceful gardens and parks. Each item in the garden was thought to have a different meaning: water lilies represented truth; chrysanthemums, culture; and bamboo, strength.

HOW WE KNOW

Have you ever wondered how we know so much about the lives of the ancient Chinese, although they lived thousands of years ago?

EVIDENCE FROM THE GROUND

Chinese emperors and important officials were often buried in elaborate tombs that contained many everyday objects. Archaeologists can find out a lot about the way these people lived by studying these objects. One tomb contained a life-sized army—6,000 pottery soldiers and horses, each one with a different face.

▲ *The pottery army was an extremely useful find for archaeologists.*

EVIDENCE FROM BOOKS

The Chinese emperors developed a huge administrative system to run their country, and detailed records were made of everything that went on. Many of these records still exist.

EVIDENCE AROUND US

Many of the things created by the ancient Chinese survive. The country is still divided into 18 provinces. The Forbidden City and other palaces still stand and tell us much about Chinese architecture.

THINK AND RESPOND

1. How did the ancient Chinese use the land and its resources to improve their lives?

2. Why did the authors use headings throughout the selection?

3. How did learning about Chinese inventions help you appreciate this ancient **civilization**?

4. Do you think you would have enjoyed living in China during ancient times? Explain why you feel as you do.

5. Which reading strategy helped you the most with this selection? Explain.

THE CHINESE DYNASTIES

from *Kids Discover*

Ancient China's first dynasty was the Shang. By 1788 B.C. the Shang family had grown so powerful that it was able to take control of much of China. Here are China's major dynasties. A representative piece of art is shown for each.

SHANG
1788–1027 B.C.

ZHOU
1027–256 B.C.

QIN
221–207 B.C.

HAN
207 B.C.–A.D. 220

SUI
589–618

298

Do this activity on a separate sheet of paper.

How long did China's major dynasties last? Here's how to make a bar graph to compare the lengths of dynasties. Subtract the lower number from the higher one to find the length of the dynasty (for the Han dynasty, which spans B.C. and A.D., add the two numbers). Then record the information on the bar graph. Above each dynasty's name, draw a thick line from the bottom of the graph to a height for the number of years of the dynasty's rule. The first one is done for you.

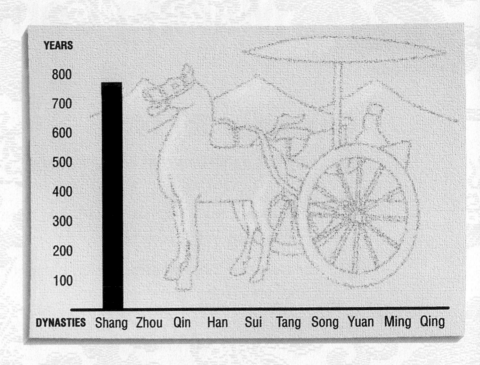

YEARS

800
700
600
500
400
300
200
100

DYNASTIES   Shang   Zhou   Qin   Han   Sui   Tang   Song   Yuan   Ming   Qing

THINK AND RESPOND

How many dynasties have ruled China? According to this time line, how long was China ruled by dynasties?

TANG
618–906

SONG
960–1279

YUAN
1279–1368

MING
1368-1644

QING
1644–1912

299

Making Connections

Compare Texts

1 Why is it important that we "unlock the past" of ancient China?

2 Why do you think the author included both illustrations and photographs in this selection?

3 Compare the kinds of information presented in "Ancient China" and "The Chinese Dynasties."

4 How is the tone of "Ancient China" different from the tone of "The Stone Age News"?

5 What questions about ancient China do you still have after reading these selections?

Write a Descriptive Paragraph

Imagine that you have gone back in time to ancient China. In a descriptive paragraph, tell what you see and draw a conclusion about the place you are in. You may need to do additional research. Use a chart to plan your paragraph.

Writing CONNECTION

Place:
Details: (what I see)
1.
2.
3.
Conclusion: (what I think)

Create a Time Line

Work with a partner to find information about important developments in China during the Shang dynasty. Record the information on a time line drawn on a large sheet of paper.

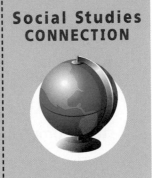

1788 B.C.   1027 B.C.

Draw a Map

Do research about the geography of China. Then draw a topographical map of the country, labeling its major features, such as mountain ranges and rivers. On a separate sheet of paper, explain how each feature affects Chinese life.

N

W   E

S

301

▲ **Ancient China**

Graphic Aids

Nonfiction books and articles often include **graphic aids**, such as maps, charts, and graphs. These graphic aids help readers understand complicated ideas quickly and easily.

The same information can be shown on more than one kind of graphic aid. What information about China is shown on the chart and the bar graph? Which do you think is the better way of showing the information?

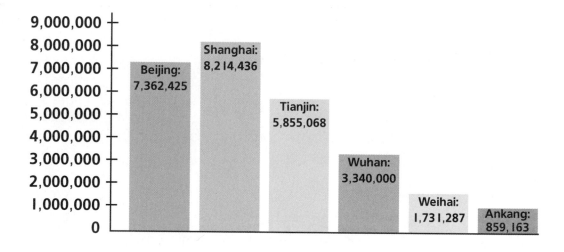

City	Population
Beijing	7,362,425
Shanghai	8,214,436
Tianjin	5,855,068
Wuhan	3,340,000
Weihai	1,731,287
Ankang	859,163

Visit *The Learning Site!*
www.harcourtschool.com

See *Skills* and *Activities*

302

Test Prep
Graphic Aids

▶ **Study the chart and map below. Then answer the questions.**

River	Length in miles
Amur	2,744
Huang He (Yellow River)	2,903
Liao He	1,448
Xi Jiang (West River)	1,630
Yangtze	3,915

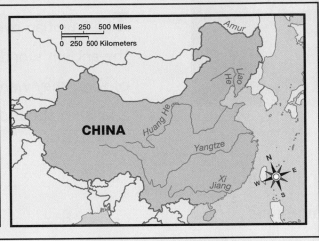

1. **The longest river in China is—**

    A Amur

    B Huang He

    C Xi Jiang

    D Yangtze

Tip

If two graphic aids provide similar information, use the one on which you can more easily find what you need to know.

2. **What river forms part of the northern border of China?**

    F Huang He

    G Liao He

    H Amur

    J Xi Jiang

Tip

The chart does not tell you where the rivers are located. Use the map and its compass rose to find the answer.

Vocabulary Power

archaeologist

ingenious

passageways

isolated

preserved

quarries

The Egyptian pyramids were one of the wonders of the ancient world. Although they weighed thousands of tons, they were made entirely by hand. Read on and learn about other wonders of the ancient world.

This giant statue, which was 110 feet high, stood near the harbor of a Greek island. Although the statue was destroyed in an earthquake, an **archaeologist** has found records that describe how it was built. They explain that **ingenious** workers built ramps of dirt around the statue. This clever idea provided a way to carry heavy materials up to the statue. Maybe there were **passageways** that then let the workers go inside the statue.

The tallest lighthouse ever built once stood on an island near the city of Alexandria in Egypt. Because it was surrounded by water, it was **isolated** from the rest of the country. At the top of the lighthouse tower, a huge mirror reflected the light of a fire for many miles.

This beautiful tomb was built for a ruler in ancient Turkey. The building itself was not **preserved**. Enemy soldiers found and destroyed it. Records from the time describe the statues that surrounded the tomb on all four sides. The statues were carved from stones brought from open pits called **quarries**.

Vocabulary–Writing CONNECTION

Imagine that you are an **archaeologist** and that you have discovered a secret **passageway** leading into a great pyramid of Egypt. Write a few sentences describing what you think you will find inside.

Expository Nonfiction

Expository nonfiction presents and explains information or ideas.

In this selection, look for

- Information about a specific time period

- Sections divided by headings

- Graphic aids that present information

P Y R

AMIDS

from *KIDS DISCOVER*

THE OUTSKIRTS OF MODERN-DAY CAIRO, the capital of Egypt, with the Pyramids of Giza in the background. The Giza Pyramids are the only one of the Seven Wonders of the Ancient World still standing.

HOW HEAVY?

The average weight of one of a pyramid's stone blocks is two and a half tons. That's the weight of two medium-sized cars. Some blocks, however, weigh up to 15 tons. That's as much as five elephants!

THE PYRAMIDS
OF EGYPT

Egypt's pyramids are the oldest stone buildings in the world. They were built nearly five thousand years ago. These ancient tombs are also among the world's largest structures. The biggest is taller than a *40-story* building and covers an area greater than that of *ten* football fields. Men built these huge structures without the help of equipment that we have today, such as cranes and bulldozers. Sometimes up to 100,000 men worked for 20 seasons on one pyramid.

More than 80 pyramids still stand today. Inside their once-smooth white limestone surfaces, there are secret passageways, hidden rooms, ramps, bridges, and shafts. Most had concealed entrances and false doors. What fun it would be to explore one!

However, the pyramids were not built for exploring. They served a very serious purpose. Ancient Egyptians had a strong belief in life after death. The kings, called pharaohs, wanted their bodies to last forever, so they had pyramids built to protect their bodies after death. Each pyramid housed a pharaoh's preserved body. It also held the goods he would need in the next life to continue living as he had when he was alive.

The pyramids of Egypt are massive monuments to the pharaohs' power. Today they are reminders of a resourceful and creative ancient civilization.

HOW TALL?
1. Eiffel Tower, 984 feet
2. **Great Pyramid at Giza, 480 feet**
3. Big Ben (Westminster Palace), 316 feet
4. Statue of Liberty, 305 feet
5. Leaning Tower of Pisa, 179 feet

309

HOW PYRAMIDS GOT THEIR START

EARLIEST TIMES

EARLY EGYPTIANS BURIED their dead under a pile of rocks. Bodies were wrapped in goatskin or reed mats. Personal goods were placed around the body.

AROUND 3000 B.C.

MASTABA (MAS tuh buh) tombs were made of sunbaked mud bricks, which gave protection against the harmful effects of nature. On the walls of mastabas were carved, painted scenes called *reliefs*. Some reliefs showed rows of people bringing offerings, such as ducks, food, water, milk, and honey.

AROUND 2700 B.C.

IMHOTEP IS CREDITED with the invention of stone architecture and the design of Egypt's first pyramid, the Step Pyramid. It was begun as a large mastaba tomb, but after going through many changes, it ended up as a pyramid of six steps. The tomb of King Djoser lies under the Step Pyramid.

KING DJOSER

IMHOTEP

PHARAOH TUTANKHAMUN, KNOWN AS KING TUT, WAS buried in the Valley of the Kings. The young king died when he was only 19 years old. Practically untouched by robbers, his tomb contained weapons, furniture, jewelry, musical instruments, clothing, and model boats—many of which were made of solid gold. The king's two stillborn daughters were buried with him, along with a lock of hair from his grandmother, Queen Tiya.

AROUND 2500 B.C.

AROUND 1500 B.C.

THE GREAT PYRAMID AT

Giza, the largest of the three Giza pyramids, is also one of the largest man-made structures in the world today. Built for Pharaoh Khufu, it was originally 480 feet high. Its base covers approximately 13 acres. The pyramid originally contained over two million blocks of limestone.

THE VALLEY OF THE KINGS

contains the tombs of many later pharaohs. These rulers were aware that robbers had taken the treasures from most of the earlier pyramids. So they decided to have their tombs built in these isolated cliffs near Thebes. Sixty-two tombs have been found there. However, even these tombs were robbed.

PHARAOH
KHUFU

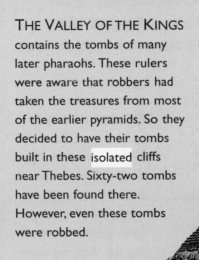

ONLY IN EGYPT

Ancient Egypt had a unique combination of ingredients for building pyramids. The country was a long, narrow, fertile strip of land in northeastern Africa. Water came from the mighty Nile River. Natural barriers protected the land from invaders. There were deserts to the east and west. There were dangerous rapids on the Nile to the south. Delta marshes lay to the north. This circle of isolation allowed the Egyptians to work in peace and security.

To build the pyramids, great supplies of raw materials were needed. Ancient Egypt had an abundance of limestone, sandstone, and granite. But these rocks had to be brought from quarries to the building sites. Egypt's most precious resource—the great Nile River—provided the means for transportation.

CAIRO

GIZA MEMPHIS

SAQQARA

DAHSHUR

TURA
(Limestone quarry)

AFRICA

VALLEY OF THE KINGS

THE NILE RIVER IS the longest river in the world. It flows for approximately 4,150 miles. The Nile flooded farmers' lands from July to October until the Aswan Dam was completed in 1970.

DESERTS CUT OFF ancient Egypt from the rest of the world. If you were trying to cross a desert on foot, you would need from four to six gallons of water per day. And, the more water you carried, the more water you would need!

THE NILE RIVER produced fertile farmland. During the flood season, when no farming could be done, farmers paid taxes to the pharaoh in labor, by helping to build the pyramids.

THE STONES WERE levered up and hauled on board. The weighed-down boat then set off for the pyramid site. Oarsmen had to work hard, and the helmsman had to be an expert, since sandbanks could easily destroy a boat.

ASWAN
(Granite quarry)
FIRST CATARACT

ANCIENT EGYPTIANS believed that a pharaoh buried in grand style would continue to bless his people. This inspired them to work cheerfully as they built the pyramids—magnificent monuments to their kings.

TWO KINDS OF rocks were used in most pyramids—limestone and small quantities of granite. These rocks were quarried close to the banks of the Nile. They were transported on the Nile in wooden boats.

MASTER BUILDERS

Building a pyramid was difficult and dangerous. It required a highly organized society. Thousands of skilled and unskilled workers were needed. To complete the Great Pyramid at Giza, one huge stone block must have been quarried, shaped, and smoothed every two minutes for 23 years!

Building plans showing how the pyramids were built have never been found. However, experts use present knowledge about construction to make some intelligent guesses. Follow the four steps in the illustration to see how ingenious—and hard working—the ancient Egyptians must have been.

1 THE ENORMOUS limestone blocks were taken off the boats near the pyramid site. If one block accidentally fell, it could crush to death hundreds of people.

2 ONCE UNLOADED, the limestone blocks were hauled on sledges over wooden rollers by gangs of men. Water or milk was poured around the sledges to help them slide.

3 RAMPS, BUILT OF MUD brick, were used to haul the heavy stones to the level where building was going on. To raise the stones higher, spiraling ramps were probably put against the pyramid sides.

4 A CAUSEWAY connected each pyramid to the Nile. Built as a highway for the sledges, it eventually served as a corridor for the funeral procession.

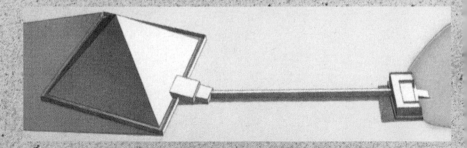

chisels

mallet

saw

drill

TODAY'S TOOLS ARE MADE OF STEEL. THE ANCIENT EGYPTIANS used tools of copper, a softer metal than steel, and wood. Their tools could cut limestone. Wooden wedges and levers were also used in building the pyramids.

MANPOWER WAS PLENTIFUL in ancient Egypt. Oxen and other beasts of burden were considered too valuable for the heavy work of building pyramids.

RELIGIOUS AND PRACTICAL REASONS CONTROLLED WHERE THE pyramids had to be built. For religious reasons, the pyramids had to be on the west side of the Nile River, where the sun set. They had to be built close to the Nile so boats could carry the stones to the construction site. They also had to be built high above the level of the river so no damage would occur during the flood season. Each side of the pyramid had to face one of the four cardinal points— north, south, east, and west. Finally, a pyramid had to be close to the pharaoh's palace so he could keep an eye on his "castle of eternity."

TRAPS, MAZES, AND SECRET CHAMBERS

The main purpose of the pyramids was to safeguard the pharaohs' bodies. Granite doors, false passages, and fake burial chambers were constructed in an attempt to confuse and deter robbers. However, in spite of all these precautions, nearly all the pyramids were robbed of their treasures by around 1000 B.C.

Take a trip through the inside of the Great Pyramid of Giza in the illustration and see how skillfully the kings planned for their bodies' final resting places.

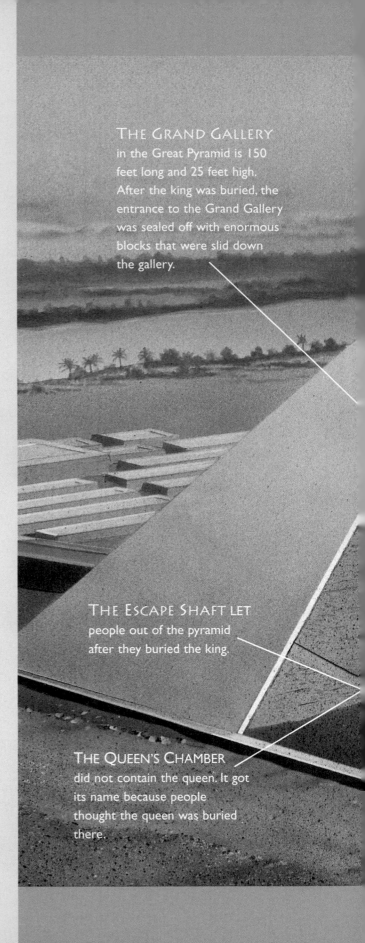

THE GRAND GALLERY in the Great Pyramid is 150 feet long and 25 feet high. After the king was buried, the entrance to the Grand Gallery was sealed off with enormous blocks that were slid down the gallery.

THE ESCAPE SHAFT LET people out of the pyramid after they buried the king.

THE QUEEN'S CHAMBER did not contain the queen. It got its name because people thought the queen was buried there.

THE SPHINX AT GIZA IS 240 FEET LONG and carved out of limestone. Built by Pharaoh Khafre to guard the way to his pyramid, it has a lion's body and the ruler's head.

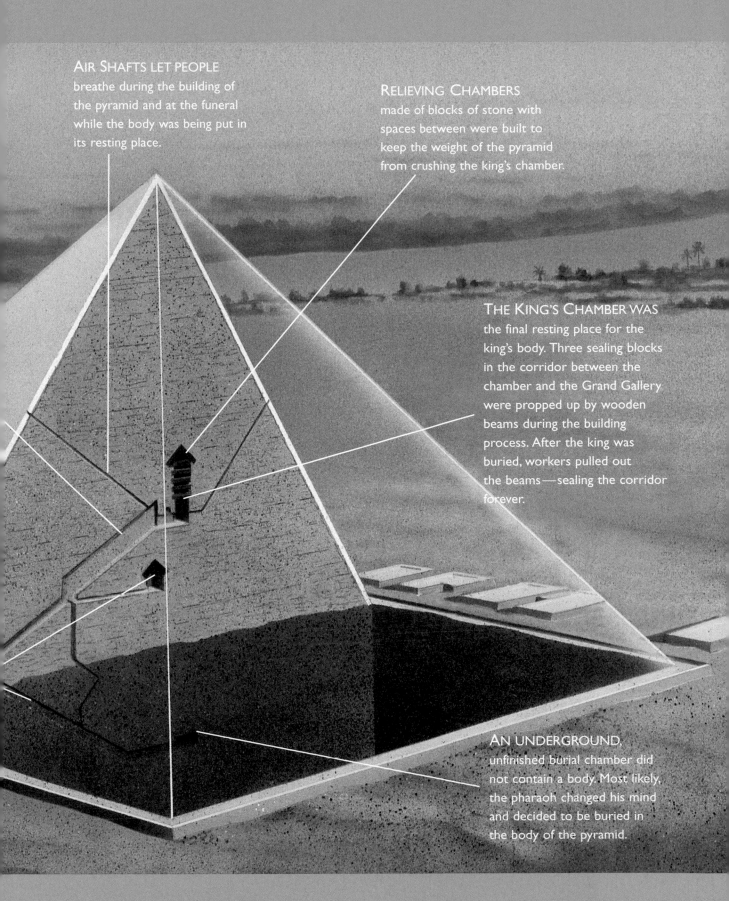

AIR SHAFTS LET PEOPLE breathe during the building of the pyramid and at the funeral while the body was being put in its resting place.

RELIEVING CHAMBERS made of blocks of stone with spaces between were built to keep the weight of the pyramid from crushing the king's chamber.

THE KING'S CHAMBER WAS the final resting place for the king's body. Three sealing blocks in the corridor between the chamber and the Grand Gallery were propped up by wooden beams during the building process. After the king was buried, workers pulled out the beams—sealing the corridor forever.

AN UNDERGROUND, unfinished burial chamber did not contain a body. Most likely, the pharaoh changed his mind and decided to be buried in the body of the pyramid.

ALL ABOUT MUMMIES

The Egyptians believed that life after death was very similar to life on earth. Their dead, therefore, had to be protected and preserved for the next life. The pyramid's job was to protect the body. To preserve the body, a process known as mummification was developed around 2600 B.C. Mummification might take as long as 70 days. The body was dried out for about 40 days. The Egyptians used a salt compound called *natron* to do this. In the next stage, the body was embalmed. That means it was treated with molten resin and perfumed oils. Finally, the body was wrapped in linen bandages.

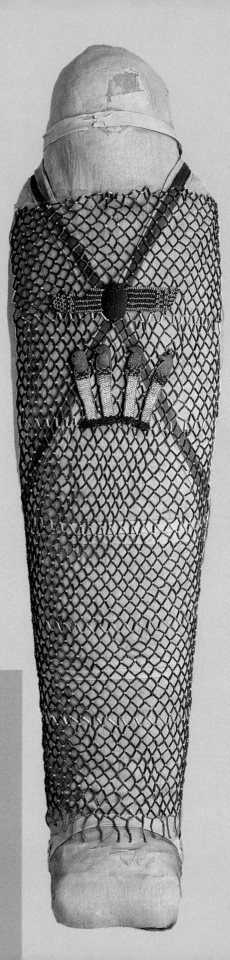

MUMMIES OF cats, dogs, ibises, crocodiles, and other animals have been found.

THE MUMMY OF Nesmutaatneru shows skillful bandaging. Bandaging took about two weeks. As many as 410 yards of linen could be used. That's about as much material as it would take to go from the top to the bottom of the Empire State Building!

FOUR SEALED JARS, CALLED *CANOPIC* (ca NOH pic) jars, held the liver, lungs, stomach, and intestines. Ancient Egyptians threw away the brain of a dead person because they didn't know what it was. They believed that the heart did all the thinking!

HOLLYWOOD'S BORIS KARLOFF modeled his mummy face and costume in the film *The Mummy* after Rameses III.

MUMMIES TELL US ABOUT LIFE IN ancient Egypt. For example, the decayed teeth in many mummies suggest that ancient Egyptians, like many people today, ate too many sweets.

CLOSED

OPEN

UNWRAPPED

TREASURES FROM A TOMB

Pharaoh Tutankhamun became king when he was about nine years old (around 1333 B.C.). Ten years later he died. Imagine ruling an entire country when you're only nine!

King Tut's is the only royal burial in the Valley of the Kings that was practically untouched by robbers. In 1922, after many years of excavating, the archaeologist Howard Carter found a sealed entrance to Tut's tomb. In the first room were thrones, vases, chariots, statues, jewelry, and ostrich-feather fans, among other items. Four coffins protected the mummy. The third coffin was made from almost 2,500 pounds of gold!

TREASURES FROM THE TOMBS of the pharaohs are now found in museums around the world.

THE CASTILLO (THE GREAT pyramid) in Chichén Itzá, Mexico, was probably built some time between A.D. 900 and A.D. 1200.

THE PYRAMID AT THE LOUVRE in Paris, France, is a transparent glass pyramid that rises to 71 feet. Designed by the architecture firm of I. M. Pei & Partners, it serves as an entrance to the museum.

THE GREAT AMERICAN PYRAMID overlooks the Mississippi River in Memphis, Tennessee. It is 321 feet high and covers approximately 6.8 acres. It is a monument to American music.

PYRAMIDS AROUND THE WORLD

The pyramids of Egypt were built over a span of one thousand years. The most splendid ones date from about 2700 B.C. to 2200 B.C.

Pyramids, however, have been built in many parts of the world at various times. All of these pyramids contain certain essential elements. They are enormous. They have rectangular bases. Most are made of stone or brick. And most have four sloping sides that meet at a point.

Think and Respond

1 How did ancient Egyptians work together to build the pyramids?

2 How did the different features in this selection bring the world of ancient Egypt to life?

3 How does the author feel about the builders of the pyramids? How can you tell?

4 Would you recommend this selection to a friend who wanted to be an **archaeologist**? Why or why not?

5 Which reading strategies did you use to help you understand the selection? When did you use them?

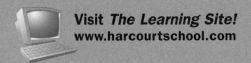

Visit *The Learning Site!* www.harcourtschool.com

Making Connections

Compare Texts

1 Why is "Pyramids" included in the theme Unlocking the Past?

2 Why do you think the author chose to include the illustrations on pages 308–309? How is the information that they show different from information in the main text?

3 How would you use the section headings in "Pyramids" to locate information? Give an example.

4 How would a biography of an Egyptian pharaoh be different from this selection?

5 What questions about pyramids do you still have?

Write a Narrative

Imagine that you are an archaeologist working at the site of an Egyptian pyramid. Write a narrative that describes your feelings as you discover various objects that tell about ancient Egyptian life. Be sure to include interesting details. Use a web to help you brainstorm ideas.

Writing CONNECTION

Egyptian Pyramid

Make a Bar Graph

Rivers played a major role in the development of ancient civilizations. Use a bar graph to compare the lengths of the Nile River in ancient Egypt, the Tigris and Euphrates rivers in ancient Mesopotamia, the Tiber River in ancient Rome, and the Yellow and Yangtze rivers in ancient China.

Social Studies/Math CONNECTION

Bar graph with y-axis labeled "Miles" ranging from 0 to 4000 (increments of 500), and x-axis labeled: Nile, Tigris, Euphrates, Tiber, Yellow, Yangtze.

Create a Diagram

Do research about the plants and animals that live in the Egyptian desert. Find out how they depend on each other for food and shelter. Use your information to create a diagram of the desert on a large piece of drawing paper or poster board. Write labels that explain briefly how the plants and animals are related in the desert ecosystem.

Science CONNECTION

Plants and Animals in the Egyptian Desert

323

Graphic Aids

Illustrations and **diagrams** are kinds of graphic aids that help you visualize the ideas in a selection. Look at this illustration from "Pyramids." Compare the illustration to the information in the paragraph beside it.

- What information is presented in the text and in the illustration?
- Which communicates the information more quickly and easily?

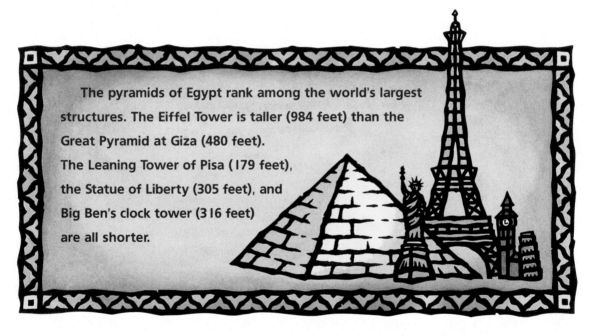

The pyramids of Egypt rank among the world's largest structures. The Eiffel Tower is taller (984 feet) than the Great Pyramid at Giza (480 feet). The Leaning Tower of Pisa (179 feet), the Statue of Liberty (305 feet), and Big Ben's clock tower (316 feet) are all shorter.

A diagram is a drawing or photograph with labels showing the parts of something. Science and social studies textbooks often include diagrams to help you visualize complex information. What information do you learn from the diagram on pages 316–317 of "Pyramids"?

324

Test Prep
Graphic Aids

▶ **Study the diagram below. Then answer the questions.**

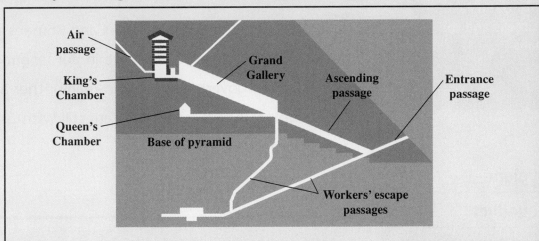

Air passage
King's Chamber
Queen's Chamber
Base of pyramid
Grand Gallery
Ascending passage
Entrance passage
Workers' escape passages

1. **One air passage leads out of the—**

   A King's Chamber

   B Ascending passage

   C Queen's Chamber

   D Base of the pyramid

Tip

Look carefully at the lines next to each label to see where they point. Otherwise, you may confuse two labels next to each other.

2. **The ascending passage leads to the beginning of the—**

   F Queen's Chamber

   G Base of the pyramid

   H Entrance passage

   J Grand Gallery

Tip

Narrow your choices by eliminating the ones that are not even close to the ascending passage. Decide between the remaining choices.

▲ Look Into the Past:
The Greeks and the
Romans

hygiene

aqueduct

mosaic

provinces

reconstruct

emblem

Vocabulary Power

The worlds of the ancient Greeks and Romans are not dead. They're very much alive in our language, in our system of government, and in many other areas. Take a look at a few scenes that are still with us from ancient times.

Aqueduct Completed

Hygiene, or cleanliness, was very important to the Romans. They bathed daily in public baths that used fresh water. It was carried from springs many miles away by a long pipe or trough called an **aqueduct,** a part of which was raised.

This beautiful **mosaic** is made from small pieces of colored glass and stone. Wall decorations like this were used in homes in many **provinces**, or political regions of the Roman Empire. Archaeologists have been able to **reconstruct** some Roman homes from their remains so that we can see how people lived.

The Olympic games began in ancient Greece. The flaming torch is an **emblem** of the modern Olympic Games. Before each Olympics, the torch is lit at this ancient temple in Olympia, Greece. Then it travels to the site of the games.

Vocabulary–Writing CONNECTION

Hygiene was an important part of life for the ancient Greeks and Romans. Think of a modern health or cleaning product. Write a descriptive paragraph about the product and how it might have been useful in ancient times.

Expository Nonfiction

Expository nonfiction presents and explains information or ideas.

In this selection, look for

- **Sections divided by headings**

- **Paragraphs with main ideas and supporting details**

LOOK INTO THE PAST

THE GREEKS

BY A. SUSAN WILLIAMS

THE ROMANS

BY PETER HICKS

WHO WERE THE ANCIENT GREEKS?

The customs and way of life of the ancient Greeks, who lived more than 2,500 years ago, have affected our lives today. The politics, language, literature, art, and sports of many countries all show links with the Greek civilization in some way. So the more we know about the history of Greece, the more we understand about how we live today.

Archaeologists use remains (called artifacts) that have been found in the area that was ancient Greece to discover how people lived hundreds of years ago.

Pictures on ancient pots, vases, and coins show us how the Greeks used to live. The ruins of buildings and the writings of poets, playwrights, and historians also give us information.

LOOK INTO THE PAST

THE GREEKS

◀ Greece is a land of mountains. In ancient times, the mountains separated groups of people from each other. This led to the development of separate communities, which were called city-states. Athens, Sparta, Argos, and Thebes were four of many city-states.

Today, the different regions of Greece are joined together by such modern inventions as the car and the telephone.

▲ The picture above shows the remains of the entrance to the Minoan palace of Knossos. It had over one thousand rooms, which were built around a courtyard in the middle. The palace was built by a group of people called the Minoans 3,500 years ago, in the fifteenth century B.C., on Crete, a large Greek island. When people talk about the greatest period of Greek civilization, they usually mean the fifth century B.C. (2,500 years ago). This is known as the classical period, which produced the art, politics, and literature that have been admired for so many years.

THE GREEK LANGUAGE

The word "alphabet" comes from the first two letters of the Greek alphabet: alpha and beta. The English alphabet is similar to the Greek alphabet, and many English words are based on Greek words. The word "telephone," for example, is made up of the Greek words for "far off" (tele) and "voice" (phone). The word "hippopotamus" is made up of the words for "horse" (hippos) and "river" (potamos).

Ancient Greek letter	Name of Greek letter
A	alpha
B	beta
Λ	gamma
Δ	delta
E	epsilon
I	zeta
H	eta
Θ	theta
I	iota
K	kappa
L	lambda
M	mu
N	nu
XE	xi
O	omicron
Π	pi
R	rho
E	sigma
T	tau
V	upsilon
Ø	phi
X	khi
ØE	psi
Ω	omega

▼ In this painting on a vase, a man at a festival in Athens is reciting two long poems written by a blind poet called Homer. Homer's poems are called the *Iliad* and the *Odyssey*. The *Iliad* is about the Trojan War, a war fought between the early Greeks and Troy. The *Odyssey* tells the adventures of Odysseus on his travels after the end of the Trojan War.

▲ Here is the old Greek alphabet. Some of our letters are different. But you could write your name in Greek letters.

Most men who lived in Athens were able to read, because boys went to school. They learned literature, music, and physical education. Girls in Athens did not go to school but stayed at home to learn how to look after a family. In Sparta, both girls and boys were taught to read and write.

A	
B	
G	
D	
E	(short)
Z	(SD)
E	(long)
Th	
I	
K	
L	
M	
N	
X	(Ks)
O	(short)
P	
R	
S	
T	
U	
Ph, F	
Kh, Ch	
PS	
O	(long)

THE CITY-STATE OF ATHENS

The city-state of Athens was very powerful and ruled a large region. It was a rich city because it owned silver mines nearby, where slaves were made to work very hard. The goddess of Athens was Athena and the emblem of the city was the owl.

▶ This is a bust of Pericles. He was a great leader of Athens in the fifth century B.C. He had the Parthenon and other beautiful temples built and had the port of the city, Piraeus, improved. He led Athens in the war against Sparta, which lasted from 431 B.C. to 404 B.C.

▼ This painting on a vase shows men voting. The people of Athens first invented the idea of democracy, which is the Greek word for "rule by the people." Because Athens was a democracy, the voters of the city could choose their leaders and be asked to serve in government.

However, not everyone was able to take part in elections—women, slaves, and freed slaves were not allowed to vote. Nowadays, most western countries are democracies, in which all adults have the right to vote for the government they prefer.

HOMES AND BUILDINGS

Greek houses were built with sun-dried bricks and wood and were arranged around an open courtyard. Women and children lived separately from the men in their families. The men lived in the more public areas, where visitors were made welcome. A stranger was not supposed to enter a room containing women, unless he had been invited to do so by the man of the house.

▲ This is a drain at the Minoan palace of Knossos, on the island of Crete, built about 3,500 years ago. The Minoans built an efficient water system to supply water to the palace and to drain it away. The queen even had running water in her bathroom and a toilet that flushed.

◄ This is the porch of the Erechtheion, a temple that was built on the acropolis of Athens, just after the Parthenon. These statues of women take the place of ordinary columns in holding up the roof.

▶ The shape and size of Greek temples were pleasing to the eye. This was because the Greeks knew a lot about mathematics and planned their buildings carefully. The mathematician Pythagoras developed ideas that children learn in school today.

▼ Public buildings were very fine and built of stone and marble. Many were temples to gods and goddesses. This is the Parthenon in Athens. It was built in the classical period and dedicated to Athena, the goddess of the city.

Over 2,000 years later, Greek temples were copied in many parts of the world. Many of the government buildings in Washington, D.C., for example, have columns like those of the temples of ancient Greece.

THE THEATER

The first public performance of a play in Athens took place in the fifth century B.C. Plays soon became very popular and were often performed at festivals. Tragedies were serious plays and had sad endings. Comedies were amusing and had happy endings. A group of dancers and singers called a *chorus* talked about the play as it went along, giving it a broader, deeper meaning.

▼ Like all the theaters built in ancient Greece, the theater at Epidaurus is outdoors. Best preserved of all Greek theaters, it seats some 14,000 people. Because it was cut into a slope, everyone could see the play. It is still in use today.

◀ The actors wore masks like the one worn by this comic actor. Some of the audience would be sitting so far away from the stage that they could not see the expressions on an actor's face. Each mask showed a different emotion very clearly, so that everyone in the audience could see how the characters were feeling. Since women did not perform, men had to play both male and female parts. Many plays were about the gods and their way of dealing with humans.

▶ Plays written in ancient Greece are still performed today. This Greek tragedy is being acted in a modern theater. The Greeks enjoyed going out to see a play, just as we do.

337

WHO WERE THE ROMANS?

The story of Rome, its people, and the empire they built is both impressive and exciting. From a city built on the banks of the Tiber River in central Italy sprang a mighty empire that stretched into three continents and lasted nearly 700 years. The Romans built lasting roads, bridges, and towns. They produced great literature and art, strong government, and a powerful army and navy.

▼ Archaeologists have discovered that nearly 4,000 years ago a tribe called the Latini were settled and farming in the region where Rome was built. The land was very fertile and the weather was good, so crops grew well. Farmers grew grain and vegetables and raised animals. The picture below shows a plowman with his team of oxen. The Latini were simple people living in thatched huts. It is believed their small farms gradually developed into villages and towns. The Roman language is called "Latin" because it developed from the language of the Latini.

▼ The area the Latini lived in was called Latium, and two powerful groups of people lived nearby: the Etruscans to the north and Greek settlers to the south. The Latini traded with these people, so it is not surprising that they picked up many ideas from them, including ideas about religion and the use of the alphabet. In fact, many of the ideas that made the Roman Empire so great came from the Etruscans and Greeks.

LOOK INTO THE PAST
THE ROMANS

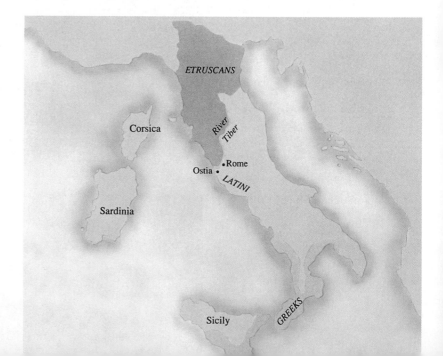

THE GROWTH OF AN EMPIRE

The cluster of tribal settlements that came together to form the city of Rome was situated on a group of hills above the Tiber River. The high ground and the river protected Rome from enemy attack.

▲ One problem Rome faced was lowland flooding near the Tiber. Once this area was successfully drained, it was made into an open space for meetings called the forum, the remains of which you can see in the picture above. The city council met in a building called the curia at the forum. People also went to the forum to trade goods and to listen to speeches.

▶ By A.D. 100, with all the wealth pouring into Rome from the Empire, the city was the largest and most impressive in the world. A million people lived there. The model of Rome gives us a good idea of what the city looked like.

As the model shows, the city was crowded with houses, apartments, public baths, and shops. The huge Colosseum stands on the right and the Circus Maximus is in the foreground. These buildings were where the Roman Games took place.

◀ Huge amounts of grain were needed for the large population and Rome, therefore, depended on receiving plentiful amounts from the Empire. Free grain was given out to the poor and, if this ran out, riots would often take place. This mosaic shows a man measuring grain, a vital crop for the Romans.

By A.D. 100 the Roman Empire was a huge area with an emperor at its head. The Empire was linked by an impressive network of roads. Many Roman roads were long and straight. Straight roads allowed troops to travel quickly and directly to any trouble spots in the Empire. Many of these straight roads built by the Romans still exist today.

The Romans also built roads to cross mountains. Here a road leads twisting and turning over the Alps. This was built by the Romans and shows what excellent engineers they were.

TOWN LIFE

Towns were very important in the growth of the Roman Empire. Roman ideas were spread through the hundreds of towns in the Empire that acted as centers of trade, religion, entertainment, and learning. They were also centers of local government, and they provided protection in times of danger. In the towns of the Empire, the local population could see Roman architecture, fashion, laws, sports, and hygiene. This encouraged them to follow Roman ways.

▲ Romans had very high standards of hygiene, and the sewage systems in their towns were remarkable. There was a plentiful supply of clean water. Since rivers and streams in towns were often polluted, a clean water spring was found, and an aqueduct was built, along which the water was carried. The Romans used more water per person than the people in New York City use today. The picture above shows part of the aqueduct that supplied water to Nîmes in France. Striding dramatically across a valley, this aqueduct carried pure water from 25 miles away.

▼ Most water was used for washing and drinking. It was supplied to fountains, and the excess water was used to flush out the drains. More important, the water was used to feed the public baths built near the town forum. Romans liked to bathe daily and were very clean. Bathing often took place after work when people visited the public baths on the way home. The baths were very cheap and the bath houses provided food and entertainment. The picture at right shows the Roman baths at Bath in England. Although everything above the bases of the pillars was added in the nineteenth century, it is easy to imagine bathers chatting and drinking on the edge or jumping in.

◀ Bathing houses were heated by a furnace and hypocaust system. The hot air from the furnace was channeled into an area under a floor supported by pillars, as shown in the picture. This made the room very hot, so the bathers would sweat before taking their bath. The hypocaust could also heat houses, which was very useful in cold parts of the Empire such as Gaul (present-day France) and Britain. In the picture the air channels are visible at the sides of the walls.

We know a lot about Roman towns from the exciting archaeological discoveries at Pompeii and Herculaneum, near Naples in Italy. Both towns were lost after the volcano Vesuvius erupted in A.D. 79, covering the towns in layers of volcanic mud, ash, and lava. For centuries they lay forgotten, until the area was carefully uncovered. The results were amazing: streets, houses, artifacts, shops, bakeries, barber shops, and laundries were preserved exactly as they were on the day the volcano erupted.

▶ Because archaeologists have found many artifacts, they have been able to reconstruct the rooms from which they came. This is a typical town house kitchen. The large storage containers are called amphorae. There is also a large cooking pot and an oven.

◀ Poor people in Roman towns lived in small apartment buildings, but the rich could afford fine stone town houses with tiled roofs, which tend to be better preserved. Many town houses had luxurious rooms, bath suites, mosaic floors, and beautiful gardens.

343

THE FALL OF ROME

By the third century A.D. tribes outside the Roman Empire began raiding provinces in the hope of taking rich pickings. In response to this threat, the boundaries of the Empire were strengthened and some cities built walls or added turrets to existing walls. Around the coasts of Gaul and Britain, special forts were built to keep a lookout for Anglo-Saxon raiders, who came in longships from what is now Germany.

▼ The huge towers of this ancient fort helped defenders see along their walls and also improved their fire power. The remains of a defensive ditch are in front of the towers. The ditch would have been much deeper 1,700 years ago.

▶ By the fifth century A.D. tribes from central Europe—the Franks, Vandals, Goths, and Huns—were making serious inroads into Roman territory. One of these tribes, the Huns, was led by Attila, who appears on this medal. The Romans called these tribes barbarians because they lived outside the Empire and were not "civilized." The writing on the medal calls Attila the "*Scourge* of God."

As the attacks on the Empire continued, it became very difficult to collect taxes: people either refused or had no money to pay. This meant that the army could not be paid, so many soldiers deserted, leaving the Empire undefended. Once the army left an area, the Roman way of life collapsed remarkably quickly. Buildings were deserted, pillaged, burned, or left in ruins.

◀ The Roman Empire was very powerful while it was growing; but defending the frontier proved to be too difficult. By A.D. 476 the Empire had broken up. This is the large city wall that bordered Constantinople (now Istanbul in Turkey), around which the Eastern Empire was based. Constantinople survived until the fifteenth century, but the once-mighty Western Empire lay in ruins.

THINK AND RESPOND

1 In what ways have the ancient Greeks and Romans influenced our lives today?

2 Why do the authors present much of the information in the selection in a caption format?

3 Why do you think the Roman way of life fell apart whenever Roman soldiers deserted **provinces**?

4 What would you have liked the most and the least about living in ancient Greece or Rome? Explain your answers.

5 How did adjusting your reading rate help you while reading this selection?

Making Connections

Compare Texts

1 How do you "unlock" the mysteries of the past by reading this selection?

2 How is the part of the selection about the Greeks similar in structure and format to the part about the Romans?

3 Which interests you more—ancient Greece or ancient Rome? Why?

4 How is "Look Into the Past" similar to and different from an encyclopedia article?

5 Where could you look for more information about Greek and Roman artifacts?

Write a Persuasive Speech

Do you think it's important to study ancient civilizations in school? Write a speech in which you present your opinion and persuade listeners to agree with your point of view. Use a chart to organize your ideas.

Writing CONNECTION

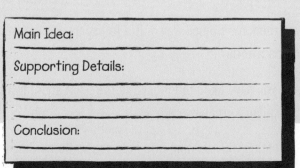

Main Idea:

Supporting Details:

Conclusion:

Write a Television News Special

Work with a partner to find more information about the eruption of Mt. Vesuvius in A.D. 79. Then imagine that you are television news reporters, and write a special news report about the event. Include information about the cause of the eruption and its effect on Roman life. Include maps and other visuals in your news report.

Science/Social Studies CONNECTION

Make a Web

The government of the Roman Republic had characteristics similar to those of the government of the United States. Use an encyclopedia and one other source to find facts about ancient Roman government. Organize your findings in a web. Think of a creative way to show on your web which characteristics also apply to American government.

Social Studies CONNECTION

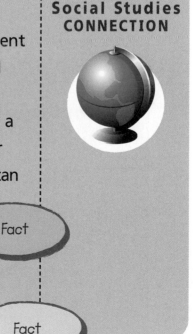

347

Text Structure: Main Idea and Details

Focus Skill

"**L**ook Into the Past" is organized according to main ideas and details. The selection covers several topics about the Greeks and the Romans. For each topic, there is a main idea that is supported by details in the paragraph or passage.

As you read "The Greeks" and "The Romans," you can connect some of the main ideas you find in the two sources. For example, both sources tell how archaeologists use artifacts to learn about ancient civilizations. This chart shows how you might connect and compare ideas on this topic from the two sources.

	The Greeks	**The Romans**
Main Idea	Archaeologists use remains to discover how the ancient Greeks used to live.	We know a lot about Roman towns from archaeological discoveries at Pompeii and Herculaneum.
Supporting Details	Pictures on pots, vases, and coins show how the Greeks lived. The ruins of buildings and the writings of the Greeks also give information.	Layers of volcanic mud and lava preserved streets, houses, artifacts, shops, bakeries, barber shops, and laundries. The rooms from which the artifacts came have been reconstructed to show how people lived.

Visit *The Learning Site!*
www.harcourtschool.com

See *Skills* and *Activities*

348

Test Prep

Text Structure: Main Idea and Details

▶ **Read the passage. Then answer the questions.**

> Archaeologists have helped us understand the lives of ancient Greeks and Romans. These scientists have found the remains of many buildings, from simple homes to great temples. They have also found artifacts such as vases, pots, and coins. These artifacts are often displayed in museums.

1. **Which is the main idea of this paragraph?**

   A These artifacts are often displayed in museums.

   B Archaeologists have helped us understand the world of the ancient Greeks and Romans.

   C These scientists have found the remains of many buildings, from simple homes to great temples.

   D Scientists have also found vases, pots, and coins.

Tip

Often the main idea can be found in the topic sentence. Is the topic sentence here the main idea?

2. **Which of these could best be added to the paragraph?**

   F Pictures on artifacts show us what people used to do.

   G Greece is a mountainous country.

   H Mathematics was an important part of ancient life.

   J Flooding often occurred near the Tiber River in Rome.

Tip

The answer you choose should support the main idea. Some of these are not related to the main idea at all.

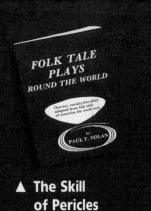

FOLK TALE
PLAYS
ROUND THE WORLD

One-act, royalty-free plays
adapted from folk tales
of countries the world over

by
PAUL T. NOLAN

▲ The Skill
of Pericles

Vocabulary Power

In "The Skill of Pericles," young people compete against each other in a contest. However, there are many other ways to compete. When the competition is friendly, everyone can win.

democratic

virtues

brutes

disguised

bellowing

rouse

THE CAMPAIGN BEGINS

Monday was the start of this year's campaign for class president. Everyone will have a chance to vote in this **democratic** election. All three candidates began by talking about their own **virtues**. Their good points appealed to many of the students. Candidate Maria Rodriguez said, "We want to campaign fairly. We're not **brutes** who act cruelly to one another."

STUDENT COUNCIL CANDIDATES DEBATE

The candidates for student council president took part in a debate Friday afternoon. They all looked **disguised**! They wore their best clothes instead of T-shirts and jeans. At first they spoke quietly, but soon they were **bellowing** loudly. Finally our principal joked, "I know you're trying to **rouse** the students from

their afternoon naps, but let's try to talk calmly." The candidates agreed to show each other more respect.

Vocabulary–Writing CONNECTION

Even very young children have their own personalities and ways of looking at things. What **virtues** do you think every young person should have? Write a few sentences explaining your ideas.

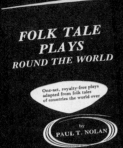

FOLK TALE
PLAYS
ROUND THE WORLD

One-act, royalty-free plays
adapted from folk tales
of countries the world over

by
PAUL T. NOLAN

THE SKILL

Genre

Play

A play is a story that is meant to be performed for an audience.

In this selection, look for

- A plot with a problem and a resolution

- Dialogue that reveals character traits

- Stage directions in parentheses

From

FOLK TALE PLAYS
'ROUND THE WORLD

by Paul T. Nolan
illustrated by David Scott Meier

OF PERICLES

Characters

CIMON *(The Athlete)*
HECTOR *(The Orator)*
AJAX *(The Warrior)*
HELENA *(The Beauty)*
LETA *(The Wise)*
IDA *(The Artful)*
NESTOR *(The Friend)*
THE OLD SAILOR
A MESSENGER
PERICLES
CITIZENS OF ATHENS

TIME: *The fifth century, B.C.*

SETTING: *The market place in Athens.*

AT RISE: THE OLD SAILOR *is telling a story about the voyages he has taken.* THE OLD SAILOR *and the young people—*CIMON, HECTOR, AJAX, HELENA, LETA, IDA, *and* NESTOR—*are downstage left and hold the center of attention, but the* CITIZENS OF ATHENS *can be seen carrying on their business upstage.* THE OLD SAILOR *pretends his tales are true; actually he takes them from the stories of Homer, "The Iliad" and "The Odyssey," but he is very interesting and a favorite with the young people.*

THE SAILOR: And there we were—Odysseus and I—and there was the great big Cyclops. . . .

CIMON: Was the Cyclops as big as ten men?

THE SAILOR: As big as fifty and he had one eye *(Points to the middle of his forehead)* right in the middle of his forehead.

CIMON: I'll bet he could run like the wind.

AJAX: And fight like an army.

HELENA: But he wasn't very pretty.

THE SAILOR: He was ugly all right, and he would have scared any other man to death—except my friend Odysseus and me.

LETA *(Doubting)*: How could you know Odysseus? He lived a long time ago.

THE SAILOR: That's a fact. A long time ago. But I was younger then.

LETA: I thought it was *a thousand years ago.*

THE SAILOR: It may have been. I was a lot younger then.

IDA: Did Homer tell the truth about
   Odysseus, old sailor?

THE SAILOR: He was a poet and
   all poets make up stories. But
   mostly he told the truth.

LETA: Why didn't he mention you?

THE SAILOR: Well, I guess Homer
   couldn't write down everything.

HELENA: Tell us about your adventures
   with our leader, Pericles.

THE SAILOR: Ah, yes, Pericles and I.

LETA: Huh. I'll bet you were never at Troy, and you
   probably don't even know Pericles.

THE SAILOR: Pericles and I have done some big things.

LETA: You made up those stories about Pericles.

NESTOR: What do you want to say that for, Leta? Now
   he won't tell us any more stories.

LETA: I said it because it's true.

THE SAILOR: Is that so, young girl? Maybe you would
   believe me if I brought Pericles here and he told you
   himself?

LETA: Yes, I would. Bring him if you can.

THE SAILOR: Maybe I just don't want to bring him.

LETA: You wouldn't know Pericles even if you saw him.
   (A MESSENGER *enters upstage center and hits a brass gong.*
   All the people stop their business to listen to him.)

MESSENGER (*Unrolling a scroll and reading it*): Hear ye,
   hear ye, hear ye. I bring news from our great leader,
   Pericles. Today Pericles will visit you to pick the youth
   who best shows he knows the skill of Pericles.

FIRST CITIZEN: The skill of Pericles? What's that?

SECOND CITIZEN: His military skill, of course.

THIRD CITIZEN: Not so. It's his speech-making.

FOURTH CITIZEN: It's his strength.

MESSENGER (*Hitting gong again to silence crowd*): Pericles is
   already among you, looking and judging. Within the

hour he shall say who best has the skill of Pericles. Parents, prepare your children. Children, be prepared. The one chosen shall win a prize. (MESSENGER *exits*.)

FIRST CITIZEN: Pericles is already among us, judging.

SECOND CITIZEN: Within the hour he will name the winner.

THIRD CITIZEN: I must go home and rouse my lazy son from sleep. But what's the use? Only if sleeping is the skill of Pericles will he win the prize.

FOURTH CITIZEN: Perhaps it is singing. My little girl has the voice of a bird.

FIFTH CITIZEN (*To* 4TH CITIZEN): The voice of a bird all right—a crow. Your daughter cannot sing.

FOURTH CITIZEN: You are jealous. You know it will bring great honor to my house if my child wins the prize. (*During the past several speeches, the* CITIZENS *have been leaving. Now only the seven main characters are left onstage. Upstage center* PERICLES, *disguised as a beggar, sits with his head bent, as though he were half-asleep.*)

CIMON: What is this skill of Pericles? Did anyone ever say?

HELENA: I have never heard of such a thing before.

NESTOR: Wouldn't it be a great honor if one of you should win the prize? I would be very proud to have a friend who has the skill of Pericles.

HECTOR: The old sailor said he knew Pericles well. The sailor can tell us. Where is he?

IDA (*Looking about*): He's gone. Leta made him angry when she said he made up stories.

LETA: I didn't make him angry. He knew that when Pericles came, we would find out his stories were not true.

AJAX: If you think he makes things up, why do you listen to him?

LETA: He tells very good stories. (PERICLES *now comes downstage and joins the group. They pay no attention to him.*)

CIMON: We Greeks are the finest athletes in all the world. We run the fastest, swim the best, hurl the javelin farther than any other people on earth. The skill of Pericles must be in our sports. Nestor, come and race me to the temple and back. If Pericles is watching he will see what a fine runner I am.

NESTOR: Gladly, my friend Cimon, if you think my running with you will help.

CIMON: Hector, tell us when to start.

HECTOR: I don't see why I should help you, Cimon. I, too, would like to win the prize.

NESTOR: Hector, if the prize is for speaking, Pericles will hear your fine voice.

HECTOR: I hadn't thought of that. All right. (CIMON *and* NESTOR *get in a starting position.*) Great runners of Athens, hear my command: Get ready, set, and go! (*The two run off.*) Didn't my voice sound well, Leta?

LETA: Don't be foolish, Hector. How can a voice sound well unless it says something?

HELENA (*Looking off*): Nestor is almost keeping up with Cimon.

LETA: Nestor is a fine runner, too, but he is more interested in making Cimon a better runner than in winning the race for himself. He will lose.

HELENA: I'm afraid so. And Nestor is nicer than Cimon, too. (NESTOR *and* CIMON *return,* CIMON *leading the race.* HECTOR *takes* CIMON's *hand and raises it.*)

HECTOR: I, Hector, judge: Cimon is the winner.

HELENA: Nestor, you might win a race if you would think about winning instead of trying to make Cimon run faster.

NESTOR: No one can beat my friend Cimon. He is the finest runner in Athens.

CIMON: But you are a great help to me, Nestor. Perhaps Pericles will give a second prize, and you will get it.

HECTOR: You are very quick to take first prize for yourself, Cimon. But I do not think the skill of Pericles is running. Pericles was a great runner in his youth, to be sure. But it takes speaking skill to win men to democracy, not running.

AJAX: Do you think you will win the prize for your speaking, Hector?

HECTOR: I don't say I will win the prize, but I would like to try. Do you remember the story of Admetus, who asked his father to die in his place? Hear me give the father's answer. . . .

LETA (*Breaking in*): Do we have to listen to that speech again?

HECTOR: Hear me, now. I am the old father speaking. (*Pretending to be an old man*) "Am I slave, son, that you treat me so? Or am I your father, a king and a freeman born? I have given you everything you own. Is it my duty to die for you as well? There is no law of the Greeks that a father must die for his son. . . ."

IDA (*Interrupting*): Are you going to give the whole speech again?

NESTOR: I think that is a good speech, and Hector gives it very well.

LETA: I don't know what we would do without you, Nestor. You make all our faults sound like virtues: Cimon's bragging and Hector's bellowing, Ajax's prancing about. . . .

AJAX: I do not prance! I walk like a warrior. And that's what I am, a warrior. You will be sorry you have said that, Leta, when I win the prize.

LETA: Do you think you have the skill of Pericles?

AJAX: What is the greatest skill of the Greeks, I ask

you? It is fighting! And who is the greatest warrior here? *(He draws his wooden sword and makes a fake thrust toward* NESTOR, *who pretends to fall dead.)* You see? Victory again. *(He pretends to place a foot on* NESTOR's *body and holds his sword aloft.)* If Pericles has seen what a great warrior I am, I am sure to win the prize.

NESTOR *(Getting to his feet again)*: One of you will win. I am sure of it. No one runs as fast as Cimon, or talks as well as Hector or fights as well as Ajax. We must all have a feast when the prize is given.

PERICLES *(All turn to him as he speaks)*: There is much in what you say, Nestor. We Greeks prize the gifts of your friends here. One of them may well win the prize.

NESTOR: I wish Pericles were here saying that.

IDA: Do you know Pericles, old man?

PERICLES: I have never seen him face to face, but I know something of the way he thinks. *(Turning to girls)* What about you girls? Helena, here, has beauty. Maybe that is the skill of Pericles.

HELENA *(Posing)*: *I* thought beauty should be the skill of Pericles, but I did not know men would agree with me.

PERICLES: We Athenians are not brutes like the Spartans, Helena. It is our greatness that we know beauty makes life worth living.

HELENA: If I win the prize, I hope it is a lovely necklace for my beautiful neck.

LETA: Do not count the beads until you have won the prize. The Goddess of Beauty won a prize from Paris, but foolish Paris was not as wise as Pericles. I do not think a pretty face will be the skill of Pericles.

PERICLES: That is a good argument for one so young. You are wise, Leta.

NESTOR: Perhaps wisdom is the skill of Pericles, Leta, and then you will win the prize.

LETA: Thank you, Nestor. I am wise enough to know I won't win. All nations have wise people, but all cities are not Athens. I don't know the skill of Pericles, but I do not think it is wisdom.

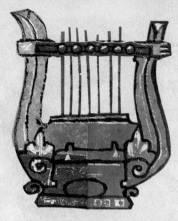

PERICLES: Perhaps it is art. I am told, Ida, that you sing and dance most wonderfully.

NESTOR: She is the finest singer and dancer in all Athens. Sing for us, Ida.

PERICLES: Yes, do, Ida. We Greeks prize our singers. Think of the honor that we have given our poet Homer these many centuries.

IDA: I'll sing if you all join in.

NESTOR: We will join in your singing and in your dancing, too. *(The following song is to be sung to the tune of Bach's "A Song of Praise." IDA sings the first verse alone. The others join her in the second verse. Then IDA and NESTOR do a ballet routine while the others sing the first verse again.)*

IDA:

We raise a song to isles we love,
For all the joys that life does bring:
For freemen's rights and heroes' deeds,
Our grateful thanks and praise we sing.

OTHERS:

We raise a song to isles we love,
For Athens, city that we prize,
For shining seas and mountains tall,
In grateful thanks our voices rise.

PERICLES *(Applauding)*: That was very good, Ida. And you did well, too, Nestor.

IDA: Nestor is my favorite partner.

NESTOR: Anyone can dance well with Ida.

PERICLES: But what is your special skill, Nestor? How do you expect to win the prize from Pericles?

NESTOR *(Laughing)*: I will not even be considered. I do not run as well as Cimon, nor talk as well as Hector. I do not fight as well as Ajax. . . .

AJAX: But you are the one I would want at my side in battle.

NESTOR: I thank you for that, Ajax.

HELENA: You are not beautiful, Nestor. But I think you are handsome. Don't you think so, old man?

PERICLES: He has a good face, one I would like in a son or friend.

NESTOR *(Laughing)*: My only skill is the luck to have such good friends. And one of them will win the prize today. I am sure of it. (MESSENGER *enters and strikes the gong again. The* CITIZENS *come onstage again.*)

PERICLES: Well, we shall soon see. Here is the messenger again. *(He leaves the group and goes upstage to the* MESSENGER.)

MESSENGER: Citizens of Greece, the time has come to announce the name of the youth with the skill of Pericles.

FIRST CITIZEN: But where is Pericles?

SECOND CITIZEN: We have not seen Pericles yet.

THIRD CITIZEN: He has not heard my lazy son snore.

FOURTH CITIZEN: He has not yet heard my little girl sing.

MESSENGER: Pericles has been with you. He has watched you work and play.

AJAX: Pericles has been here? *(The* OLD SAILOR *comes onstage.*)

HELENA: Look, the old sailor! He's back.

MESSENGER: Pericles has been here, and he is here. He has come disguised. But now he will speak.

IDA: Pericles is here disguised.

CIMON: I'll bet the old sailor is Pericles.

HECTOR: You will not win, Leta, because you said he made up stories.

AJAX: The old sailor said he knew Pericles, and surely a man knows himself. (PERICLES *now steps up beside the* MESSENGER.)

LETA: Look! The old beggar is standing next to the messenger. It is not the old sailor, but the old beggar who is Pericles in disguise.

HECTOR: It can't be. He said he had never seen Pericles face to face.

LETA: No man ever sees himself face to face.

MESSENGER: Citizens of Athens! Pericles! (PERICLES *drops the ragged cloak he has had about him, removes the hood from his head, and stands erect.*)

CITIZENS: Pericles! It is Pericles.

FIRST CITIZEN: I have seen him talking to the children by the river's edge.

SECOND CITIZEN: I have seen him listening to the children sing.

THIRD CITIZEN: He has heard my lazy son snore.

FOURTH CITIZEN (*Pleased*): He has heard my little girl sing.

PERICLES: Citizens of Athens, I have come disguised not to trick you, but because I wanted to know you as you know each other—as friend knows friend and fellow-citizen knows fellow-citizen.

FIFTH CITIZEN: That is the democratic way.

PERICLES: I have watched and been pleased. Here are many youths with skills and gifts that make life good.

NESTOR (*To his friends*): You see! He is going to give one of you the prize.

PERICLES: I have seen Cimon race. He will win many palms in the games.

NESTOR: You see, Cimon. He knows.

PERICLES: I have heard Hector speak and seen Ajax fight. With such voices and willing hearts, Athens will long remain free.

NESTOR: Perhaps he will give three prizes.

PERICLES: And I have seen Helena's beautiful face and Ida's grace, and I have heard the wise words of Leta. All our poets will sing of these three.

NESTOR: He's going to give six prizes!

PERICLES: And there are other youths, too. Jason, who works with his father in the olive groves, and Hymen, who sails a boat so well across the waters. Each has skills I wish I had. But my only skill is in knowing that all men have skills.

FIRST CITIZEN: That is true. He knows men have skills that they do not know they have.

PERICLES: Now which youth among you best knows your virtues? What say you, Cimon?

CIMON: My friend, Nestor.

PERICLES: What say you, Hector?

HECTOR: My friend, Nestor.

PERICLES: What say you, Ajax?

AJAX: My friend, Nestor.

PERICLES: What say you, Citizens of Athens?

ALL: Our friend, Nestor.

FIRST CITIZEN: He listens to me when I am sad.

SECOND CITIZEN: He sings with me when I am happy.

THIRD CITIZEN: He is happy when I am fortunate.

PERICLES: Then, my friends, *your* choice is Nestor. He is our friend, and before the sun sets, we will honor him today as he honors us every day of his life. Go to your homes to prepare, and return before the sun sets. (*All except the* OLD SAILOR, PERICLES, *and the seven young people depart, speaking as they go.*)

FIRST CITIZEN: It was a good choice.

SECOND CITIZEN: He has always been a friend to all.

THIRD CITIZEN: And he says my son is not lazy, just thinking, and one day he will be a fine man.

FOURTH CITIZEN: He loves to hear my little girl sing. *(All exit.)*

PERICLES *(Who has made his way down to the seven)*: Well, my young friends, I know you all agree, but what did you learn from this?

LETA: Something we should have known: the first prize in a democracy goes to those who give, not to those who have.

PERICLES: You are wise, Leta, and if you have the wisdom to comfort people, you will be honored all the days of your life. *(The* OLD SAILOR *attempts to move offstage without being noticed.* PERICLES *shouts to him.)* Wait a minute, old sailor, my friend. *(To the others)* I must go see my old friend, the sailor. He fought alongside me in many a battle. I must seek his advice on how to make our country better. *(As he is leaving)* He was with Odysseus when they escaped from the Cyclops, you know. *(He goes to the* OLD SAILOR *and they exit together.)*

CIMON: Did you hear, Leta? The old sailor *was* with Odysseus. You were wrong.

AJAX: You said that he did not even know Pericles. And now you have seen what great friends they are.

LETA: They are now. That is Pericles' skill, to use one's gift to help others. I don't know if the old sailor ever saw Pericles before, but he will never forget him now. *(Curtain)*

Think and Respond

1 Why does Pericles give the prize to Nestor?

2 Why do you think Pericles disguised himself to judge the contest?

3 How does reading this play help you identify the **virtues** that were important to the ancient Greeks?

4 If you had the opportunity to award a prize for personal skills, what qualities would you look for? Why?

5 What reading strategy was useful to you in reading the play? When did you use it?

Meet the Illustrator

DAVID SCOTT MEIER

David Scott Meier has been painting since he was four, but he only recently started illustrating children's books. He especially enjoyed illustrating this play because his pet parrot is named Pericles! Meier enjoys collecting artifacts from ancient Greece. He also enjoys traveling, singing, and acting when he can spare the time from his busy illustrating career.

Visit *The Learning Site!*
www.harcourtschool.com

Aesop's Fables

retold by Margaret Clark
illustrated by Charlotte Voake

THE NORTH WIND and THE SUN

The north wind and the sun were having an argument. The north wind claimed to be stronger than the sun, and the sun said, "No, I am the strongest." At last they agreed to have a competition to see who could make a traveler take off his cloak. The wind blew and blew furiously, but the harder it gusted, the tighter the man clutched his cloak around him.

Then it was the sun's turn. At first the sun warmed the traveler gently with its rays so that he soon had to unbutton his cloak. Then the sun shone more and more brightly, until the man was so hot that he threw off his cloak and went on his way without it.

Persuasion is better than force.

366

THE FOX and THE CROW

One day a crow snatched a piece of cheese from an open cottage window and flew up into a tree, where she sat on a branch to eat it. A fox, walking by, saw the crow and at once wanted the cheese for himself.

"O Crow," he said, "how beautiful your feathers are! And what bright eyes you have! Your wings shine like polished ebony, and your head sparkles like a glistening jewel. If your voice is as sweet as your looks are fair, you must be the queen of the birds." The unwary crow believed every word, and, to show how sweet her voice was, she opened her mouth to sing. Out dropped the cheese, which the fox instantly gobbled up.

"You may have a voice," he said to the crow as he went on his way, "but whatever happened to your brains?"

Do not be fooled by flattery.

Think and Respond

The crow is meant to seem silly. Do you think the fox is an admirable character?

▲ The Skill of Pericles

Making Connections

Compare Texts

1 Why is "The Skill of Pericles" in a theme about past civilizations?

2 How do the feelings expressed by the Greek citizens at the beginning of the play change by the end?

3 Which character in "Aesop's Fables" do you think Pericles is most like? Explain your answer.

4 Compare "The Skill of Pericles" with another play you have read.

5 What sources would you use to find more information about Pericles and his achievements?

Write a Fable

Write your own fable, using talking animals as the main characters. Include a sentence at the end of the fable that sums up its moral, or message about life. Use a story map to plan your fable.

Writing CONNECTION

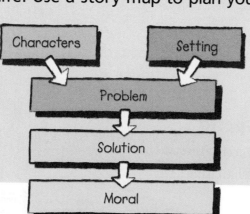

Characters → Setting → Problem → Solution → Moral

Make a Chart

At one point in the play, Pericles says, "We Athenians are not brutes like the Spartans." Do research to find out more information about ancient Athens and Sparta. Then make a two-column chart that compares and contrasts these two Greek city-states.

Athens	Sparta
1. developed democracy	

Make a Poster

Many letters of the Greek alphabet have meanings in English. The Greek letter pi, or π, stands for a number used to figure out the circumference of a circle. Use your math book or another source to find out more about π. Then make a poster showing what the number π represents, as well as the formula for determining the circumference of a circle.

369

Prefixes, Suffixes, and Roots

Focus Skill

Knowing the meanings of word parts will help you figure out the meanings of unfamiliar words. Remember that prefixes, suffixes, and roots are word parts that carry meaning. A **root** is the part of a word to which prefixes and suffixes are added. Many English roots were borrowed from the Greek and Latin languages.

Notice the underlined words in the sentences below. The chart shows how you can figure out the meanings of the words if you know what the roots mean.

1. We signed a <u>contract</u> saying we would respect the law.
2. Pericles will soon <u>interrupt</u> us and identify the winner.
3. The citizens of ancient Athens lived in a <u>democracy</u>.

Word	Meaning of Root	Meaning of Word
con<u>tract</u>	"draw, pull"	"an agreement pulling together two people"
inter<u>rupt</u>	"break, burst"	"to break the course of"
dem<u>ocr</u>acy	"people"	"government by the people"

Visit *The Learning Site!*
www.harcourtschool.com

See *Skills* and *Activities*

370

Test Prep
Prefixes, Suffixes, and Roots

▶ **Read the passage. Then answer the questions.**

> Pericles ruled Athens during the city's "golden age." Under his leadership, there were many changes in the Athenian government. For the first time, elected officials were paid a salary. The new *democratic* government allowed the common people to hold any state office. Pericles also hired the greatest architects in the world to build beautiful temples, theaters, and other fine *structures*. During his rule many famous Greek writers and philosophers lived and worked in Athens.

1. **What is the meaning of the word** *democratic* **in this passage?**

   A without people

   B against the people

   C treating people equally

   D full of people

Tip

Figure out the meaning by first identifying any word parts you know. Then make sure your answer makes sense in the passage.

2. **The word** *structures* **means—**

   F plans

   G museums

   H bridges

   J buildings

Tip

If you don't know the meaning of the root, think of similar words you know, such as <u>construct</u> or <u>construction</u>.

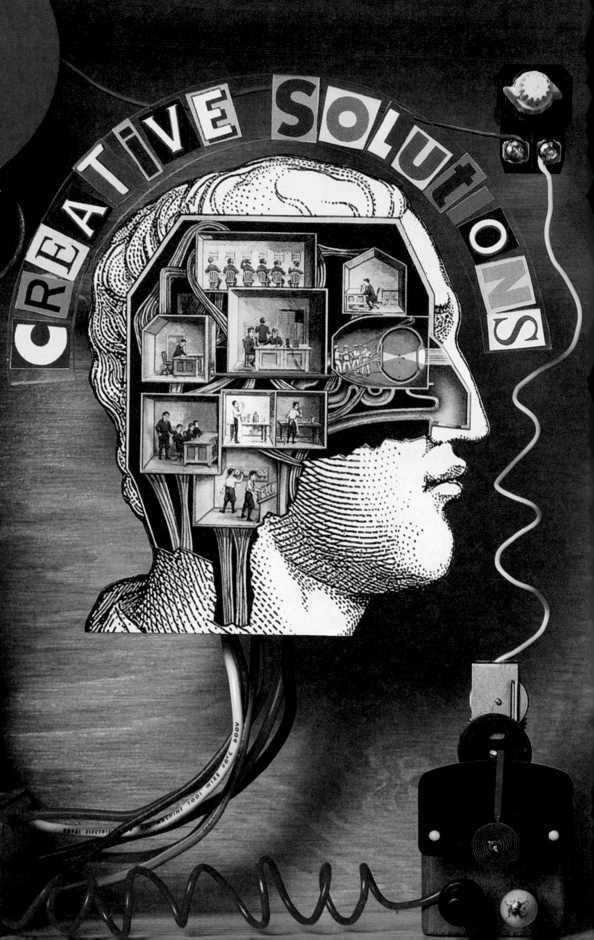

CREATIVE SOLUTIONS

CONTENTS

My Side of the Mountain 374
by Jean Craighead George

Focus Skill Literary Devices

Fall Secrets 392
by Candy Dawson Boyd

Kids Did It! 408
from *National Geographic World*

Focus Skill Word Relationships

Girls Think of Everything 414
by Catherine Thimmesh

Focus Skill Text Structure: Compare and Contrast

A Do-It-Yourself Project 438
by Anilú Bernardo

Preface to *The Other Side* 456
by Angela Johnson

Focus Skill Text Structure: Compare and Contrast

Catching the Fire:
Philip Simmons, Blacksmith 462
by Mary E. Lyons

The Road Not Taken 478
by Robert Frost

Focus Skill Word Relationships

▲ My Side of the
Mountain

Vocabulary Power

discouraging

edible

nourishing

remote

cavity

foundation

migration

Many people enjoy the outdoors. On the following pages, you'll read about a boy named Sam who moves to the mountains and lives off the land. What does it take to survive on your own outdoors? Here are some tips to follow.

Finding and cooking your own food can be **discouraging** at first. Don't give up! Begin by deciding what is **edible**. If the food can be eaten, then decide if it is **nourishing**, or good for you. Fruits and nuts are usually good choices.

You may need to store leftover food to eat on another day. Choose a **remote** location where hungry animals will not find it. The **cavity** of this tree is a hollowed-out space that makes a perfect hiding place for fruits and nuts.

Plan the **foundation**, or base, for your tent carefully. The tent will be your home for the night. If you're camping in the fall, you may notice the **migration** of birds as they fly south to their winter homes. Their journey south means that cold weather is on the way.

Vocabulary–Writing CONNECTION

Suppose you are lost in a forest without food or water. What could you eat to survive? List some **edible** foods that you might be able to find in the woods.

Genre

Realistic Fiction

Realistic fiction tells about characters and events that are like people and events in real life.

In this selection, look for

- One main character

- Descriptive language that helps readers picture the setting

MY SIDE of the MOUNTAIN

by Jean Craighead George   illustrated by Allen Garns

Sam Gribley leaves crowded New York City for the peace and quiet of the Catskill Mountains. With the help of some maps provided by Miss Turner, the local librarian, he finds the part of a mountain that once belonged to his great-grandfather. Sam plans to live on this land, using his knowledge of nature and the few supplies he has with him. But how will he find food and shelter, alone on a mountain with fall and winter approaching?

The following morning I stood up, stretched, and looked about me. Birds were dripping from the trees, little birds, singing and flying and pouring over the limbs.

"This must be the warbler migration," I said, and I laughed because there were so many birds. I had never seen so many. My big voice rolled through the woods, and their little voices seemed to rise and answer me.

They were eating. Three or four in a maple tree near me were darting along the limbs, pecking and snatching at something delicious on the trees. I wondered if there was anything there for a hungry boy. I pulled a limb down, and all I saw were leaves, twigs, and flowers. I ate a flower. It was not very good. One manual I had read said to watch what the birds and animals were eating in order to learn what is edible and nonedible in the forest. If the animal life can eat it, it is safe for humans. The book did suggest that a raccoon had tastes more nearly like ours. Certainly the birds were no example.

Then I wondered if they were not eating something I couldn't see—tiny insects perhaps; well, anyway, whatever it was, I decided to fish. I took my line and hook and walked down to the stream.

I lay on a log and dangled my line in the bright water. The fish were not biting. That made me hungrier. My stomach pinched. You know, it really does hurt to be terribly hungry.

A stream is supposed to be full of food. It is the easiest place to get a lot of food in a hurry. I needed something in a hurry, but what? I looked through the clear water and saw the tracks of mussels in the mud. I ran along the log back to shore, took off my clothes, and plunged into that icy water.

I collected almost a peck[1] of mussels in very little time at all, and began tying them in my sweater to carry them back to camp.

But I don't have to carry them anywhere, I said to myself. I have my fire in my pocket, I don't need a table. I can sit right here by the stream and eat. And so I did. I wrapped the mussels in leaves and sort of steamed them

[1] *peck:* a measure for fruits and vegetables equal to eight dry quarts

in coals. They are not quite as good as clams—a little stronger, I would say—but by the time I had eaten three, I had forgotten what clams tasted like and knew only how delicious freshwater mussels were. I actually got full.

I wandered back to Great-grandfather's farm and began to explore. Most of the acreage was maple and beech, some pine, dogwoods, ash; and here and there a glorious hickory. I made a sketch of the farm on my road map, and put x's where the hickories were. They were gold trees to me. I would have hickory nuts in the fall. I could also make salt from hickory limbs. I cut off one and chopped it into bits and scraps. I stuck them in my sweater.

The land was up and down and up and down, and I wondered how Great-grandfather ever cut it and plowed it. There was one stream running through it, which I was glad to see, for it meant I did not have to go all the way down the mountain to the big creek for fish and water.

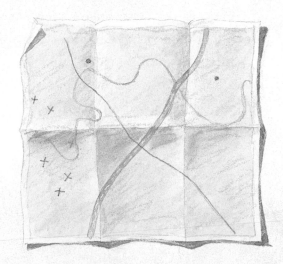

Around noon I came upon what I was sure was the old foundation of the house. Miss Turner was right. It was ruins—a few stones in a square, a slight depression for the basement, and trees growing right up through what had once been the living room. I wandered around to see what was left of the Gribley home.

After a few looks I saw an apple tree. I rushed up to it, hoping to find an old apple. No apples beneath it. About forty feet away, however, I found a dried one in the crotch of a tree, stuck there by a squirrel and forgotten. I ate it. It was pretty bad—but nourishing, I hoped. There was another apple tree and three walnuts. I scribbled *x*'s. These were wonderful finds.

I poked around the foundations, hoping to uncover some old iron implements that I could use. I found nothing. Too many leaves had fallen and turned to loam, too many plants had grown up and died down over the old home site. I decided to come back when I had made myself a shovel.

Whistling and looking for food and shelter, I went on up the mountain, following the stone walls, discovering many things about my property. I found a marsh. In it were cattails and arrow-leaf— good starchy foods.

At high noon I stepped onto a mountain meadow. An enormous boulder rose up in the center of it. At the top of the meadow was a fringe of white birch. There were maples and oaks to the west, and a hemlock forest to the right that pulled me right across the sweet grasses, into it.

Never, never have I seen such trees. They were giants—old, old giants. They must have begun when the world began.

I started walking around them. I couldn't hear myself step, so dense and damp were the needles. Great boulders covered with ferns and moss stood among them. They looked like pebbles beneath those trees.

Standing before the biggest and the oldest and the most kinglike of them all, I suddenly had an idea.

I knew enough about the Catskill Mountains to know that when the summer came, they were covered with people. Although Great-grandfather's farm was somewhat remote, still hikers and campers and hunters and fishermen were sure to wander across it.

Therefore I wanted a house that could not be seen. People would want to take me back where I belonged if they found me.

I looked at that tree. Somehow I knew it was home, but I was not quite sure how it was home. The limbs were high and not right for a tree house. I could build a bark extension around it, but that would look silly. Slowly I circled the great trunk. Halfway around the whole plan became perfectly obvious. To the west, between two of the flanges of the tree that spread out to be roots, was a cavity. The heart of the tree was rotting away. I scraped at it with my hands; old, rotten insect-ridden dust came tumbling out. I dug on and on, using my ax from time to time as my excitement grew.

With much of the old rot out, I could crawl in the tree and sit cross-legged. Inside I felt as cozy as a turtle in its shell. I chopped and chopped until I was hungry and exhausted. I was now in the hard good wood, and chopping it out was work. I was afraid

December would come before I got a hole big enough to lie in. So I sat down to think.

You know, those first days, I just never planned right. I had the beginnings of a home, but not a bite to eat, and I had worked so hard that I could hardly move forward to find that bite. Furthermore, it was discouraging to feed that body of mine. It was never satisfied, and gathering food for it took time and got it hungrier. Trying to get a place to rest it took time and got it more tired, and I really felt I was going in circles and wondered how primitive man ever had enough time and energy to stop hunting food and start thinking about fire and tools.

I left the tree and went across the meadow looking for food. I plunged into the woods beyond, and there I discovered the gorge and the white cascade splashing down the black rocks into the pool below.

I was hot and dirty. I scrambled down the rocks and slipped into the pool. It was so cold I yelled. But when I came out on the bank and put on my two pairs of trousers and three sweaters, which I thought was a better way to carry clothes than in a pack, I tingled and burned and felt coltish. I leapt up the bank, slipped, and my face went down in a patch of dog-tooth violets.

You would know them anywhere after a few looks at them at the Botanical Gardens and in colored flower books. They are little yellow lilies on long slender stems with oval leaves dappled with gray. But that's not all. They have wonderfully tasty bulbs. I was filling my pockets before I got up from my fall.

"I'll have a salad-type lunch," I said as I moved up the steep sides of the ravine. I discovered that as late as it was in the season, the spring beauties were still blooming in the cool pockets of the woods. They are all right raw, that is if you are as hungry as I was. They taste a little like lima beans. I ate these as I went on hunting food, feeling better and better, until I worked my way back to the meadow where the dandelions were blooming. Funny I hadn't noticed them earlier. Their greens are good, and so are their roots—a little strong and milky, but you get used to that.

A crow flew into the aspen grove without saying a word. The little I knew of crows from following them in Central Park, they always have something to say. But this bird was sneaking, obviously trying to be quiet. Birds are good food. Crow is certainly not the best, but I did not know that then, and I launched out to see where it was going. I had a vague plan to try to noose it. This is the kind of thing I wasted time on in those days when time was so important. However, this venture turned out all right, because I did not have to noose that bird.

I stepped into the woods, looked around, could not see the crow, but noticed a big stick nest in a scrabbly pine. I started to climb the tree. Off flew the crow. What made me keep on climbing in face of such discouragement, I don't know, but I did, and that noon I had crow eggs and wild salad for lunch.

At lunch I also solved the problem of carving out my tree. After a struggle I made a fire. Then I sewed a big skunk cabbage leaf into a cup with grass strands. I had read that you can boil water in a leaf, and ever since then I had been very anxious to see if this were true. It seems impossible, but it works. I boiled the eggs in a leaf. The water keeps the leaf wet, and although the top dries up and burns down to the water level, that's as far as the burning goes. I was pleased to see it work.

Then here's what happened. Naturally, all this took a lot of time, and I hadn't gotten very far on my tree, so I was fretting and stamping out the fire when I stopped with my foot in the air.

The fire! Indians made dugout canoes with fire. They burned them out, an easier and much faster way of getting results. I would try fire in the tree. If I was very careful, perhaps it would work. I ran into the hemlock forest with a burning stick and got a fire going inside the tree.

Thinking that I ought to have a bucket of water in case things got out of hand, I looked desperately around me. The water was far across the meadow and down the ravine. This would never do. I began to think the whole inspiration of a home in the tree was no good. I really did have to live near water for cooking and drinking and comfort. I looked sadly at the magnificent hemlock and was about to put the fire out and desert it when I said something to myself. It must have come out of some book: "Hemlocks usually grow around mountain streams and springs."

I swirled on my heel. Nothing but boulders around me. But the air was damp, somewhere—I said—and darted around the rocks, peering and looking and sniffing and going down into pockets and dales. No water. I was coming back, circling wide, when I almost fell in it. Two sentinel boulders, dripping wet, decorated with flowers, ferns, moss, weeds—everything that loved water—guarded a bathtub-sized spring.

"You pretty thing," I said, flopped on my stomach, and pushed my face into it to drink. I opened my eyes. The water was like glass, and in it were little insects with oars. They rowed away from

me. Beetles skittered like bullets on the surface, or carried a silver bubble of air with them to the bottom. Ha, then I saw a crayfish.

I jumped up, overturned rocks, and found many crayfish. At first I hesitated to grab them because they can pinch. I gritted my teeth, thought about how much more it hurts to be hungry, and came down upon them. I did get pinched, but I had my dinner. And that was the first time I had planned ahead! Any planning that I did in those early days was such a surprise to me and so successful that I was delighted with even a small plan. I wrapped the crayfish in leaves, stuffed them in my pockets, and went back to the burning tree.

Bucket of water, I thought. Bucket of water? Where was I going to get a bucket? How did I think, even if I found water, I could get it back to the tree? That's how citified I was in those days. I had never lived without a bucket before—scrub buckets, water buckets—and so when a water problem came up, I just thought I could run to the kitchen and get a bucket.

"Well, dirt is as good as water," I said as I ran back to my tree. "I can smother the fire with dirt."

Days passed working, burning, cutting, gathering food, and each day I cut another notch on an aspen pole that I had stuck in the ground for a calendar.

THINK AND RESPOND

1 How does the main character use his inventiveness to find food and shelter in a **remote** area in the woods?

2 Why do you think the author chose the first-person point of view for this story?

3 How does the author help you picture the story's setting? Give an example.

4 Would you like to live in the woods, as Sam does in the story? Why or why not?

5 How did you use strategies to help you understand what you read?

Meet the Author
JEAN CRAIGHEAD GEORGE

Award-winning author Jean Craighead George called upon her lifelong interest in nature to help her write *My Side of the Mountain.* Here she answers questions about her childhood experiences.

What was your childhood like?
I grew up in Washington, D.C., and at the old family home at Craighead, Pennsylvania. Both my father and mother were entomologists (scientists who study insects), and my twin brothers were among the first falconers in the country and the first to track grizzly bears using radio collars.

Did you have any memorable times in the wilderness?
My brothers took me with them on hunting and camping trips. We went to the tops of cliffs to look for falcons, down the whitewater rivers to fish and swim, and over the forest floors in search of mice, birds, wildflowers, trees, fish, salamanders, and mammals. My childhood seems like one leaping, laughing adventure into the mysteries and joys of the earth.

Did you have pets when you were growing up?
Our home was always full of pets—falcons, raccoons, owls, and opossums, and dozens of sleeping insects. Hounds and kids ran in and out. It was a rollicking childhood.

Jean Craighead George

Visit *The Learning Site!*
www.harcourtschool.com

387

Making Connections

Compare Texts

1 How does "My Side of the Mountain" relate to the theme Creative Solutions?

2 How does the setting of the selection affect Sam's problem and the way he solves it?

3 Think about another example of realistic fiction with an outdoor setting. How important is the setting to the main problem of each story?

4 How would a nonfiction selection about the plant and animal life of the Catskill Mountains be different from "My Side of the Mountain"?

5 Would you like to read the rest of the novel from which this selection was taken? Why or why not?

Write a Paragraph

Sam loves the peace and quiet of his new mountain home. Think of a place where you would like to live. Then write a paragraph explaining why you would like to live there. Use a chart to help organize your ideas.

Writing CONNECTION

My Place: _____

Reasons: _____

_____

_____

_____

Conclusion: _____

Make a Food Chain

Sam finds many nourishing foods to eat in his new outdoor home. Do research to find out more about the plant and animal life in the Catskill Mountains. Draw a food chain to show which living things are food for other living things.

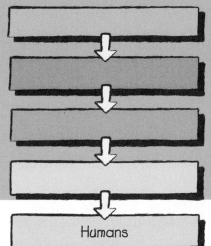

Humans

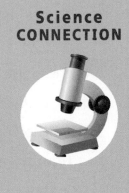

Create a Time Line

The Catskill Mountains are part of the Appalachian Mountain System. Work with a partner to find out how changes in the Earth's structure over a period of time created the Appalachian Mountains. Record your findings on an illustrated time line.

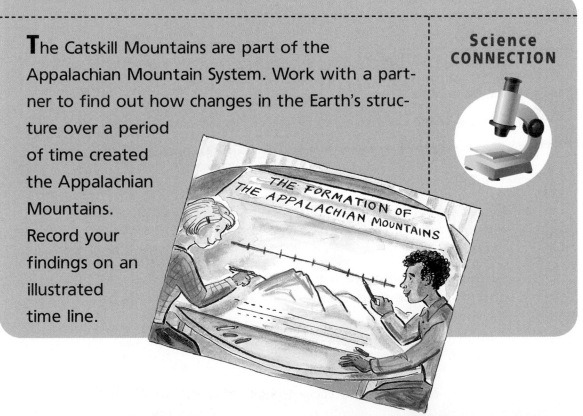

THE FORMATION OF THE APPALACHIAN MOUNTAINS

Literary Devices

Authors use various techniques for telling a story. These techniques, or **literary devices**, create different kinds of effects. In "My Side of the Mountain," Jean Craighead George uses **point of view** and **figurative language** to tell Sam Gribley's story.

Remember that an author uses point of view to control what the reader finds out about the characters. In first-person point of view, one of the characters is the narrator, who tells the story in his or her own words. First-person pronouns such as *I* and *my* are clues that "My Side of the Mountain" is told in first-person point of view. You learn more about Sam by knowing what he thinks and feels.

> **I lay on a log and dangled my line in the bright water. The fish were not biting. That made me hungrier. My stomach pinched. You know, it really does hurt to be terribly hungry.**

Authors often use figurative language, such as **metaphors** and **similes**, to create a mood or image. These vivid descriptions help you picture scenes from the story in your mind. What do you see in your mind when you read each of these descriptions from the selection?

> **Never, never have I seen such trees. They were giants— old, old giants. They must have begun when the world began.**

> **With much of the old rot out, I could crawl in the tree and sit cross-legged. Inside I felt as cozy as a turtle in its shell.**

Visit *The Learning Site!*
www.harcourtschool.com

See *Skills* and *Activities*

390

Test Prep
Literary Devices

▶ **Read the passage. Then answer the questions.**

When my sister Meg and I arrived at the beach, the sand was still cool. By ten o'clock, it burned our skin like tiny flames. My mother had warned us to stay under the beach umbrella when the sun became too hot. "David," she had said, "you can get a bad sunburn even when you're in the water. Be careful!" But Meg and I loved to swim. As Meg swam, she was a mermaid gliding through the water. We came out of the water only after my grandmother called to us from the shore.

1. What is the author comparing in this sentence?
   "As Meg swam, she was a mermaid gliding through the water."

   A   A mermaid and a fish

   B   Meg and a mermaid

   C   Meg and the water

   D   A mermaid and the water

Tip

Think about why the author uses figurative language in the description. What picture do you see when you read the sentence?

2. The narrator of the passage is—

   F   David

   G   Grandmother

   H   Mother

   J   Meg

Tip

Remember that pronouns help you figure out point of view. What pronouns do you see? Do you see any other clues?

presentation

flawless

persevered

melodious

lilting

legacy

Vocabulary Power

The four students in the next selection, "Fall Secrets," all want to perform. What does it take to stand up in front of people and dance or sing? These journal entries give you some idea.

Monday, March 10

The dance **presentation** at the community center was terrific! Mom videotaped my performance so I could watch it later. She said my dancing was **flawless**. I didn't make a single mistake. Practicing two hours every day wasn't easy. There were times when I wanted to give up, but I'm glad I **persevered**. My success tonight was worth all the hard work.

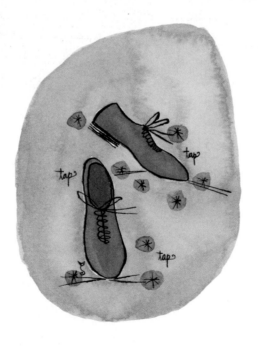

Thursday, June 2

We were all so proud of my sister's singing in the school talent show. Her teacher, Mr. Fisher, said she has a naturally **melodious** voice that's truly musical. The high, **lilting** tone of her singing was so pleasant to listen to. Dad said that Jenny's talent is a **legacy** she inherited from our grandmother, a very fine singer. I wish Gran could have been here with us tonight.

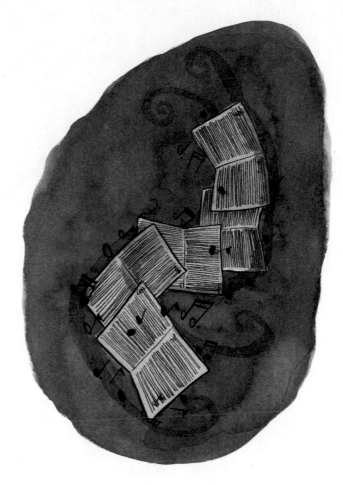

Vocabulary-Writing CONNECTION

Think about your family members and their different talents. Do you have a talent like one of theirs? Write a few sentences describing a **legacy** of talent passed on to you from a family member.

Genre

Realistic Fiction

Realistic fiction tells about characters and events that are like people and events in real life.

In this selection, look for

- **Characters who have feelings that real people have**

- **A plot with a problem and a resolution**

FALL SECRETS

by
Candy Dawson Boyd

illustrated by
Floyd Cooper

Jessie Williams and her three friends have just performed in auditions at OPA—the Oakland Performing Arts Middle School. All four girls have high hopes:

- Jessie hopes to get a leading role in a play.
- Mkiwa (mm-KEE-wah) Cooper (also known as Addie Mae) hopes to be placed in the first line of dancers.
- Maria Hernandez hopes to play the piano flawlessly.
- Julie Stone, with her broken leg, just hopes for the best when she stands to play the violin.

In addition to their separate talents, the girls perform together in a group called the Fours. The Fours perform in order to give something to the community. Today, though, the community will give something to them.

On Wednesday the results of the auditions were posted at various places in the school. Crowds of students gathered around. Groans and whoops of joy were heard up and down the corridors of OPA.

Jessie hung back. At last she got the courage to read the list by the theater door. The part of the elderly Harriet Tubman had gone to Dorothy Foster. Jessie bit her bottom lip. Sylvia Duncan was listed after "Harriet Tubman as a young woman." *That figures.* And Jamar had been selected as Harriet's second husband. Jessie searched for any mention of her name. There it was. The part of Harriet's sister, Mary Ann, went to Jessie Williams.

"Hey. How did you do?" Jamar stood behind her.

Unable to respond, Jessie fled down the hall. What could she tell Dad, Mom, Cass, and Mamatoo? She was a failure. At the front of the school building she saw the other three.

"I didn't get the part of Harriet as an old woman. I got the part of Harriet's younger sister," said Jessie, the words coming out in a rush. "And I wore all of my good-luck clothes and jewelry!"

Tears glistened in Maria's eyes. "I practiced three hours a day! No matter what else I want to do—I practice and then I fall apart!"

"Maria, it can't be that bad!" said Julie, leaning against the wall, one crutch on the floor.

"I tried out for a simple solo part in the Winter Festival concert. Instead I get to play one song that a two-year-old could play, with the rest of the orchestra!" Maria wiped at the tears falling from her eyes.

"Here." Mkiwa handed her some Kleenex. "Maria, everybody blows it sometimes. Even me. Try being placed in not the first, not the second, but the third line of dancers! My mother will be disappointed, but I know that my father will understand. He's always in my corner. No matter what."

The girls just stared at her.

Jessie decided to let any questions about Addie Mae and her family drop. Everybody waited for Julie to say something.

"I don't feel bad. I get to play a short solo. Nothing really exciting. But to tell the truth, I was surprised and happy. I didn't expect to get to do much of anything," she said.

"Like my grandmother says, 'There's always next time.' And next time we'll do better. I'm glad we all tried." Jessie struggled to sound upbeat.

"I feel the same way, Jessie." Maria handed Julie her crutch.

Jessie bit her bottom lip. "Anyway, we have other opportunities. There's the Spring Fund-Raiser. That's the one that counts the most."

"We don't have time to stand around here," said Addie Mae.

Maria nodded. "They're expecting us at Evergreen in fifteen minutes. If we mess this up, there goes our grade."

"I don't feel much like performing," Jessie confessed.

"We have to." Julie added, as she limped off, "If we're serious artists we have to work even when we don't want to."

The girls carried Julie's things with their own. She walked well on the crutches. The sky was overcast. The chill in the air hurried them along.

Once inside Evergreen Residential Manor, they stowed their belongings in a small room off the dayroom. Mrs. Winters had arranged the furniture in the dayroom. Mrs. Hernandez rushed in with the video camera. The girls changed clothes. They had decided to dress up and appear as professional as possible.

Jessie broke the silence. "Julie's right. Professionals give their best, no matter what," she said.

Addie Mae spoke up. "Let's put our hands on top of each other's and say—"

"Four, three, two, one. We're the best. Let's have some fun!" Jessie quipped.

"I like it!" Maria put her hand out.

One after the other they placed their hands on top of each other's. The girls chanted, "Four, three, two, one. We're the best. Let's have some fun!"

Residents and members of the staff crowded the dayroom. The senior citizens sat on chairs or couches, or in wheelchairs. The Fours walked out to smiles and applause. Mrs. Winters introduced them. There was more applause.

The girls took their places. Julie sat on a chair, holding her violin. Her green taffeta dress shimmered. Maria, dressed in a long velvet skirt and white blouse, stood by the piano. Clad in a black bodysuit with a leopard print skirt and head wrap, Addie Mae crouched down on the side. Jessie had on the same black pants, white T-shirt, and *kente* cloth scarf she had worn for the reader's theater performance. The gold hoop earrings glowed against her skin.

"Good afternoon, Evergreen residents. My name is Jessie Williams. My friends and I are sixth graders at the Oakland Performing Arts Middle School. We are very happy to be here. Each one of us has a special dream and talent. We want to share each of our stories with you. Our first Dreamgirl is Maria Hernandez. No one works harder than Maria to make her dream come true. When she succeeds she will open another door for her people." She nodded to Maria, who stepped forward. Jess moved back.

"My name is Maria Hernandez. I live a few blocks from here. When I was five years old, my godmother took me to a piano recital in Mexico City. I saw a beautiful lady sit down at a huge grand piano. The concert hall looked like a castle and she was the queen. She started to play and minutes later I was lost in the most wonderful, magical music I had ever heard in my life. It all came from her mind and hands. When I told my father I wanted to learn how to be a concert pianist, he said that it was not a wise choice. There were few, if any, Mexican female concert pianists. But my godmother and mother persuaded him to let me take piano lessons."

Maria moved to the piano. "My dream is to become a world-class concert pianist. I will now play the audition piece that won me entrance into the castle, the Oakland Performing Arts Middle School." More applause filled the room. Maria nodded.

The lilting strains of the *New World Symphony* flowed over the audience. Jessie listened closely. Maria wasn't making any mistakes. Mrs. Hernandez videotaped the presentation. When Maria finished and took her place by the side of the piano, the room shook with approval. More relaxed, Jessie walked to the center of the room.

"Our next Dreamgirl is Mkiwa Cooper. She has chosen a rough road to dance on. Her heroines represent the most brilliant shining stars in the world of dance. When she succeeds she will continue the legacy they have left behind for her people." Jessie nodded to Addie Mae as she turned on the taped music. African drums and percussion instruments created an exciting mood.

"My name is Mkiwa Cooper. All of my life I have wanted to be a dancer like Judith Jamison of the Alvin Ailey Dance Company. For years I have taken classes in ballet, tap, modern dance, and African dance. I continue to take classes on Saturdays and practice every day. Dance is the only way I can really communicate how I feel and who I am. I'd like to perform the African dance I did when I auditioned for the Oakland Performing Arts Middle School. This is part of a dance by the Kikuyu (ke-KOO-yoo) people to celebrate a good hunt."

Jessie fast forwarded the tape to the number on her script. This music was pulsating and melodious. Addie Mae's movements, combined with the commanding African music, electrified the audience. She stomped, leaped, gestured, and swayed. Jessie saw several of the elderly people lift their hands in appreciation. As the last drumbeat drifted away, Addie Mae sank into a crouch, her head bowed. Again, applause thundered. One man pounded his cane.

This is going a lot better than we hoped. We are talented, thought Jessie.

"Our next Dreamgirl, Julie Stone, selected one of the oldest instruments in the world to master. In the face of enormous hardship, she has persevered."

Jessie moved the chair to the center. She carried Julie's violin and handed it to her after she was seated, the crutches by her side. Keeping Julie's part short had been deliberate. Julie wanted her violin to speak for her. The group had agreed.

"My name is Julie Stone. Like Mkiwa, I can't remember when I didn't want to play the violin. I take lessons on Saturday and practice every night. Whenever I play, I am happy. This is my favorite piece. I hope you like it."

There were moments when Julie's playing touched Jessie so deeply that she wanted to cry. Julie was oblivious to the audience. As her bow moved across the strings for the last time, Jessie saw a tear fall on her cheek. The silence in the audience lasted for several seconds. It ended with applause and shouts of "Brava!" Julie grinned. Addie Mae and Maria helped her move to the back.

Jessie exhaled. No one had made any mistakes. In fact, they had been at their best. *I just hope that I can do my part as well.*

"Now, I switch from narrator to performer. I am still Jessie Williams."

People chuckled.

Jessie continued. "My grandmother, Mamatoo, is the artistic director of a repertory theater company here in Oakland. I've been going to plays since I was born! My dream is to become a famous dramatic actress. I realize that this will be difficult. Not many make it, and there are few parts for African-Americans, but I am determined. To audition for acceptance at the Oakland Performing Arts Middle School, I selected Sojourner Truth's speech, 'Ain't I a Woman?' It is my pleasure to share her powerful words with you."

Like the rest of her group, Jessie delivered a flawless performance. This time she was able to erase everyone before her. In moments she escaped back to 1851 and that packed hall.

The words and intonations flowed like music. The audience's response startled her. Maria's mother was leading the cheers! Jessie was relieved that their work had been videotaped. Their stories plus the interviews with some of the residents about their lives would make a great project.

After two bows, Mrs. Winters explained that from now on the girls would be entertaining the residents twice a month. A table laden with punch, sandwiches, and cake stood in the corner. She invited everyone for refreshments. Before the girls could even change clothes, people came up to shake their hands and thank them.

Jessie watched an elderly black woman who walked with a cane beckon to Julie. The woman walked with a distinctive style, her eyes clear. The two of them sat down together. So Julie had already begun her interviews. Both Maria and Cooper were talking with certain residents.

For a second, the girls gazed at one another. An understanding passed between them. Going home depressed and dejected about the audition results would have been foolish and irresponsible. Coming here and performing was great.

Think and Respond

1. What do the girls learn about themselves as a result of their **presentation** to Evergreen Residential Manor?

2. How does the author help you know what each girl's character is like?

3. What do you learn about failure and success from this story?

4. Jessie and her classmates have big dreams. What dreams do you have?

5. Give an example of a reading strategy that you used as you read.

MEET THE AUTHOR
Candy Dawson Boyd

Candy Dawson Boyd's writing career began when she was a teacher in Chicago. She was always on the lookout for good books that represented different cultures. They were hard to find, so she decided to write some herself. Boyd's stories often show African American children winning out against the odds they face in life. She believes, "If books help children or give them a safe place to go, then that's the biggest reward for writing." This belief, along with her writing talent, has helped Candy Dawson Boyd become an award-winning author.

MEET THE ILLUSTRATOR
Floyd Cooper

Floyd Cooper drew his first picture as a young child in Tulsa, Oklahoma, when he sketched "a duck of some sort" on the side of his father's house. "I had to erase it," he recalls, "but I've been drawing ever since."

Actually, Cooper still erases quite a bit. He creates his warm, sunny illustrations using a technique called oil-wash-on-board. "What I do is cover the board with paint and then erase the images out of the paint using these little things called kneaded erasers."

Cooper does not draw many ducks nowadays, but his skillful illustrations of people in books such as *Grandpa's Face* and *Meet Danitra Brown* have earned him several awards. He currently lives in West Orange, New Jersey, with his wife, his two children, and a fish named Little Foot.

Visit *The Learning Site!*
www.harcourtschool.com

Kids Did It!

Keys to Success

Randy Chang, 16

"When I first started piano lessons at age 9, it was quite a struggle," says Randy Chang of Dover, Delaware. Randy was born with a disability called Down's syndrome that makes it hard to learn new skills. But little by little, he practiced, learned, and began performing. Today Randy has played more than 30 concerts, performed on TV fund-raisers, and represented Delaware at the International Very Special Arts Festival in Brussels, Belgium.

"Music has inspired me and helped me learn about myself," says Randy. "Performing a piece called 'Waterwheel,' I began to think of myself as a small waterwheel powered by my faith, always spinning, always trying."

Randy loves playing and listening to music by composers such as Mozart and Bach. He is an excellent student in school and has gradually become a skilled public speaker. If something is hard, he advises: "Practice every day. Never give up. Learning is fun!"

Bridging Generations

Kristen DeForrest, 14

After her grandmother died three years ago, Kristen DeForrest noticed that her grandfather was sad and lonely. "He was all alone in his apartment and needed us to visit him," she says. "I wondered if other older people needed companionship, too."

Kristen organized an Adopt-an-Elder program for kids at her school in Rowley, Massachusetts. She matched 20 kids in grades 6–8 with seniors who were patients at a nearby rehabilitation center. The kids phoned their seniors, sent them cards, and visited them at home. "The elders were really happy to see the kids," says Kristen. "But the kids enjoyed it, too."

For her idea Kristen won $3,000 in a contest to help the community. She uses the money to buy gift baskets and other items for the seniors. Kristen says her best reward is "seeing all the smiles of the pairs together."

Kristen still spends a lot of time with her own grandfather (above). He says he loves her idea and is proud to be the one who inspired it.

Think and Respond

Why are Randy's and Kristen's accomplishments important?

Making Connections

Compare Texts

1 Why is this selection included in the theme Creative Solutions?

2 Look at the illustrations on pages 397 and 404. How do they help you understand the girls' feelings at the beginning and at the end of the selection?

3 What do "Fall Secrets" and "Kids Did It!" say about the "keys to success"?

4 Compare the way "Fall Secrets" and "Kids Did It!" show the idea of "bridging generations."

5 Would you like to read the rest of the novel *Fall Secrets*? Why or why not?

Write a Poem

Writing CONNECTION

Write a short poem about one of the themes in "Fall Secrets," such as friendship, helping others, believing in yourself, or artistic accomplishments. You may express your own feelings or write from the point of view of one of the characters in the story. Use the web diagram to help you brainstorm ideas.

Details

Theme

Make a Poster

Julia plays the violin and Maria plays the piano. Work with a partner to find out about musical instruments that were used in two of the following ancient civilizations: Greece, Rome, China, or India. Organize your information in a two-column chart. Then use the facts to make a poster that includes pictures of the instruments you have researched.

Social Studies CONNECTION

Ancient Greece	Ancient Rome

lyre:
    small, harplike
    used to accompany
    singers	

Role-Play an Interview

In "Fall Secrets," Addie Mae says that she wants to be a dancer like Judith Jamison of the Alvin Ailey Dance Company. Work with a partner to find information about a famous dancer. You might research ballet, modern, or other types of dance. Then role-play an interview between the dancer and a reporter. Present your role-play in class.

Language Arts CONNECTION

411

Word Relationships

Focus Skill

The words in a sentence or paragraph take on meaning by the way they are related to each other. Each word appears in a **context** that helps you understand it. Read this sentence from "Fall Secrets":

> **Going home depressed and dejected about the audition results would have been foolish and irresponsible.**

The underlined words are **synonyms**, or words with similar meanings. If you were not sure of the meaning of *dejected*, its connection to the word *depressed* may have helped you understand it.

Suppose the writer had used this sentence to describe the girls' feelings after their performance: *The girls went home excited rather than dejected.* Here you can tell that *dejected* means the opposite of *excited*. These two words are **antonyms**, or words with opposite meanings.

When a word has more than one meaning, you can use **context clues** to tell which meaning is intended. The selection word *strains* is an example of a **multiple-meaning word**. This chart shows some of its meanings.

Example	Meaning
The lilting <u>strains</u> of the *New World Symphony* flowed over the audience. (p. 400)	Passages of music (noun)
Reading without glasses <u>strains</u> my eyes.	Injures or damages (verb)
The dog <u>strains</u> at its leash.	Pulls with great force (verb)

Visit *The Learning Site!*
www.harcourtschool.com

See Skills and Activities

Test Prep
Word Relationships

▶ **Read the sentence in the box. Then select the answer that uses the underlined word in the same way.**

1. During the storm, the water rose above the creek's <u>banks</u>.

   A The local <u>banks</u> are closed on national holidays.

   B We began our hike near the <u>banks</u> of the river.

   C The plow <u>banks</u> the snow on the side of the road.

   D The race cars slowed down at the <u>banks</u> of the track.

Tip

Picture the situation in the sentence in the box. Then decide which answer choice gives you a picture that is similar.

2. My parents buy <u>produce</u> from the grocery store.

   F I hope to <u>produce</u> a movie one day.

   G The lawyer will <u>produce</u> evidence of her client's innocence.

   H Certain types of <u>produce</u> need to be refrigerated.

   J Her kind words always <u>produce</u> a positive reaction.

Tip

The correct answer will be the same part of speech as the word in the box. Is the word a verb or a noun?

▲ Girls Think of Everything

persistence

acknowledged

visibility

ingenuity

initial

inquiries

milestone

Vocabulary Power

Think about the thousands of inventions we use every day. Without them, even the simplest chore could take hours. Read more about the ways inventors have changed our lives.

When Frank Epperson was a boy, he mixed water and powdered soda water, and stirred it with a wooden stick. It then froze by accident on his back porch. This gave him the idea for a treat that others could enjoy. Fortunately, he had great **persistence** and didn't give up. Years later he is **acknowledged** by many people as the inventor of one of America's favorite frozen treats, the Popsicle!

James Naismith was asked to invent a game that could be played at night. People couldn't see outside in the dark, of course. Because of this poor **visibility**, the game would have to be played indoors. The inventor used his **ingenuity** and cleverly nailed two peach baskets to the walls of a gym. This was the **initial**, or first, step in his invention. Next he wrote the rules of his new game. What do you think he called it?

Did you ever wonder who invented some well-known toy? The answers to your **inquiries** might surprise you. About fifty years ago, children rode scooters made from the boards of wooden crates. The next **milestone** in the history of scooters occurred when someone added roller-skate wheels to them. Later, plastic wheels became available, and the modern skateboard was invented.

Vocabulary-Writing CONNECTION

You can do just about anything with a little hard work and **persistence**. Think about something you would like to invent. Write an advertisement for your new product.

by Catherine Thimmesh

illustrated by **Melissa Sweet**

ink of Everything

Ingenious Inventions by Women

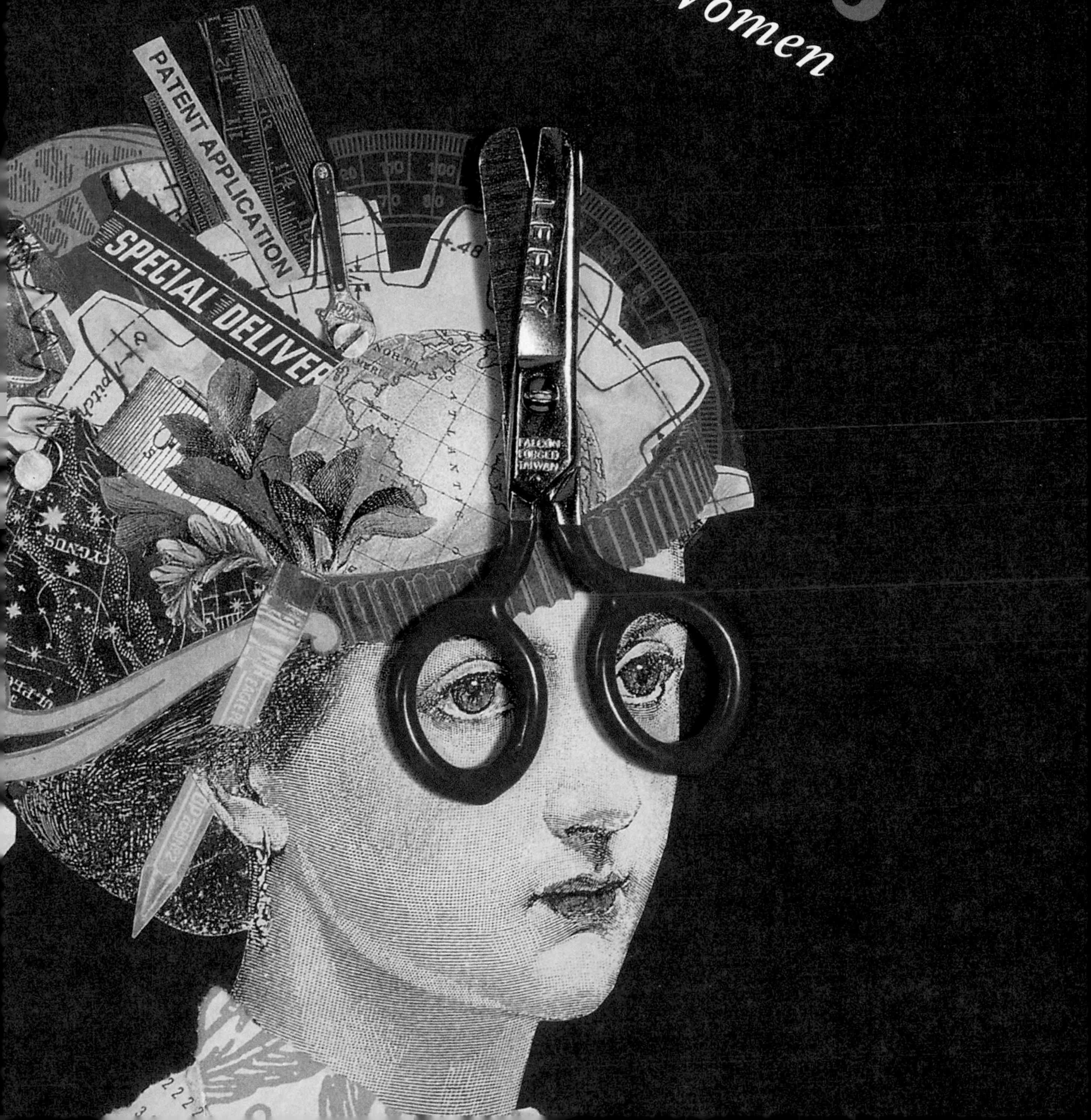

Against the odds, women have invented. They succeeded when many thought they'd fail. Madam C. J. Walker—the daughter of former slaves—invented hair care products for African-American women and a new method for selling them. She was born Sarah Breedlove, was orphaned at the age of seven,

married at fourteen, and widowed at twenty. For nearly twenty years she labored doing other people's laundry. Madam Walker began her business with a single product, a lot of confidence, and $1.50. She went door-to-door giving free demonstrations and showing before-and-after photos of herself. Within seven years, she had several hair care products and a thriving business. Madam C. J. Walker went on to become the first American woman self-made millionaire.

Today, in living rooms and labs, women are inventing. They are combining their curiosity and creativity with persistence and optimism. They are imagining. They are thinking and talking. "What if?" they ask. "How about?" they wonder. "Ah-ha!" they exclaim.

And gradually their ingenuity emerges. An inventiveness that touches all our lives, and perhaps energizes our own creativity—women and men, girls and boys alike.

Mary Anderson
Windshield Wipers

It was a dreadful day, weatherwise. Snow and sleet pelted the pavement, and people burrowed deep within their coats. Hoping to catch the sights and escape the blustery cold, Mary Anderson of Birmingham, Alabama, climbed aboard a New York City streetcar. The year was 1902. It turned out to be a ride she would never forget, but not because of the scenery. Instead, the ride would inspire her to invent the very first windshield wiper. And simply because she felt sorry for the streetcar driver, who struggled to see through the glass. The invention would not only improve conditions for all drivers, but would save countless lives as well.

Earlier, top-notch engineers had tackled the problem of poor visibility in bad weather and came up with a solution. They split the windshield. Once the glass became covered with rain or snow, the streetcar driver could fling open the middle for a clear view. Trouble was, it didn't work. At least not very well. Mary watched helplessly as the driver desperately tried to see. When he opened the split glass, he was greeted with a burst of icy cold air and a blast of heavy, wet snow.

"Why doesn't someone create a device to remove the snow?" Mary reportedly asked the people around her.

"It's been tried many times," they told her. "Can't be done."

Nonsense, thought Mary, as she scribbled in her notebook. Why can't there be a lever on the inside that would move an arm on the outside to swipe off the snow? To her, it seemed perfectly simple.

Later, when she returned to her home in Birmingham, she studied her sketches. She spent some time refining her drawings—making them more elaborate, adding more details. Satisfied at last, she brought her design

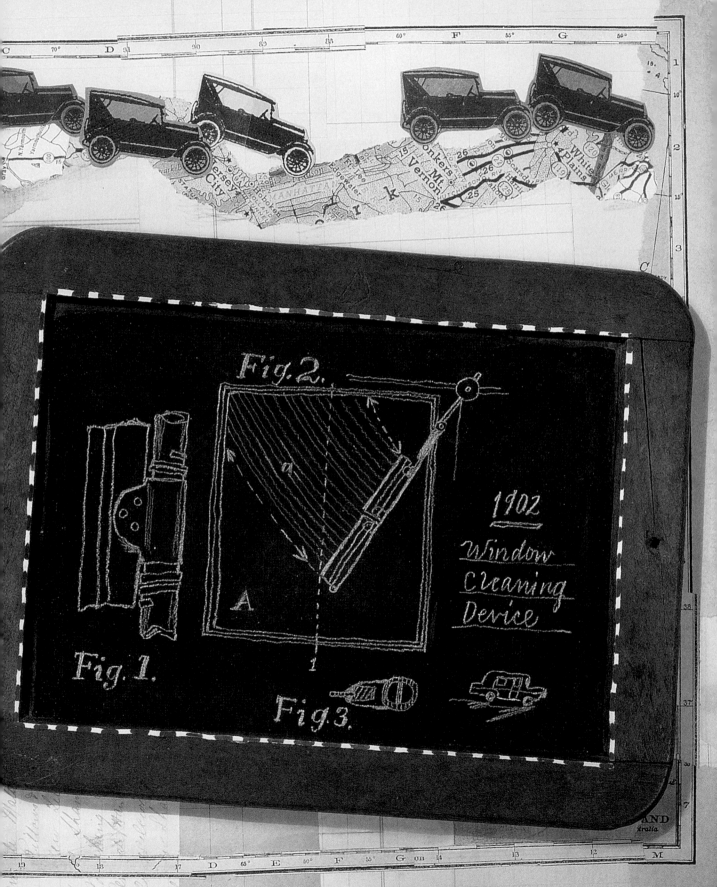

Fig. 2.

1902
Window
Cleaning
Device

A

Fig. 1.

Fig. 3.

to a small manufacturing company in Birmingham and hired them to make a model. Then, she filed a patent application.

"My invention relates to an improvement in window-cleaning devices in which a radially-swinging arm is actuated by a handle from inside of a car-vestibule," Mary stated in her patent specification.

In other words, a lever on the inside that would move an arm on the outside. Mary's wiper was made of wooden strips and pieces of rubber. She designed it to be removed in good weather so that it would not interfere with the appearance of the streetcar. One of her most important elements was the addition of a counterweight.

This was used, she writes, "to provide means for maintaining a uniform pressure upon the glass throughout the entire area swept by my improved window-cleaning device."

In other words, it would swipe off the snow. Mary was awarded a patent in 1903 for a window-cleaning device—a windshield wiper. Once the invention was protected by patent, she wrote a large Canadian company offering to sell her rights. They weren't interested. After reviewing her proposal, they decided that her invention had little, if any, commercial value. They simply didn't think it would sell. They encouraged her, however, to submit any other "useful patents" she might have for their consideration.

Mary put the patent in a drawer and, eventually, it expired. Several years later, someone else revived her idea, patented it, sold it, and made a very large sum of money. Every day, lives are saved due to increased visibility during bad weather. Even in our high-tech society, the windshield wiper remains one of the greatest safety inventions of the modern-day automobile. And tourists can now see the sights despite the snow, sleet, or rain.

Before windshield wipers were widely available, drivers used to smear pieces of carrots or onions across the glass to create an oily film that they hoped would repel water.

Margaret E. Knight
Paper Bags

They're used every minute of every hour of every day by millions of people in thousands of stores across the United States and throughout the world. When she invented a machine that made flat-bottomed paper bags, Margaret E. Knight not only revolutionized the paper bag industry, but she forever changed the way people shopped. No longer did they have to pack their milk, meats, and cheeses into heavy, wooden crates. No longer did shoppers struggle to stuff jam and bread into bags shaped like envelopes. With the flat-bottomed paper bag, life suddenly got a whole lot easier.

Margaret's job at the Columbia Paper Bag Company was relatively simple. She needed to gather, stack, and tie the company's finished bags into neat bundles. Regular bags were made by machine; flat-bottomed bags by hand. She had been at work barely a week before the idea came to her.

"I had plenty of leisure time for making observations," Margaret said. "And such time was employed in watching the movement of the machines and the manufacture of square-bottomed bags by hand."

Why did flat-bottomed bags have to be made by hand, she wondered? It was time-consuming and very costly. Few customers could afford them. Margaret was told there was no such thing as a machine that could fold and paste flat bottoms. This seemed odd to her since the flat bottom was clearly a better bag.

Margaret had no formal training in engineering, but she had been working with or around machines—in cotton mills and manufacturing plants—from her earliest memory. In fact, as a child, she much preferred a jackknife, gimlet, and pieces of wood to dolls and other such toys.

She began by making drawings of her ideas. Next, she constructed a cutting tool that she called a guide finger, and created a folding tool from a piece of tin that she called a plate-knife folder. The result? A successfully folded square-bottomed bag.

"My next experiment was on one of my machines in the shop, to which I rigged these same two devices, my guide finger and plate-knife folder," she

United States Patent Office.

MARGARET E. KNIGHT, OF BOSTON, MASSACHUSETTS.

Letters Patent No. 109,224, dated November 15, 1870.

IMPROVEMENT IN PAPER-FEEDING MACHINES.

No. 109,224.

Fig. 2.

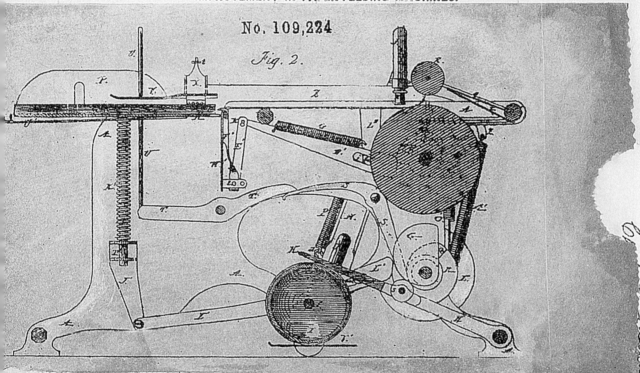

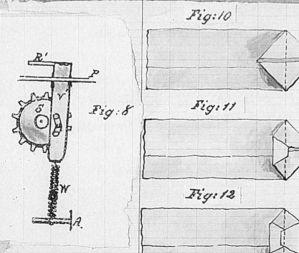

Fig: 10

Fig: 11

Fig: 12

Fig: 8

March 9, 1867

I've been to work all this evening trying the clock work arrangement for making the square bottoms. It works well, so far so good. Have done enough for one day.

PAPER FEEDING MACHINE.

Inventor,
Margaret E. Knight
By her attorney

beneath the upper plate V, the lower surface of which is in contact with the upper sheet of paper. When in this position the upper sheet is "cockled," in the middle by the approach of the fingers X toward each other, so as to pass over the separator I', when the sheet is fed forward, (see fig. 6.) The upper plate presses down upon the paper until the cockle is made, and rises away from it to release the upper sheet at the instant when it is taken hold of by the feed-mechanism to be drawn forward toward this cylinder.

explained. "By this means the paper tube followed along the guide finger entering it and flushing it back over the plate-knife folder. I did succeed in folding square bottoms."

Once she established that a machine could, in fact, fold and paste square bottoms, Margaret was more determined than ever. A year after her initial idea, she successfully built a wooden model, about two and a half feet in length and one foot wide.

"In July of 1868, I then completed making it a perfect working model," stated Margaret. "I should say that I made thousands of bags from it."

She then hired a skilled machinist to build an iron version, which she needed to submit along with her patent application. Unfortunately, and unknown to Margaret, a man named Charles Annan saw her machine in the shop while it was being cast in iron. He copied it and tried to patent it as his own.

Determined to set the record straight, Margaret went to Washington, D.C., with her diary, patterns, photos, records, models, folded bags, witnesses, and her lawyer in tow to fight Annan's claims before the commissioner of patents.

After sixteen days of testimony, she won. The invention of the machine that makes flat-bottomed paper bags was acknowledged as Margaret Knight's and she was awarded a patent in 1870. She joined forces with a business partner and established the Eastern Paper Bag Company in Hartford, Connecticut, to manufacture her machines. She also set up a lab where she worked on other inventions—amassing a total of twenty-seven patents—and prompting the media of the time to dub her "Lady Edison."

Margaret Knight's paper bag machine remains a milestone in the history of mechanical engineering. It's remarkable that during this era of high-tech gadgetry, a simple paper bag has remained a staple of everyday life. So, shoppers, toss some more chips and salsa into your cart. Your bag will hold them.

Although Margaret's invention has stood the test of time, she didn't get rich. Reportedly, she was offered $50,000 for her machine—the equivalent of more than half a million dollars today—but turned it down. It was noteworthy, then, that at her death her estate was worth a mere $275.05.

Girls (Even the Young Ones) Think of Everything

Becky Schroeder

A person has to be sixteen to drive, seventeen to see certain movies, and eighteen to vote. People can get terrific discounts on all sorts of stuff—provided they're over sixty-five. Everywhere we look there are age limits that define what people can and can't do. But creativity has no boundaries, no limitations. Anyone can invent. And they do. Inventors are popping up at the youngest of ages.

Sitting in the car waiting for her mom to return from shopping, Becky decided she might as well try to finish her math homework. But it was growing dark and getting hard to see the paper.

"I didn't have a flashlight, and I didn't want to open the car door because then the whole car would light up," recalled Becky. "So I thought it would be neat to have my paper light up somehow, and that's when the idea came to me."

It isn't every day that a ten-year-old invents a product eagerly sought by several businesses, but that's exactly what Becky Schroeder did when she created a tool that enabled people to write in the dark. Her invention? The Glo-sheet.

That night Becky went home trying to imagine different ways of making her paper glow in the dark. She remembered all sorts of glow-in-the-dark toys—like balls and Frisbees™—and wondered how they were made. She was determined to find a solution. So the very next day, Becky's dad took her on an outing to the hardware store. They returned with a pail of phosphorescent paint. She took the paint and stacks of paper into the darkest room in the house—the bathroom. There, she experimented.

"I'd turn on the light, turn it off, turn it on," said Becky. "My parents remember me running out of the room saying, 'It works, it works! I'm writing in the dark!'"

She used an acrylic board and coated it with a specific amount of phosphorescent paint. She took a complicated idea and made it work rather

Things that glow in the dark:

man made

flashlights
candles
Frisbee™
☆ ☆ ☆
-Sticker Stars
(that you put on
your ceiling).

in nature

fireflies
the moon
phosphorescent
fish:
Stars and Planets
glow-worms

It worked! The paper
glowed. I painted stacks
of paper in the bathroom
~~~~ ~~~~ of the house

As a below named inventor, I hereby declare that:

I believe I am the original, first and sole inventor (if only one name is listed below) or an original, first and joint inventor (if plural names are listed below) of the subject matter which is claimed and for which a patent is sought on the invention entitled:

GLO SHEET

the specification of which
☐ is attached hereto
OR
☐ was filed on (MM/DD/YYYY)

(Title of the Invention)

Application Number   as United States Application Number or PCT International

I hereby state that
amended b

simply. When the coated clipboard is exposed to light, it glows. The glowing board then illuminates, or lights up, the paper that has been placed on top. Two years after her initial inspiration, in 1974, Becky became the youngest female ever to receive a U.S. patent.

She didn't actively market her Glo-sheet. She didn't need to. The *New York Times* wrote an article about an incredible invention—patented by a twelve-year-old—and the inquiries and orders streamed in. Professionals who needed to write in the dark started ordering her Glo-sheet: photographers for their darkrooms, critics who took notes in darkened theaters, emergency medical people for use in ambulances.

"Some of the Glo-sheets I was handmaking and some I had a company manufacture for me," Becky explained. *"There were more expensive versions and less expensive ones—electric-operated and light-activated models."*

Several large companies offered to buy her patent rights, but Becky and her father decided to sell the Glo-sheet on their own.

What began as a personal project, just for fun, blossomed into a business, with Becky as the president of the company. Proof that success can come at any age with a good idea and a little imagination.

After reading about Becky's invention, NASA sent her a letter. They wanted to know if she was a former employee because the Glo-sheet sounded similar to one of their projects (and if so, they would own her patent). They had no idea she was a kid.

Alexia Abernathy

And here's more proof. One day, about a dozen managers at some very large companies received a letter in the mail. "Hi. I'm Alexia Abernathy, and I'm an eleven-year-old inventor." Based on that letter, six companies asked for more information on her product—the no-spill feeding bowl. One company eventually bought it. Beginner's luck? Maybe. A great idea? Definitely.

Every morning, it was the same story. Her babysitter's little boy carried his breakfast to the table, spilling every step of the way. Alexia knew there had to be a way to stop the cereal from slopping over the sides. So she took it upon herself to do something about it.

"The idea actually came pretty easily," said Alexia. "I was just thinking, OK, he's walking and spilling over the side, so what you need is some way to collect what spills. And I thought, what if you had a bigger bowl to hold onto it?"

At the time, she was involved in the program "Invent, Iowa!" through her elementary school and had to come up with an invention anyway and thought this would be a good, practical problem to solve. So Alexia created the nonslosh bowl—a product that, within a couple of years, would find its way onto the shelves of major stores.

"I thought I needed the simplest materials possible," she explained. "So I went and bought Tupperware™ bowls. My dad helped me cut the top out of one of the containers to form a rim. And the only thing I had to do was put the small bowl inside the large bowl."

Originally, Alexia wanted the bowls to snap together but didn't have the materials or means to do that, so she settled for glue. She experimented with all sorts of glues, but nothing worked. The bowls always came apart when they were being washed. Eventually, she tried hot glue, and finally it held. That was it; she was done. She entered her clear, nonslosh bowl with the blue lid in the "Invent, Iowa!" contest and won. She advanced to the next two levels of the contest, but ultimately lost at the state competition.

Alexia Abernathy

rim

handles

Big bowl

al
p

mall
bowl

Inventor's signature(s):

Alexia Abernathy

DATE: January 17, 1992

y dad suggested a new problem, that was Charlie, (our babysitters 2½

ear old). So I began to think of things he does and things he gets

into. That's when it hit me, just this morning when he was walking to

the table he spilled half his milk and cereal out of the bowl onto the

floor. So my new invention is, that you have a little bowl super glued

FIG. 2

Little Kids

Oops! Proof™

NO-SPILL FEEDING BOWL

Prevents messy meal spills!
Bowl-within-a-bowl catches spills before they happen!

When the Little Kids company bought Alexia's invention in 1994, they changed the name to Oops! Proof No-Spill Feeding Bowl and made the bowls so they could snap together. They also added a piece that makes it completely spillproof.

Encouraged by others who saw her invention, Alexia decided to try and market her bowl. So she wrote her letters.

"If everyone would have said no, I never would have pursued it," confessed Alexia. *"It wasn't like I was doing this for money; it was just kind of fun."*

But she did get money. She got her name on a patent, and she got to see her invention sitting on the shelves of major stores. Just think what else could be done with a simple idea, a solid solution, and a stack of first-class stamps. And it really *doesn't* matter how old you are. . . .

Your Turn

Suppose you have an invention of your own. It's different, it's new, it's neat. Now what? Obtaining a patent may be an important first step. A patent is the legal document issued by the government to protect an idea. Utility patents are for inventions that are either mechanical or electrical in nature. Design patents cover inventions that are new and original designs of existing products.

To patent an invention, you must prove that it is new and useful and that you are the very first person to have invented the item. It is important that you apply for a patent immediately, and you are required to use a patent attorney or patent agent to do so. A patent application must be complete with diagrams, notes, and models. If your invention proves to be unique, you pay the fees and are assigned a patent number. Your invention is then legally protected for twenty years (from the date of filing), and you alone have the right to profit from it.

Not all inventions, however, will benefit from having a patent. The patent process can be extremely expensive, and depending on the invention, might not be really necessary. A good patent attorney should be able to advise you on the merits of obtaining a patent for your specific invention.

For more information on the patent process, contact:

U.S. Patent and Trademark Office
Washington, D.C. 20231
(800)786-9199
www.uspto.gov

Think and Respond

1 How does each invention discussed in this selection help people?

2 What purpose do the headings and diagrams serve in this selection? Explain your answer.

3 What qualities did all the inventors share in the **initial** stage of their careers?

4 Think about the inventions you read about in this selection. What invention would you like to develop to solve a problem?

5 What strategies did you find helpful for reading the selection?

Meet the Author
Catherine Thimmesh

Catherine Thimmesh lives with her two young children and her husband in Minneapolis, Minnesota. Like the women she tells about in her first book, *Girls Think of Everything*, Catherine Thimmesh has many creative ideas. She invents ways to help children around the house, including a spill-free way to make powdered drinks called "Swim Fishies."

Meet the Illustrator
Melissa Sweet

Melissa Sweet has had some great ideas of her own. When she was just ten years old, Melissa worked with a neighborhood bakery and delivered their doughnuts to customers on her bicycle, fresh and hot.

Sweet has since become the illustrator of many children's books, including James Howe's *Pinky and Rex* books and Charles Zolotow's *Snippets*. Her cheery watercolors and collages have appeared in cookbooks, on notecards, on posters, and in private collections.

Melissa Sweet

▲ Girls Think of
Everything

Making Connections

Compare Texts

1 Think about the theme Creative Solutions. How do the inventors in "Girls Think of Everything" show that one person's creativity can affect many people?

2 Why do you think the author chose to focus on women inventors in this book?

3 Choose two inventors from the selection, and compare the way they solved a problem.

4 How is this selection different from articles about inventors that you might find in an encyclopedia?

5 Would you like to read more about famous inventors? Why or why not?

Write a Paragraph That Explains

The selection describes a number of inventions that have changed our lives. Think about an invention you use that affects your daily life. Write a paragraph that explains what the invention is, how you use it, and why it's important to you. Use a circle map to organize the details you will use in your paragraph.

Writing CONNECTION

name of invention

how you use it

why it is important

Make an Invention Tree

Choose one of the following ancient civilizations—Mesopotamia, Greece, Rome, or China. Find out about several inventions or processes developed by people in that civilization. Make an invention tree to show your findings. On the trunk of the tree, write the name of the civilization. On each branch, write the name of an invention or process and the date or time period when it was developed. Put the earlier inventions on the lower branches.

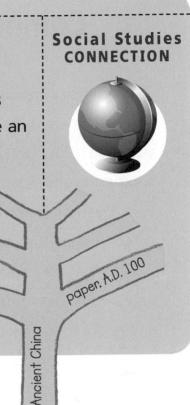

Paper, A.D. 100

Ancient China

Make a Bar Graph

Work with a partner. Use the website for the U.S. Patent and Trademark Office to find out the number of patents applied for in the United States in 1900, 1920, 1940, 1960, 1980, and 2000. Use the information to create a bar graph on a large sheet of drawing paper. Display your completed bar graph in the classroom.

▲ Girls Think of
Everything

Text Structure:
Compare and Contrast

Focus
Skill

Sometimes informational text is organized in a way that helps you see how two or more topics are similar and different. As you read "Girls Think of Everything," you probably found yourself **comparing** the inventors, or noticing what they had in common. Each inventor identified a problem, looked at it critically, and persisted in figuring out a solution.

You may also have **contrasted**, or noticed differences in, the way people did something before and after each invention came along. This chart shows a contrast the author makes in the section "Mary Anderson: Windshield Wipers."

	Before Windshield Wipers Were Invented	After Windshield Wipers Were Invented
How cars were designed	Cars had a split windshield with a middle that could be opened. It didn't work well because it let in cold air and snow.	Cars had a lever on the inside that moved an arm on the outside to swipe off the snow. Driving in bad weather was much safer.

What contrast do you find in the section "Margaret E. Knight: Paper Bags"?

Visit *The Learning Site!*
www.harcourtschool.com

See *Skills* and *Activities*

436

Test Prep

Text Structure: Compare and Contrast

▶ **Read the passage. Then answer the questions.**

> If you invented a new product, would you name it after a company that already exists? Hugh Moore and Walter Morrison invented products that you probably know. In 1908, Moore convinced a wealthy business-man to manufacture paper drinking cups. Previously, people had used unsanitary public dipping tins to get water. Moore named the product after the Dixie Doll Company, a company in the building where he worked. In 1948, Walter Morrison learned that students on college cam-puses were playing with metal pie tins from a local bakery called the Frisbie Baking Company. Morrison created a plastic version of the toy, but he was not successful in selling it. Years later, two men bought Morrison's invention and named it after the bakery.

1. **How are the inventions similar?**

   A The same person invented them.

   B They were invented in the same year.

   C They were used for the same purpose.

   D They were both named after existing companies.

Tip

Look at the organization of the passage. Then compare and contrast the inventions.

2. **Which statement shows a contrast in the passage?**

   F A businessman made paper cups.

   G Before paper cups were invented, people used unsanitary dipping tins.

   H Morrison could not sell his plastic toy.

   J Drinking cups can be paper or plastic.

Tip

Each statement is true, but only one shows a contrast in the passage.

▲ A Do-It-Yourself
Project

miniature

realistic

three-dimensional

recognition

represent

dependent

Vocabulary Power

On the following pages you'll read about a girl named Mari and her do-it-yourself project. Are you a do-it-yourself type? Can you solve problems using whatever is handy? That's what these students did.

The figures in my **miniature** model are so small that they were hard to create. It took me many hours of work to make them look **realistic**. I made them seem true-to-life by making their costumes look just like clothes worn in the U.S. a century ago.

The planets in my **three-dimensional** model all have height, width, and depth. My classmates awarded me the first prize in **recognition** of my hard work. Their approval was very important to me.

When this model is finished, it will **represent**, or stand for, a desert habitat in the United States. By studying it, you will be able to see how desert plants and animals are **dependent** on one another for meeting their needs.

Vocabulary–Writing CONNECTION

Imagine that you, too, have been assigned the project of creating a diorama of the solar system. Make a list of objects you could use in your diorama to **represent** the planets.

Fitting In
by Anilú Bernardo

Genre

Realistic Fiction

Realistic fiction tells about characters and events that are like people and events in real life.

In this selection, look for

- A setting that is familiar to most readers

- Challenges and problems that could happen in real life

440

It-Yourself

PROJECT

by Anilú Bernardo

illustrated by

Karen Blessen

Mari is worried that her school project, a diorama of the local ecosystem, won't be as fancy as those of her classmates. She has no money to buy materials from the store, so she will have to use her creativity.

The next day, Mari had a chance to visit the library during her English class. Her English teacher usually let four students go to the library during the last fifteen minutes of class. There, she opened a heavy dictionary and searched under 'D.'

"di-o-ram-a: noun. A scene reproduced in three dimensions by placing objects, figures, etc. in front of a painted background."

Finally, she had an answer! Mrs. Graham wanted them to make a miniature scene of the life of the bay. She had to show how each living thing was dependent on another for food by making little models of them. After all the worry, Mari felt a flood of relief. But the work was still ahead. Now, she had to decide how she would do it. She had never seen a diorama before.

When she got up to put the dictionary away, Mrs. Frank, the librarian, asked if Mari needed help. Mari had always turned down her sweet offers, but this time she said yes.

"I have to make a diorama for my Natural Science class," Mari told her. "I have never made one. I have never even seen one," she laughed nervously.

"I have photographs of some that students made in years before. Would you like to see them?" Mrs. Frank led her to her office and took five pictures from her desk drawer.

They were beautiful small scenes of landscapes. One showed a river with a cow pasture on one side and a sugar cane field on the other. The river flowed into a marshy area in which the plants were shown to be dying. A girl glowing with pride and holding a red ribbon stood by the project. In another photo, a pimply-faced boy held a diorama of sand dunes with sea oats growing on them. The ocean was made out of clear dark-blue cellophane. Each project had won a ribbon.

"I'd like to show you my favorite one," said Mrs. Frank. She opened the door to a storage case. "This scene shows the daily life of the Seminoles living in the Everglades."

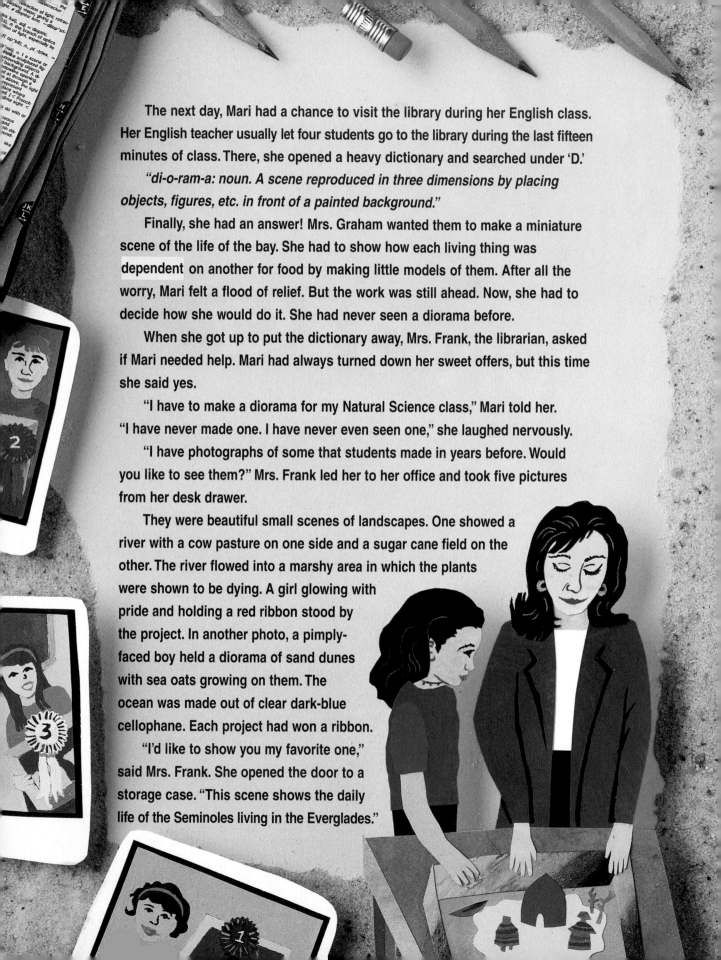

Mrs. Frank brought the diorama out and set it on a table. "I like it very much because it was made with natural materials."

On a sandy island in the middle of the box, there was a small *chickee* hut, the palm-frond house used by the Native American tribe of South Florida. It was made out of reeds and grasses. A tiny wooden canoe, resembling the kind the Seminoles carved from a single log, rested on the painted water. Straw dolls were dressed in colorful calico clothes Seminole women take pride in making.

"The student made the dolls, too?" Mari asked, amazed.

"No, I think he bought them at a souvenir shop. But he made everything else. He even carved the canoe." Mrs. Frank ran a finger down the side of the rough, miniature boat.

"It's beautiful!" Mari exclaimed. "What kind of box did he use?" She walked around the table to view the back of the four-sided stage.

"Just about any grocery-store carton would do. You can cut out the top and one side and paint a background scene on the in—" The loud sound of the bell interrupted Mrs. Frank's words. She didn't fight the ringing. She waited quietly for it to end. "What is your topic?"

"The food chain in Biscayne Bay," Mari said. She anxiously glanced at the other students, who picked up their books and were moving on to other classes.

"Would you like me to find some books on the subject? I can have them ready for you after school," Mrs. Frank asked, realizing Mari had to go.

"Yes, that would really help me." Mari thanked her and ran out of the library.

Sitting on her bed that afternoon, Mari leafed through the three books Mrs. Frank had selected for her. One was a biology book which had a chapter on food chains. Another was a book on marine life of southern Florida. The third book showed examples of three-dimensional models and directions for making them. Mari's mind raced with ideas on how to design her project. She could buy crinkly cellophane for the light-green water of the bay. And she'd get the beautiful, shiny

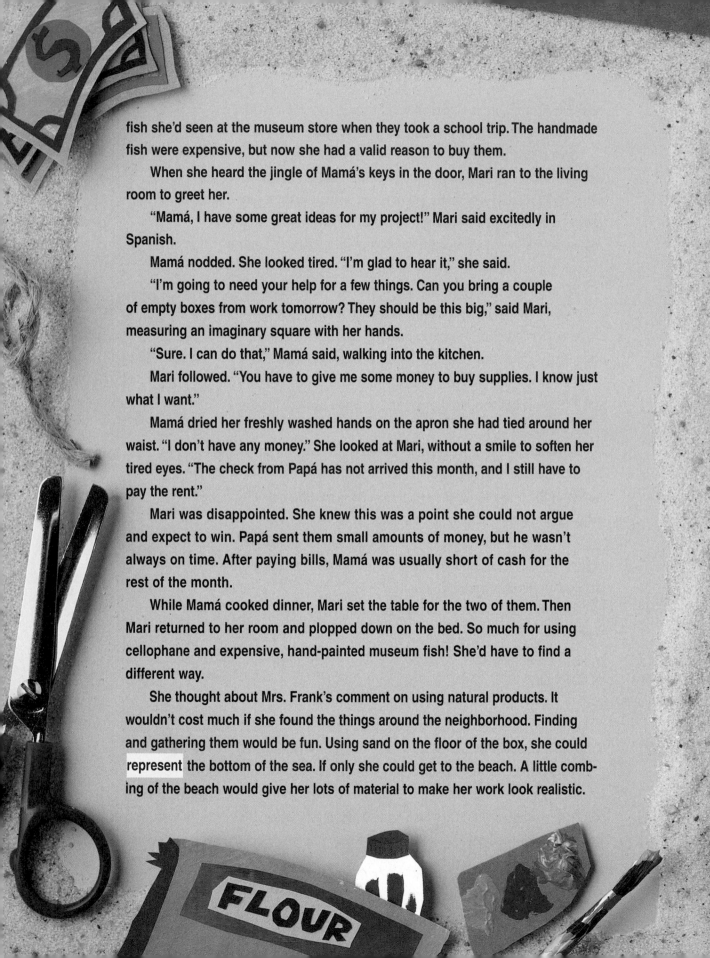

fish she'd seen at the museum store when they took a school trip. The handmade fish were expensive, but now she had a valid reason to buy them.

When she heard the jingle of Mamá's keys in the door, Mari ran to the living room to greet her.

"Mamá, I have some great ideas for my project!" Mari said excitedly in Spanish.

Mamá nodded. She looked tired. "I'm glad to hear it," she said.

"I'm going to need your help for a few things. Can you bring a couple of empty boxes from work tomorrow? They should be this big," said Mari, measuring an imaginary square with her hands.

"Sure. I can do that," Mamá said, walking into the kitchen.

Mari followed. "You have to give me some money to buy supplies. I know just what I want."

Mamá dried her freshly washed hands on the apron she had tied around her waist. "I don't have any money." She looked at Mari, without a smile to soften her tired eyes. "The check from Papá has not arrived this month, and I still have to pay the rent."

Mari was disappointed. She knew this was a point she could not argue and expect to win. Papá sent them small amounts of money, but he wasn't always on time. After paying bills, Mamá was usually short of cash for the rest of the month.

While Mamá cooked dinner, Mari set the table for the two of them. Then Mari returned to her room and plopped down on the bed. So much for using cellophane and expensive, hand-painted museum fish! She'd have to find a different way.

She thought about Mrs. Frank's comment on using natural products. It wouldn't cost much if she found the things around the neighborhood. Finding and gathering them would be fun. Using sand on the floor of the box, she could represent the bottom of the sea. If only she could get to the beach. A little combing of the beach would give her lots of material to make her work look realistic.

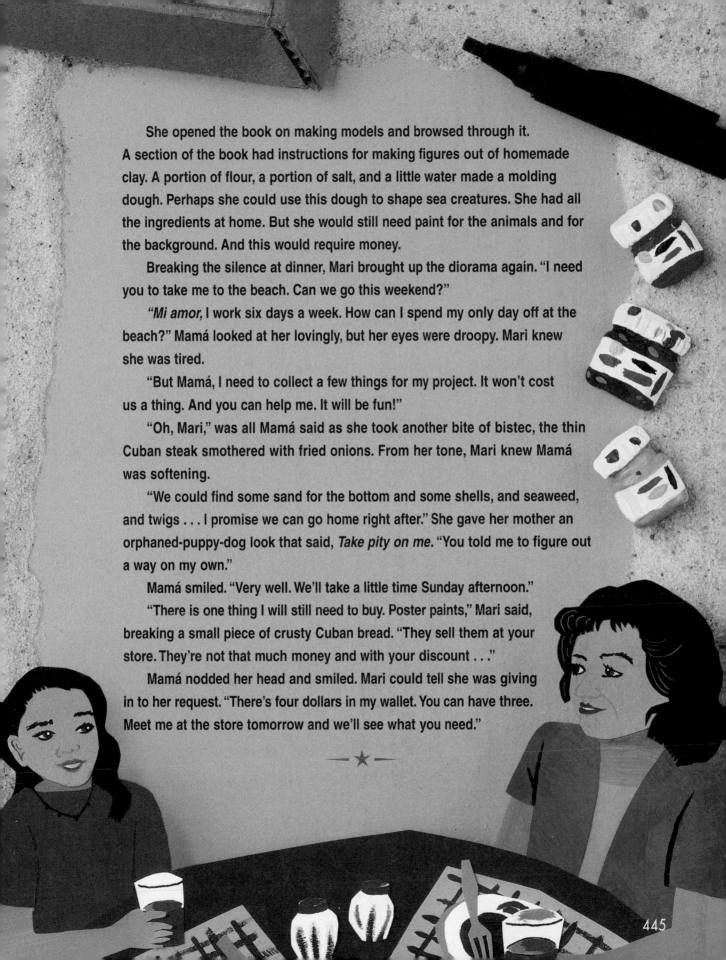

She opened the book on making models and browsed through it. A section of the book had instructions for making figures out of homemade clay. A portion of flour, a portion of salt, and a little water made a molding dough. Perhaps she could use this dough to shape sea creatures. She had all the ingredients at home. But she would still need paint for the animals and for the background. And this would require money.

Breaking the silence at dinner, Mari brought up the diorama again. "I need you to take me to the beach. Can we go this weekend?"

"*Mi amor,* I work six days a week. How can I spend my only day off at the beach?" Mamá looked at her lovingly, but her eyes were droopy. Mari knew she was tired.

"But Mamá, I need to collect a few things for my project. It won't cost us a thing. And you can help me. It will be fun!"

"Oh, Mari," was all Mamá said as she took another bite of bistec, the thin Cuban steak smothered with fried onions. From her tone, Mari knew Mamá was softening.

"We could find some sand for the bottom and some shells, and seaweed, and twigs . . . I promise we can go home right after." She gave her mother an orphaned-puppy-dog look that said, *Take pity on me.* "You told me to figure out a way on my own."

Mamá smiled. "Very well. We'll take a little time Sunday afternoon."

"There is one thing I will still need to buy. Poster paints," Mari said, breaking a small piece of crusty Cuban bread. "They sell them at your store. They're not that much money and with your discount . . ."

Mamá nodded her head and smiled. Mari could tell she was giving in to her request. "There's four dollars in my wallet. You can have three. Meet me at the store tomorrow and we'll see what you need."

——★——

445

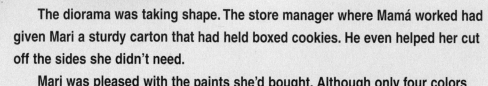

The diorama was taking shape. The store manager where Mamá worked had given Mari a sturdy carton that had held boxed cookies. He even helped her cut off the sides she didn't need.

Mari was pleased with the paints she'd bought. Although only four colors had been in the package, Mari had a knack for mixing them to get all the shades she wanted. She painted a background divided horizontally into sky, water surface, and underwater levels. Using different shades of soft blue and clear light green, it was easy to tell the sea apart from the sky with its puffy, white clouds.

The trip to the beach had been a success. Mari found many colorful shells and cut small bits of sea grass and weeds that had dried up above the surf line. Mari's enthusiasm spilled over to Mamá, who kept her eyes lowered to the sandy beach looking for useful things. Mamá discovered small bits of coral and sponges that had washed up on shore. She handed Mari a large paper cup to bring back sand. Mari was glad Mamá had taken the time to go to the beach and relax. She could tell Mamá had a good time.

Maybe Mrs. Graham was right after all. Making a diorama was turning out to be fun!

After school, she opened her locker and decided which books she would need for homework. As she filled her backpack, Erica and Cathy, the two girls from Natural Science class, came up to their lockers.

"My diorama is looking great!" Cathy said. "We used iridescent paper to show the water and plaster to make the shore. Wait till you see it!"

"My dad is helping me," Erica said. "He takes an underwater camera when he goes diving. He gave me great pictures to use as our background. Maybe I should say I'm helping him!"

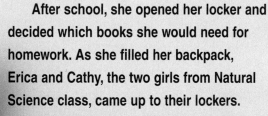

Great! Mari thought. Erica is getting help from her father. Her diorama will look perfect, like an adult worked on it. She continued to listen, pretending to be busily sorting through the junk in her locker.

"My dad built a wooden box to display my diorama," said Jake, the smart kid, who had now joined them at the wall of lockers. "He's really handy and has lots of ideas for it. I guess our project will be very scientific."

"Well, my mom is an artist. She's giving me a hand, too," Cathy told them. "If she weren't, my diorama would look awful! I'm not handy at all."

It seemed like everyone's parents were getting in on the act. It wasn't fair. Mari had no one to help her make hers.

"No, I'm not artistic either," Erica told Cathy. "Mine would look homemade without my dad's help. I'd probably just have sand and a few shells."

Mari was devastated. Hers looked homemade! It was decorated with sand and a few shells, just as Cathy had said.

"How's yours coming along, Mari?" Erica asked, turning to her.

The question took Mari by surprise. She had fallen deep into her sad thoughts, regretting her choice of materials and angry that her father was not around to help her.

"Have you started working on it?" Jake asked her.

"Yes. I've been working on it. It's coming along fine," Mari said, her Spanish accent coming through her words and annoying her. She padlocked the door to her locker and picked up her backpack. "I've got to go now."

The school library was almost empty after class the next day. Shyly, Mari approached Mrs. Frank. The librarian put her book down and looked up at her over her reading glasses.

"Hello, Mari. Did you find the books useful?" she asked, smiling sweetly.

"Yes. Thank you. I'm finished with them now." Although Mari was grateful, she could not bring herself to smile. She was too disappointed in her work.

"What did you decide to do about your diorama?" Mrs. Frank questioned her with interest.

"I'm using things found in nature, like you said." Mari saw Mrs. Frank's face light up. But Mari didn't think she had cause to feel proud.

"That sounds like an excellent choice," Mrs. Frank said.

"Well, I'm afraid it wasn't." Mari hung her head. "All the other kids have their parents helping them. My mother can't help me. She hardly speaks English and doesn't understand what the teacher wants. My father moved away. My diorama will look like a kindergartner made it!"

Mrs. Frank removed her glasses and set them on her desk. She took her time to speak, and for a moment Mari thought she had nothing to say. Then the soft-spoken librarian asked, "Why don't you tell me what materials you used?"

"I got beach sand for the bottom of the bay and scattered a few shells and bits of coral in it." Mari examined her fingernails nervously. "To make it look realistic, I put dried sea grass growing from the bottom of the sea. I found some twigs, that I glued to the shallow end, to represent red mangrove. The roots reach into the salt water. I cut tiny leaves from bits of green gift wrap and glued them to the tops of the twigs."

"So far, it sounds wonderful!" said Mrs. Frank.

"I know, but the others are using fancy paints and pictures, and even special wooden boxes instead of grocery-store cartons. My mom says we don't have money to spare for such things."

"Well, it doesn't matter what you use. The teacher will be looking for the amount of care each student puts into her work," Mrs. Frank said, looking into Mari's sad, brown eyes. "What are you using for the animals?"

Mari reached in her book bag and pulled out a small box held together with a rubber band. She opened it and took out a cotton-wrapped figure. It was a little, white fish, unpainted and delicate.

"I made these out of dough, from the recipe in the book you gave me." Mari watched Mrs. Frank for a reaction to her work.

Mrs. Frank took the little fish in her hand gently. She put her reading glasses back on and examined it. "Why, you've carved out little circles for the eyes and tiny half moons for scales. You've even scraped little lines down the length of the fins," Mrs. Frank said, clearly impressed.

Mari smiled. "I used a pin from my mother's sewing basket and carved out the lines and curves while the dough was soft." She removed the cotton from a few other figures and set each one on Mrs. Frank's desk.

"Let's see. You've made bigger fish and a tiny crab." The librarian looked the dough figures over carefully.

"Well, the little crab has no legs yet," Mari said, laughing at the little white shell in Mrs. Frank's hand. "I'm going to make them out of soft, thin wire that I found among my dad's tools. I might even paint it with pink nail polish."

Mrs. Frank nodded her head and smiled. "And this bird is beautiful!" She pointed to the spread wings, too afraid to take the delicate figure in her hand.

"That's an osprey," said Mari proudly. "They hunt for fish as they fly above the bay. I left a ceiling on my display box so I could hang a bird from it."

Mrs. Frank shook her head with disbelief. "Your work is wonderful!"

Mari thanked her. She raised her shoulders, still unsure of herself. "Well, I still have to paint the animals. I hope they look as realistic when I finish."

Mrs. Frank opened her desk drawer. She took out a small bottle and handed it to Mari. "See if you'd like to put glitter on the sides of the fish. It will make them look like the summer sun is reflecting off their scales."

"Thank you. This is great!" Mari shook the silver dust happily. "Maybe I can mix it with the paint I use."

Mrs. Frank helped her wrap the dough creatures back in their protective cotton coats. "You know, Mari," the librarian said, "I wouldn't worry about the work the other students are doing. It seems to me, you're doing a great job all by yourself."

— 🐚 —

Soon, the big day arrived. Mrs. Graham and Mrs. Frank had arranged tables in the library into a large rectangle. The students brought their projects in the morning and set them up for the judges. They would go to classes and return later in the day, after the dioramas had been examined and judged.

Mari looked around the room. Everyone had a different way of representing the same idea: the food cycle of the creatures of Biscayne Bay. She was amazed at the variety of materials selected to build the models. Some used bright, shiny paints and glittery, shredded tissue paper. One student used fabric with a beach scene as a background. Mari thought she even detected a fishy smell coming from one of the dioramas. One diorama was lighted with a black light which made the bottom of the ocean and the creatures in it glow. Many had the sharp polish of an adult behind all the fine work.

One of the students had used the pretty museum fish Mari had liked. Mari was sorry she had not been able to make her diorama as pretty as this one was.

Mari knew her project was not going to impress the other students. Even so, she was proud of all the effort she had put into it. It looked like a real bay scene. Three glittery fish chased each other with open mouths by order of their size. She'd elevated the fish above the sandy bottom with small sections of clear drinking straws. But, the smallest of the three was held up by the spring of a ball-point pen. The littlest fish bounced at the slightest touch, as though it were attempting to jump out of the water to capture the tiny pink crab. The shiny, polished crab rested on a leggy mangrove root, peacefully eating a rotting leaf. Above it were the remains of the osprey's last meal, a small dead fish whose white bones showed through, dangling from the mangrove branches. The bird flew against the sky of the diorama, suspended by fishing line, and eyed the biggest of the three fish below.

What her diorama lacked, Mari thought, deflated, was the attention-grabbing smoothness and glow that the store-bought materials gave. Anyone could tell that little money had been spent on hers. She was glad the projects would be displayed in the library. She wouldn't like to have her diorama in the classroom all day, pointed at when people asked who made the homemade one.

— ★ —

Later, during Natural Science class, Mrs. Graham announced they would go to the library to find out the results of the judging. The students were restless.

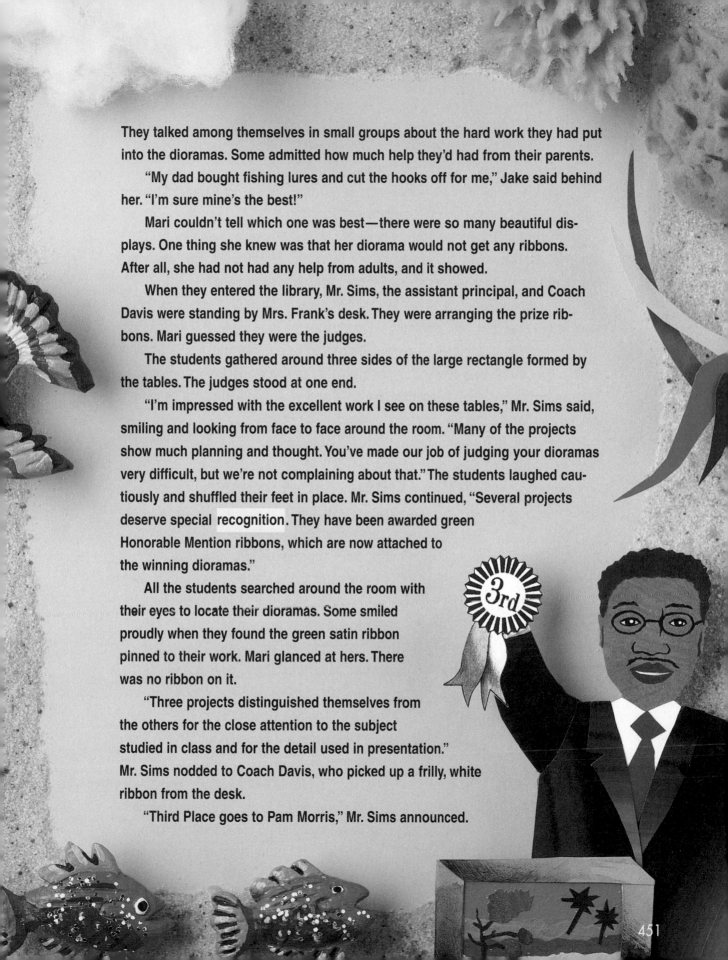

They talked among themselves in small groups about the hard work they had put into the dioramas. Some admitted how much help they'd had from their parents.

"My dad bought fishing lures and cut the hooks off for me," Jake said behind her. "I'm sure mine's the best!"

Mari couldn't tell which one was best—there were so many beautiful displays. One thing she knew was that her diorama would not get any ribbons. After all, she had not had any help from adults, and it showed.

When they entered the library, Mr. Sims, the assistant principal, and Coach Davis were standing by Mrs. Frank's desk. They were arranging the prize ribbons. Mari guessed they were the judges.

The students gathered around three sides of the large rectangle formed by the tables. The judges stood at one end.

"I'm impressed with the excellent work I see on these tables," Mr. Sims said, smiling and looking from face to face around the room. "Many of the projects show much planning and thought. You've made our job of judging your dioramas very difficult, but we're not complaining about that." The students laughed cautiously and shuffled their feet in place. Mr. Sims continued, "Several projects deserve special recognition. They have been awarded green Honorable Mention ribbons, which are now attached to the winning dioramas."

All the students searched around the room with their eyes to locate their dioramas. Some smiled proudly when they found the green satin ribbon pinned to their work. Mari glanced at hers. There was no ribbon on it.

"Three projects distinguished themselves from the others for the close attention to the subject studied in class and for the detail used in presentation." Mr. Sims nodded to Coach Davis, who picked up a frilly, white ribbon from the desk.

"Third Place goes to Pam Morris," Mr. Sims announced.

The blond girl walked up to Coach Davis to receive her award. Her pale, freckled complexion glowed pink as she accepted the ribbon and thanked him.

"Second Place goes to Jeff McIntosh," said Mr. Sims.

Jeff's friends elbowed him teasingly as he made his way up to collect his red ribbon. Coach Davis shook the curly-haired boy's hand.

Mari shrugged her shoulders. She would not get any recognition for her diorama. Maybe it was better this way, no one would figure out which one was hers. She could come back for her project after school, when everyone had left.

"The highest honor of all . . ." Mari half listened as Mr. Sims continued, "is awarded to someone who worked hard to present the food cycle of Biscayne Bay in a most realistic fashion. The project appears to be a miniature version of what goes on in nature. Very few of the materials used in this model are man-made. This project shows that using your own head and your own hands can be more rewarding than asking for help from others."

Please end this agony, Mari thought, I want to go back to the class before I have to identify my diorama to anyone.

Mr. Sims continued, "First Place goes to Mari Espina."

Mari was jolted back to the room as if from a dream. She had heard her name mentioned. Now Mr. Sims was looking straight at her and holding up a large, frilly blue ribbon.

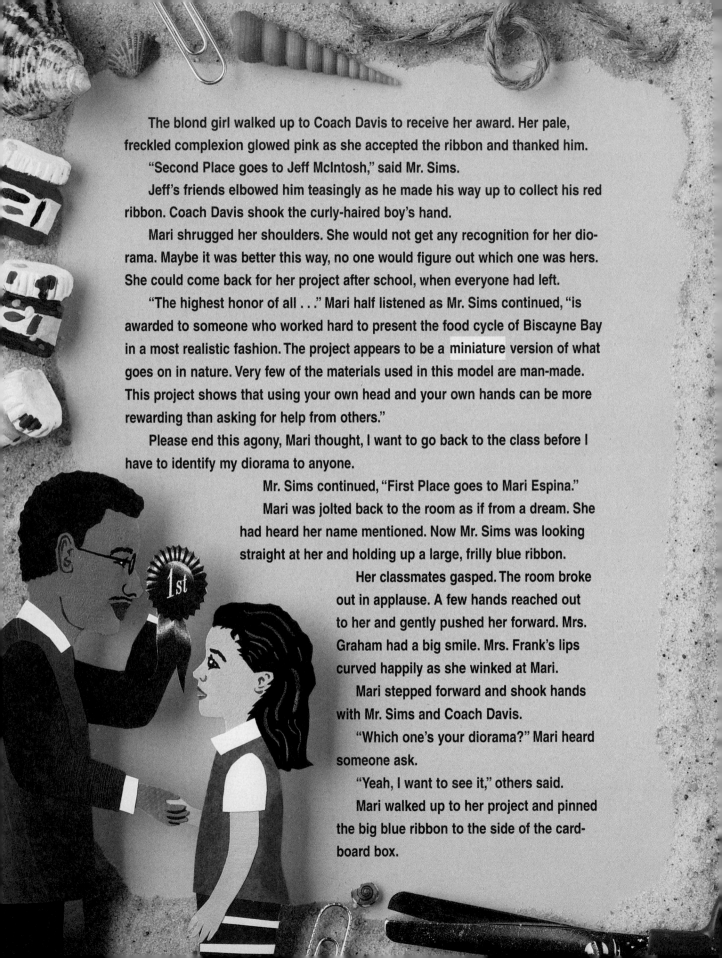

Her classmates gasped. The room broke out in applause. A few hands reached out to her and gently pushed her forward. Mrs. Graham had a big smile. Mrs. Frank's lips curved happily as she winked at Mari.

Mari stepped forward and shook hands with Mr. Sims and Coach Davis.

"Which one's your diorama?" Mari heard someone ask.

"Yeah, I want to see it," others said.

Mari walked up to her project and pinned the big blue ribbon to the side of the cardboard box.

"It's so realistic!" Cathy said.

"Look at the materials she used," said Erica, clearly impressed.

Mrs. Frank brought out her camera. "Stand by your diorama and hold up the ribbon," she told Mari.

"I'm sure your picture will be put on the library bulletin board. Everyone will see it when they come in," Liz said.

"Better than that," said Mrs. Graham. "We'll have the diorama on display for a month, right here in the library."

"Can I take it home tonight and show my mother?" Mari asked. "I promise to bring it back tomorrow."

"Sure, dear. But right now I want to see a big, fat smile!" said Mrs. Frank, looking through the camera lens.

Mari couldn't hide her pride. A satisfied smile broke out across her face.

— 🐟 —

"Mamá, look! Look what I won!" Mari yelled happily in Spanish. She had been controlling her excitement since she got home and now she ran to the door as her mother entered their apartment. "I won a ribbon for my project!" Mari held the frilly medallion against her chest so that the long, blue ribbons hung down to her waist.

453

Mamá reached for the satin streamers and stroked them with her fingers. "It's beautiful! Congratulations!" she told her daughter in Spanish, and smiled lovingly.

"Read what it says," said Mari.

In her best English, Mamá read slowly, "First Place."

"They said mine was the best!" Mari said excitedly in Spanish. "You should have seen the other dioramas. They were so beautiful. But they said mine was the best!"

"Well, I'm not surprised, *mi amor*," Mamá said. "You worked so hard on it every night and it turned out perfect."

"Mr. Sims told everyone they could tell I had worked on the project without any help from others." Mari took a breath and watched her mother's reaction. Mamá smiled and nodded. "You know what, Mamá? Mr. Sims was wrong. I did have some help."

"I don't see how, *mi amor*. You worked alone at this table every night," Mamá said, resting her purse on the kitchen table.

"Well, Mamá," Mari said tenderly. "You gave me the best help anyone could get. You told me to figure things out on my own."

Mamá's eyes filled with tears. "I wish I could have helped more."

"But, Mamá, this was the kind of help I needed. I needed to realize I could do it by myself."

"I'm proud of you." Mamá didn't need to tell her that. Mari already knew. Mamá wrapped her arms around Mari. "Let's take a picture of you standing by your project. In your next letter to Papá, you can send it to him and tell him all about your project and your ribbon."

"Yes," said Mari, grinning happily. "I bet he'll be very proud of me, too!"

Think and Respond

1 What does Mari learn by taking part in and winning this contest?

2 How does Mari feel about herself at the beginning and at the end of the story?

3 What is the author's message about being **dependent** on other people? How do you know?

4 How do you think teachers should judge students' projects? List at least two suggestions.

5 Which reading strategies did you use for this selection? Why?

Meet the Author

Anilú Bernardo

Like Mari, author Anilú Bernardo was born in Cuba and moved to the United States when she was young. She knows the challenge of fitting in—she spoke very little English, and her classmates could not speak Spanish.

Bernardo loved to write, and she began to write poems in Spanish. Later, she drew on her childhood experiences to make her stories about young Cuban immigrants realistic. Anilú Bernardo has used her creativity to become a successful author of stories for young readers.

Anilú Bernardo

Visit *The Learning Site!*
www.harcourtschool.com

Preface

by Angela Johnson
Illustrated by
Cornelius Von Wright

When I was very young and had just begun to write,
I considered myself a poet.

In my self-centered fourteen-year-old world,
poetry was immediacy
and spoke to longing, loss, hope, and absurdity.

You could not tell lies when you wrote poetry.
Poetry was sudden impact and the truth.
Poetry was odd characters in sometimes
odder circumstances.

I didn't understand meter, but
I knew what I felt and
what I saw and,
because I was very young,
when I thought myself a poet
there were no barriers. . . .

My poetry doesn't sing the song of the sonnets, but then
I sing a different kind of music—
which is what it's all about anyway.

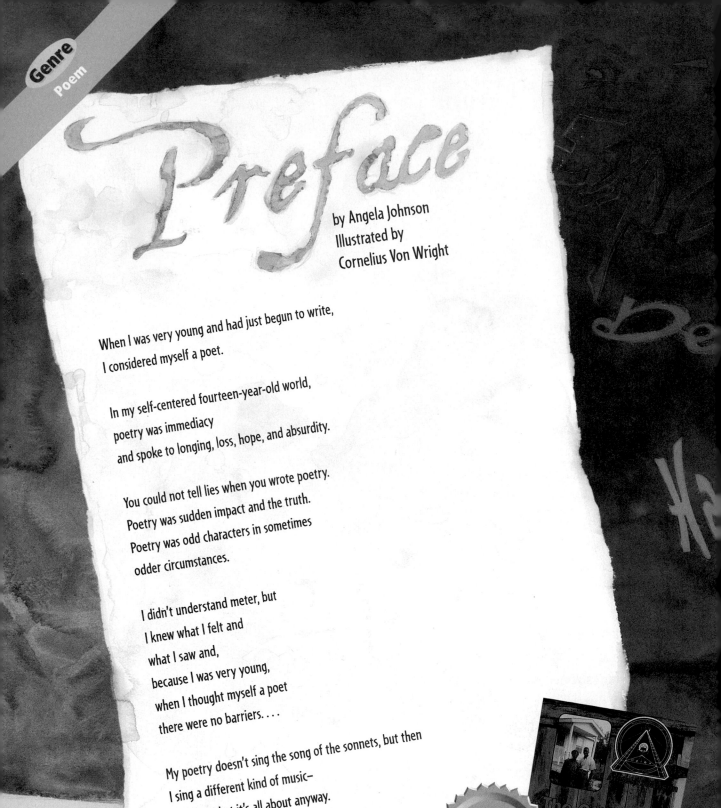

The Other Side

Coretta Scott
King Honor

Making Connections

Compare Texts

1 How does "A Do-It-Yourself Project" express the theme of creative problem-solving?

2 How do Mari's feelings about her diorama project at the beginning of the story change by the end?

3 Think about the story "A Do-It-Yourself Project" and the poem "Preface." What do the author and the poet want readers to learn about being creative?

4 What do the character Mari and the poet who wrote "Preface" have in common?

5 Would you like to read other stories by Anilú Bernardo? Why or why not?

Write a Letter

Imagine that you are Mari. Write a letter to your father about your diorama and the school contest. Describe how you felt when you were awarded the first prize. Use the form of a personal letter.

Writing CONNECTION

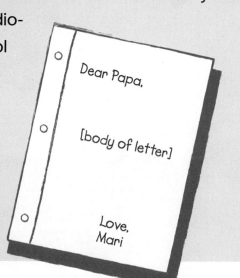

Dear Papa,

[body of letter]

Love,
Mari

Create a Beach Poster

Mari researched the food chain in Biscayne Bay. Work with a partner to find information about the plant and animal life on a beach in the United States. Choose a beach on either the Atlantic or the Pacific Ocean. Then create a poster of the beach, with labeled illustrations of the plants and animals that live there. Display your poster and take your classmates on a "nature tour" of the beach ecosystem.

Science CONNECTION

Make a Chart

The underwater coral reef in Biscayne Bay is one of the United States' five undersea national parks. Do research to find out about coral reefs and how they change over time. Record your findings on a chart like this one.

Science CONNECTION

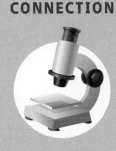

A marine polyp attaches itself to skeletons of dead polyps.

459

Text Structure:
Compare and Contrast

Authors of fiction often **compare** and **contrast** important elements in a story to make connections for readers. The relationships between ideas may be presented within one paragraph or in different paragraphs.

In "A Do-It-Yourself Project," the contest judges recognize that Mari's diorama is different from those of the other students. The author contrasts the dioramas in different paragraphs of the story. The organization of these paragraphs helps readers understand the different ways of doing the same assignment.

Look at the paragraphs on page 450. What details does the author use to describe the dioramas made by the other students? What details describe Mari's diorama? How are the dioramas alike?

Mari's Diorama

1. Materials from home or in nature
2. Work done independently
3. Spent little money

Shows the food cycle of Biscayne Bay creatures

Other Students' Dioramas

1. Store-bought materials
2. Help from adults
3. Spent more money

Visit *The Learning Site!*
www.harcourtschool.com

See *Skills* and *Activities*

Test Prep
Text Structure: Compare and Contrast

▶ **Read the passage. Then answer the questions.**

> Adam and Ellen each created a display about life in ancient countries. Adam made a model of the Greek city of Athens. He included outdoor markets and houses with central courtyards. Ellen chose a different subject. She made a model of ancient Rome that included the Tiber River and the houses, apartments, and public baths in the city. Both Adam and Ellen displayed their work in class. Unlike Ellen, who was pleased with her model, Adam felt bad because he thought Ellen's was better. While Ellen's model had miniature figures of Roman men, women, and children, Adam had not included any figures of Athenian citizens.

1. **What is the main difference between Adam's and Ellen's displays?**

   A Adam included figures of people, and Ellen did not.

   B Ellen made a map of Rome, and Adam made a model of Rome.

   C Adam made a model of ancient Athens, and Ellen made a model of ancient Rome.

   D Adam made a model of ancient Egypt, and Ellen made a model of ancient Rome.

Tip

Use the organization of the paragraph. Notice that similar information is grouped together.

2. **Contrast the way that Adam and Ellen feel about their work. Use details from the passage in your answer.**

Tip

Look for words such as *both*, *however*, *but*, and *unlike*, which often signal similarities and differences.

461

Vocabulary Power

Do you have a favorite painting or other artwork? In the next selection, you will learn about a blacksmith known for his metal artwork. Artists use their creativity in many ways to make things for people to enjoy.

ornamental

install

forge

portable

rugged

tributes

Blacksmiths were among the first artists in the United States. They made things for daily living, such as horseshoes. They also made fancy, **ornamental** things, such as iron gates. Wealthy people would **install** iron gates at the entrances to their homes. Blacksmiths worked at a **forge**, where they could heat the iron and pound it into shape.

Artists who use more **portable** tools can move their supplies from place to place. A painter can study the rocky, **rugged** beauty of the mountains from up close.

Artists may make a living from their work, or they may create art just for the joy of it. Some artists receive **tributes** for their best work. They may be honored by the government, by a museum, or by other artists.

Vocabulary–Writing CONNECTION

There are many kinds of **tributes**. Write a tribute to your favorite artist or author. Choose the form of writing that best suits your purpose, such as a poem or a letter.

463

Booklist Editors'
Choice

CATCH

I n 1925, when Philip Simmons was thirteen, he became a blacksmith's apprentice in Charleston, South Carolina. After more than ten years of hard work, Philip had acquired the skills to run his own shop. To find work during hard times, Philip started fixing people's iron gates and fences. Sometimes he added animal figures to bring his ironwork to life. Before long, people started to take notice of his skill and artistry. In 1976 Philip was invited to demonstrate his talent in front of the entire nation.

ING THE FIRE

Philip Simmons, Blacksmith

by Mary E. Lyons

"Y ou must be Philip Simmons," the young man said. Sixty-year-old Philip looked up from his pile of scrap iron. The year was 1972, and he was working in his shop yard on Blake Street. Philip shook the visitor's hand. Who was this fellow, anyway? He said he was a graduate student from Indiana, but he had Washington, D.C., plates on his car.

Philip Simmons forges a scroll in the early 1970s.

Was he lost? Well, yes, he was. John Michael Vlach had been wandering around the one-way streets near Philip's shop, looking for the man who knew "the old ways of ironwork." John seemed a little nervous, maybe because a scruffy dog named Brownie was barking at him. But the blacksmith liked to talk about old times, so the scholar soon relaxed.

Philip explained the history of his business to John.

In the late 1930s, the federal government gave Charleston enough money to build two East Side housing projects: one for black citizens and one for whites. So Philip had to move his shop "for the improvement of the city."

The smith moved four times and landed on Blake Street in 1969. It was here that he replaced the spiteful bellows with an electric forge blower.

By the time America entered World War II in 1941, most of the city's blacksmiths were gone. When the Charleston Naval Ship Yard wanted parts for ships, they went to Philip Simmons. But after the war was over in 1945, business slowed down.

"I needed to make some money on the side," Philip told John. He drove a taxi, ran a dry-cleaning business, and opened and closed a restaurant. There must be a faster way to "grab a few more pennies," he thought.

Peter Simmons had died in 1953, two days before his ninety-eighth birthday. About this time, Philip decided to modernize his own shop. He bought an electric arc welder that was three times faster than riveting. And he attached an old washing machine motor to his hand drill. Both tools speeded up the work.

When John Vlach wanted to compare the old ways to the new ones, Philip took him on a tour of Charleston. He led John down a narrow alley to one of his first "fancy" pieces. Philip was proud of the old-time rivets he had used to join the wiggle tail to the gate.

Next, the two men looked at a bird gate. The customer had given Philip a drawing of an egret. "Can you make it?" the fellow had asked.

Sure he could. Philip knew egrets like the calluses on his

hands. He used an acetylene torch to cut the metal talons, and he made a bended knee so the bird was "looking ready to go."

Philip drove John over to East Bay Street to see his Snake Gate. It took him one month to forge that gate. He thought he'd never finish the eye. At first, it stared as if it were dead. Philip "heat and beat, heat and beat, heat and beat," until the snake looked as real as a diamond head rattler. "If it bites you," Philip joked, "you better get to the doctor fast. Blood get up to your heart, you know what happens!"

John Vlach was impressed. These were no ordinary pieces of ornamental ironwork. They were sculpture! Philip Simmons was not just a blacksmith. He was an artist.

John saw Philip often over the next four years. He helped install gates, took photographs, and tape-recorded conversations. And in 1976, John offered Philip the greatest test of his career: an invitation to make a gate at the Festival of American Folklife, a summer-long event in Washington, D.C.

The two men discussed the trip in the dim light of Philip's shop. As they spoke, pinpoints of sun poked through the sheet metal walls. At first the artist didn't want to go.

"No, no, no, no, no," Philip said. He held two scrolls up to the light to see if they matched. "I got business to do."

This wasn't going to be easy. John raked his hands through his dark brown hair. "You'll only be gone fifteen days," he said.

"Any special piece that you want me to make?" Philip asked.

"The choice is yours," John sweet-talked him. "We just want you to come up and demonstrate what you're doing in Charleston."

This offer made sense to the businessman. He could make

468

Egret Gate, 2 St. Michael's Alley, Charleston, South Carolina

Overthrow of Snake Gate, 329 East Bay Street, Charleston, South Carolina

something small to bring home and "sell for a profit."

"What about the materials? How will I move them?"

"We'll put everything in the trunk of your car."

"Only so much I can do without my 'prentice boys."

"Bring the apprentices with you. We'll pay their expenses, and they can drive the car."

The blacksmith ran out of arguments. "Yes, I'll come," he finally agreed.

There were a few other hurdles. First, Philip needed a portable forge. He always "liked to make the odd thing," so he cut the top off an old hot water heater and packed it with fire clay. He didn't spend more than fifty dollars on his homemade invention.

Second, what kind of gate should he make? Philip "set to

the desk," but nothing came to mind. He lay awake at night. Still no ideas. Six weeks passed. Suddenly he realized he was leaving—tomorrow!

Would this be the first test the blacksmith failed? When the airplane left Charleston the next day, Philip peeked out the small oval window next to his seat. He took a long look at the rivers and marshes that hugged Charleston on three sides.

"I'm just crazy about the water," he thought. "Maybe I'll show the stars in the water."

He considered fish. "Fish represents Charleston. It's known for fishing."

Philip imagined the moon over the Cooper River and decided to show a "quarter-moon, just racing along."

But like the old Sea Island tale says, "'sidering and 'cidering won't buy Sal a new shirt." The artist pulled out a scrap of paper and began to draw. By the time the plane landed an hour later, he had solved the puzzle.

He would make a fish in the water and a double star in the sky, one inside the other. "Like watchin' a star," he thought, "it get smaller on you." Two quarter-moons would shine over it all.

Maybe this wouldn't be his prettiest gate, but it would be his most important one. It would be his "sacrificial piece." The one made in front of thousands of people and forged with the ancient tools of ironworking: fire, hammer, and a blacksmith's rugged hands.

THE FESTIVAL

Washington, D.C., was almost as hot as Charleston. Especially the last week of July and first week of August 1976. For these two weeks, Philip and his apprentices, Joseph

Pringle and Silas Sessions, worked on the grassy Mall near the Lincoln Memorial. When the sun grew too bright, they moved under a striped tent.

The United States was two hundred years old, and the festival was a birthday party. It celebrated the skills of people from all over the world. Philip was impressed with the other talented folks he saw on the Mall: singers, dancers, cooks, hairdressers, gospel singers, woodcarvers, and seamstresses.

"Everybody on this ground," he noticed, "is doing it the old way."

At first, he and his helpers forged simple chandeliers and plant stands. The rain of sparks and ring of hammers drew a stream of visitors to the demonstration. Philip answered their questions, just as Peter Simmons had done fifty years before.

Then the blacksmiths began the Star and Fish Gate. They cut lengths of iron bars, forged pecan leaves, welded J-curves inside of S-curves. Philip used several pieces of metal to create an open effect in the spot-tailed bass. Finally he made the striking star within a star.

Toward the end of Philip's stay in Washington, John noticed something curious about the outside star.

"The center point is off by twenty degrees," he commented.

"A star can shine all different ways," the artist explained.

That evening Philip started thinking. Nothing is right until it's right. His grandfather had taught him that as a boy on Daniel Island. Peter Simmons had drilled it into him as a young man. And what about his customers? "If it weren't for them," Philip thought, "I wouldn't even be in Washington."

The blacksmith tossed all night in his dormitory bed at George Washington University. The next day, he hurried to the Mall before anyone else was around. It took him fifteen min-

"In sixty-two years," Philip says, "I never went in the shop and didn't need a hammer."

utes to cut the star out of the gate and weld it back in place.

By the time the demonstrations began at eleven A.M., the star pointed straight up toward the enamel blue sky. Philip Simmons had proved himself once more. And though he didn't know it yet, he had hooked his future to that star.

Afterword

The Star and Fish Gate sparked a national interest in Philip Simmons's work. Festival officials invited him again in 1977, and in 1981 John Michael Vlach published *Philip Simmons, Charleston Blacksmith*. That year John suggested his friend's name for a Heritage Fellowship. The federal government gives this award to artists who are considered "national treasures."

Philip Simmons was one of "fifteen head" of people who

won. He returned to Washington in 1982 to accept the award and to join the festival again. The same year, the Smithsonian Institution bought his Star and Fish Gate. Now it's a national piece that travels to museums around the country.

State awards followed. In 1988 the blacksmith won a South Carolina Folk Heritage Award. He was admitted into the South Carolina State Hall of Fame in 1994.

The city of Charleston was the last to "get on the bandwagon." Some say this is because Charlestonians take African-American craftsmen for granted. Local officials finally followed the example of state and national agencies. In 1995 they gave Mr. Simmons a Conservation Craftsman Award.

Every year, more tributes come the blacksmith's way. He doesn't dwell on the success. Instead, like Peter Simmons, he concentrates on his role as a teacher.

Philip Simmons, 1996

Since 1955, Philip Simmons has taught at least five apprentices. Two of them, Joseph Pringle, a cousin, and Carlton Simmons, a nephew, are now fully trained smiths. Both are the latest in a long line of African-American blacksmiths in Charleston.

The silver-headed Mr. Simmons puts it this way: "I say to people, 'There won't be another Philip, but there will be another Joseph or Carlton.'"

Star and Fish Gate, 1976

Like generations of blacksmiths before him, Mr. Simmons has passed on the tradition. And now the Historic Charleston Foundation plans to open a Philip Simmons training center for young blacksmiths. The center will grant the artist his deepest wish: "to teach more kids."

"You got to teach kids while the sap is young," he believes, "just like you got to beat the iron while it's hot."

Students from Buist Academy on Visitor's Center Gate, Charleston, South Carolina

Think and Respond

1 What design did Philip Simmons create for the festival in Washington, D.C.? What was his inspiration?

2 How did the author organize the events in the selection? How did she divide the selection?

3 How would you describe Philip Simmons's reaction to the many **tributes** he has received?

4 Did the selection help you better appreciate a blacksmith's work? Why or why not?

5 What reading strategy did you use for this selection? How did this strategy help you?

MARY E. LYONS

Author Mary E. Lyons with Philip Simmons in his blacksmith shop in Charleston, South Carolina

Problem: Many of Mary Lyons's students wanted to learn more about an African American author named Zora Neale Hurston. They had trouble finding information that was written for children.

Solution: Mary Lyons researched and wrote a biography of Zora Neale Hurston that was both entertaining and informative.

Problem: Little has been written about the work of talented African American craftspeople.

Solution: Mary Lyons created a series called "African American Artists and Artisans." While researching *Catching the Fire*, Mary visited with Philip Simmons to learn as much as she could about this artist and his craft.

Visit *The Learning Site!*
www.harcourtschool.com

The Path by the River, **Ernest Albert**
1936. Oil on canvas 32" x 40". Grand Central Gallery, New York

THE ROAD NOT TAKEN

by Robert Frost

Two roads diverged in a yellow wood,
And sorry I could not travel both
And be one traveler, long I stood
And looked down one as far as I could
To where it bent in the undergrowth;

Then took the other, as just as fair,
And having perhaps the better claim,
Because it was grassy and wanted wear;
Though as for that, the passing there
Had worn them really about the same,

And both that morning equally lay
In leaves no step had trodden black.
Oh, I kept the first for another day!
Yet knowing how way leads on to way,
I doubted if I should ever come back.

I shall be telling this with a sigh
Somewhere ages and ages hence:
Two roads diverged in a wood, and I—
I took the one less traveled by,
And that has made all the difference.

Making Connections

Compare Texts

1 How does "Catching the Fire" add to your understanding of the theme Creative Solutions?

2 How is the section subtitled "Afterword" different from the rest of the selection?

3 What connection do you see between "Catching the Fire" and the poem "The Road Not Taken"? How does each treat the theme of making personal choices?

4 Compare the ways that Mari—in "A Do-It-Yourself Project"— and Philip Simmons accept a challenge.

5 What questions do you have about training to be a blacksmith like Philip Simmons?

Write a Paragraph to Compare and Contrast

Think about an activity that you do well, such as playing a musical instrument. Write a paragraph that compares and contrasts Philip Simmons's special talent and feelings about it with your own. Use a Venn diagram to organize your ideas.

Writing
CONNECTION

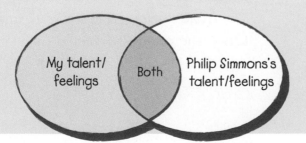

My talent/feelings — Both — Philip Simmons's talent/feelings

Make a Chart

In the selection, Philip Simmons tells how he works with iron. Do research to find out how various metals were used in two of the following ancient civilizations: Greece, Rome, India, China, Mesopotamia, or Kush. Record your information in a chart like this one.

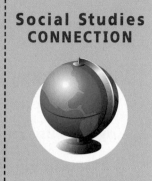

Ancient Egypt	Ancient China
1. Gold was used to make coffins for pharaohs.	

Make a Poster

Research the life and work of an American sculptor or architect. Use the Internet to find pictures of the artist's most famous sculptures or buildings. Use your research to create a poster advertising a museum exhibition of the artist's work. Display your poster in class.

VISIT
The Exhibition!
LOUIS SULLIVAN:
AMERICAN ARCHITECT

▲ Catching the Fire: Philip
Simmons, Blacksmith

Word Relationships

To figure out the meaning of a word, look for **context clues** in the surrounding words, sentences, or paragraphs. Notice how *rivets* is used in this sentence from "Catching the Fire":

> **Philip was proud of the old-time <u>rivets</u> he had used to join the wiggle tail to the gate.**

The important context clue in this sentence is *join*. Since you know from earlier paragraphs that the blacksmith is joining iron pieces, you can tell that *rivets* are the parts that he uses to join them. For a more specific definition, you can look in the dictionary and find out that rivets are metal pins used to join metal objects.

If you look up *rivet* in the dictionary, you may also notice that it is a multiple-meaning word. The meaning "to set or fix firmly" is used in this sentence: *This new computer game rivets my attention.*

There are also other kinds of words with more than one meaning. They are shown in this chart.

Kind of Word	Definition	Examples
Homographs	Words that are spelled the same but are pronounced differently and have different meanings.	The city built a housing <u>project</u>. (proj´ekt) *noun* When do you <u>project</u> the work will be finished? (pro·jekt´) *verb*
Homophones	Words that sound the same but have different spellings and meanings	The offer made <u>sense</u> to the customer. The boy paid ten <u>cents</u> for the whistle.

Visit *The Learning Site!*
www.harcourtschool.com

See *Skills* and *Activities*

482

Test Prep
Word Relationships

▶ **Read the passage. Then answer the questions.**

> The artist was delighted to be interviewed by the newspaper reporter about her life and work. The reporter enjoyed the interview as well. The artist's *congenial* nature made it easy for him to ask questions. She had received her first paintbrush and piece of *canvas* when she was a child. "I decided right away to paint the tree outside my bedroom window," she said. "I still paint trees sometimes. Each one is full of life and mystery."

1. **What is the meaning of the word *congenial* in this passage?**

   A   Interesting

   B   Pleasant and agreeable

   C   Unusual

   D   Easy to understand

Tip

More than one of the answers might describe the artist's nature. Which quality makes the interview easy and enjoyable for the reporter?

2. **What is the meaning of the word *canvas* in this passage?**

   F   An examination or discussion

   G   Getting votes or contributions from people

   H   A material on which an artist paints

   J   A strong, heavy cloth used for tents and sails

Tip

Look for clues in the surrounding words and sentences. You know that G is wrong because this passage is not about voting.

MAKING A DIFFERENCE

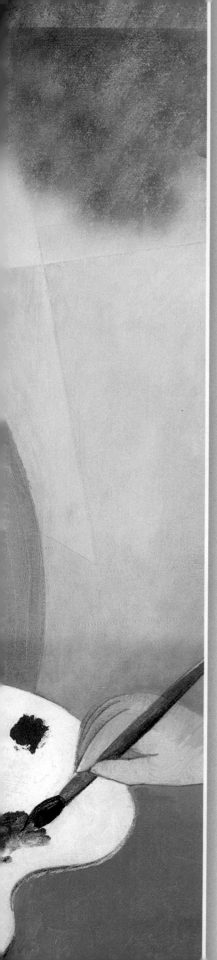

CONTENTS

Seventh Grade.................................486
by Gary Soto

Focus Skill Draw Conclusions

My Name Is San Ho...........................506
by Jayne Pettit

Dia's Story Cloth..............................522
by Dia Cha

Focus Skill Author's Purpose and Perspective

Out of Darkness:
The Story of Louis Braille................530
by Russell Freedman

Focus Skill Draw Conclusions

Anne of Green Gables 548
by Lucy Maud Montgomery, adapted by Jamie Turner

Tea Biscuits....................................570
by Carolyn Strom Collins and Christina Wyss Eriksson

Focus Skill Word Relationships

Cowboys: Roundup on an
American Ranch.............................576
by Joan Anderson

This Big Sky...................................592
by Pat Mora

Focus Skill Author's Purpose and Perspective

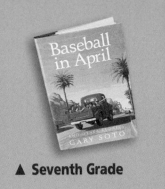

▲ Seventh Grade

Vocabulary Power

bustled

elective

sheepishly

scowl

conviction

propelled

uncertainly

In the next selection, you'll read about a seventh-grade boy's first day of school. Do you remember the first day of school this year? Here are some scenes from some other students' first days.

Today the gym **bustled** with activity as students hurried about, asking questions. Teachers helped everyone choose an **elective** course, such as chorus or archery, in addition to the required classes. Seventh-grade student Scott Allen stared **sheepishly** at his class schedule. He was embarrassed because he had signed up for two classes that met at the same time.

These two seventh graders have nothing to **scowl** about. They're grinning because they were both chosen for the school basketball team. "This will be a great year for us," Sally Hughes said with **conviction**. Let's hope the other players share her strong belief in our team's chances this season.

When the bell rings, a large crowd of students is **propelled** down the hallway. What drives them forward? They're excited about going to their first class of the year. No one talks **uncertainly** or doubtfully about what is ahead. All of them are sure it will be a good year.

Vocabulary–Writing CONNECTION

People often behave **uncertainly** when they try something new, such as a new sport or a new class. Write a journal entry describing a time when you tried something new.

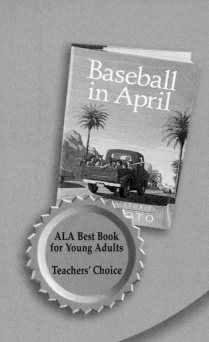

ALA Best Book
for Young Adults

Teachers' Choice

Genre

Short Story

A short story is a fictional narrative that is not part of a novel.

In this selection, look for

- **A plot with a problem and a resolution**

- **A main character who learns something**

- **Third-person point of view**

SEVENTH GRADE

BY GARY SOTO
ILLUSTRATED BY STEPHANIE GARCIA

SCHOOL

On the first day of school, Victor stood in line half an hour before he came to a wobbly card table. He was handed a packet of papers and a computer card on which he listed his one elective, French. He already spoke Spanish and English, but he thought some day he might travel to France, where it was cool; not like Fresno, where summer days reached 110 degrees in the shade. There were rivers in France, and huge churches, and fair-skinned people everywhere, the way there were brown people all around Victor.

Besides, Teresa, a girl he had liked since they were in catechism classes at Saint Theresa's, was taking French, too. With any luck they would be in the same class. Teresa is going to be my girl this year, he promised himself as he left the gym full of students in their new fall clothes. She was cute. And good at math, too, Victor thought as he walked down the hall to his homeroom. He ran into his friend, Michael Torres, by the water fountain that never turned off.

They shook hands, *raza*-style,[1] and jerked their heads at one another in a *saludo de vato*.[2] "How come you're making a face?" asked Victor.

"I ain't making a face, *ese*.[3] This *is* my face." Michael said his face had changed during the summer. He had read a *GQ* magazine that his older brother borrowed from the Book Mobile and noticed that the male models all had the same look on their faces. They would stand, one arm around a beautiful woman, and scowl. They would sit at a pool, their rippled stomachs dark with shadow, and *scowl*. They would sit at dinner tables, cool drinks in their hands, and *scowl*.

"I think it works," Michael said. He scowled and let his upper lip quiver. His teeth showed along with the ferocity of his soul. "Belinda Reyes walked by a while ago and looked at me," he said.

Victor didn't say anything, though he thought his friend looked pretty strange. They talked about recent movies, baseball, their parents, and the horrors of picking grapes in order to buy their fall clothes. Picking grapes was like living in Siberia, except hot and more boring.

---

[1] *raza-style*: a special way of shaking hands
[2] *saludo de vato*: greeting
[3] *ese*: man

"What classes are you taking?" Michael said, scowling.

"French. How 'bout you?"

"Spanish. I ain't so good at it, even if I'm Mexican."

"I'm not either, but I'm better at it than math, that's for sure."

A tinny, three-beat bell propelled students to their homerooms. The two friends socked each other in the arm and went their ways, Victor thinking, man, that's weird. Michael thinks making a face makes him handsome.

On the way to his homeroom, Victor tried a scowl. He felt foolish, until out of the corner of his eye he saw a girl looking at him. Umm, he thought, maybe it does work. He scowled with greater conviction.

In homeroom, roll was taken, emergency cards were passed out, and they were given a bulletin to take home to their parents. The principal, Mr. Belton, spoke over the crackling loudspeaker, welcoming the students to a new year, new experiences, and new friendships. The students squirmed in their chairs and ignored him. They were anxious to go to first period. Victor sat calmly, thinking of Teresa, who sat two rows away, reading a paperback novel. This would be his lucky year. She was in his homeroom, and would probably be in his English and math classes. And, of course, French.

The bell rang for first period, and the students herded noisily through the door. Only Teresa lingered, talking with the homeroom teacher.

"So you think I should talk to Mrs. Gaines?" she asked the teacher. "She would know about ballet?"

"She would be a good bet," the teacher said. Then added, "Or the gym teacher, Mrs. Garza."

Victor lingered, keeping his head down and staring at his desk. He wanted to leave when she did so he could bump into her and say something clever.

He watched her on the sly. As she turned to leave, he stood up and hurried to the door, where he managed to catch her eye. She smiled and said, "Hi, Victor."

He smiled back and said, "Yeah, that's me." His brown face blushed. Why hadn't he said, "Hi, Teresa," or "How was your summer?" or something nice?

As Teresa walked down the hall, Victor walked the other way, looking back, admiring how gracefully she walked, one foot in front of the other. So much for being in the same class, he thought. As he trudged to English, he practiced scowling.

In English they reviewed the parts of speech. Mr. Lucas, a portly man, waddled down the aisle, asking, "What is a noun?"

"A person, place, or thing," said the class in unison.

"Yes, now somebody give me an example of a person—you, Victor Rodriguez."

"Teresa," Victor said automatically. Some of the girls giggled. They knew he had a crush on Teresa. He felt himself blushing again.

"Correct," Mr. Lucas said. "Now provide me with a place."

Mr. Lucas called on a freckled kid who answered, "Teresa's house with a kitchen full of big brothers."

After English, Victor had math, his weakest subject. He sat in the back by the window, hoping that he would not be called on. Victor understood most of the problems, but some of the stuff looked like the teacher made it up as she went along. It was confusing, like the inside of a watch.

After math he had a fifteen-minute break, then social studies, and, finally, lunch. He bought a tuna casserole with buttered rolls, some fruit cocktail, and milk. He sat with Michael, who practiced scowling between bites.

Girls walked by and looked at him.

"See what I mean, Vic?" Michael scowled. "They love it."

"Yeah, I guess so."

They ate slowly, Victor scanning the horizon for a glimpse of Teresa. He didn't see her. She must have brought lunch, he thought, and is eating outside. Victor scraped his plate and left Michael, who was busy scowling at a girl two tables away.

The small, triangle-shaped campus bustled with students talking about their new classes. Everyone was in a sunny mood. Victor hurried to the bag lunch area, where he sat down and opened his math book. He moved his lips as if he were reading, but his mind was somewhere else. He raised his eyes slowly and looked around. No Teresa.

He lowered his eyes, pretending to study, then looked slowly to the left. No Teresa. He turned a page in the book and stared at some math problems that scared him because he knew he would have to do them eventually. He looked to the right. Still no sign of her. He stretched out lazily in an attempt to disguise his snooping.

Then he saw her. She was sitting with a girlfriend under a plum tree. Victor moved to a table near her and daydreamed about taking her to a movie. When the bell sounded, Teresa looked up, and their

eyes met. She smiled sweetly and gathered her books. Her next class was French, same as Victor's.

They were among the last students to arrive in class, so all the good desks in the back had already been taken. Victor was forced to sit near the front, a few desks away from Teresa, while Mr. Bueller wrote French words on the chalkboard. The bell rang, and Mr. Bueller wiped his hands, turned to the class, and said, "*Bonjour.*"[4]

"*Bonjour,*" braved a few students.

"*Bonjour,*" Victor whispered. He wondered if Teresa heard him.

Mr. Bueller said that if the students studied hard, at the end of the

[4] *Bonjour:* hello; good day

year they could go to France and be understood by the populace.

One kid raised his hand and asked, "What's 'populace'?"

"The people, the people of France."

Mr. Bueller asked if anyone knew French. Victor raised his hand, wanting to impress Teresa. The teacher beamed and said, *"Très bien. Parlez-vous français?"*[5]

Victor didn't know what to say. The teacher wet his lips and asked something else in French. The room grew silent. Victor felt all eyes staring at him. He tried to bluff his way out by making noises that sounded French.

"La me vava me con le grandma," he said uncertainly.

Mr. Bueller, wrinkling his face in curiosity, asked him to speak up.

Great rosebushes of red bloomed on Victor's cheeks. A river of nervous sweat ran down his palms. He felt awful. Teresa sat a few desks away, no doubt thinking he was a fool. Without looking at Mr. Bueller, Victor mumbled, "Frenchie oh wewe gee in September."

[5] *Très bien. Parlez-vous français?:* Very good. Do you speak French?

Mr. Bueller asked Victor to repeat what he had said.

"Frenchie oh wewe gee in September," Victor repeated.

Mr. Bueller understood that the boy didn't know French and turned away. He walked to the blackboard and pointed to the words on the board with his steel-edged ruler.

"*Le bateau*," he sang.

"*Le bateau*," the students repeated.

"*Le bateau est sur l'eau*,"[6] he sang.

"*Le bateau est sur l'eau*."

Victor was too weak from failure to join the class. He stared at the board and wished he had taken Spanish, not French. Better yet, he wished he could start his life over. He had never been so embarrassed. He bit his thumb until he tore off a sliver of skin.

The bell sounded for fifth period, and Victor shot out of the room, avoiding the stares of the other kids, but had to return for his math book. He looked sheepishly at the teacher, who was erasing the board, then widened his eyes in terror at Teresa, who stood in front of him. "I didn't know you knew French," she said. "That was good."

Mr. Bueller looked at Victor, and Victor looked back. Oh please, don't say anything, Victor pleaded with his eyes. I'll wash your car, mow your lawn, walk your dog—anything! I'll be your best student, and I'll clean your erasers after school.

Mr. Bueller shuffled through the papers on his desk. He smiled and hummed as he sat down to work. He remembered his college years when he dated a girlfriend in borrowed cars. She thought he was rich because each time he picked her up he had a different car. It was fun until he had spent all his money on her and had to write home to his parents because he was broke.

Victor couldn't stand to look at Teresa. He was sweaty with shame. "Yeah, well, I picked up a few things from movies and books and stuff like that." They left the class together. Teresa asked him if he would help her with her French.

"Sure, anytime," Victor said.

"I won't be bothering you, will I?"

"Oh no, I like being bothered."

---

[6] *Le bateau est sur l'eau:* The boat is on the water.

"*Bonjour*," Teresa said, leaving him outside her next class. She smiled and pushed wisps of hair from her face.

"Yeah, right, *bonjour*," Victor said. He turned and headed to his class. The rosebushes of shame on his face became bouquets of love. Teresa is a great girl, he thought. And Mr. Bueller is a good guy.

He raced to metal shop. After metal shop there was biology, and after biology a long sprint to the public library, where he checked out three French textbooks.

He was going to like seventh grade.

Think and Respond

1. How do other characters change Victor's outlook during the first day of school?

2. Why is Mr. Bueller an important character in the story?

3. Do you think this story describes the school life of a seventh-grade student in a realistic way? Explain your answer.

4. Victor acts confused and uncertain when he's embarrassed. What advice would you give him about avoiding embarrassing situations in the future?

5. How did using the reading strategy of making and confirming predictions help you understand what you read?

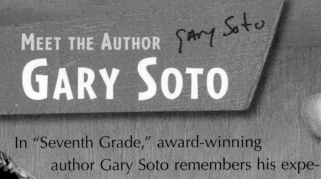

MEET THE AUTHOR
GARY SOTO

Gary Soto

In "Seventh Grade," award-winning author Gary Soto remembers his experiences growing up in Fresno, California. Like Victor in the story, Soto liked a girl who didn't notice him, and he wanted to fit in at a new school. Soto says that he wrote "Seventh Grade" because he likes "taking the past and reshaping it into a story."

MEET THE ILLUSTRATOR
STEPHANIE GARCIA

Before illustrator Stephanie Garcia begins to bring a story to life, she tries to identify with the main characters. Her sixth-grade nephew was the model for Victor in "Seventh Grade." Garcia says that her family and friends often see themselves in her work and that a little part of her is in every illustration.

Stephanie Garcia

Visit *The Learning Site!*
www.harcourtschool.com

Making Connections

Compare Texts

1 Why is "Seventh Grade" placed in the theme Making a Difference?

2 Why does Victor behave so differently in math class and in French class?

3 Identify and explain one example of figurative language that the author uses to describe Victor's feelings in French class.

4 Compare "Seventh Grade" with "The Marble Champ" (pages 86–97), also written by Gary Soto. What similarities do you see?

5 If you could interview Gary Soto, what question would you ask him about this story?

Write a Story Episode

Think of another problem that Victor might face in school. Then write another story episode about Victor and his friends that takes place during the school year. Use a chart to plan your story.

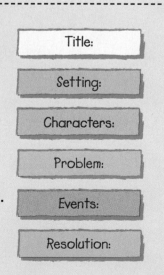

Title:

Setting:

Characters:

Problem:

Events:

Resolution:

Writing CONNECTION

Make a Poster

Victor and his friends live in Fresno, California, where residents experience earthquakes. Find information about an earthquake in California. Then make a poster to share your findings with classmates. Include information such as the earthquake's magnitude, the location of the epicenter, and how the earthquake affected residents.

Science CONNECTION

⊙ **Fresno**

Make a Foreign-Language Guide

Victor is studying French, and his friend is studying Spanish. With a partner, make a language guide that gives the meanings of foreign words used in the English language. If you wish, use illustrations to make the meanings clear. Exchange your guide with another pair of students, and compare the words you know.

Social Studies CONNECTION

Draw Conclusions

Focus Skill

A conclusion is a judgment that is based on evidence or clues plus personal knowledge. This evidence may be stated directly in the story, or it can be implied by other information in the story. Sometimes readers must recognize conclusions that have been drawn by others, such as by a story character or by the author. When you identify conclusions drawn by a story character or by the author, look for story clues that led to these conclusions.

Ask yourself:

• Do these clues make sense?

• Did the story character or the author draw a valid or correct conclusion based on these clues?

Read this passage from "Seventh Grade" (pages 496–498).

> **Mr. Bueller, wrinkling his face in curiosity, asked him to speak up.**
>
> **Great rosebushes of red bloomed on Victor's cheeks. A river of nervous sweat ran down his palms. He felt awful. Teresa sat a few desks away, no doubt thinking he was a fool. Without looking at Mr. Bueller, Victor mumbled, "Frenchie oh wewe gee in September."**
>
> **Mr. Bueller asked Victor to repeat what he had said.**
>
> **"Frenchie oh wewe gee in September," Victor repeated.**
>
> **Mr. Bueller understood that the boy didn't know French and turned away.**

Mr. Bueller draws the conclusion that Victor cannot speak French. Do you think Mr. Bueller's conclusion is valid?

Visit *The Learning Site!*
www.harcourtschool.com

See *Skills* and *Activities*

504

Test Prep
Draw Conclusions

▶ **Read the passage. Then answer the questions.**

> Norma knew that her younger brother, Tommy, hadn't studied at all for his math test. Instead of reviewing the chapters in his textbook for the midterm exam the night before, he had played basketball with his best friend, José. Norma got home from school first. She was sitting in the kitchen when the front door opened. Tommy threw his backpack on the living room floor. He didn't even pay attention when the family dog, Rosie, ran to greet him. "How did the test go?" Norma asked. Tommy just shrugged. Norma knew he hadn't done very well on the test. "You can make up for it by studying hard for the final," she said. Tommy hadn't answered a single question on the test, so he knew he'd be taking it again—in summer school.

1. **What conclusion does Norma draw about Tommy?**

   A   He will go to summer school.

   B   He tried hard to pass the exam.

   C   He didn't do well on the test.

   D   He and José passed the exam.

Tip

Find what Norma thinks and why. Eliminate answers that are not supported by story evidence.

2. **What conclusion does Tommy draw about himself?**

   F   He will study harder next time.

   G   He will go to summer school.

   H   He will probably pass the exam.

   J   José did better on the exam than he did.

Tip

Tommy's conclusion is different from Norma's. Remember that a character's conclusion may or may not be valid.

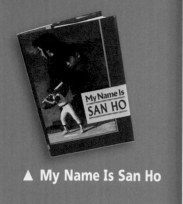

▲ **My Name Is San Ho**

Vocabulary Power

In this selection a boy finds that you don't need words to feel at home in a new country. Sometimes just learning the meaning of *friend* is enough.

tentative
gestured
appreciatively
mystified
significance
muster

May 10

The boy standing on the sidewalk seemed **tentative** and unsure of himself. When he realized I wanted to help, he held up his map. I **gestured** toward the bus stop. Once I pointed out the sign, he seemed to understand me. Although we didn't speak the same language, he smiled **appreciatively**. I could tell he was grateful for my help.

August 4

I was **mystified** when I had to buy some groceries for my mother at the Mexican market. I was puzzled by the signs. Since I can't read Spanish, the words had no **significance**, or meaning, for me. I felt very shy, but finally I was able to **muster** the courage to ask some- one for help. A girl who lived in the village understood me and helped me find everything I needed.

Vocabulary–Writing CONNECTION

Sometimes a possession has great **significance** for us because of the way we came to own it. Write a few sentences telling why something of yours has special meaning for you.

My Name Is
SAN HO

Award-Winning
Author

Genre

Realistic Fiction

Realistic fiction tells about
characters and events that
are like people and events in
real life.

In this selection, look for

- A setting that challenges
  the main character

- The way the main character
  changes through his
  experiences

My Name Is
SAN HO

by Jayne Pettit
illustrated by Amy Ning

The South Vietnamese village where San Ho was born was destroyed during the Vietnam War. San Ho's father joined the army and never returned, and San Ho and his mother became separated by the events of war. After three years, San Ho found out that his mother had married an American Marine and moved to America. Her letters to the Vietnamese government had finally been answered, and in 1975, San Ho was allowed to come to America. He began attending school in Philadelphia in early May and developed a special friendship with his teacher. At home San Ho was building a relationship with his stepfather, Stephen. Here San Ho tells about some of his experiences during his first year in a new country.

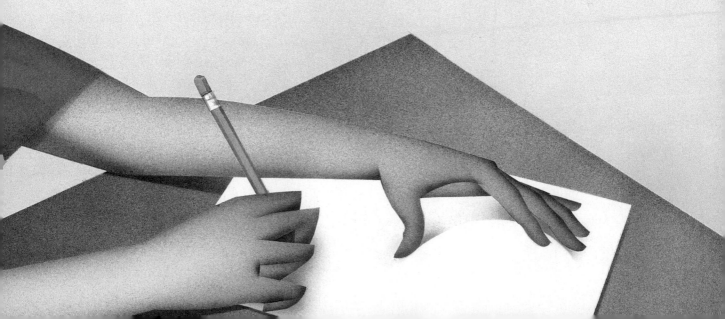

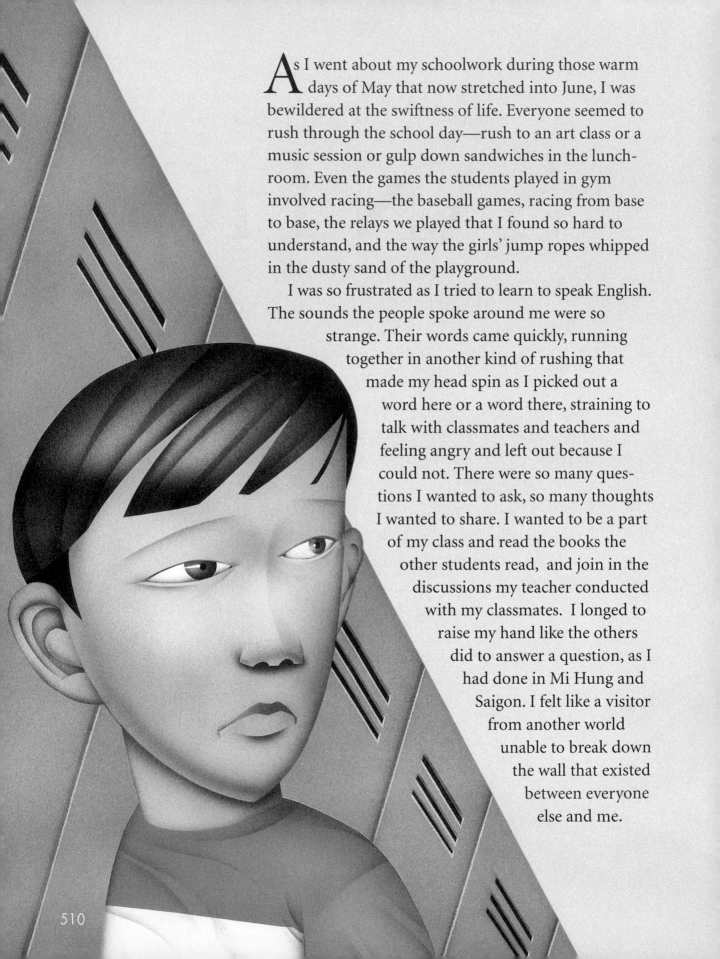

As I went about my schoolwork during those warm days of May that now stretched into June, I was bewildered at the swiftness of life. Everyone seemed to rush through the school day—rush to an art class or a music session or gulp down sandwiches in the lunchroom. Even the games the students played in gym involved racing—the baseball games, racing from base to base, the relays we played that I found so hard to understand, and the way the girls' jump ropes whipped in the dusty sand of the playground.

I was so frustrated as I tried to learn to speak English. The sounds the people spoke around me were so strange. Their words came quickly, running together in another kind of rushing that made my head spin as I picked out a word here or a word there, straining to talk with classmates and teachers and feeling angry and left out because I could not. There were so many questions I wanted to ask, so many thoughts I wanted to share. I wanted to be a part of my class and read the books the other students read, and join in the discussions my teacher conducted with my classmates. I longed to raise my hand like the others did to answer a question, as I had done in Mi Hung and Saigon. I felt like a visitor from another world unable to break down the wall that existed between everyone else and me.

And then, one day, I discovered a little crack in that wall. I was in a gym class meeting outside on the school ground. I stood listening to the teacher's voice as he gave directions for a relay race, dividing us into six teams of four runners. I watched as the gym teacher moved about the school ground in a circle, setting down markers at specific places, each the same distance from the other. When he had finished, he returned to where we were and handed a short plastic baton to the student who headed each of the six teams. Turning to us, the teacher moved to where I was standing and gestured that when it became my turn, I was to grab the baton from the person in front of me and run around the huge circle as fast as I could, coming back to the finish line he had chalked in the dirt. Then, I was to hold up my hand to indicate that I had finished, since I would be the last member of my team to run.

The whistle blew and the race was on. The first boy on our team charged ahead, as the students in the other five lines ran as fast as they could to outrace all the others. The boys and girls shouted and laughed, clapping their hands and chanting words I could not understand. What I did understand was that I was to run as fast as I could with the baton, pass each marker, return to my team, and hold up my baton. I was the anchor for my team. The last to run. *Whether my team won or lost depended largely on me.*

One after another, the students took their turns, cheering each other on, arguing and pounding each other on the back as the game progressed. One after another they moved to the ends of their lines as the next teammate took off. Then it was my turn.

I looked around me to see that on four of the other teams, a number of students waited to take their turns. On the other remaining team, there was but one student left—the dark-haired boy from my desk group. The student in front of me had completed his run, racing to where I was standing. I nervously held out my hand to him, grabbed the baton, and with a quick glance at the dark-haired boy, I darted off.

The students' voices were now at a fever pitch as the two of us raced around the circle, passing first one marker and then another. Those on the other teams fell behind. The dark-haired boy was ahead of me, his long legs striking out in front of him and his arms flying, his elbows pointed outward, his fists clenched. I felt my breath coming in short gasps as I pushed with all the strength I could muster to reach yet another marker.

As the boys and girls in our two lines screamed to each of us to win the game, a fresh burst of energy swept through me. My heart pounded as my feet touched the ground with a new rhythm, faster and surer, as I passed the last marker before the finish line. I wanted to see where the other boy was, but I couldn't risk the chance of a false move—a step that might put me behind. All I knew was that I couldn't see him now, and that meant but one thing. *He wasn't ahead of me.*

Suddenly, I was back at the finish line, breathless and numbed by the excitement of the race. Clutching my baton, I thrust my arm high into the air. The students on my team crowded around me, shaking my hand and pounding me on the back. I had won the race!

The instructor blew his whistle and pointed toward my team. Then, holding up two fingers, he looked at me with a smile and made a V with his fingers. I wondered what the sign meant, but I could guess—and as my teammates crowded around me, I sensed the pride that had come to my team with the winning of the race. I was glad for them, glad that we had won. But there was something else that brought me greater joy. The feeling that I was not alone anymore, that I was an important part of our team and of my class. I had finally broken through the wall and I

was a stranger no longer.

Later, as we took our seats in class, I looked across my desk to see the dark-haired boy grinning at me. Raising an arm, he held up two fingers and made the V sign that our instructor had made after the race.

"Good, San Ho! Very, *very* good!" he laughed. Then he pointed to himself and then to me. "Friends, okay?"

He is not angry with me, I thought. I've won a relay race and beat him and he is not angry. Instead, he wants to be my friend!

After a moment, a smile slowly crossed my face as I became aware of the significance of his words.

"Friends," I said, trying to imitate his word. "Okay!"

The others in my group giggled, and first one and then another pointed to themselves and to me saying, "Friends, okay?"

"Friends," I answered, nodding my head and smiling at each one.

The dark-haired boy spoke once again.

"My name is Bruce. I am your friend!" he said, pointing to himself again and speaking his words slowly so that I could catch the sound and the meaning of what he said.

I thought very hard for a minute and then answered, "My—name—is San Ho. I am *your* friend!!"

I glanced around the room, which

by now had grown still. The students in all the other groups had stopped their chatter and were looking at me with faces lit by friendly smiles.

Then a girl clapped softly, and then more loudly as others in the room joined her. Soon the whole class was applauding my first real sentence in English.

"Friends, okay?" I heard each of them say, as I looked at one, then another and another.

"Friends," I answered, laughing and repeating the word over and over until my teacher came to my desk and held out her hand to me. "Friends, San Ho!" she said, as she swept her other hand around the room to include all the members of my class.

I can still remember how happy I felt on that wonderful day. That very special day when I discovered that in America people could, after all, become friends whom you could trust and believe in. I felt good inside as I sat there at my desk, grateful to be a part of things at last.

Arriving home from school one afternoon with my mother, I saw Stephen's car parked in the driveway.

"Stephen is home early, today, San Ho," my mother said. "I hope nothing is wrong at the naval base."

Setting my books down on the front steps, I approached the car. As I did so, I saw that the trunk was slightly open in the back, a rope fastened between it and the fender. A portion of a rubber tire was sticking out of the gap, and a shiny bicycle shone in the sunlight.

"Stephen says he thinks it's high time that you learned to ride an American bike," my mother announced, as I ran to the back of the car to investigate.

Stephen quickly untied the rope and opened the trunk of the car. There inside was the most beautiful bicycle I had ever seen. Big and green and shiny, totally unlike those used by my people in Vietnam. Those ridden by peasants in our hamlet who could afford them were ancient, handed down by older members of a family, rusted and bent, like anything would be after years of handling. This bicycle was wonderful!

With my mother translating for me, Stephen explained that the bike had special gears to allow for ten different speeds. He cautioned me about following safety rules when I rode in the street. I listened intently, waiting for Stephen to finish and eager to try my luck at riding.

After a few tentative wobbles, I took off down the driveway and out into the street. I rode slowly at first and then, as my confidence grew, I increased my speed. The warm air touched my cheeks as I rode down the block, my hair flying from my forehead and my legs stretching out beneath me as I pumped along. I hadn't a care in the world that afternoon, and I couldn't ever remember having had that feeling before.

At last, I returned to Stephen and my mother, standing at the entrance to our driveway and smiling from ear to ear as I rode up to meet them.

Bringing the bike to a halt at the curb, I got off and wheeled it to the garage door, setting it carefully against the door frame. Then, running down to where Stephen stood, I threw my arms around his neck and gave him a big hug. It was the first time that I had done so since my arrival, and when I finally released my arms from Stephen's neck, I looked up shyly to see that he had been very pleased and surprised by my gesture.

During the weeks that followed, Stephen and I spent more and more time together, and I grew increasingly relaxed with this tall American. Stephen would watch as I rode my bike, giving me tips about handling it and even showing me how to do special tricks with it. Some evenings, we tossed a ball back and forth to each other in the driveway, laughing and teasing each other as we raced around the car.

The weeks passed quickly for me as I learned many new things in school, plodding away at my studies and gaining strength and confidence as the days went by. I continued to use the tape recorders, building my English vocabulary until I was practicing with short phrases. I began to read short sentences and carried my books home to show my mother and Stephen all that I was learning. I was excited and proud of my progress, and I sensed that they were quite proud of me, too. Sometimes I would read aloud to Stephen, and my mother would listen as my eyes moved from word to word. Stephen would giggle appreciatively as I concentrated to pronounce my *th*'s and some of the other funny letters,

and he would try again and again to explain to me why it was that Americans spoke English and not American. On many occasions, my mother would try reading from my books.

My greatest pride, however, during those beginning weeks at school, was my skill at math. As I grew accustomed to working without my abacus, I became quite independent, completing complicated problems quickly and entering contests with the other students. My classmates began to believe that I was something of a whiz! My ability in math and in athletics contributed much to my becoming part of the school life.

Here were two areas beyond the language barrier that I was working so hard to break down, where I could excel.

I continued to make new friends and to discover new wonders in this land across the sea—a land that was less frightening with each passing day. Bruce and a few other boys from my class began coming to my house after school, and we spent many hours riding bicycles and playing kickball on a big, empty lot down the street from my house.

I learned to help my mother and Stephen as they worked in their garden, and I planted four little tomato plants that I cared for each day, watering them and propping them up with sticks to help them grow straight and tall.

And then it was over.

One morning in class, I stared as my classmates began emptying their desks and returning books to the shelves that lined the closets and walls in our room. Boys and girls had brought brown paper bags with them that morning and were stuffing their belongings into them. We sang songs and played games on the school ground afterward, and then two students came to our room carrying trays of ice cream. We ate quickly so that the swirls of chocolate and vanilla wouldn't melt into soup. Then the students began moving toward the door. My teacher said something to each of them as they passed through the door. When my turn came, she reached down and gave me a big hug.

I was mystified by the shortness of the school day and wondered why the students had been so busy emptying out their desks and returning books. There was something very unusual about it all. This wasn't like the other days when we said

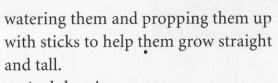

good-bye to each other and ran down the hallways, calling to each other and promising to meet for a game on the school ground before going home.

This must have been what my mother had meant earlier that morning when she spoke with me as I ate my rice and drank my tea before going to school.

"The Americans call it a summer vacation, San Ho," she tried to explain, as I looked at her with questioning eyes.

"You will not have school tomorrow, nor the day after that, nor even the day after that. You will not return to your school until the month of September."

September, I thought. *Why no school until September*? Summer vacation, I repeated to myself in disbelief. The words sounded so strange. I didn't want my school days to end. I didn't want to say good-bye to my new friends or to my teacher who had become my special friend.

THINK AND RESPOND

1 How does San Ho's life change after he joins his mother and stepfather in America?

2 Which event in the story changed San Ho's attitude about school? Explain the significance of the event.

3 How would you describe San Ho's reaction to finding out that school is over for the summer?

4 If San Ho had been a student in your class, what could you have done to help him get used to his new school?

5 What reading strategies helped you understand this selection?

Jayne Pettit

Award-winning author Jayne Pettit has been writing children's books since 1990. Her works often deal with the personal impact that a major historical event has had on people's lives. In addition to writing historical fiction novels like *My Name Is San Ho*, Pettit enjoys writing biographies about courageous people who have worked hard to accomplish their goals.

In addition to writing for younger people, Pettit teaches English as a second language to adults. She likes to think of her writing as another way of teaching— that is, telling young people really good stories outside the classroom.

MEET THE ILLUSTRATOR

Amy Ning

Amy Ning was born in Japan. Although she moved to the United States at the age of ten, she says that much of her art is influenced by Japanese design and style.

In 1985 Amy Ning graduated from California State University in Long Beach. Soon afterward, she illustrated *Good Night, Sleep Tight*, her first children's book. Since then she has published her art in many magazines and books. She has won numerous awards for her work.

Now Amy Ning lives in Long Beach, California, with her husband, son, and cat. "My son inspires much of my work," she said. In addition to her own projects, she works as a staff illustrator at her local newspaper.

**Visit *The Learning Site!*
www.harcourtschool.com**

DIA'S
STORY CLOTH

Notable Trade
Book in Social
Studies

*The Hmong People's Journey
of Freedom*

by Dia Cha • stitched by Chue and Nhia Thao Cha

This story cloth shows the journey of my people. We are called Hmong, which means "free people." Our journey begins long ago in China, and continues to Laos and then the refugee camps in Thailand. For over 125,000 Hmong people, the journey ends in the United States.

My Aunt Chue and Uncle Nhia Thao Cha sent this story cloth to me and my mother from the Chiang Kham refugee camp in Thailand. I will never forget the day the story cloth arrived in the mail five years ago. When I looked at the pictures in the cloth, I remembered how my own family came to the United States in 1979, when I was 15 years old.

Everything in a Hmong story cloth is hand-embroidered. Only the women used to do needlework, but since so many of our

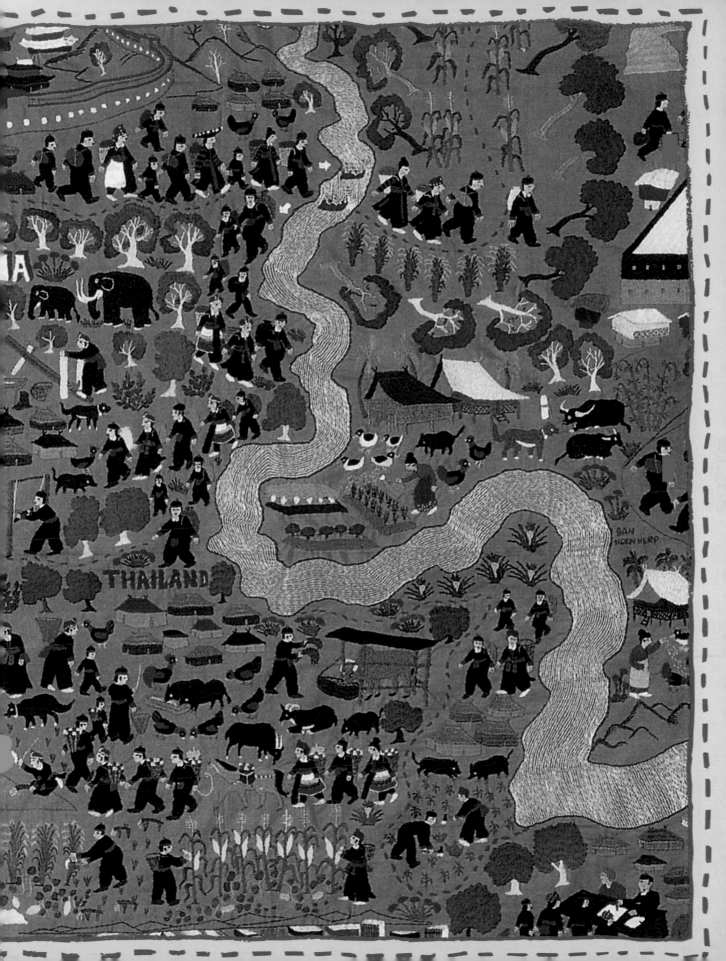

people have been detained in refugee camps, men, like my Uncle Nhia, help make story cloths to pass the time and earn money. It takes many months to complete a story cloth. No patterns are used; no measurements are made. The needlework is done by eye, and comes out perfectly every time.

Here in the United States, stories are told in a different form, through illustrations in a book. But Hmong people living here today continue the tradition of needlework. The stitches in a Hmong story cloth make pictures of life.

When my people first arrived in America, most didn't speak or write English. Many families had sponsors, who picked us up at the airport.

Everything about life in America was different for the Hmong.

I was 15 years old when I came to this country. I'd never been to school, so I had to start everything from scratch. They wanted to put me in high school, but I didn't know anything. Then they wanted to put me in an adult school, but the teachers said I was too young.

Finally, I started high school. Thirteen years later, I received my master's degree from Northern Arizona University. I went back to Laos as an anthropologist in 1992 to work with Hmong and Lao women in the refugee camps in Thailand.

This story cloth reminds me of the history of my family and of my people. Some of the memories it brings are good, and some are bad. But it is important for me to remember everything the Hmong have been through.

Hmong women in America continue to stitch new story cloths. We all have vivid memories about our lives and culture and history. The story cloth is a bridge to all the generations before us. When I show the story cloth to my niece and nephew, who were both born here in the United States, I point to different pictures and tell them that this is what it was like.

Think and Respond

Why do the Hmong in America continue to make story cloths?

Making Connections

Compare Texts

1 How does "My Name Is San Ho" show the importance of belonging to a community?

2 Explain how San Ho's feelings about his classmates and his feelings about his stepfather change.

3 How are the experiences of San Ho and Dia Cha similar?

4 How is "My Name Is San Ho" like an autobiography? How is it different from one?

5 How could you find out more about Vietnam?

Write to Explain

San Ho tells how he feels when he moves to a new country. Write a paragraph telling how you would treat a girl or boy from another country who is new at your school. Make a web to organize your thoughts.

Writing CONNECTION

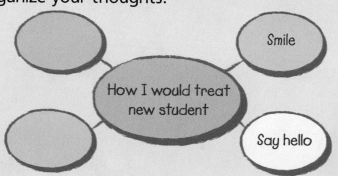

How I would treat new student

Smile

Say hello

Construct a Time Line

Because Vietnam and China share a border, the two countries also share a history that can be traced back to ancient times. Research China and Vietnam. Identify important events in the developments of these countries by constructing and labeling a time line.

Social Studies CONNECTION

ancient times ——————————————— present

Hold a Debate

Which do you think is the more important quality in a team player—talent or good sportsmanship? With a partner, hold a debate with another pair of classmates. Use characters from "My Name Is San Ho" to demonstrate your position.

Health CONNECTION

527

Author's Purpose and Perspective

Focus Skill

An **author's purpose** is the reason an author writes a selection. The three general purposes for writing are

- to **entertain**: to provide amusement or enjoyment
- to **inform**: to provide information about a topic
- to **persuade**: to get the reader to think in a certain way

The general purpose of a fiction story, such as "My Name Is San Ho," is to entertain readers. An author also has a specific purpose. In "My Name Is San Ho," Jayne Pettit wanted to show readers what it was like for a Vietnamese immigrant to come to the United States and start a new life. Why do you think she chose a fiction story to show this?

Identifying the author's purpose for writing will help you figure out the **author's perspective**, or viewpoint. This is the author's opinion or feeling about a subject. Authors can express their perspectives through their characters' thoughts and actions.

Character's Thoughts and Actions
San Ho feels frustrated and left out.
+
San Ho helps win a relay race at school.
+
San Ho's classmates accept him as a friend.

↓

Author's Perspective
Jayne Pettit sympathizes with San Ho and the Vietnamese who came to the United States at the end of the Vietnam War.

Visit *The Learning Site!*
www.harcourtschool.com

See *Skills* and *Activities*

Test Prep
Author's Purpose and Perspective

▶ **Read the passage. Then answer the questions.**

> The teacher introduced Alma to the class on the first day of school. Marcie saw Alma and said hello that afternoon as they were getting on the bus. Alma just nodded at Marcie before taking a seat by herself at the back of the bus. "I guess she's not very friendly," Marcie thought. The next day, Marcie saw Alma at the checkout counter of the grocery store. She noticed that Alma didn't speak English very well. Marcie walked over and said, "Maybe I can help you." When they walked home, Alma told Marcie how much she missed her friends in her home country. "Maybe we can go to a movie this weekend," Marcie said. Alma smiled. Marcie could tell that Alma was glad to have a new friend.

1. **What is the author's main purpose for writing the passage?**

   A   to inform

   B   to influence

   C   to entertain

   D   to persuade

Tip

The first clue to knowing an author's purpose is identifying the genre.

2. **What is the author's perspective on getting to know people?**

   F   It's easy to meet people who live in your community.

   G   Stores are good places to meet people.

   H   You should avoid unfriendly people.

   J   You shouldn't make judgments about people until you know them.

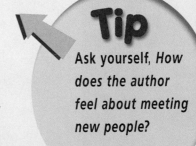

Tip

Ask yourself, *How does the author feel about meeting new people?*

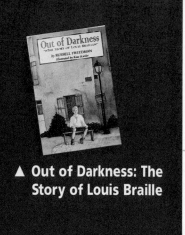

▲ Out of Darkness: The Story of Louis Braille

Vocabulary Power

Can a student help other students? Can a person who is visually impaired help other people who are blind? The answer to both questions, of course, is yes.

devised

gradually

stylus

precision

dormitory

transcribed

Louis Braille **devised** a way for people who are blind to read. After he invented his system, he **gradually** changed it over time so it would be easier to use. Now many things are printed in braille, and there are signs in braille in all public buildings.

Originally the letters in Louis Braille's system were made with a **stylus**. This sharp-pointed instrument could cut through paper with great **precision** and make very clear marks.

This college student is reading a book printed with braille letters, in the **dormitory** room where he lives. Today many books are **transcribed**, or copied, into braille.

**Vocabulary–Writing
CONNECTION**

Louis Braille **devised** a way to enable people who are blind to read. Describe something else that has been devised to help people with disabilities.

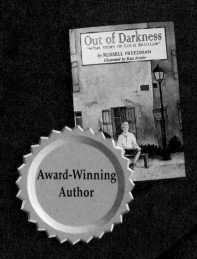

OUT of DARKNESS

THE STORY
OF LOUIS BRAILLE

Genre

Biography

A biography is a story about
a person's life written by
another person.

In this selection, look for

● Events in time order

● Information showing how
the person made a difference

by Russell Freedman
illustrated by Glenn Harrington

Louis Braille was living at a school for
the blind in Paris when he first heard
about Captain Barbier's reading system.
That system, called sonography, used
dots and dashes to stand for sounds.
Louis learned the system eagerly, but
he was soon disappointed. It took too
long to use, and it had no spelling or
punctuation. Louis decided that he
himself could create a better system.

ᘏ

Visions of dots and more dots danced in Louis's head. He wanted to simplify Captain Barbier's system so that each dotted symbol could be "read" with a quick touch of the finger.

His days were filled with classes and school activities, so he experimented whenever he could find the time—between classes, on weekends, at night in the dormitory. When everyone else had gone to bed, and the only sound was the breathing of his sleeping classmates, he would take out his stylus and paper and begin to juggle dots. Often, he would doze off himself, his head nodding, the stylus grasped in his hand as though he wanted to keep on working in his sleep.

On some nights, he lost all track of time. He would be sitting on the edge of his bed, punching dots, when the rumbling of wagons on the cobblestones outside told him that morning had come.

After staying up all night, he fell asleep in class. And like several other students, he developed a hacking cough. Winter coughs were common at the Institute. The old school building always felt damp and cold.

Louis's mother worried about him when he came home for vacation. He looked so pale and gaunt. She wanted to fatten him up, and she insisted that he go to bed early. Monique would climb the stairs to the garret bedroom, tuck Louis in, and kiss him good-night, as though he were still a little boy.

A few weeks of fresh country air did wonders. Louis's cough vanished. He felt revived. On fine mornings, he would walk down the road with his cane, carrying a stylus, writing board, and paper in his knapsack. He would sit on a grassy slope, basking in the sun and working patiently as he punched dots into paper. People would pass by and call out, "Hello there, Louis! Still making pinpricks?" They weren't sure what he was trying to do, but whatever it was, he was obviously lost in thought.

Gradually, Louis managed to simplify Captain Barbier's system, but he wasn't satisfied. The dotted symbols he came up with were never simple enough. Sometimes he shouted in frustration and ripped the paper he was working on to shreds.

Then an idea came to him—an idea for an entirely different approach. It seemed so obvious! Why hadn't he thought of it before?

Captain Barbier's symbols were based on *sounds*—that was the problem! There were so many sounds in the French language. With sonography, a dozen dots or more might be needed to represent one syllable, as many as a hundred dots for a single word.

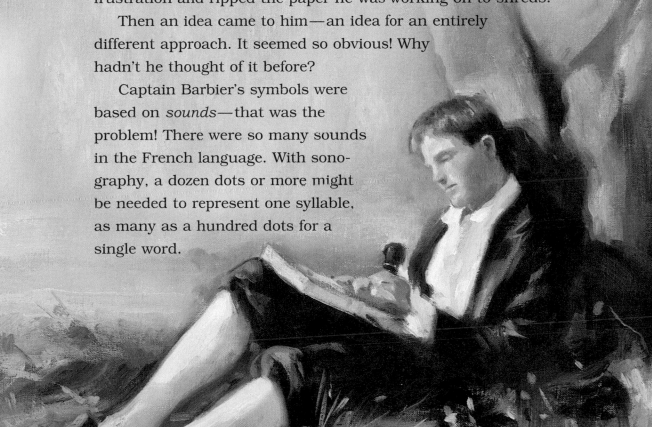

Instead of sounds, suppose the dot-and-dash symbols represented *letters of the alphabet*? The alphabet would be so much easier to work with.

Of course, Louis could not simply have one dot stand for *a*, two dots for *b*, and so on. That way, a blind reader would have to count twenty-six dots to read the letter *z*. Additional dots would be needed for numbers and punctuation marks.

But now that he had changed his thinking, Louis made real progress. He invented a simple code that allowed him to represent any letter of the alphabet within the space of a fingertip. At the beginning of the fall term in 1824, he was ready to demonstrate his new system. He had been working on it for three years.

First, he asked for a meeting with the school's director, Dr. Pignier. Louis sat in a big armchair opposite Pignier's desk, a writing board and paper on his lap, a stylus in his hand. He asked the director to select a passage from a book, any book he chose. "Read from it slowly and distinctly," Louis said, "as if you were reading to a sighted friend who was going to write down all your words."

Pignier picked a book from the shelf behind him. He opened it and began to read. Louis bent over his writing board and paper, his hand flying as he punched dots. After a few lines, he told Pignier, "You can read faster."

When Pignier finished reading the passage, Louis ran his finger over the raised dots on the back of the paper, as if to reassure himself. Then, without hesitating, he read every word he had taken down, at about the same speed as the director had read them.

Pignier couldn't believe his ears. He picked out another book, another passage, and asked Louis to repeat the demonstration. Then, rising from his desk with a burst of emotion, the director embraced Louis and praised him.

Soon the entire school was talking about Louis's new language of raised dots. Dr. Pignier called an assembly to introduce the students and teachers to the new system. Louis sat in the middle of a big classroom, working with his stylus as one of the sighted teachers read a poem aloud. The other sighted teachers leaned forward in their seats, watching Louis's hand move across the paper. The blind instructors and students cocked their heads and listened as the point of the stylus punched out dots.

Then Louis stood up. He cleared his throat and recited the poem, his fingers moving as he spoke, without missing a word or making an error. When he finished, an excited murmur filled the room and everyone crowded around him.

Louis was just fifteen years old when he demonstrated the first workable form of his system. During the next few years, he would continue to improve and add to his system, but he had already devised the basic alphabet that would open the doors of learning to blind people all over the world.

At first, he used dots combined with small dashes. But as his system was put to use, he found that dashes, while sensitive to the touch, were difficult to engrave with the stylus. Eventually, he got rid of the dashes, perfecting an alphabet made up entirely of dots.

Braille's system seems simple at first glance. That is the true sign of its genius. A simple system is exactly what Louis had spent three years trying to perfect.

To begin with, Louis reduced Barbier's dot clusters to a basic unit small enough to fit within the tip of a finger. This unit, now known as the braille cell, has space for six dots—two across and three down:

1 ● ● 4
2 ● ● 5
3 ● ● 6

Within this cell, Louis worked out different arrangements of dots. Each dot pattern represented a letter of the alphabet. As used today, the first ten characters of the system represent the first ten letters of the alphabet and the ten Arabic numerals:

A	B	C	D	E	F	G	H	I	J
1	2	3	4	5	6	7	8	9	0

Additional letters are formed by adding dots at the bottom of the cells:

K	L	M	N	O	P	Q	R

S	T	U	V	W	X	Y	Z

Using this basic six-dot cell, Louis eventually worked out sixty-three characters, representing the entire alphabet, numbers, punctuation symbols, contractions, some commonly used words, and later, musical notation and mathematical signs.

For use in writing his system, he adapted a device Barbier had used to write sonography—a grooved slate to hold the paper, and a sliding ruler to guide the stylus. The ruler was pierced by little windows. By positioning the stylus in these openings, a blind person could punch dots across the page with precision, then slide the ruler down to the next line.

The stylus produces depressions on the paper. One must therefore write from right to left and turn over the paper in order to read it.

With this system, Louis swept away all the shortcomings of embossing. The raised-dot characters were simple and complete. They could be read quickly with a light touch of a finger. They took up little more space than conventional printed letters. The braille system, as it came to be known, made it possible to place all the world's literature at the fingertips of blind readers.

The new alphabet of raised dots was mastered quickly by Louis's fellow students. Now, they could take notes in class, write letters and essays, keep journals, record their thoughts and feelings on paper. Louis personally transcribed parts of a standard textbook, *Grammar of Grammars*, into his new alphabet. It became the first text that blind students could read with ease.

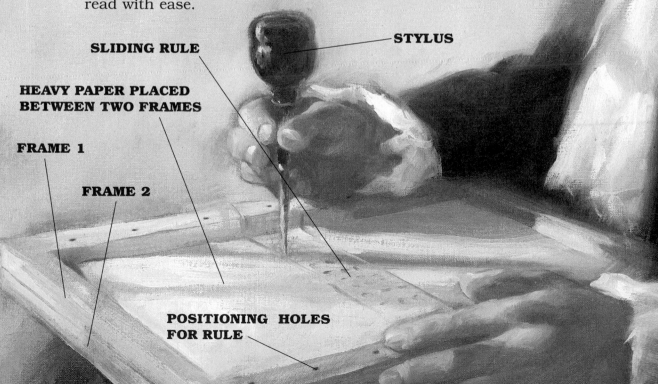

STYLUS

SLIDING RULE

HEAVY PAPER PLACED
BETWEEN TWO FRAMES

FRAME 1

FRAME 2

POSITIONING HOLES
FOR RULE

Yet he still wasn't satisfied. During his remaining years as a student, he continued to add to his system. Meanwhile, he did not neglect his studies. "Each year," wrote a classmate, "the name of Louis Braille rang out among the winners of the various prizes."

In 1826, while Louis was still a student, both he and his friend Gabriel Gauthier became teaching assistants at the Institute. When Louis graduated in 1828, Dr. Pignier asked him to stay on as a full-time instructor of grammar, geography, and arithmetic. Louis accepted gladly. By now, the school had become a real home to him.

When Louis celebrated his twentieth birthday in 1829, his raised-dot alphabet had been perfected to the point where it was substantially the same as the braille system used today.

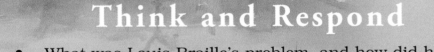

Think and Respond

1. What was Louis Braille's problem, and how did he **gradually** solve it?

2. Why do you think the author chose to show how Louis Braille's alphabet looks?

3. How do you think Louis Braille felt when neighbors who saw him working said, "Hello there, Louis! Still making pinpricks?" How can you tell?

4. If you could interview Louis Braille, what questions would you ask him?

5. What strategies did you use while reading the selection?

Meet the Author
RUSSELL FREEDMAN

Russell Freedman has written over 30 books for young readers. His work has earned many awards, including the Newbery Medal for *Lincoln: A Photobiography*.

Freedman got the idea for his first book after reading a newspaper article about a blind sixteen-year-old who invented the braille typewriter. He learned that Louis Braille himself was only fifteen when he invented the braille alphabet. Freedman decided to write about Louis Braille and other outstanding young people in *Teenagers Who Made History*. He told Louis Braille's life story many years later in *Out of Darkness*.

Meet the Illustrator
GLENN HARRINGTON

Born and raised in New York, illustrator Glenn Harrington has always had a love of art. He began drawing at a young age, and his parents encouraged him to take art lessons.

Harrington has now been illustrating books for 20 years. He says that he gets the ideas for his illustrations from the words of the story. He wants his drawings to make those words come alive for readers.

Harrington also enjoys writing poetry and children's books. His hobbies are baseball, spending time with his two sons, and woodworking.

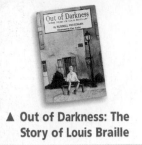
Making Connections

Compare Texts

1 Why do you think "Out of Darkness" is included in the theme Making a Difference?

2 What information can you find in the illustration on page 541 that you can't find in the illustration on page 537?

3 Compare "Out of Darkness" with "Girls Think of Everything." How are the two selections alike? How are they different?

4 How would an encyclopedia article about the braille alphabet be different from "Out of Darkness"?

5 What else would you like to learn about Louis Braille?

Write a News Feature

Imagine that you are a reporter for a French newspaper in 1829. Write a feature article about the raised-dot alphabet that Louis Braille has invented. Use details from the selection in your article. Before you write, organize your ideas in a chart.

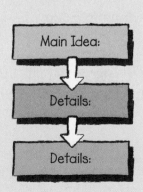

Main Idea:

Details:

Details:

Writing CONNECTION

Make a Chart That Compares

"Out of Darkness" describes the writing system developed by Louis Braille. With a partner, find information about the writing systems developed by two of these ancient peoples: the Egyptians, the Chinese, the Greeks. Record your information on a chart that compares the writing systems.

Ancient Egyptians	Ancient Greeks
1. used hieroglyphs 2. Hieroglyphs stood for ideas.	

Role-Play a Radio Interview

Work with a partner to write and perform a radio interview with Louis Braille. The interviewer should ask questions about the writing system Louis developed and how it changed people's lives. Use details from the selection to make your script realistic.

Draw Conclusions

When you read, you **draw conclusions** by looking for evidence or clues. In a nonfiction selection, you may also find conclusions drawn by the author. A conclusion is like a main idea, and it should have evidence that leads to it and supports it. As you read, ask yourself:

- Does this evidence make sense?

- Did the author draw a valid conclusion based on this evidence?

Read this passage from "Out of Darkness: The Story of Louis Braille." Look for the author's conclusion and the evidence that supports it.

> With this system, Louis swept away all the shortcomings of embossing. The raised-dot characters were simple and complete. They could be read quickly with a light touch of a finger. They took up little more space than conventional printed letters. The braille system, as it came to be known, made it possible to place all the world's literature at the fingertips of blind readers.

Conclusion	Selection Evidence	Evaluate Conclusion
The braille system enabled blind readers to read all the world's literature.	The raised-dot characters were simple and complete. They could be read quickly with a light touch of a finger. They took up little more space than conventional printed letters.	The author based his conclusion on factual evidence. Therefore, the conclusion is valid.

Visit *The Learning Site!*
www.harcourtschool.com

See *Skills* and *Activities*

546

Test Prep

Draw Conclusions

▶ **Read the passage. Then answer the questions.**

> Helen Keller lost her sight and hearing as a result of a serious illness when she was nineteen months old. In 1887, when Helen was six, her parents hired a teacher, Anne Sullivan, to help Helen learn. Anne developed a special method to teach her young student to read. She traced the alphabet letters into the palm of Helen's hand to teach her the names of objects. Soon Helen learned that things had names. When Helen was ten, Anne taught her to speak by putting Helen's fingers against her throat as she spoke so that she could feel the movement of Anne's vocal cords. Helen later learned to read and write in braille. When she attended college, Anne spelled the lectures into her hand. Helen Keller became a famous writer and used her talents to help people understand and appreciate the blind.

1. **What conclusion does the author draw about Helen Keller?**

   A Nobody knew why she lost her sight.

   B Helen had great talent.

   C Helen was slow to learn that things had names.

   D Anne Sullivan became Helen's teacher in her adult life.

Tip

You know that A is wrong because the passage tells how Helen lost her sight. Can you eliminate any other choices?

2. **Is the author's conclusion valid? Support your opinion with information from the passage.**

Tip

Make your opinion clear. Select from the passage the *best* evidence to support your position.

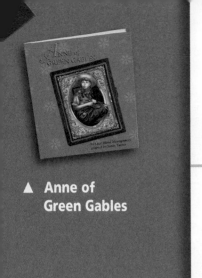

▲ Anne of
Green Gables

fluster

solemnly

bewildered

dramatically

sublime

irresistible

Vocabulary Power

Are you willing to try new things? Anne Shirley, in "Anne of Green Gables," always is, but not everyone is like her. These two dialogues show characters who are about to try something new.

Joey: I think it's great that you're going back to college, Mom.

Mother: I'm so excited, I'm in a real **fluster** .

Joey: Don't worry about anything. You'll be fine.

Mother: Maybe I should act very seriously and **solemnly** .

Joey: You'll have more fun if you just act like yourself.

Jessica: I can't do it, Sarah! I can't go back to that school.

Sarah: I don't get it, Jessica. I'm totally **bewildered** by the way you're acting.

Jessica: Don't you see? I *am* acting! I'm behaving **dramatically** because I want to be an actress.

Sarah: Why don't you join the school drama club?

Jessica: That's a **sublime** idea—the best idea I've ever heard. In fact, it's **irresistible**. I just can't say no.

Sarah: Great. Now can we get to school?

Vocabulary–Writing CONNECTION

When might someone behave in an emotional or a dramatic way? Write a short dialogue in which one of the characters behaves **dramatically.**

Play

A play is a story that is meant to be performed for an audience.

In this selection, look for

- **The setting of each scene**

- **Dialogue that tells what the characters say**

- **Stage directions that tell how the characters act and speak**

550

ANNE of GREEN GABLES

by Lucy Maud Montgomery

adapted by Jamie Turner

illustrated by Mitchell Heinze

Characters

MARILLA CUTHBERT
MATTHEW CUTHBERT
ANNE SHIRLEY
MRS. RACHEL LYNDE
MRS. BARRY
DIANA BARRY
PEDDLER
REVEREND ALLAN
MRS. ALLAN

Scene 1

Time: *Early 1900's.*

Setting: *Kitchen in Green Gables, a farm on Prince Edward Island. Dining table and chairs are center. Rocking chair, footstool, another chair and lamp are at left. Cupboard or long table across back of stage holds dishes, kitchen utensils, etc. Stove with pots on it is at right. Large window attached to back curtain shows view of trees in bloom, lake, etc. Working door is left.*

At Rise: Marilla Cuthbert *sits in rocking chair, sewing.*

Marilla (*To herself*): Where is that brother of mine? He should be back from the station by now. (*Rises and crosses to stove*) This stew will be cold if he doesn't come soon. (*After a moment,* Matthew Cuthbert *and* Anne Shirley *enter,* Anne *holding a battered suitcase.* Marilla *turns, then gasps.*)

Marilla (*Pointing to* Anne): Matthew Cuthbert, who's *that?* Where's the *boy* we sent for? (*During following conversation,* Anne *looks back and forth at* Marilla *and* Matthew.)

Matthew: There wasn't any boy at the train station, Marilla. Just this girl.

Marilla: But there must be a mistake. We sent word to Mrs. Spencer at the orphanage to bring us a *boy.*

Matthew (*Matter-of-factly*): Well, she didn't. She brought *her,* and I couldn't very well leave her at the station, mistake or not.

Marilla (*Throwing up hands*): Well, this is a pretty state of affairs. How is a *girl* going to be able to help us with all our work on the farm?

Anne (*With spirit*): You don't want me! You don't want me because I'm not a boy! (*Dramatically*) I might have expected it! Nobody ever did want me! I should have known all this was too good to last. Oh, what shall I do? (*Throws herself into chair, buries head in her arms and sobs loudly.*)

Marilla (*Sharply*): Well, well, there's no need to cry about it.

"Where is that brother of mine? He should be back from the station by now."

ANNE (*Looking up*): Yes, there is need. You would cry, too, if you were an orphan and had come to a place you thought was going to be home and found they didn't want you because you're not a *boy*. (*Dramatically*) Oh, this is the most *tragical* thing that ever happened to me! (*More sobs*)

MATTHEW: Marilla, we'd best let her get a night's sleep. She's had a hard day.

MARILLA (*To* ANNE *a bit soothingly*): Now, now. Don't cry anymore. We're not going to turn you out of doors tonight. What's your name?

ANNE (*Wiping eyes*): Well...I wish my name were *Cordelia*. It's such an elegant name. But my real name is Anne — with an *e* on the end. A-n-n-e looks so much more distinguished than plain old A-n-n, don't you agree?

MARILLA: I don't see what difference it makes. (*Shakes head, puzzled*) Come, let's have our supper, and then you can get to bed.

ANNE: Oh, I couldn't possibly eat, thank you anyway.

MARILLA: And why not?

ANNE: Because I'm in the depths of despair. Can *you* eat when you're in the depths of despair?

MARILLA: I've never been in the depths of despair, so I can't say.

ANNE: Well, it's a very uncomfortable feeling indeed. When you try to eat, a lump comes right up in your throat and you can't swallow a thing, not even a chocolate caramel. (*Looks at pot on stove*) Everything looks extremely nice, but I still cannot eat. I hope you won't be offended.

MATTHEW: I guess she's too tired to eat, Marilla. Come on, Anne, let me show you your room. (*Exits*)

MARILLA: Good night, Anne.

ANNE (*Starting to exit*): I'm sorry, Miss Cuthbert, but I can't bear to say *good* night when I'm sure it's the very worst night I've ever had! (*Exits.* MARILLA *ladles stew from pot to bowl, sets it on table.* MATTHEW *re-enters, sits at table, and begins to eat.*)

MARILLA: Well, Matthew, this is a pretty kettle of fish! The girl will have to be sent back to the orphanage, of course.

MATTHEW (*Unhappily*): Well, yes, I suppose so.

MARILLA: You *suppose* so? Don't you *know* it?

MATTHEW (*Uneasily*): Well, she's a nice little thing, Marilla.

MARILLA (*Sharply*): Matthew Cuthbert! You don't mean to say you think we ought to keep her! We need a boy to help out on the farm. What good would she be to us?

MATTHEW (*Firmly*): *We* might be some good to *her*, Marilla.

MARILLA (*Crossing arms*): I can see as plain as plain that you want to let her stay.

MATTHEW: It does seem kind of a pity to send her back when she's so set on staying. (*Chuckling*) She's quite an interesting little girl, Marilla. You should have heard her talk coming home from the station.

MARILLA: Oh, she can talk, all right, but talk is…

MATTHEW (*Interrupting*): I can hire a boy to help out with the farm, Marilla.

MARILLA: Well, I…(*Exasperated*) Matthew! You're a stubborn one, for sure. (*Sighs heavily*) I can fight forever, but I may as well give in now as later. All right, Matthew. She can stay.

MATTHEW (*Smiling*): You won't regret this decision, Marilla. It will be nice to have a lively little girl on the farm.

MARILLA (*Shaking head*): Marilla Cuthbert, did you ever suppose you'd see the day when you'd be adopting an orphan girl? (*Curtain*)

Scene 2

TIME: *Next morning.*

SETTING: *Same.*

AT RISE: MARILLA *is setting food on table for breakfast.* MATTHEW *is seated at table.*

MARILLA (*Calling off*): Anne! Time to be up and dressed for breakfast! (ANNE *enters.*)

ANNE: Oh, aren't mornings a wonderful thing? Though my heart is still aggrieved, I'm not in the depths of despair anymore. I'm glad it's such a sunshiny morning; it's easier to bear up under afflictions when the sun is shining, isn't it?

MARILLA (*Grumpily*): Never mind all your talk now. Let's sit down to eat. (ANNE *and* MARILLA *join* MATTHEW *at table. They start to eat.* MARILLA *puts down fork and speaks to* ANNE *in businesslike tone.*) I suppose I might as well tell you that Matthew and I have decided to keep you (MATTHEW *smiles.*)—that is, if you will try to be a good little girl. (ANNE *looks disturbed.*) Why, child, whatever is the matter?

ANNE (*Bewildered*): I'm crying. And trembling. I can't think why. I'm as glad as glad can be. But *glad* doesn't seem the right word at all. I was glad when I saw that wild cherry tree blooming outside my window, but this—oh, Miss Cuthbert, this is something more than glad! (*Sniffs loudly, wipes eyes*)

MARILLA: Well, there's no sense in getting so worked up. I'm afraid you're too emotional for a little girl. And you must not call me Miss Cuthbert. That would make me nervous. We'll be just Marilla and Matthew.

ANNE: Oh, Miss—I mean, Marilla—I'll try ever so hard to be good — *angelically* good.

MARILLA (*Looking toward door*): Well, here comes your first opportunity. Our neighbor Mrs. Rachel Lynde is headed up the path to pay us a visit. Finish your breakfast quickly.

MATTHEW (*Standing*): I'm going out to plant the rest of my turnip seed. (*Exits right, as knock at door is heard.* MARILLA *rises, goes to door, and lets in* MRS. RACHEL LYNDE.)

MARILLA: Why, Rachel, you're out early this morning. (*They walk back to table.*)

MRS. LYNDE (*Sitting down with a groan*): Oh, Marilla, I'm coming down with a terrible case of the rheumatics. I can just feel myself stiffening up something fearful! (*Sighs heavily*) Well, well, life is full of suffering. (*Turns to peer over her glasses at* ANNE) Well! And who is *this*, Marilla?

"Why, Rachel, you're out early this morning."

556

MARILLA: This is Anne Shirley, Rachel. Mrs. Spencer sent her to us from the orphanage. Anne, this is Mrs. Lynde.

MRS. LYNDE: I thought you said you were getting a boy from the orphanage. She's terribly homely and skinny, Marilla. Merciful heavens, did anyone ever *see* such freckles? And hair as red as carrots!

ANNE (*Jumping to feet; angrily*): How dare you call me homely and skinny! You are a rude, impolite woman! How would you like to be told that you are fat and clumsy? You've hurt my feelings *excruciatingly*, and I shall never forgive your unkindness! Never! Never! (*Stamps foot and runs from stage, crying.* MARILLA *and* MRS. LYNDE *sit in stunned silence.*)

MRS. LYNDE: Well! Did anybody ever see such a temper? I don't envy you your job of bringing *that* up, Marilla!

MARILLA: What Anne just did was very naughty, Rachel, but I wish you hadn't called attention to her looks. (*Sighs*) I'll have to give her a good talking to.

MRS. LYNDE (*Primly*): You'll have trouble with that child, mark my words! (*Rises and goes to door*) Goodbye, Marilla! I'm going to look around in your garden for a few minutes before I go, if you don't mind. I want to have a word with Matthew, too. (*Exits.* MARILLA *turns, shakes head, and sighs.*)

MARILLA (*Calling*): Anne, come here. (ANNE *enters, head down.*) Now, aren't you ashamed of the way you spoke to Mrs. Lynde?

"*Y*ou'll have trouble with that child, mark my words!"

ANNE: She had no right to say those things.

MARILLA: And you had no right to fly into such a fury. You must ask her forgiveness.

ANNE: Oh, I can never do that, Marilla. (*Dramatically*) You can shut me up in a dark, damp dungeon inhabited by snakes and toads, but I *cannot* ask Mrs. Lynde to forgive me.

MARILLA (*Sternly*): Anne, disrespect in a child is a terrible thing. I'm disappointed in you. (ANNE *hangs her head and is silent for a few moments.*) You did tell me that you would try to be good, didn't you?

557

ANNE (*Looking up*): Now that my temper has died down, I suppose I am truly sorry for speaking so to Mrs. Lynde.

MARILLA: And you will tell her so?

ANNE: Yes, Marilla. I will. (MARILLA *goes to door.*)

MARILLA (*Calling*): Rachel! Anne has something to say to you. Will you please come back in for a minute? (ANNE *is mouthing words to herself.*) What are you doing, Anne?

ANNE: I'm imagining out what I must say to Mrs. Lynde. (MRS. LYNDE *enters, and* ANNE *approaches, falling down on her knees and extending her hands.*) Oh, Mrs. Lynde, I am so extremely sorry. (*In a quivering voice*) I could never express all my sorrow, no, not if I used up a whole dictionary. You must just try to *imagine* the extent of my grief. I have been dreadfully wicked and ungrateful. Oh, Mrs. Lynde, *please, please* forgive me. If you refuse, it will be a life-long sorrow to me. (MRS. LYNDE *and* MARILLA *exchange surprised glances.*)

MRS. LYNDE (*Embarrassed*): There, there, child. Get up. Of course I forgive you. I guess I was a little too harsh and outspoken.

ANNE (*Rising*): Oh, thank you, Mrs. Lynde. Your forgiveness is like a soothing ointment to my heart.

MRS. LYNDE (*Patting* ANNE *on head*): Good day, Anne. Good day, Marilla. (*Aside, to* MARILLA) She's an odd little thing, but you know, on the whole I rather like her. (*Exits. Curtain*)

Scene 3

TIME: *Next day.*

SETTING: *Same.*

AT RISE: MARILLA *sweeps floor while* ANNE *dries dishes.*

MARILLA: Anne, the Barrys are coming over this morning. Mrs. Barry is going to return a skirt pattern she borrowed, and you can get acquainted with her daughter, Diana. She's about your age.

ANNE (*Dropping dish towel*): Oh, Marilla, what if she doesn't like me?

MARILLA: Now, don't get into a fluster. I guess Diana will like you well enough. Just be polite and well behaved, and don't make any of your startling speeches.

ANNE: Oh, Marilla, *you'd* be flustered, too if you were going to meet a little girl who might become your best friend. I've never had a best friend in my whole life. My nerves are absolutely *frazzled* with excitement!

MARILLA: I do wish you wouldn't use such long words. It sounds funny in a little girl. (*Knock at door is heard.*) For pity's sake, calm yourself, child. (*Goes to answer door.* MRS. BARRY *and* DIANA *enter.*) Hello, Margaret, Hello, Diana.

MRS. BARRY: How are you, Marilla?

MARILLA: Fine. I'd like you both to meet the little girl we've adopted. (*Gestures*) This is Anne Shirley.

ANNE: That's "Anne" spelled with an *e.*

DIANA: Hello, Anne. I'm Diana.

MRS. BARRY (*Taking* ANNE's *hand*): How are you, Anne?

ANNE: I am well in body although considerably rumpled in spirit, thank you, ma'am. (*Aside, to* MARILLA) There wasn't anything startling in that, was there?

MARILLA: Anne, why don't you take Diana outside, and show her the flower garden while Mrs. Barry and I talk? (*Ladies sit down.*)

ANNE: All right, Marilla. (*Girls walk stage front, sit side by side with legs hanging over edge, looking at each other shyly.*)

MRS. BARRY (*To* MARILLA): I'm glad for the prospect of a playmate for Diana. Perhaps it will take her more out of doors. She spends too much time inside, straining her eyes over books. (*Ladies continue to talk in background as focus shifts to* ANNE *and* DIANA.)

ANNE (*Fervently*): Oh, Diana, do you think…do you think you can like me well enough to be my best friend?

DIANA (*Laughing*): Why, I guess so. I'm glad you've come to live at Green Gables. It'll be fun to have somebody to play with.

ANNE (*Seriously*): Will you swear to be my friend for ever and ever?

DIANA (*Gasping*): Why, it's dreadfully wicked to swear!

ANNE: Oh, no, *my* kind of swearing isn't wicked. There are two kinds, you know.

DIANA: I've heard of only one kind.

ANNE: My kind isn't wicked at all. It just means vowing and promising **solemnly**.

DIANA: Oh. Well, I guess it wouldn't hurt to do that. How do you do it?

ANNE: First, we stand up. (*Girls stand.*) Then we just join hands—so. (*They join hands.*) I'll repeat the oath first. (*Closes eyes*) I solemnly swear to be faithful to my best friend, Diana Barry, as long as the sun and the moon shall endure. Now you say it and put my name in.

DIANA: I solemnly swear to be faithful to my best friend, Anne Shirley, as long as the sun and moon shall endure. (*Laughs*) I can tell we're going to have lots of fun together, Anne Shirley! Will you go with me to the Sunday School picnic next week? It's going to be ever so much fun! Everyone takes a picnic basket, and we eat our lunch down by the lake and go for boat rides—and then we have *ice cream* for dessert!

ANNE: Ice cream! Oh, Diana, I would be perfectly *enraptured* if Marilla would let me go with you. I'll go ask her right now. Come on. (*Still holding hands, girls approach* MARILLA *and* MRS. BARRY.) Oh, Marilla! Diana has invited me to go to the Sunday School picnic with her next week! I've never been to a picnic, though I've dreamed of them often. Oh, and Marilla— think of it— they are going to serve *ice cream! Ice cream*, Marilla! And there will be boats on the lake and everyone will take a picnic basket—and, oh, dear Marilla, may I go, *please*, may I? I would consider my life a graveyard of buried hopes—I read that in a book once, doesn't it sound pathetic?—if I couldn't go to the picnic! *Please* say that I can go, Marilla.

MARILLA (*Shaking head and clicking tongue*): Anne, I've never seen the like for going on and on about a thing. Now, just try to control yourself. As for the picnic, I'm not likely to refuse you when all the other children are going.

ANNE (*Throwing her arms around* MARILLA): Oh, you dear, good Marilla! You are so kind to me.

MARILLA: There, there, never mind your hugging nonsense. I'll make you up a nice lunch basket when the time comes.

MRS. BARRY: Anne may ride over to the picnic with Diana if you like, and we'll bring her home, too. (*Rises*) We must be going home now, Diana. Tell Anne goodbye. Maybe you can play together tomorrow. Thank you, Marilla, for the nice visit. (BARRYS *exit.*)

ANNE: Oh, Marilla, looking forward to things is half the pleasure of them, don't you think? I do hope the weather is fine next week. I don't feel that I could endure the disappointment if anything happened to prevent me from getting to the picnic. (*Curtain*)

Scene 4

TIME: *Several days later.*

SETTING: *Same. Brooch is on floor, under chair. Loose flowers and vase are on table.*

AT RISE: ANNE *sits with patchwork in lap, day-dreaming.* MARILLA *enters.* ANNE *begins stitching vigorously.*

ANNE: I've been working steadily, Marilla, but it's ever so hard when the picnic is *this very afternoon.* I keep trying to imagine what it will be like.

MARILLA (*Looking around, puzzled*): Anne, have you seen my amethyst brooch? I thought I put it right here in my pin cushion, but I can't find it anywhere.

ANNE (*Nervously*): I—I saw it last night when you were at the Ladies Aid Society. It was in the pin cushion, as you said.

MARILLA (*Sternly*): Did you touch it?

ANNE (*Uncomfortably*): Yes. I pinned it on my dress for just a minute—only to see how it would look.

MARILLA (*Angrily*): You had no business touching something that didn't belong to you, Anne. Where did you put it?

ANNE: Oh, I put it right back. I didn't have it on but a minute, and I didn't think about it being wrong at the time, but I'll never do it again. That's one good thing about me. I never do the same naughty thing twice.

MARILLA (*Sternly*): You did not put it back, or else it would be here. You've taken it and put it somewhere else, Anne. Tell me the truth at once. Did you lose it?

ANNE (*Upset*): Oh, but I did put it back, Marilla. I'm perfectly certain I put it back!

MARILLA (*Angrily, her voice rising*): If you had put it back, it would be here, Anne. I believe you are telling me a falsehood. In fact, I know you are.

ANNE: Oh, but, Marilla…

MARILLA (*Harshly*): Don't say another word unless you are prepared to tell me where the brooch is. Go to your room and stay there until you are ready to confess. (ANNE *starts to exit, downcast.*)

ANNE: The picnic is this afternoon, Marilla. You *will* let me out of my room for that, won't you? I *must* go to the picnic!

MARILLA: You'll go to no picnic nor anywhere else until you've confessed, Anne Shirley. Now, *go!* (ANNE *exits.*)

MATTHEW (*Entering*): Where's Anne? I wanted to show her the new geese down at the pond.

MARILLA (*Coldly*): She's in her room. The child has lost my amethyst brooch and is hiding the truth from me. She's *lied* about it, Matthew.

MATTHEW: Well now, are you certain, Marilla? Mightn't you have forgotten where you put it?

MARILLA (*Angrily*): Matthew Cuthbert, I'll remind you that I have kept the brooch safe for over fifty years, and I'm not likely to lose track of it now.

MATTHEW: Don't be too hasty to accuse Anne. I don't think she'd lie to you. *(Exits. MARILLA begins to arrange flowers in vase on table as ANNE enters.)*

ANNE: Marilla, I'm ready to confess.

MARILLA: Well, that was mighty quick. What do you have to say, Anne?

ANNE *(Speaking quickly, as if reciting from memory)*: I took the amethyst brooch, just as you said. I pinned it on my dress and then was overcome with an irresistible temptation to take it down by the Lake of Shining Waters to pretend that I was an elegant lady named Cordelia Fitzgerald. But, alas, as I was leaning over the bridge to catch its purple reflection in the water, it fell off and went down—down—down, and sank forevermore beneath the lake. Now, will you please punish me, Marilla, and have it over so that I can go to the picnic with nothing weighing on my mind?

MARILLA *(Staring at ANNE in anger)*: Anne, you must be the very wickedest girl I ever heard of to take something that wasn't yours and to lose it and then to lie about it and now to show no sign of sorrow whatever! Picnic, indeed! You'll go to no picnic! That will be your punishment, and it isn't half severe enough either for what you've done!

ANNE *(Sobbing)*: Not go to the picnic! But, Marilla, that's why I confessed! Oh, Marilla, you promised! Think of the ice cream, Marilla! How can you deny me the ice cream and break my heart?

MARILLA *(Stonily)*: You needn't plead, Anne.

You are *not* going to the picnic, and that is final. (ANNE *runs to table and flings herself into a chair, sobbing and shrieking wildly.*) I believe the child is out of control. (MARILLA *walks around, wringing her hands. She suddenly catches sight of brooch under chair and picks it up with a startled cry.*) What can this mean? Here's my brooch, safe and sound! And I thought it was at the bottom of the lake! (ANNE *looks up.*) Anne, child, whatever did you mean by saying you took it and lost it?

ANNE: Well, you said you'd keep me in my room until I confessed, so I thought up an interesting confession so I could go to the picnic. But then you wouldn't let me go after all, so my confession was wasted.

MARILLA *(Trying to look stern, but finally laughing)*: Anne, you do beat all! But I was wrong—I see that now. I shouldn't have doubted your word when you had never told me a lie before. Of course, you shouldn't have made up that story, but I drove you to it. So if you'll forgive me, I'll forgive you. Now, go upstairs and wash your face and get ready for the picnic.

ANNE: It isn't too late?

MARILLA: No, they'll just be getting started. You won't miss a thing—especially the ice cream. That's always last.

ANNE *(Squealing happily)*: Oh, Marilla! Five minutes ago I was in the valley of woe, but now I wouldn't change places with an angel! *(Exits)*

"Here's my brooch, safe and sound! And I thought it was at the bottom of the lake!"

Scene 5

TIME: *Next day.*

TIME: *Next day.*

SETTING: *Same.*

AT RISE: MARILLA *is dusting furniture. Anne enters.*

ANNE: When I woke up just a while ago, Marilla, I spent a good ten minutes at my window just remembering yesterday's splendid picnic. I could hardly bear to face a plain old ordinary day after such a romantic experience. Words fail me to describe the ice cream, Marilla. I assure you it was *scrumptiously* sublime.

MARILLA: I'm glad you had a pleasant time, Anne, but you must come back down to earth. I've invited the new minister, Mr. Allan, and his wife for tea this afternoon.

ANNE (*Clasping hands*): Oh, Marilla! How divine! I think Mrs. Allan is perfectly lovely. I've watched her during sermons every Sunday since they've been here. She wears such pretty hats and has such *exquisite* dimples in her cheeks!

MARILLA: Hmph! You'd do better listening to the sermon instead of studying hats and dimples.

ANNE: Marilla, will you let me make a cake for the Allans? I'd love to do something special for them.

MARILLA: Well, I suppose you can — if you'll be very careful to measure properly and then clean up afterward.

ANNE: Oh, I will, I will—I promise! Thank you, Marilla! (ANNE *starts to measure, stir, etc. As she works, she alternately hums and talks.*) I do hope the minister and Mrs. Allan like layer cake. Diana says she has a cousin who doesn't even like ice cream. Can you *imagine*, Marilla? (*Pause*) I wonder if Mrs. Allan will ask for a second piece of cake? She's probably a dainty eater, judging from her waistline, don't you think? But then, sometimes it's hard to tell. (*Pours batter into pan*) I can eat quite a bit, and I'm awfully skinny, but Diana eats hardly anything and is ever so plump. (*Puts pan into oven*) There, now. The cake's in the oven, Marilla.

Oh, I don't see how I can ever wait till this afternoon! I'm bound to *explode* before the Allans arrive.

MARILLA: Goodness, child, let's hope not. That would be quite a spectacle. Now, why don't you go outdoors and run off a little of your excitement? I'll keep a close eye on your cake and take it out when it's done.

ANNE: Thank you, Marilla! (*Exits and comes out side door,* PEDDLER *comes out other side, and they meet on floor on front of stage.* MARILLA *may work in kitchen or sew during conversation.*)

PEDDLER: Hello there, miss. Would you be interested in buying some of my wares?

ANNE: Uh—well—what kinds of things do you have?

PEDDLER (*Walking around* ANNE, *looking at her hair and shaking his head*): Well, right here in my bag, miss, I have a bottle of Mr. Roberts' Hair Potion that is guaranteed to turn you into the raven-haired beauty of Prince Edward Island. (*Takes bottle from bag, holds it up*) One simple application will give your hair a glossy ebony sheen.

ANNE (*Touching her hair*): My red hair *is* a sore affliction to my soul. And I *have* always dreamed of having beautiful black hair. But I have only fifty cents. (*Fishes in pocket*)

PEDDLER: Well, now, I'll tell you what, miss. The regular price of Mr. Roberts' Hair Potion is seventy-five cents, but just for today I'll give it to you for only fifty cents. (*Takes her money and gives her the bottle; exits quickly*)

ANNE: What a kind-hearted man! (*Excited*) Now I can be the dark-haired beauty I've always wanted to be! I'll go home right now and put the potion on before the Allans come. With my cake and my beautiful new hair, I'm sure to impress them! (*Exits.* MARILLA *takes cake from oven, rearranges flowers in vase, straightens napkins at table.*)

MARILLA: Now, I must call Anne in. The Allans will be here any minute. (*Calls offstage*) It's time for tea! Anne! Anne! (MATTHEW *enters.*)

MATTHEW: I didn't see Anne outside, Marilla. (*Knock on door is heard.*)

MARILLA: Oh, dear. That must be the Allans. Now, where could Anne be? (*Goes to door.* REVEREND *and* MRS. ALLAN *enter.*) Hello, Reverend Allan. Mrs. Allan. Do come in! We're mighty glad you could come.

MRS. ALLAN: How lovely of you to invite us for tea, Marilla.

REV. ALLAN: We've been looking forward to it. (*To* MATTHEW) Hello, Matthew.

MATTHEW (*Shaking hands with* ALLANS): Welcome to our home.

MARILLA (*Gesturing to chairs*): Please have a seat. Anne will be right here to greet you.

ANNE (Entering, wearing a large, floppy hat, head down): Here I am, Marilla.

MARILLA (*Startled*): Why, Anne, what in creation are you doing with a hat on your head?

ANNE: Uh—my head feels a little chilly, Marilla. Good day, Reverend and Mrs. Allan. It's an honor to have you come for tea. (*Curtsies with a flourish. Her hat falls off, and* ANNE's *hair, bright green, tumbles down.*)

MARILLA (*Stepping back; covering mouth*): Anne Shirley! What have you done to your hair?

MATTHEW (*Amused*): Well now, it looks *green*!

ANNE (*Miserably*): Oh, please don't scold me. I'm utterly wretched as it is, and scolding would only make it worse. (*Covers face with hands*) I wanted to have beautiful raven hair—the peddler promised—but...

MARILLA (*Sternly*): Peddler? What peddler?

MATTHEW: I saw one of those traveling peddlers around town this morning. I'll warrant he came out this way after he finished in Avonlea.

MARILLA: Anne, what did you buy from the peddler?

ANNE: Mr. Roberts' Hair Potion. My hair was supposed to turn glossy black, but it turned...(*Holding up a strand*) green.

MARILLA (*Shaking head*): Oh, Anne, goodness only knows what's to be done with you. You can get yourself into more scrapes. It appears to me that you would run out of ideas for mischief one of these days. Now I hope you've learned...(MATTHEW *begins laughing quietly.*) Matthew, what *are* you doing? (ALLANS *join in; soon everyone is laughing.*)

REV. ALLAN (*Smiling, holding hand out to* ANNE): I don't believe we've ever been greeted in such a unique fashion, Anne. We're pleased to be here.

MRS. ALLAN (*Shaking* ANNE's *hand*): Hello, Anne. Don't be upset. I like little girls with imagination and an adventurous spirit.

MARILLA: Well, I do hope you'll pardon us. I certainly hadn't expected to greet you in such a fashion. Anne, we'll have to try to see what we can do with your hair after tea. But for now, let's all sit down. Everything's ready. (*All sit.*) Let me serve the cake first. Anne made this all by herself.

MRS. ALLAN: My, what an accomplished girl to bake such a lovely cake!

"*M*y hair was supposed to turn glossy black, but it turned...*green.*"

REV. ALLAN: Yellow layer cake is my favorite, Anne. (*Everyone takes a bite at the same time. Peculiar looks cross faces; everyone begins to cough, take drinks from cups, fan faces, etc.*)

MARILLA: Anne Shirley! What did you put into that cake?

MATTHEW: Well now, it does taste a mite peculiar.

ANNE (*Forlornly*): I put in what the recipe said. Oh, it must have been that baking powder!

MARILLA: Baking powder, fiddlesticks! What flavoring did you use?

ANNE: Only vanilla.

MARILLA: Go and bring me the bottle of vanilla you used. (ANNE *gets up and brings back small brown bottle from cupboard.*) Mercy on us, Anne, you've gone and flavored our cake with Matthew's cough medicine! (ANNE *utters a cry of distress and runs off stage. Curtain closes. ANNE enters in front of curtain and sits down, crying dejectedly. MRS. ALLAN enters from other side and stands quietly while ANNE talks.*)

ANNE (*Crying*): Oh, I'm disgraced forever and forever. I shall never live this down, not if I live to be a hundred years old. I can never look the Allans in the face again. First my hair and then the cake—oh, I'm doomed to bounce from one tragedy to another! How can I ever tell Mrs. Allan that the cake was an innocent mistake? What if she thinks I tried to *poison* her?

MRS. ALLAN (*Stepping closer*): Oh, I doubt that she'll think that. (ANNE *looks up and rises quickly, wiping eyes.*) You mustn't cry like this, Anne. It's only a funny mistake that anybody might make.

ANNE: Oh, no, it takes me to make such a mistake, Mrs. Allan. And I so wanted to have that cake perfect for you.

MRS. ALLAN: In that case, I assure you I appreciate your kindness and thoughtfulness just as much as if it had turned out all right. Now, you mustn't cry anymore, but come down to the flower garden with me. Miss Cuthbert tells me you have a little plot all your own. I want to see it, for I love flowers. (*They begin walking across stage together.*)

ANNE: Well, I suppose there's one encouraging thing about making mistakes. There *must* be a limit to the number a person can make, and when I get to the end of them, then I'll be through with them for good. (*They exit.*)

Think and Respond

1. How does Anne change Marilla's and Matthew's lives?

2. How would you compare and contrast the personalities of Marilla and Matthew?

3. Anne often behaves **dramatically**. Why do you think she acts this way?

4. If you were an actor in the play, which character would you want to be? Why?

5. Explain how the structure and format of the play helped you understand the events.

About the Author

LUCY MAUD MONTGOMERY

Lucy Maud Montgomery (1874-1942) grew up in a small town on Prince Edward Island, a province of Canada. At the age of eleven, Lucy began sending her writing to publishers. Four years later, a Canadian magazine published her first poem. She once said she was born with "an itch for writing."

Montgomery had a lot in common with her most famous character, Anne Shirley. Montgomery was raised by grandparents similar to Anne's adoptive parents, Marilla and Matthew Cuthbert. Like Anne, she had an outgoing, lively personality. Instead of getting into trouble, however, Montgomery put her energy into writing. She wrote ten novels about Anne and her family as well as hundreds of stories and poems.

Lucy Maud Montgomery's lively characters and the humor in her stories made her books popular around the world. Today, tourists visit her home in the Canadian province of Ontario, where she did most of her writing as an adult. Many more visit Prince Edward Island to experience for themselves the setting of their favorite story, *Anne of Green Gables*.

Visit *The Learning Site!* www.harcourtschool.com

Tea Biscuits

Mrs. Rachel and Marilla sat comfortably in the parlour while Anne got the tea and made hot biscuits that were light and white enough to defy even Mrs. Rachel's criticism. (ANNE OF GREEN GABLES)

"The Tea," about 1880, Mary Stevenson Cassatt
M. Theresa B. Hopkins Fund, Courtesy, Museum of Fine Arts, Boston

570

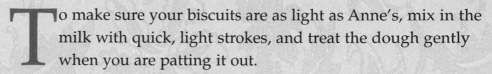

To make sure your biscuits are as light as Anne's, mix in the milk with quick, light strokes, and treat the dough gently when you are patting it out.

Ingredients

1¼ cups	all-purpose flour	300 mL
1¼ tsp	baking powder	6 mL
¼ tsp	baking soda	1 mL
pinch	salt	pinch
6 tbsp	cold butter, cut in small pieces	90 mL
6 tbsp	milk or buttermilk	90 mL

1. Preheat your oven to 400°F (200°C).
2. In a large bowl, combine the flour, baking powder, baking soda, and salt.
3. Add the butter to the dry ingredients and, using a pastry blender, your fingers, or a fork, blend it in thoroughly until the mixture has the look of coarse crumbs.
4. Add the milk and mix it in just until blended.
5. Turn the dough out onto a lightly floured board. Flour your hands and pat out the dough until it is about ½ inch (1.25 cm) thick.
6. Cut out biscuits with a 1½-inch (3.75-cm) floured cutter. (Do not twist the cutter.) Place the biscuits about ½ inch (1.25 cm) apart on an ungreased baking sheet.
7. Bake the biscuits for 10 to 12 minutes, or until they are just golden-brown. Butter the tops of the biscuits lightly as soon as they come out of the oven. Serve them hot, if possible, with butter and jam.

Makes about 16 biscuits.

Think and Respond

What do you think would happen if you didn't follow the directions?

Making Connections

Compare Texts

1 How does "Anne of Green Gables" express the theme that joining a new community changes our lives and the lives of those around us?

2 What characteristics of Anne's personality are shown in the illustrations on page 554 and page 567?

3 What is the difference between the purpose of the playwright who adapted "Anne of Green Gables" and that of the author who wrote "Tea Biscuits"?

4 This play was adapted from a novel. Would you rather read "Anne of Green Gables" in play form or in the original novel form? Explain.

5 Would you like to read more about Anne and her new family? Explain your answer.

Write a Descriptive Paragraph

The play tells what happens after Anne arrives at Green Gables. Write a paragraph describing Anne. Remember to use vivid details to help your reader understand more about Anne's personality. Use an organizer to plan your paragraph.

Writing CONNECTION

```
           Main Idea
     ┌────────┼────────┐
  Detail    Detail    Detail
```

Make a Web

Plays were written and performed many centuries ago in ancient Greece. Use print and online sources to find information about ancient Greek theater. Record your information in a bubble web on a large sheet of drawing paper.

Ancient Greek Theater

Make a Number Line

Measurements in recipes need to be exact so that the food turns out the way it should. Make a number line showing the measurements of the ingredients in "Tea Biscuits" from the smallest to the largest amount. Use other numbers to fill in the spaces on your number line.

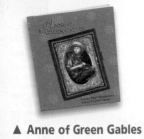

Word Relationships

Focus Skill

"**A**nne of Green Gables" contains many words about feelings. Read this speech of Anne's, and notice the underlined words.

> Oh, aren't mornings a wonderful thing? Though my heart is still <u>aggrieved</u>, I'm not in the depths of despair anymore. I'm glad it's such a sunshiny morning; it's easier to bear up under <u>afflictions</u> when the sun is shining, isn't it?

This speech contains many **context clues** to help you understand the meanings of the underlined words. The word *heart* is a clue that Anne is talking about feelings. Anne makes a contrast between sadness and happiness. This chart shows the words and phrases Anne uses to express these feelings.

Sadness	Happiness
aggrieved	wonderful
depths of despair	glad
afflictions	sunshiny, sun is shining

For the word *aggrieved*, the phrase *depths of despair* is a strong context clue. Both express sadness and pain. What are *afflictions* if they are easier to bear when the sun is shining? They must be things that are hard to bear, or hardships.

Visit *The Learning Site!*
www.harcourtschool.com

See *Skills* and *Activities*

Test Prep
Word Relationships

▶ Use the words in each sentence to help you figure out what the underlined word means. Then answer the question.

1. We thought that our seats for the game would be good, but a camera platform <u>obstructed</u> our view of the football field. <u>Obstructed</u> means —

    A helped

    B noticed

    C blocked

    D cleared

Tip

The word *but* tells you that the seats were probably not very good. Do any other clue words help you choose the correct answer?

2. Although I usually believe the stories that she tells me, I am <u>skeptical</u> about the one I heard yesterday. <u>Skeptical</u> means —

    F doubtful

    G sure

    H excited

    J hopeful

Tip

The clue words here are *although* and *believe*. Does the person believe the story? Which of the choices makes sense in the sentence?

▲ Cowboys: Roundup on an American Ranch

corralled

compliant

ornery

craggy

permeates

full-fledged

diversion

Vocabulary Power

In the next selection, you'll learn about the lives of cowboys on a western ranch. The cowboy still represents American life to people all over the world. Look into the past at some scenes of cowboy life 150 years ago.

Cowboys keep their cows and horses **corralled** in large, fenced-in pens on the ranch. When they choose horses to ride, they look for **compliant** animals that follow their commands easily. A horse that is **ornery** would be difficult to handle.

Each day the men ride twenty miles over **craggy**, rough ground. At night the tired cowboys rest around a campfire. They enjoy the smell of prairie grass and wildflowers that **permeates** the night air every spring.

Working on a ranch is hard work, even for a **full-fledged** cowboy trained for the job. Barn dances are a pleasant **diversion**, and people look forward to this change in their daily routine. The music they dance to includes tunes they all know and like.

Vocabulary–Writing CONNECTION

Cowboys are experts at handling horses. Write a few sentences describing a skill at which you hope to become a **full-fledged** expert.

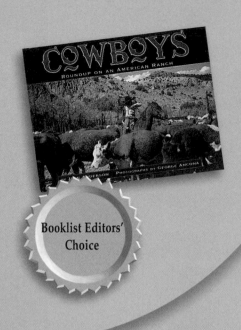

Booklist Editors' Choice

Genre

Nonfiction

Nonfiction tells about people, things, events, or places that are real.

In this selection, look for

- Details describing places and events
- Dialogue that tells what people really said
- The author's viewpoint

COW

ROUNDUP ON AN

BY JOAN ANDERSON

BOYS
AMERICAN RANCH
PHOTOGRAPHS BY GEORGE ANCONA

It is spring roundup time at the Eby Ranch in Faywood, New Mexico. Leedro and Colter Eby have reported to work to help their father. Their mission: to round up 800 cattle on the 75-square-mile range.

Eby Ranch brand

The smell of saddle soap and neat's-foot oil, used to keep saddle leather soft, permeates the air. The cowboys haul saddles and blankets out of the tack room. They brush the snarls out of their horses' backs and speak tenderly to them.

"There's no vehicle that can go where these horses go," says Leedro, pulling the saddle strap tight, making sure the rigging has no extra play. "They give us so much. We've got to take care of 'em."

Just then he notices his horse favoring her hind leg. He rubs his hand gently over her ankle. It feels hot. "You're not goin' anywhere," he says, realizing she must have strained a tendon on yesterday's ride. "You need a couple days' rest." He pats her neck and leads her back to a pen.

The once-tranquil corral is now alive. Boots pound the hardened earth, and spurs clink as the cowboys head for their horses, hiding bridles behind their backs.

"The horses don't like a bridle on," says Leedro, "so we kinda creep up on 'em."

Meanwhile, experienced horse trainer Randy Biebelle has cornered the high-spirited filly that he's been breaking for the past thirty days. All eyes are on Randy to see how he handles her. He talks gently to the barely tame horse. After some initial balking, she lets him secure the bit in her mouth.

"I think you're ready to ride," Randy says, patting her and swiftly saddling her up. "We'll soon see," he says, thinking ahead to the challenge of riding her all day. Just then the horse bucks, as if to assert that she's still free.

All the cowboys are mounted and ready to go when Leedro and Colter's mom, Rose Ann, pulls up. She tucks freshly made burritos into saddle-bags and grabs the reins of her horse, Tommy. A full-fledged cowgirl herself, Rose Ann would rather work alongside her husband and boys than stay behind.

"Time to head out," Larry says. The cowboys gather for their orders, some still shivering in the cool early-morning air. It's been a dry winter and an even drier spring. Larry is anxious to sell off as many cows as he can before he loses them to the drought.

Larry has divided up his territory into sections like a checkerboard. Each cowboy is assigned a section, where he will search for and bring in every last grazing cow.

"Leedro, you head east up the canyon. Colter, you go with Johnny and Abe. The rest of you come with me to the high country. See you at Tom Brown Basin in a couple of hours." They trot off toward the red clay mesas, into the wind, eyes squinting to avoid the dust, felt hats pulled down around their ears. The lilt of voices bounces off the canyon walls for a time and then fades away.

Leedro feels safe mounted on Comanche, a surefooted horse who can handle rugged terrain. They proceed slowly at first, navigating around craggy mesquite bushes and paddle cactus plants.

Leedro keeps his eyes open for rattlesnakes, knowing horses buck when they see one. The buzz of hummingbirds and the clack of Comanche's hooves against the shale rock keep him company. These wide-open spaces are his backyard, a place he's been playing in and riding over since he was a baby. They pass rock caves where Apaches corralled their horses, spots where his dad found weapons left behind by Spanish conquistadores, and rock carvings drawn by Mimbres Indians.

Seconds later his horse stops. She neighs and jumps backward. Leedro looks around to see what is upsetting her. Nearby lies a dead baby calf, probably killed by a hungry predator. Coyotes and mountain lions, desperate for food when there is a drought, ravage anything they can find. Leedro has never seen conditions this bad on the range, and he's worried.

On the other side of the mountain, Larry Eby stares at the brown rubble that was once hearty food for his cattle. He is concerned about the health of his herd as well as the condition of his land.

As he rides, he scans the quiet hills for signs of life, cows grazing or the movement of deer and antelope. It takes a while to find the cattle with Larry's method of ranching. "I spread 'em out, only about eight or ten on each section. That way I'm bein' kinder to the land. It does take a little longer to round 'em up." But Larry doesn't mind.

"Comin' up here, smellin' the sage, breathin' clean air, I forget about everything back in the valley.

"I love this place," he says of the ranch his family has worked for one hundred fifty years. "My dad used to say that you didn't need church when you lived out here under the big sky — you can see God's been here." Even so, Larry would feel much better if the sky turned dark with rain clouds.

The cowboys usually begin to spot cows after about an hour of riding. "It's like findin' a needle in a haystack," Leedro says. "You gotta think like a cow. What would they be feedin' on? Where would they be hidin' their newborns? If they finished breakfast, would they be sleepin' under trees by the waters?"

Just then he sees a momma with a newborn close beside, fur still damp, legs unsteady. Leedro smiles. The new life makes up for the animal that didn't make it.

"When you finally start collectin' them," Leedro continues, "it takes a lot of cow jibberish to get 'em movin'. Hey, hey, hey, yup, yup, c'mon girlie, git up there," he hollers and then prods them with a stick or taps them with his lasso until they get going.

"There's a time to rush a cow and a time to be slow with her. A cowboy's got to know which way a cow's goin' to run, and the shortest way to head her off."

It doesn't take long after finding the first cow to have a string of ten or twelve. The trick is to push them along and together.

Just when the riding gets lonely, Leedro spots his dad up above him on a mesa ledge. He hears a whistle and looks below. Randy is chasing a frisky yearling who doesn't want to stay with the others.

"Head 'em off," Larry shouts, just as a heifer breaks free and follows the yearling. Leedro charges after Randy as his dad gallops down from the mesa in hopes of blocking them from straying too far. Before long, half the team is in the chase, six cowboys running after two cows. Three miles and forty-five minutes later, they finally lasso the skittish runaways and drag them back to the rest of the herd.

What can start out as a short day frequently turns into a long one. "You can never tell when they'll break up on you," Leedro says. "You can have a real smooth drive goin', and then somethin' will happen. They'll get spooked, or a bull will get ornery, and boom, they just take off."

Now the fun begins. Each cowboy on his own has found ten or twenty head of cattle, and they are slowly, cautiously moving them toward one of the many corrals that dot the range. With combined herds, the cowboys begin pushing fifty or sixty cows, trying to keep them together even though each cow has a favorite direction.

"There was a stampede down on the flats last week," Leedro says, a smile in his eyes. "The cows are kinda wild there in the open spaces. They don't like bein' bunched and driven. Sure enough, as we neared the pen the lead cow took off. Colter and I followed her, ridin' forever to catch up, when the other cows got the same idea. They went in the opposite direction. We had cows goin' everywhere, hats flyin' off, dust swirlin' . . . all you could hear were poundin' hooves and cowboys yellin'."

Just before noon, half of the cowboys are at a corral called The Box, where they lead the cattle into a pen and close the gate.

They refresh themselves near a windmill, which creaks and rattles as the wind catches its blades and water pours into the tank. As the horses eagerly slurp, Leedro takes off his jacket and grabs his canteen for a drink. It feels good to stop. The corral, tucked between giant rocks and steep embankments, is a cool place to rest from the blazing sun.

These watering spots are vital for the cattle, who are struggling to survive and raise their young. The Ebys have seventeen windmills that pump water up from underground springs. Since the forty natural water holes and creek beds have dried up in the drought, the windmills must be kept in perfect working order if the animals are to survive.

After ten minutes or so, Larry gives the order to move out. "We can't keep the others waitin'," he says, referring to the rest of the crew on the other side of the mountain. Leedro opens the pen containing the newly herded cows, and they rush out, their heavy bodies rubbing up against each other, dust clouds rising from the weight of their hooves. They look confused and angry about being pushed and prodded. One utters a long "moo" and then another, until a chorus of guttural groans fills the valley that was once silent.

"C'mon, girlie, thataway," a cowboy coaxes a big fat momma. "Yo bully, git up there."

This time the cattle are compliant. It only takes half an hour to drive them to Tom Brown, an enormous basin scooped out of the barren landscape. Eyes squinting, the cowboys scan the hills for signs of the rest of the crew. Randy points east, spotting Rose Ann's blue shirt. Leedro sees Colter herding a bunch of cows through a thicket. The hills are now dotted with cowboys leading strings of cattle toward the valley.

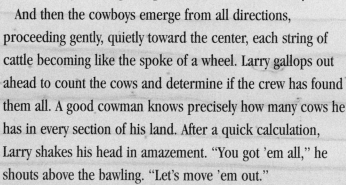

And then the cowboys emerge from all directions, proceeding gently, quietly toward the center, each string of cattle becoming like the spoke of a wheel. Larry gallops out ahead to count the cows and determine if the crew has found them all. A good cowman knows precisely how many cows he has in every section of his land. After a quick calculation, Larry shakes his head in amazement. "You got 'em all," he shouts above the bawling. "Let's move 'em out."

The drive is on. "Keep 'em together," Larry shouts above the thunder of hooves. The point is to gather cattle, not scatter them. "It's like keepin' a bunch of marbles on the table," Larry says as he prods them into line.

"Yippee!" Colter shouts, twirling his rope and lassoing first one calf and then another, more for his own amusement than anything else. "Once you get 'em goin' forward, you don't want 'em goin' back," he says.

The cows duck and dodge, startled by the slightest diversion. In order to keep them together, several cowboys ride swing, along the sides of the herd, to keep the line from bulging. Larry rides point, up front, heading them to the next watering place. Colter, Leedro, and their friends and mom ride flank, behind, staring at rear ends and getting most of the dust in their faces.

Even so, this part of the roundup is fun. After hours of riding alone, whistling to themselves, the cowboys can now talk to one another, munch on burritos, and drink soda.

Think and Respond

1. How do Leedro and Larry solve problems during the spring roundup?

2. How do the photographs in this selection help you understand what happens on a cattle roundup?

3. To write this story, the author rode with the cowboys. What message does she share about this experience?

4. What would you enjoy most about becoming a **full-fledged** cowboy and working on a cattle ranch? What wouldn't you enjoy?

5. What reading strategies helped you understand the selection? Explain.

589

Meet the Author

JOAN Anderson

What do acting, teaching English, hosting a cable television show, and being a radio reporter have in common? Joan Anderson has drawn on the experiences of each of these former jobs to help her become a better writer. She enjoys writing magazine articles about exotic adventures in Peru, the south of France, and the Grand Canyon. She and photographer George Ancona have worked on fifteen books together.

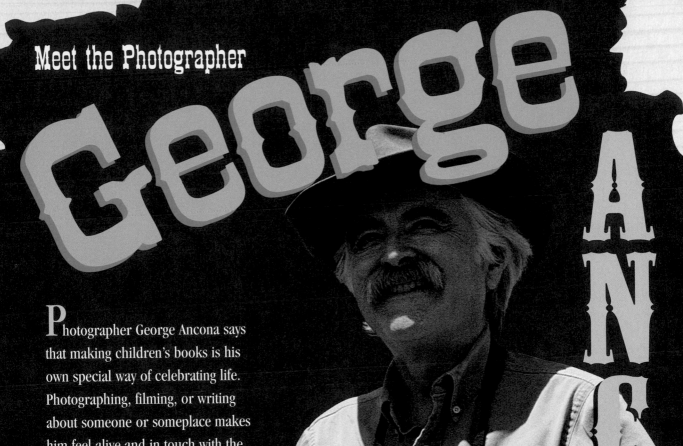

Meet the Photographer

George

ANCONA

Photographer George Ancona says that making children's books is his own special way of celebrating life. Photographing, filming, or writing about someone or someplace makes him feel alive and in touch with the world around him. Ancona says that when he begins working on a book, he travels to the place where the book will be set. "I meet the people, live with them for a while, listen to their stories, photograph their lives. As the book grows, we become friends, and it's always difficult to say good-bye."

Visit *The Learning Site!*
www.harcourtschool.com

THIS BIG SKY
BY PAT MORA

This sky is big enough
for all my dreams.

Two ravens burst black
from a piñon tree
into the blare
of blazing sun.

I follow their wide ebony flight
over copper hills,
down canyons shimmering gold
autumn leaves.

Two ravens spread their wings, rise
into whispers
of giant pines, over mountains blue
with memories.

This sky is big enough
for all my dreams.

ILLUSTRATED BY STEVE JENKINS

Making Connections

Compare Texts

1 How does "Cowboys: Roundup on an American Ranch" express the theme that people in a community are connected to one another in many ways?

2 Look at the photographs on pages 581 and 586. What do they mainly show about life on the Eby ranch?

3 Compare the way Larry Eby in "Cowboys" and the speaker in "This Big Sky" feel about being outdoors on the western plains.

4 How is the purpose of the photographs in "Cowboys" different from the purpose of the illustration for "This Big Sky"?

5 What questions about the life of a modern cowhand do you still have?

Write a Poem

Think about the attractive way that nature is described in this selection. Then write a poem that describes a natural setting that is attractive to you. Think about how this setting makes you feel. Use details to create an image for readers. Use a graphic organizer to collect your ideas.

Writing CONNECTION

Looks

Sounds

Feels

Topic/ Main Idea

Tastes

Smells

Make a Food Web

Work with a partner to find more information about prairie ecosystems in the western United States. Then create a food web that shows how prairie plants and animals depend on one another. Begin your food web by showing how sunlight is transformed into chemical energy through photosynthesis.

Sunlight + photosynthesis = chemical energy

Make a Map

Use print and online resources to find information about the earliest hunters who came to the Americas from Asia. Record your information on a map that shows what North America and Asia may have looked like when linked by a land bridge. Use symbols to show the direction of this human migration. Include a compass rose and a map legend.

HUNTERS REACH THE AMERICAS

Author's Purpose and Perspective

Focus Skill

You have learned that authors write for one of these main **purposes: to entertain**, **to inform**, or **to persuade**. The purpose of "Cowboys" is to inform readers about how modern-day cowboys live and work. To achieve this purpose, Joan Anderson presents many factual details about the cowboys.

Anderson chooses details in a way that reveals her **perspective** on the topic. As you have learned, an author's perspective is his or her viewpoint or feeling about something. Joan Anderson writes from the perspective of someone who is investigating the work of the cowboys and is very interested in what she learns. How does Anderson feel about the cowboys? Does she lead you to see them as she does?

Details
Dialogue that shows what the cowboys think and feel
+
Details about the cowboys' skills and their hard work
+
Details about the cowboys' concern for their herds and for the land

↓

Author's Perspective
Joan Anderson admires the cowboys and appreciates the work that they do.

Visit *The Learning Site!*
www.harcourtschool.com

See *Skills* and *Activities*

Test Prep

Author's Purpose and Perspective

▶ **Read the passage. Then answer the questions.**

> In the late 1800s, cattle drives from Texas began in the early spring. Driving a herd of 2,500 cattle was always hard work, but nothing was more difficult than making the cattle cross a large river along the route. The cowboys had to plan these river crossings carefully. The foreman, who directed the cattle drive, always looked for a shallow place with a firm bottom so the cattle wouldn't slip. It could take hours or sometimes days to get a few cattle to start to cross a river. Eventually, the other cattle would follow the leader. Cowboys worked hard to make sure the herd kept moving instead of turning back and running out of the water.

1. The author's perspective about getting a herd of cattle to cross a river is that it was —

   A the most enjoyable part of the cattle drive

   B easy because the cattle moved quickly

   C frightening to watch

   D the hardest part of the cattle drive

Tip

Ask what the writer's opinion is about the main topic. You can quickly eliminate answers you know are incorrect.

2. What is the author's purpose for writing this passage?

   F to inform

   G to persuade

   H to narrate

   J to entertain

Tip

Different genres have different purposes. Does the passage contain facts, reasons, or events the writer made up?

EXPANDING WORLDS

CONTENTS

Atlas in the Round 600
by Keith Lye and Alastair Campbell

A Strange Sled Race 618
retold by Vivian L. Thompson

> **Focus Skill** Text Structure: Cause and Effect

Dive! My Adventures in the Deep Frontier 626
by Sylvia A. Earle

Some Like It Wet! 638
from *Contact Kids*

> **Focus Skill** Fact and Opinion

I Want to Be an Astronaut 644
by Stephanie Maze and Catherine O'Neill Grace

What It's Like Up There 658
by Karen Romano Young

> **Focus Skill** Text Structure: Cause and Effect

CyberSurfer 666
by Nyla Ahmad

In the Next Three Seconds 684
by Rowland Morgan

> **Focus Skill** Fact and Opinion

The Case of the Shining Blue Planet 692
by Seymour Simon

> **Focus Skill** Draw Conclusions

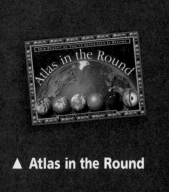

▲ Atlas in the Round

Vocabulary Power

How can people learn more about our planet Earth? These daring scientists have discovered new and important information about our world.

cylinder

submerged

transparent

microscopic

traditional

collide

This underwater explorer carries a tank shaped like a **cylinder** on his back. By breathing the air in it, he can stay **submerged** deep under the ocean's surface. As he swims, he looks out through his **transparent** face mask to see the underwater world around him.

600

These scientists want to learn more about a volcano. They collect samples of soil that contain small pieces of volcanic rock. They will study these soil samples in their laboratory. They will examine **microscopic** details too small to see without special equipment.

In the past, volcanoes not only ended **traditional** ways of life by destroying farmland, they ended many lives as well. Today, scientists try to prevent this loss of life by determining when and where volcanoes will erupt. Special equipment keeps track of the movements of the rocky plates that make up the Earth's crust. Where two plates **collide**, a volcano or an earthquake can result.

Vocabulary-Writing CONNECTION

What is the **traditional** way of life in your part of the world? Write a few sentences about how people live, work, and play.

Expository Nonfiction

Expository nonfiction presents and explains information or ideas.

In this selection, look for

- **Factual information**

- **Sections organized by headings**

- **Illustrations and captions that present information**

602

ATLAS
in the
ROUND

by KEITH LYE and ALASTAIR CAMPBELL

The views of the world in *Atlas in the Round* are like those you can see on globes, which are models of our round Earth. Globes accurately show distances, areas, directions and the correct shapes of land and sea areas.

Unlike globes, flat maps of large areas can never be completely accurate. This is because it is impossible to show a round surface on a flat piece of paper. You can understand why this is so if you peel an orange. There is no way you can flatten the orange peel without breaking it up and stretching the pieces.

One way of showing the round Earth on a map is to divide the globe into segments, as shown here. But maps made in this way break up land and sea areas. This makes it hard to see the true shapes of the continents and the oceans.

Another way to make a world map is to imagine a paper cylinder wrapped around a transparent globe. If you place a light at the center of the globe, it will cast, or project, shadows of the lines on the map onto the cylinder. These shadows would form a world map. This map "projection" is accurate along the equator, where the paper touches the globe. But areas near the poles look much bigger than they really are.

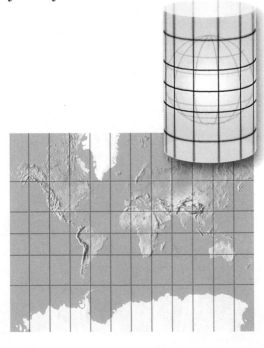

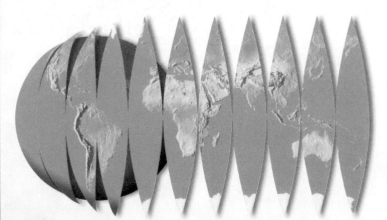

Measuring the Earth

Globes are models of the Earth, showing how our planet looks from a spacecraft. But globes also have names and lines drawn on them. One point marked on the top of a globe is the North Pole, while the point at the bottom is the South Pole. An imaginary line joining the North Pole to the center of the Earth and the South Pole is called the Earth's axis. The axis, around which the Earth rotates, is tilted by 23.5 degrees. Most globes are mounted on stands and tilted, just like Planet Earth.

Halfway between the poles is another imaginary line running around the globe. This line is called the equator. It divides the world into two equal halves, called hemispheres. (The word "hemisphere" means half a sphere.) The equator is a line of latitude, as are the other lines drawn around globes parallel to the equator. Globes also show lines of longitude, which run at right angles to the lines of latitude.

Globes accurately show areas, shapes, directions and distances on Earth. The surfaces of globes also contain networks of lines of latitude and longitude. Every place on Earth has its own latitude and longitude.

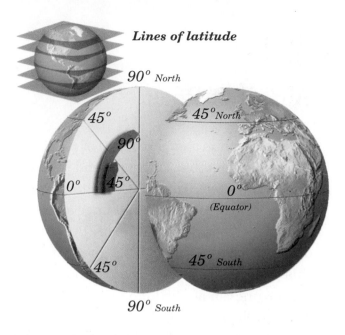

Lines of latitude

Latitude and longitude are measured in degrees. The equator is 0 degrees latitude. The cutaway globe, above, shows that latitudes 45° North and South are measured by the 45° angle at the center of the Earth.

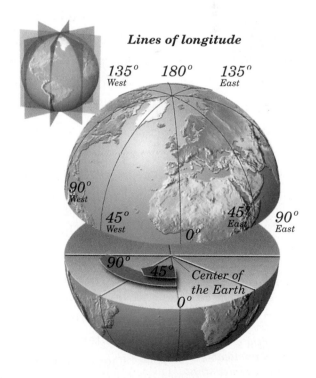

Lines of longitude

Lines of longitude, or meridians, run at right angles to the lines of latitude, passing through the North and South Poles. Longitudes 45° West and East are shown on the cutaway globe.

A Ball of Rock

The Earth is a sphere (ball) of rock. It is one of nine planets that travel around the Sun in the solar system. Its surface contains large land areas, called continents, and huge oceans. The oceans look smooth from space. But if we could drain off the water, as shown in the globes on this page, we would see that the ocean floor is just as uneven as the land areas, with mountains, valleys, and plains.

When the Earth first formed, around 4.6 billion years ago, hot molten (liquid) rock covered the surface. As the Earth cooled, the surface hardened to form a thin crust. Steam from volcanoes formed clouds. Rainwater from storms collected in hollows in the surface. These were the first oceans.

The Earth's hard outer layers are split, like a cracked egg, into several large blocks, called plates. The plates move around because of slow movements in the partly molten rocks below them. As a result of this, the Earth's surface is always changing.

The large globes show the Earth's surface with the water drained away.

The small globes show the same views as they look from space, with the oceans in place.

If you cut through an apple, you will see that it has a skin that protects the fleshy interior. The apple skin is thin, like the Earth's hard crust. Just like the Earth, the apple also has a core. Between the skin and the core is the flesh of the apple. This is the equivalent of the part of the Earth that scientists call the Earth's mantle.

The ocean floor contains mountains, volcanoes, deep trenches, and plains.

The gently sloping areas near the continents are called continental shelves.

A Ball of Water

Water covers nearly 71 percent of the Earth's surface. The four oceans, which are all joined together, are the Pacific, Atlantic, Indian, and Arctic. Each ocean contains smaller areas called seas, gulfs, or bays.

The water in the oceans is always moving. Winds blowing over the surface create up-and-down movements, called waves. Warm currents flow across the surface from the hot regions toward the poles, while cold currents flow toward the equator. Tides are rises and falls in sea level that occur twice every 24 hours and 50 minutes, caused by the gravitational pull of the Moon and, to a lesser extent, the Sun, on the Earth.

North Pole

RUSSIA

NORTH AMERICA

SOUTH AMERICA

MICRONESIA

MELANESIA

AUSTRALIA

NEW ZEALAND

POLYNESIA

PACIFIC OCEAN

ANTARCTICA

This area represents the surface of the Earth.

This area represents the oceans.

The diagram shows that the oceans cover much of the Earth's surface.

Water covers just over seven-tenths of the Earth's surface. If you looked down from the window of a spacecraft over the Pacific, the largest of the world's four oceans, you would see very little land. You might think that our planet should be called "Ocean" or "Water" instead of "Earth."

ARCTIC OCEAN

ATLANTIC OCEAN

INDIAN OCEAN

The Atlantic Ocean, far left, is the second largest ocean, while the Indian Ocean, left, ranks third. The Arctic Ocean is around the North Pole.

The Story of the Earth

The Earth has seen many changes in its 4.6-billion-year-long history. At first, the Earth's surface was probably ablaze with molten rocks, so no rocks formed more than about 4 billion years ago have been found. The earliest known fossils, of microscopic organisms, are around 3.5 billion years old. But amphibians, the first land animals, did not appear until between 408 and 360 million years ago. Dinosaurs lived between about 220 and 65 million years ago. Mammals became common in the last 65 million years.

Plate movements have changed the face of the Earth. Aliens visiting our planet around 200 million years ago would have seen only one super-continent, which we call Pangaea. But in the last 180 million years, Pangaea has broken apart and the continents have moved to their present positions.

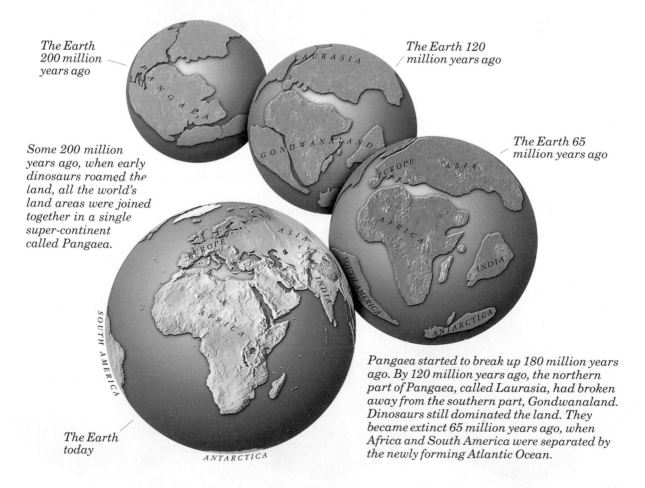

The Earth 200 million years ago

The Earth 120 million years ago

The Earth 65 million years ago

Some 200 million years ago, when early dinosaurs roamed the land, all the world's land areas were joined together in a single super-continent called Pangaea.

The Earth today

Pangaea started to break up 180 million years ago. By 120 million years ago, the northern part of Pangaea, called Laurasia, had broken away from the southern part, Gondwanaland. Dinosaurs still dominated the land. They became extinct 65 million years ago, when Africa and South America were separated by the newly forming Atlantic Ocean.

The Restless Earth

The Earth's outer layers, including the crust and the top, rigid layer of the mantle, are split into huge plates. The plates, which are about 62 miles (100 km) thick, rest on the mostly solid mantle. But the mantle also contains some molten material that moves around in slow currents. These currents move the plates and the continents resting on them. Plates move apart along ocean ridges and collide along ocean trenches. Sometimes, when plates push against each other, the rocks between them are squeezed up into mountain ranges. Some plates move alongside each other. They are separated by long faults (cracks) in the Earth's surface.

Plates sometimes move in violent jerks, causing earthquakes. On the average, plates move by only 0.8 to 4 inches (2-10 cm) a year. This sounds slow. But over the course of millions of years, plate movements change the face of the Earth.

When molten magma emerges through holes in the ground, called volcanoes, it is called lava. When some volcanoes erupt, they explode shattered bits of lava high into the air. Other volcanoes send out streams of runny lava. Most volcanoes lie near the plate edges in the ocean trenches. Some lie in the middle of plates, above heat sources in the mantle.

The globes show the plates that form the Earth's hard outer layers.

Below · The Earth contains a solid inner core, made up mainly of iron, and a liquid outer core. The core is about 4,190 miles (6,740 km) across. Around the core is the rocky mantle, which is about 1,800 miles (2,900 km) thick. The crust averages 2.3 miles (6 km) under the oceans and 22 miles (35 km) under the continents.

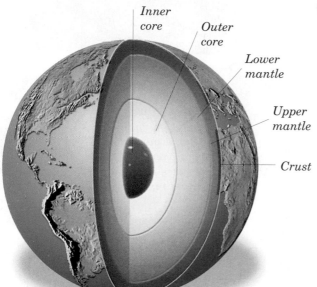

Inner core

Outer core

Lower mantle

Upper mantle

Crust

Above · Some plates move sideways alongside each other. Most of the time, the jagged plate edges are locked together, but friction occasionally breaks the rocks, causing the plates to move suddenly. This causes earthquakes.

Hidden beneath the oceans are mountain ranges, called ocean ridges. Deep valleys in the middle of the ridges form the edges of plates that are moving apart. When plates move apart, molten magma from the mantle rises and fills in the gaps.

When two plates collide, one plate sinks down beneath the other alongside the ocean trenches, the deepest places in the oceans. The edge of the descending plate melts, and some of the molten rock rises and erupts out of volcanoes on the Earth's surface.

Magma rising through the crust to form a volcano

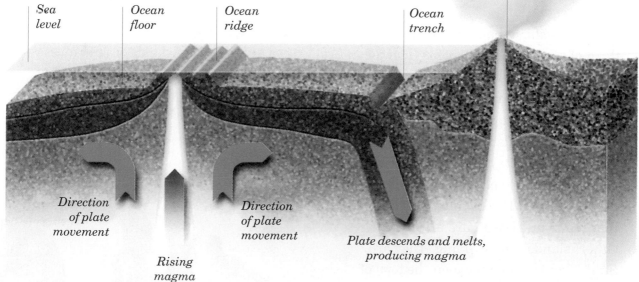

Sea level

Ocean floor

Ocean ridge

Ocean trench

Direction of plate movement

Direction of plate movement

Plate descends and melts, producing magma

Rising magma

Molten lava
spills into
the sea on
the island
of Hawaii.

Many houses
on coral
islands are
built on stilts.

Pacific Ocean

The Pacific Ocean covers about a third of the globe. It is bigger than all the continents put together. It stretches from the frozen Arctic Ocean to the icy continent of Antarctica.

Some of the Pacific Ocean islands are mountainous. They are the tops of active or extinct (dead) volcanoes that rise from the ocean floor. For example, the islands that make up Hawaii are all volcanic. Other islands are low-lying. They are coral islands which form on the tops of

submerged volcanoes or in the shallow seas around other islands or land masses. Some coral islands form in the shapes of rings or horseshoes, called atolls.

Easter Island has
impressive but mysterious
ancient monuments.

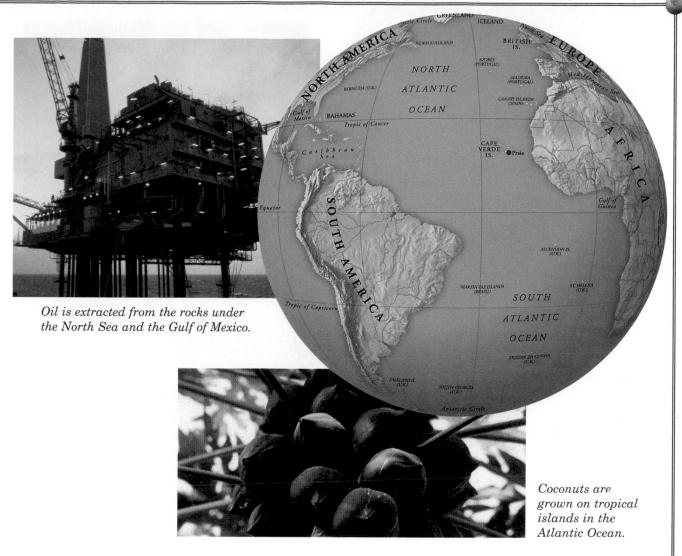

Oil is extracted from the rocks under the North Sea and the Gulf of Mexico.

Coconuts are grown on tropical islands in the Atlantic Ocean.

Atlantic Ocean

The Atlantic is the world's second largest ocean. It is a busy ocean, with ships crisscrossing its waters, carrying goods from one continent to another. It also contains large fishing grounds, although overfishing has caused fish stocks to drop to low levels.

The ocean's chief feature is mainly hidden from view. This is the mid-Atlantic ridge, a huge mountain range rising from the deep ocean floor and running north-south through the ocean. The ridge is the place where plates are moving apart and where molten lava is rising to the surface to form new crustal rock. As a result, the Atlantic Ocean is becoming wider by about one inch (2.5 cm) a year. The volcanic island of Iceland rises from the ridge. It, too, is becoming wider as the plates on either side move apart. Newfoundland in eastern Canada, the British Isles, and the sunny islands of the Caribbean Sea are also Atlantic islands.

The island of Madagascar is home to these ring-tailed lemurs.

Fishing boats called dhows are common in the Arabian Sea.

Indian Ocean

The Indian Ocean, the world's third largest ocean, extends from southern Asia to Antarctica. The northern part of the ocean contains busy shipping lanes. Huge tankers, for example, cross the ocean to transport oil from the Persian Gulf to many parts of the world. Fishing vessels also sail the ocean, especially off the west coast of India. But fish spoils quickly in the hot weather in the northern and central parts of the Indian Ocean.

Hidden beneath the waves are long ocean ridges and deep trenches. These features are the edges of plates that form the Earth's hard outer layers. Around 180 million years ago, India was located near Antarctica. But a plate carrying India broke away and moved north, colliding with Asia around 50 million years ago. These plate movements created the modern Indian Ocean.

A small iceberg at Ellesmere Island, in northern Canada.

Polar bears live around the coasts of North America and Asia and also on many Arctic islands. They feed by hunting seals and other animals.

Most Inuit now live in modern towns. Some of the houses are shaped like igloos (traditional snow houses).

The Arctic

The Arctic Ocean, the smallest of the world's four oceans, lies around the North Pole on the top of the world. Ice covers much of the ocean for most of the year. Ships carrying goods must be accompanied by icebreakers that cut paths through the ice.

The region called the Arctic also includes the northern parts of Asia, Europe, and North America surrounding the Arctic Ocean. Ice sheets cover some areas. Greenland, for example, is blanketed by the world's second largest ice sheet. However, in parts of the Arctic, the snow and ice melt in the summer and plants grow. Various peoples, such as the Inuit of North America, live in the Arctic. Their traditional way of life has depended mainly on hunting such animals as polar bears, and fishing.

Leopard seals feed on young seals, penguins, and other creatures around Antarctica.

Penguins are flightless birds found in Antarctica.

The Antarctic

Antarctica, the world's fifth largest continent, lies around the South Pole at the bottom of the globe. From space, you would see that it is mainly covered by the world's largest ice sheet, and surrounded by frozen seas. But you would also see high mountains jutting through the ice in places. In some parts of the continent, the ice is 15,700 feet (4,800 m) thick.

This frozen land is the world's coldest place. It is swept by strong winds that blow loose snow across the surface, causing blinding blizzards. Some scientists go there to study the continent and its weather, and some tourists now visit the continent. But no one lives in Antarctica all the time.

Huge icebergs break away from the ice sheet of Antarctica and drift northward. About eight-ninths of the ice is hidden beneath the water.

Think and Respond

1. Why is the Earth's surface constantly changing?

2. Why do you think the author begins this selection with information about **traditional** maps?

3. What information about the four oceans can you find out by studying the pictures of the globes on pages 612–615?

4. How do you think your reading of this selection will affect the way you look at maps and globes?

5. How did the text structure and format help you understand the selection?

A Strange

Sled Race

A Hawaiian myth retold by Vivian L. Thompson
illustrated by Leslie Wu

The goddess of snow, Poliahu, lives high on the slopes of Mauna Kea on the northern side of Hawaii. That side is free of lava flows because of the goddess's skill at sled-racing . . . .

Poliahu and her snow maidens one day covered their dazzling snow mantles with mantles of golden sunshine. They took their long, slender sleds to the race course below the snowfields. There a narrow, grassy track had been laid, dropping swiftly toward the sea.

High, tinkling laughter filled the air as the maidens urged the goddess to race. Poliahu was very willing. She made a running start, threw herself upon her sled, and plunged down. Far below she came to a stop, marked the spot, and lifted her sled aside.

One after another the snow maidens followed, but none reached the goddess's mark. As they gathered below, they discovered a stranger in their midst, a handsome woman dressed in black mantle and robe.

Fixing gleaming black eyes upon the goddess of snow, she spoke. "I should like to race with you, but I have no sled."

"You may use one of ours," Snow Goddess said, and a maiden quickly offered hers.

The stranger took it without a word of thanks. Then she and Poliahu climbed up the mountain slope. The maidens watched from below. The stranger swooped down the slope and flashed past them. There was no doubt she was skillful. Poliahu followed and passed the other's stopping place.

"That sled did not fit me!" said the dark-eyed stranger.

A taller maiden offered her sled. Again the long, slow climb. Again the short, swift descent. Both sleds went farther than before, but Poliahu's still led.

"An inferior sled!" the woman said with scorn.

"We have no inferior sleds," Snow Goddess replied coldly. "Let us race again, and you shall take mine."

"I have always raced on a longer course," said the woman. "Let us go higher up the mountain. You shall race first this time."

They exchanged sleds and climbed to the snow line. The stranger waited until Poliahu had started down; then she stamped her foot. The earth trembled. A jagged crack split open across the lower part of the racing course.

The snow maidens, watching below, lost sight of their goddess as steam rose from the crack and formed a curtain. They ran up the slope.

For a moment, the steam cleared. They caught a glimpse of Poliahu racing toward the widening crack. The woman in black was close behind her, standing upright on her speeding sled. In horror they saw her black robe turn red and her eyes glow like burning coals. They knew now! She was Pele—Volcano Goddess!

She stamped again. They felt the molten lava come rumbling through underground passages in answer to her signal. It spurted out along the crack.

Swiftly the snow maidens raised their arms toward the snowy peaks and began to chant. The air grew chill as gray cloud goddesses gathered to aid Poliahu. They sent snow swirling down from the top of the mountain, hissing as it struck the heated earth. The spurting lava died.

Pele, in a fury, gave a crackling shout. The lava leaped up again, forming a row of fiery fountains directly ahead of Poliahu.

The snow maidens watched fearfully. There was no way that Poliahu could slow her sled nor turn it aside. She plunged through the wall of fire.

Her golden mantle burst into flame. Throwing it off and leaping from her sled, Snow Goddess stood robed in dazzling white. A red-gold river raced toward her from the fire fountains. On its crest rode Pele. Poliahu waited, unmoved.

Volcano Goddess burst through the flames without harm. She sprang from her sled to face the young woman who dared to defy her.

Snow Goddess swung her
mantle in a wide arc. A blast of icy
wind swept down the mountain. Her silvery hair and dazzling garments streamed out
behind her.

Volcano Goddess shivered. The leaping fountains
dwindled. The racing river slowed.

She screamed at the lava, "Swallow her up!"

But the lava fountains died. The lava river grew sluggish. Still
deadly, it flowed to the very feet of Snow Goddess. She flung her
arms wide. The river split in two, leaving her unharmed in the center. It made its way beyond her, moving slowly down to the sea.
There it formed a long, flat point of land, known to this day as
Leaf-of-Smooth-Lava.

Volcano Goddess stared, unable to believe what she saw.
Her red mantle turned black again. Her glowing eyes dulled.
Shivering with cold, she disappeared as mysteriously as she
had come.

High, tinkling laughter filled the air once more as the
snow goddess and her maidens picked up their sleds and
returned to their snowy home.

Pele never again crossed over Mauna Kea to
Poliahu's side of the island, although she still sent
lava pouring down the southern side.

Think and Respond

What explanation does this story give for
earthquakes and volcanoes?

Making Connections

Compare Texts

1 Why is "Atlas in the Round" in a unit about exploring new ideas and places?

2 What information can you learn by studying the diagrams in the section titled The Restless Earth?

3 Explain how the authors of "Atlas in the Round" and "A Strange Sled Race" approach similar topics in different ways.

4 How is "Atlas in the Round" different from other atlases you have used?

5 What questions about Earth's history do you still have?

Write a Myth

Write a myth that explains one of the physical changes described in "Atlas in the Round." Your myth can include talking animals or make-believe characters. Use a story map to plan your myth before beginning to write.

Writing
CONNECTION

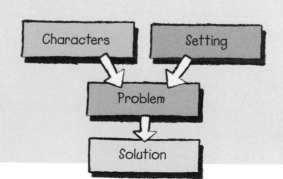

622

Make a Diagram

"**A**tlas in the Round" includes a diagram showing how plates move and how they change the surface of Earth. Do research in books and online to find out why plate movement causes earthquakes. Then create your own diagram that shows what you have learned.

Science CONNECTION

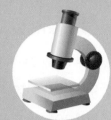

The Causes of an Earthquake

Design a Building

Architects in certain parts of the world are especially concerned with improving the safety of buildings during earthquakes. Find one way in which architects in earthquake areas have changed the design of buildings. Then design a building for an earthquake-prone area, and list its features. Display your work for your classmates.

Science/ Visual Arts CONNECTION

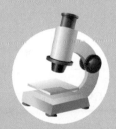

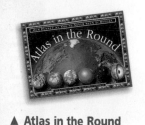
Text Structure:
Cause and Effect

You know how important it is to pay attention to the way material is organized in a nonfiction selection. "Atlas in the Round" is divided into sections with headings and main ideas. Often, the author organizes the information to show how one event or action causes something else to happen.

- The cause is an action or event.
- The effect is what happens because of the action or event.

Sometimes the topic sentence in a section or paragraph states the effect, and then the supporting details tell the causes. Reread the section titled A Ball of Water from "Atlas in the Round." What topic sentence identifies an effect? What are the supporting details that identify its causes?

Effect
The water in the oceans is always moving.

Cause	**Cause**
Winds blowing over the surface create up-and-down movements, called waves.	The gravitational pull of the Moon and the Sun creates tides.

Visit *The Learning Site!*
www.harcourtschool.com

See *Skills* and *Activities*

Test Prep
Text Structure: Cause and Effect

▶ **Read the passage. Then answer the questions.**

> People fear earthquakes because they can cause terrible destruction. Buildings are weakened by the earth's movement. Structures that weren't built to withstand the force of an earthquake may collapse. In places where the ground is mostly gravel or sand, the shaking of the particles may turn the ground into a muddy liquid, and buildings may sway and sink. Other destruction occurs if broken gas pipes and electrical wires catch fire. In mountainous areas, earthquakes can trigger landslides that cause further damage.

1. **What may cause buildings to sink into the ground during an earthquake?**

   A The shaking of particles of gravel or sand

   B Broken gas pipes

   C Weak structures

   D Landslides

Tip

Find the sentence that tells about buildings sinking. What does the sentence describe?

2. **What is this passage mainly about?**

   J The causes of earthquakes

   K The effects of earthquakes

   L Safety measures to take during an earthquake

   M Staying calm during an earthquake

Tip

Look at the whole paragraph. What kinds of facts are used to organize the paragraph?

▲ **Dive! My Adventures in the Deep Frontier**

- buoyancy
- gauge
- acoustic
- diversity
- abounded
- salvage
- dissipate

Vocabulary Power

Scientists such as the woman you will meet in the next selection explore every corner of our world. Some of these modern-day explorers even travel into space.

These astronauts float inside their spacecraft because they're weightless in space. They practiced for this on Earth, using their **buoyancy** in a tank of water. One of them studies a **gauge** that measures the amount of air in their cabin. Later they will test their **acoustic** ability to see if they hear normally in space.

There is a great **diversity** of plants and animals in the world's rain forests. Before logging of the trees began, countless numbers of plants and animals **abounded** there. They filled the land, water, and sky. Now scientists hope to **salvage** the damaged forests and save the remaining wildlife from destruction.

Every year scientists from all over the world visit Antarctica. Some of them study information collected by a giant telescope. Others work to learn why the ozone layer of Earth's atmosphere is beginning to **dissipate**, or become thinner, above Antarctica.

Vocabulary-Writing CONNECTION

The great **diversity** of life in the oceans includes many unknown animals. Imagine that on a visit to the seashore you discover a new type of animal. Write a list of the characteristics of this new creature.

Genre

Nonfiction

Nonfiction tells about people, things, events, or places that are real.

In this selection, look for

- **First-person point of view**

- **Information shared through the author's own experiences**

- **The use of vivid words and details**

If you want to be the first to go where no one has ever been before, you can. If you want to discover new kinds of animals, new plants, and whole new systems of life, they are there, deep in the sea. You can be the first to explore any of thousands of undersea mountains and cross unknown plains; be the first to figure out how barely known creatures live, how they spend their days and nights, how their lives influence us — and how we who live on the land affect them.

You can also dream up ways to explore the sea — with submersibles, underwater laboratories, robots, new sensors, cameras, and other instruments. If you want to, you can even build your own. I know such things are possible because I have had the fun of doing them and have glimpsed how much more there is to discover.

Sylvia A. Earle

Dive!

My Adventures in the Deep Frontier

by Sylvia A. Earle

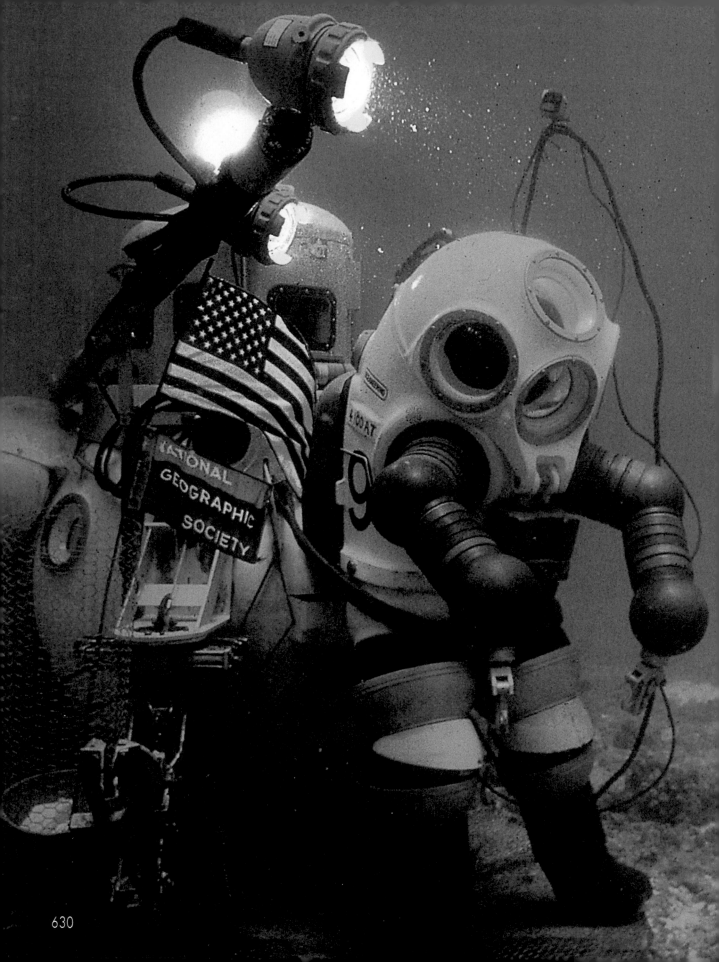

ONWARD & DOWNWARD

*L*ike a hawk gliding, I swam in clear blue water far offshore in the Bahama Islands. A large Nassau grouper circled around me, his great brown eyes meeting mine. Then, with a gentle flip of his tail, he swam down into an underwater canyon. I longed to follow but looked at my watch and depth gauge. I was 120 feet down and had been underwater for 15 minutes. If I stayed longer, I would have to decompress — stopping along the way back to allow compressed nitrogen that had accumulated in my bloodstream to gradually dissipate. My air supply was too limited for me to take the time needed to do that, so with a sigh, I turned back toward the surface. I dreamed of finding a way to go really deep into the sea.

Soon after, I heard about a special diving suit called Jim. It looks like the suits astronauts wear in space. Commercial divers use it for underwater salvage operations and to maintain oil rigs. I thought it could also be used for scientists to explore and conduct research.

In this diving suit, called Jim, I descended 1,250 feet from sunlight into darkness. On the bottom, I stepped off the platform attached to the little submarine Star II.

Jim was named for the first person willing to try it — Jim Jarrett. In a special training tank in southern California I learned how to climb in and out of the thousand-pound suit, how to put on the helmet, and how to move.

At sea level the weight of the atmosphere above puts 14.7 pounds of pressure on every square inch of whatever is below — including us. That pressure, "one atmosphere," is doubled 33 feet underwater and increases by 14.7 pounds per square inch, or another atmosphere of pressure for every additional 33 feet of descent. Inside Jim the pressure is always the same as it is at the surface: one atmosphere.

After weeks of preparation the time came to test the concept of using Jim for research.

Strapped to the front of a little submarine, *Star II*, I descended inside Jim through the brightly illuminated surface to intensely blue depths that finally merged with black. At 1,250 feet the sub and I landed with a gentle bump. A strap that held me in place was released.

I stepped into a forest of whiskerlike bamboo coral. Lights from the little submarine beamed on a pink sea fan, and I watched as bright red crabs

swam to it and hung on like shirts drying in a deep-sea wind. A great pale crab as large as a cat crept into the light, then paused to look at a strange joint-legged creature unlike anything it had ever encountered before — me.

In some ways I might as well have been on the moon, but there are no lacy pink corals, bright red crabs, or crabs that look like cats on the moon.

There may be living creatures elsewhere in the universe, perhaps even on Mars where water once abounded. Maybe there is life on Europa, one of Jupiter's moons where an ocean has been discovered. But we know of nowhere else, not even in the richest rain forests of our planet, where there is greater diversity of animals, plants, and microbial life than in Earth's vast saltwater realm.

More than 30 major divisions of animals are known, and all have some

To enter Jim (above), I climbed in from the top. Then, strapped to a platform attached to the Star II *sub, I descended to the ocean floor. To return to the surface, the* Star II *sub ascended, towing me with it.*

representation in the sea: from sponges and jellies to many kinds of beautiful worms and mollusks; from starfish and their relatives to moss animals, lamp shells, and creatures with backbones — fish, turtles, whales, and even diving seabirds. Only about half of these categories of life occur on land, but on a single dive I often encounter more than two dozen.

Although I was excited by explorations that could be made with Jim, I wondered, why stop at 1,250 feet? The ocean, after all, has an average depth of two and a half miles, more than 13,000 feet. Why not have one-atmosphere diving systems like Jim

Like an alien spacecraft, this jellyfish pulses through the sea.

that can go all the way to the deepest part of the ocean: to the bottom of the Mariana Trench, east of the Philippine Islands — seven miles down?

It is amazing that only two people in all of the history of humankind have been there. Their diving system was the bathyscaphe *Trieste*. Their historic dive took place in 1960 — nine years before the first humans landed on the moon. Since then dozens of people have left Earth's atmosphere as astronauts, instruments have landed on Mars, and cameras in deep space have inspected the outer reaches of the solar system. Meanwhile, no one has returned to the deepest sea, and no submersibles exist now that can take us there and back.

I wanted to explore the deepest parts of the ocean, but *Trieste* no longer was being used. To do what I wanted to do would take something new.

I described the problem to an engineer friend, Graham Hawkes, who had helped modernize Jim for work on offshore oil rigs. At first he told me why my "dream sub" wasn't possible.

"Pressure is the biggest problem," he said. "You could build a submersible out of a metal such as steel or titanium. Both are strong, but not transparent. Also, to go deep the best shape isn't something that fits over arms and legs like Jim does. A sphere is ideal because pressure is equally distributed overall.

Like birds in a forest, blue damselfish flit among the tangled branches of a sponge off Bonaire, in the Netherlands Antilles.

"Glass would be wonderful to use because you would be inside a clear bubble; you wouldn't need to have windows. You could use a kind of clear acrylic plastic — the same stuff that is used to make the thick windows in the giant fish tanks in aquariums."

We talked about other problems. Light penetrates underwater only a few hundred feet in many coastal areas, and even in very clear water it is completely dark below about 1,500 feet. I wanted to go much deeper than that and be able to dive at night when many special creatures are most active.

"Even with lights," Graham reminded me, "it's not possible to see very far underwater. You should have an acoustic system — sonar — like dolphins and whales have naturally so you can 'see' with sound."

"That's easy to add," I said. "What else do we have to worry about?"

"To be safe, you should have an extra air supply, and what about arms? Those on Jim won't work below about 1,500 feet. What about having mechanical arms?"

The more we talked, the more real the idea became. The first step would be to start with a basic design. Building a small, clear, spherical submersible with mechanical arms and a generous supply of air seemed a logical place to begin.

Deep Rover soon became more than a dream.

Graham and I started a submarine company and found an ally in a fellow explorer, Phil Nuytten. Four years and a lot of hard work later, I looked through the clear, curved acrylic dome of the first *Deep Rover*. Our company, Deep Ocean Engineering, built the little sub; Phil's company, Can Dive Services, owned it. Graham, Phil, and I were the first to use it for its deepest dives — to 3,000 feet. There was still a long way to go to get seven miles down, but we were heading in the right direction.

As I descended into a dark sea several miles offshore from San Diego, California, thousands of small creatures flowing over *Deep Rover*'s sphere sparkled with blue-green light. Like falling into a galaxy, I thought.

In my dream machine, the submersible Deep Rover, *I explored deep reefs in the Bahamas.*

*Lights from a submersible illuminate
a deep reef in the Bahamas.*

I was alone as a human being but surrounded by living things whose existence was unknown to most of my species.

I reached overhead to turn a valve that adjusted *Deep Rover's* buoyancy and for a while simply hovered, neither rising nor falling—much like one of the gelatinous creatures I had come to see. With the lights on I could see tiny jellies, small shrimp, the glint of silver from a curious fish, and the translucent form of a speckled octopus clinging to the outside of the sphere. With the lights off I could see showers of bioluminescence as creatures brushed by—small jewel-like

ingredients in a vast, living soup. Again adjusting buoyancy, I continued downward, wondering what might be in the depths below.

As I neared maximum depth, I turned on the sub's lights and could see soft, brown mud marked with the burrows and mounds of numerous creatures who make their homes in the seafloor. I tried to land gently so as not to disturb the local residents, and as I did, something on the bottom seemed to flash in the sub's lights—

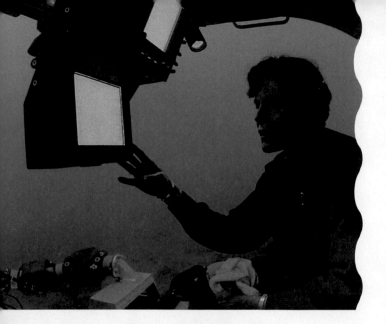

Inside a two-person Deep Rover II, *I viewed marine life among California's Channel Islands.*

something silvery with a reddish glint.

Cautiously, I moved closer, hoping I wouldn't startle the strange creature. Many deep-sea fish move slowly, and most would likely be stunned by the unfamiliar glare of lights from the sub. This whatever-it-was did not move, and I carefully reached forward with the manipulator. The silvery red, sparkling object remained motionless, and I held my breath and tilted the lights to a new angle. Suddenly I knew what it was. A soda can!

It was not really a surprise. Whatever gets tossed into the sea doesn't just go away; it settles down in some other place, out of sight but not really gone. Some bits of junk are quietly being transformed into homes for sponges and small fish, like miniature shipwrecks in the sea, but I felt like apologizing on behalf of my species for raining debris on the unsuspecting communities of life in the deep.

THINK and RESPOND

1 What was the main problem that kept the author from exploring the **diversity** of life in the deepest parts of the ocean?

2 How did the photographs and captions help you as you read the selection?

3 Why do you think the author compares underwater exploration to space exploration?

4 After reading this selection, would you like to be an underwater explorer? Explain your answer.

5 What reading strategies did you use to help you understand this selection? When did you use them?

SYLVIA EARLE

Sylvia Earle is one of the world's leading oceanographers. She has traveled to the ocean's deepest valleys, discovering new life forms along the way. Earle's fame grew when she headed a team of female researchers who lived 50 feet underwater for two weeks. This underwater expedition heightened her appreciation of the ocean's living treasures. "I'm changed forever because I lived underwater for two weeks in 1970. I wish that everybody could go live underwater if only for a day," she said.

When Sylvia Earle speaks to young people, she challenges them with these words: "Anyone can put on a magic faceplate and go into the sea. There is so much new to find. I hope you can all go there."

Some Like

from **Contact Kids** magazine

When Curry and his staff aren't checking coral reefs, they might be examining historic shipwrecks.

It Wet!

Richard Curry is all wet. That's because 95 percent of his "office" is underwater! Biscayne is one of America's five undersea national parks. Curry spends much of his time studying and repairing the park's coral reefs: underwater ridges that are home to fish, plants, and other marine life.

Lots of things can be dangerous to the coral reefs. "Anchors that drop on the reefs cause the most damage," Curry told CONTACT KIDS. Fishing lines, spear guns, and debris from boats are also to blame for broken coral.

Damaged coral reefs can throw off the whole marine ecosystem. It's Curry's job to make sure that doesn't happen. To help reverse the problem, he started his own coral reef recovery program.

Growing coral is no easy task. First, Curry places mini concrete pyramids underwater. He glues damaged coral to the pyramids. When the coral matures, Curry attaches it to a real coral reef.

So far, the program's been a success. "One of the sites has had a 100-percent survival rate," says Curry. Spoken like a proud papa!

Curry on his way to build a coral nursery.

Curry and a fellow diver position the pyramid.

Think and Respond

How does Curry's recovery process work?

Making Connections

Compare Texts

1 How does "Dive! My Adventures in the Deep Frontier" relate to the theme Expanding Worlds?

2 How is the tone in the author's introduction different from the tone in the rest of the selection?

3 Compare the reasons why Sylvia Earle in "Dive!" and Richard Curry in "Some Like It Wet!" spend so much of their time under water.

4 How is "Dive!" like "Cowboys: Roundup on an American Ranch" or another nonfiction selection you've read? How are the two selections different?

5 What question would you like to ask Sylvia Earle?

Write a Science Fiction Story

Think about the challenges that Sylvia Earle faces during her underwater adventures. Write a science fiction story set in the future about explorers who travel to the bottom of the ocean. Use a story map to organize your ideas.

Writing
CONNECTION

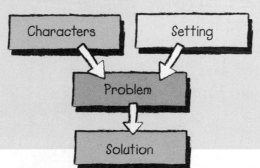

Characters   Setting

Problem

Solution

Make a Pie Chart

Use an almanac to find out the areas of the four oceans: Pacific, Atlantic, Indian, and Arctic. Add the figures to determine the total area of Earth's oceans. Using a calculator, determine the percentage of total ocean area for each ocean. Record your findings on a pie chart.

Science/Math CONNECTION

PACIFIC

Create a Poster

Work with a partner to find information about the ways in which the plants, fish, and other marine life in Biscayne National Park depend on one another. Then create a poster for an ad campaign to protect this underwater ecosystem. Display your poster in class. Describe the other elements that your ad campaign would include.

Science CONNECTION

Fact and Opinion

Focus Skill

The author of "Dive! My Adventures in the Deep Frontier" uses many facts to support her opinions about underwater exploration.

- A **fact** is something that can be proved to be true. It is a statement based on direct evidence, and it tells what really happened or what is really the case.

- An **opinion** is what someone thinks about a subject. It is a statement of belief, judgment, or feeling. A signal word or phrase such as *I believe*, *I think*, *probably*, *perhaps*, or *usually* often introduces an opinion. Descriptive words such as *amazing*, *beautiful*, and *important* also signal opinions.

Although opinions cannot be proved true or false, they give readers a better understanding of the author. They are especially valuable if the author is an expert on the subject.

This chart shows the opinion that Sylvia Earle expresses in the second paragraph on page 631, and the facts that support the opinion.

> ### Facts:
> I heard about a special diving suit called Jim.
> It looks like the suits astronauts wear in space.
> Commercial divers use it for underwater salvage operations and to maintain oil rigs.

↓

> ### Opinion:
> I thought it could also be used for scientists to explore and conduct research.

Visit *The Learning Site!*
www.harcourtschool.com

See *Skills* and *Activities*

Test Prep
Fact and Opinion

▶ **Read the passage. Then answer the questions.**

> Oceanographers are scientists who study the oceans, including the creatures and plants that live there. They use many different instruments in their daily work. For example, a special kind of ship, called a research vessel, enables scientists to collect fish and plants for study as well as to explore the ocean bottom.
>
> Oceanographers also use a device called an echo sounder to measure ocean depth and map the ocean bottom. Certain oceanographers, called marine biologists, study the living things in oceans all over the world. The information that these oceanographers have discovered is valuable because it helps people appreciate and protect the underwater world.

1. **Which of these is an *opinion* in the passage?**

   A Scientists called oceanographers explore the oceans.

   B An echo sounder measures the depth of the ocean.

   C The information that marine biologists have discovered is valuable.

   D A marine biologist is a kind of oceanographer.

Tip
To identify an opinion, ask yourself: Can this statement be proved, or is it just the way someone thinks?

2. **Do you agree with the author's opinion? Support your answer with facts from the passage.**

Tip
Evaluate the information in the passage. Does it convince you to agree with the author?

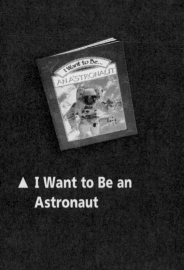

▲ I Want to Be an
Astronaut

high-tech

maneuver

navigation

mission

facilities

simulation

Vocabulary Power

People have always wanted to fly, but until recently they never could. In the last 100 years, however, people have at last left the ground. They have flown higher and higher, even into space.

This balloon flies without the use of advanced, **high-tech** equipment. To go up, the pilot heats the air inside the balloon. To go down, the pilot lets the air cool. The pilot tries to **maneuver** the balloon by adjusting the controls carefully.

This early type of airplane had two sets of wings. **Navigation**, or controlling the course of the plane, was done from an open space in the middle. This early plane had an important **mission**—to deliver the mail.

Today people can learn to fly airplanes at flight schools. These **facilities** are well-equipped with planes and instructors. Some of them offer students a **simulation**, or imitation, of a real plane ride so they can practice without ever leaving the ground.

Vocabulary-Writing CONNECTION

Imagine that you are an astronaut preparing for a **mission** into space. Write a journal entry telling how you feel about your adventure into the unknown.

Award-Winning Author

I Want to Be
★ an ★
Astronaut

by Stephanie Maze and Catherine O'Neill Grace

Can you picture yourself in a space suit? Do you dream about traveling in space or going to other planets? Can you imagine climbing aboard a space shuttle?

Astronauts Bernard A. Harris and C. Michael Foale had dreams like yours that came true. The astronauts blasted off on the space shuttle *Discovery* in 1995. In this picture, Harris (top) and Foale are on their way out of the shuttle orbiter for some extravehicular activity (EVA). This means that they're getting ready to leave the vehicle for a space walk, protected by their high-tech space suits.

Harris was payload commander and Foale was a mission specialist on the flight. Payload crew members are scientists or engineers who run and analyze experiments during a mission. Mission specialists are technical/scientific astronauts who also run experiments in flight and work with the pilots to keep the shuttle running smoothly.

Whether you hope to fly the shuttle or to supervise experiments on board, taking math and science courses now will help you prepare. These two astronauts studied hard to get into the space program. Harris earned a doctorate of medicine at Texas Tech. Foale earned a doctorate in astrophysics from Cambridge University in England.

Education is essential for astronauts. Fields in which they train include mathematics, astronomy, engineering, geology,

chemistry, biology, physics, and electronics. Although you don't have to be a championship athlete, fitness is important, too. You must be in top physical condition to go into space, so prepare your body with healthful food and exercise.

(LIVING IN SPACE ☀

In space you have to take care of yourself as you do on Earth—but it's more difficult. Right, astronaut William B. Lenoir, an electrical engineer by training, tries his hand at being a barber. He trims the sideburns of space shuttle *Columbia*'s pilot, Robert F. Overmyer, during a mission in 1982. Aboard *Endeavour* in 1992, Japanese astronaut Mamoru Mohri (below) lathers up for a dry shampoo.

Washing your hair, brushing your teeth, having a snack, going to the bathroom, getting some exercise, or taking a snooze all sound like ordinary things to do, don't they? How about performing all those daily tasks while you're weightless—and the tools you need to use

are weightless, too? That's the challenge astronauts deal with every day while they're on a mission. They use lots of straps to hold things down. Even the toilet has a seatbelt!

Of course, weightlessness can be fun. Sometimes astronauts fool around a bit when they're relaxing during a mission. Astronauts Daniel W. Bursch and Frank L. Culbertson did as they brushed

their teeth before going to bed aboard the space shuttle *Discovery* one evening in 1993 (below). No, Culbertson isn't standing on his head. He's floating upside down! In the background you can see sleep restraints attached to the wall. The straps will keep the astronauts from floating around the cabin while they're sleeping.

It takes many years of training to become an astronaut. After they are selected, astronauts-to-be train at facilities in Texas, Alabama, and Florida. At the Weightless Environment Training Facility, part of the Lyndon B. Johnson Space Center in Houston, trainees learn everything they need to know to do their extravehicular jobs correctly in zero-gravity conditions in space. Astronauts-in-training wearing extravehicular mobility units (EMUs)—the suits that make it possible to survive outside a space-craft—practice for the Hubble Space Telescope repair mission (see photo below). They may look as if they're in space but they're not. The bubbles—and the diver in the background—are clear signals that they are underwater. Working conditions in the giant pool are like those that the astronauts would find in space. This helps them learn how to

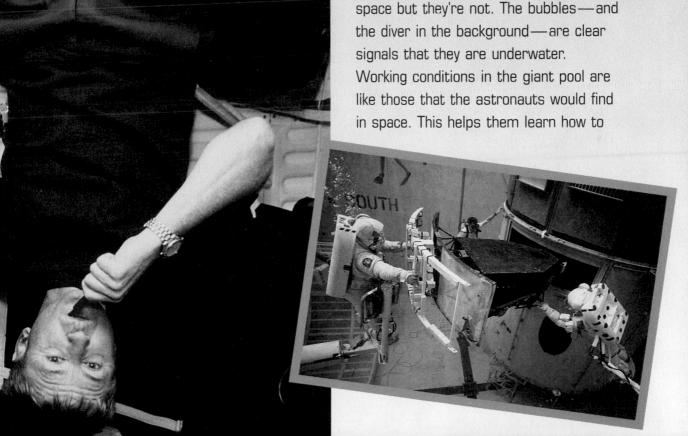

maneuver and to use tools in the bulky space suits.

Trips in a modified jet airplane give astronauts-in-training a chance to actually experience the feeling of weightlessness—if only for a few seconds. The airplane produces weightlessness by diving from thirty-five thousand to twenty-four thousand feet. *Zoom!* People inside are weightless for about twenty seconds during the dive. One of the side effects of this training is airsickness. Some astronauts feel queasy in weightless conditions during missions in space, too. But they get used to it and feel better after a while. During training, the nose dives may be repeated as often as forty times in one day. Riding a roller coaster must seem pretty tame after that!

Astronauts prepare for many different situations they might encounter if their craft landed somewhere other than at a fully equipped space center. Below, astronaut Mae C. Jemison—who in 1992 became the first African American woman in space when she flew on the space shuttle *Endeavour*—takes part in land survival training. Astronaut candidates learn parachute jumping, scuba diving, and sea survival skills, too. When they finally lift off, they are ready to deal with just about anything.

Practicing the checklist run-through in a shuttle cockpit simulator are Charles F. Bolden, Jr. and NASA's Steven A. Nesbitt.

EDUCATION AND ☾ TRAINING ✳

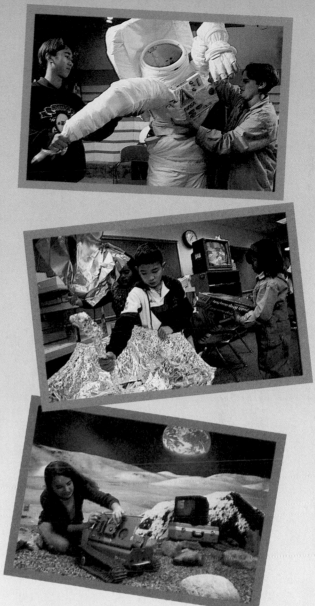

Student Liana Lorigo manipulates a lunar robot, which she built at the Massachusetts Institute of Technology's Artificial Intelligence Lab.

You don't have to wait until college to learn more about space science. Tell your teacher or principal about the National Aeronautics and Space Administration's (NASA) Teacher Resource Centers, a nonprofit program that provides videotapes, slides, computer software, and other materials about the space program to schools. Many spaceflight centers, universities, and science-and-technology museums offer hands-on programs for kids. Top right, students from E. Brooke Lee Middle School in Silver Spring, Maryland, try on a space suit at NASA's Goddard Space Flight Center in Maryland. Goddard was the first major U.S. spaceflight lab. It has been operating since 1959. Other students at Patrick Henry Elementary School in Arlington, Virginia (middle right), build space satellites with aluminum foil in class. They are participants in the Young Astronauts program.

In Huntsville, Alabama, a space camper tries out a mission control station.

Young Astronauts is a national program headquartered in Minnesota. It offers schools around the country a challenging and fun space curriculum that covers astronomy, flight, rocketry, shuttle missions, and life in space. Below, ninth graders at Montgomery Blair High School in Silver Spring, Maryland, learn the fundamentals of physics by building a catapult to launch coins.

(LEARNING PROGRAMS ✱

Going to camp means doing crafts, swimming, sitting around a fire and telling stories . . . right? Not at space camp. There you try out astronaut water survival training, launch your own model rocket, and take part in a simulated space shuttle mission.

There are several space camps in the United States. Two of the best known camps are located at the U.S. Space and Rocket Center in Huntsville, Alabama, and in Florida near NASA's Kennedy Space Center. At space camp you learn about the space program and the science of spaceflight. But the programs involve more than that. Space camps focus on teamwork and problem-solving ability, too—skills astronauts need.

Students in Charleston, South Carolina, who got involved with NASA's Can Do program actually launched experiments into space. Their experiments were loaded into one of the shuttles' "Get Away Special" (GAS) cans, which NASA provides for special educational and research purposes. Their work went into space aboard the space shuttle *Endeavour* in 1993.

A space camper tries out a reduced gravity chair.

Below, high school students at NASA's Ames Research Center in Mountain View, California, wear special glasses to observe heat patterns from sources out in the universe.

(CHALLENGER ✸ LEARNING CENTER

In 1986 the space shuttle *Challenger* exploded seventy-three seconds after blastoff. Seven astronauts—among them Christa McAuliffe, the first teacher to prepare for spaceflight—died. After the disaster the families of the seven astronauts did not turn their backs on the space program. Instead, they founded an education program in memory of the *Challenger* crew.

The program, called the Challenger Center, uses space exploration to get kids excited about science, math, and technology. It also encourages young people to pursue careers that use those skills—like becoming an astronaut.

The Challenger Center experience begins in the classroom. Student crews prepare for a simulation of a space mission. They do team assignments in navigation, communication, life support, and space-probe assembly.

The mission itself takes place at one of twenty-five learning centers located in science museums, schools, and other educational institutions throughout the United States and Canada—including

Below, Maria Ibarra checks Jacqueline Zacatales's blood pressure. In space, astronauts monitor their bodies—so Challenger Center students do, too.

The shuttle flight deck is command central during a simulated mission. Above, communications officer Trang Phan unloads data from a computer.

the Challenger Research, Development & Training Center in Washington, D.C., shown on these pages. During their simulated spaceflights, students may launch a space probe into the tail of a comet, land on the Moon, relieve a research team stationed on Mars, or study Earth's environment from space. Student crews work in mission control and aboard a model spacecraft. It's very realistic!

The students in these photographs go to Bailey Elementary School for the Arts and Sciences in Fairfax, Virginia. Above right, classmates John Paez and Michael Osorto work with a glove-box laboratory that's free of contaminants. They're examining rocks and other substances for radioactivity and magnetism. Meanwhile, Trang Phan, wearing a headset, serves as a communications officer, linking the space station with mission control.

The thousands of young people who take part in Challenger Center programs every year share the mission of astronauts on *Challenger*'s last flight—to learn, to explore, and to inspire.

Think and Respond

1. How is living in space different from living on Earth?

2. What kinds of information do you find under the headings on pages 648–652 compared to the information under the headings on pages 653–657?

3. What is the author's purpose in writing this selection? How do you know?

4. After reading this selection, are you interested in becoming an astronaut and being part of a space **mission**? Explain your answer.

5. What strategy helped you read this selection? When did you use it?

What It's Like up There

An interview with Astronaut Franklin Chang-Diaz

Astronaut Franklin Chang-Diaz spent his boyhood in Costa Rica imagining what life in space might be like.

But nothing could have prepared him for the awesome beauty of the view from a space shuttle. "Our planet dominates the view," says Chang-Diaz. "You can see a lot of features on the ground, but the most interesting one is Earth's atmosphere. It looks like a veneer of dust on a big blue jewel. How easy it would be to wipe off that dust . . . but think about the consequences. It makes you think about the fragility of the planet and how much we need to take care of it. Each of us is a citizen of this planet, not of a country.

"If you want to spend time looking at the sky when you're on the shuttle, you have to wear goggles in the daytime," says Chang-Diaz. On a shuttle orbiting Earth, the sun rises and sets every forty-five minutes. It's easy for astronauts to get confused by the constant day-night action, but they come prepared. "We condition ourselves to this change on Earth through a new program that uses very intense light." By being exposed to the same amounts of strong light they'll experience on the shuttle, the astronauts' bodies adjust before they take off. "On Earth, people live by circadian rhythm, which goes along with morning and evening," Chang-Diaz explains. "When the sun rises, you get up. When it sets, you go to bed, more or less. It can get weird when the sun rises and sets so often."

In space Chang-Diaz wears a watch set to the time in Houston, where he lives and where the shuttle's control center is. "It helps to keep track of what's happening on the ground," he says. Meanwhile his life is organized by the folks at Houston Space Center. They set a wake-up alarm in Chang-Diaz's computer, but rouse all the astronauts beforehand with a musical selection of some kind. "It might be 'Happy Birthday,' or country-and-western, or a marching song from one of our schools. They like to get us laughing—and moving." After that,

Chang-Diaz aboard the shuttle *Columbia*

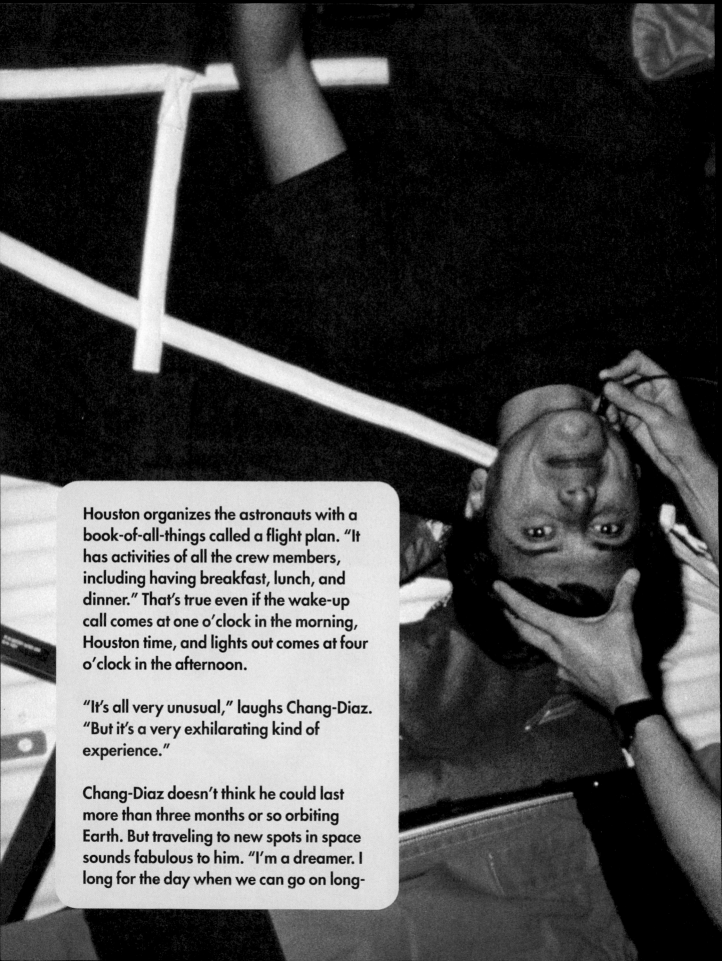

Houston organizes the astronauts with a book-of-all-things called a flight plan. "It has activities of all the crew members, including having breakfast, lunch, and dinner." That's true even if the wake-up call comes at one o'clock in the morning, Houston time, and lights out comes at four o'clock in the afternoon.

"It's all very unusual," laughs Chang-Diaz. "But it's a very exhilarating kind of experience."

Chang-Diaz doesn't think he could last more than three months or so orbiting Earth. But traveling to new spots in space sounds fabulous to him. "I'm a dreamer. I long for the day when we can go on long-

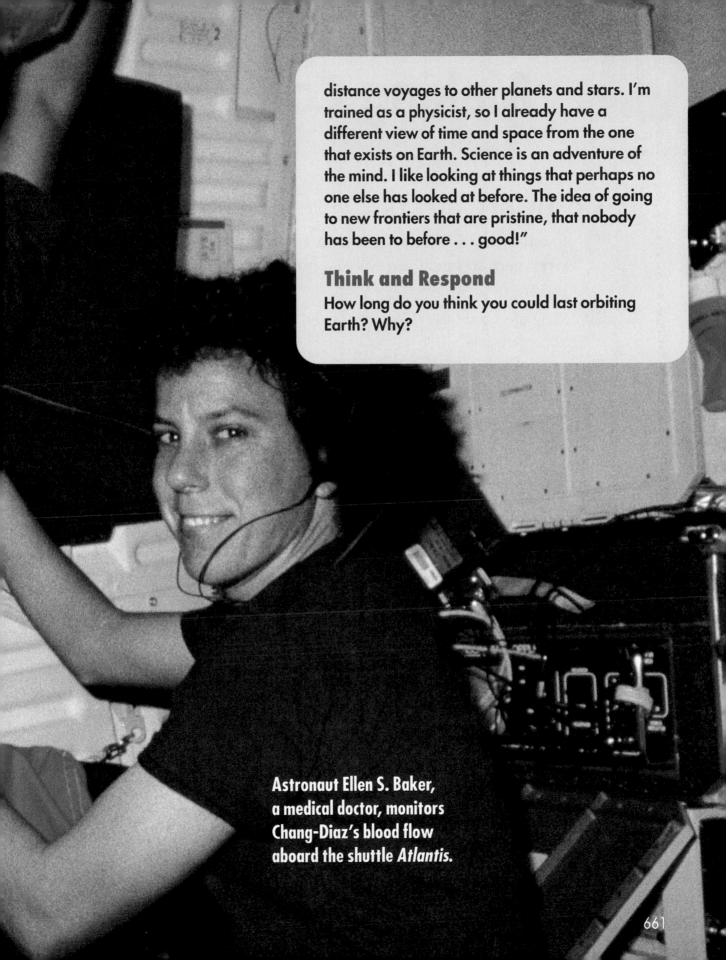

distance voyages to other planets and stars. I'm trained as a physicist, so I already have a different view of time and space from the one that exists on Earth. Science is an adventure of the mind. I like looking at things that perhaps no one else has looked at before. The idea of going to new frontiers that are pristine, that nobody has been to before . . . good!"

Think and Respond
How long do you think you could last orbiting Earth? Why?

Astronaut Ellen S. Baker, a medical doctor, monitors Chang-Diaz's blood flow aboard the shuttle *Atlantis.*

Making Connections

Compare Texts

1 In what way is "I Want to Be an Astronaut" about people who reach beyond their everyday world to achieve their goals?

2 Why are books like "I Want to Be an Astronaut" useful for young people?

3 Compare "I Want to Be an Astronaut" and "What It's Like Up There." How does each give a different perspective on being an astronaut?

4 If you could send an e-mail to Franklin Chang-Diaz, what questions would you ask him?

5 Would you like to study space science at a space camp or at the Challenger Center? Explain your answer.

Write a Persuasive Paragraph

Write a paragraph presenting your opinion about the following question: Should courses in space science be offered in your school? Include reasons to support your point of view. Use a web to organize the main idea and supporting details of your paragraph.

Writing CONNECTION

Details

Main Idea

Make a List

One reason astronauts go into space is to study Earth from a different perspective. From space they can appreciate how the sun is the major source of energy for life on Earth. Make a list of ways that the sun affects Earth's surface. Use a nonfiction book or another reference source to get started.

Earth

sun

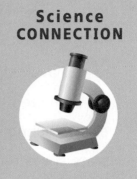

Present a Skit

Work with two other students to act out how astronauts live and work in space during their missions. Use details from the selection to make your dramatization realistic. Perform your skit in class.

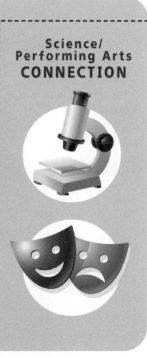

A DAY IN THE LIFE OF A SPACE SHUTTLE CREW

663

Text Structure: Cause and Effect

Focus Skill

You have learned that information in a nonfiction selection can be organized to show how one event or action causes something else to happen. The author may first state the cause and then state the effect. The author may also reverse the order by stating the effect first and then the cause.

Reread the section Challenger Learning Center, which begins on page 655. How does the organization help you understand the cause-and-effect relationships?

Cause
Creation of Challenger Learning Center

Effect
Students become excited about science, math, and technology.

Effect
Young people are encouraged to pursue careers that use science, math, and technology skills—such as becoming an astronaut.

Visit *The Learning Site!*
www.harcourtschool.com

See *Skills* and *Activities*

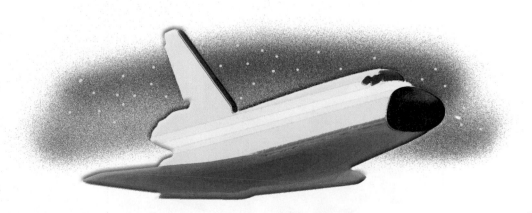

664

Test Prep
Text Structure

▶ **Read the passage. Then answer the questions.**

There's a big problem in outer space, and it's called "space junk." There may be more than 100,000 human-made objects in space—the leftovers of thousands of space launches. This problem began to be taken seriously in 1986, after the shuttle *Challenger* exploded during takeoff. NASA officials did not want an accident to happen in space. They knew that space shuttles could possibly be hit by space junk. The windows on shuttles often had to be replaced because of damage from tiny particles of space junk. Engineers added extra shielding to the space shuttles and created repair kits for astronauts to use. To solve the problem, however, methods of removing objects from orbit need to be developed.

1. **According to the passage, one effect of space junk is—**

   A damage to space shuttle windows

   B more than 100,000 human-made objects in space

   C thousands of space launches

   D a new way to solve the problem

Tip

Eliminate any choice that is a cause of the problem. Which choice states an effect?

2. **What event caused NASA officials to begin taking the problem of space junk seriously?**

   F They discovered new objects in space.

   G They wanted to build a space station.

   H Engineers added shielding to shuttles.

   J The shuttle *Challenger* exploded.

Tip

More than one of the statements may be true; however, only one answers the question.

Vocabulary Power

▲ **CyberSurfer**

Do you surf the Internet? Before you start, make sure you've done your homework. Learn which computer equipment to buy and how to use it.

- modem
- online
- interactive
- transmission
- bombarded
- barrage

Cyber Store

To celebrate the grand opening of Cyber Store, there will be a one-day **modem** sale. Use these amazing devices to connect to the Internet. You can go **online** and use the Internet for free from 9 to 5 on June 1 at our new store.

Connections, Inc.

Become part of an **interactive** world where your computer connects to computers everywhere. Learn how to send and receive e-mail. Find out what to do if your **transmission** wasn't received.

Computer Center

At Computer Center you won't be **bombarded** by ads to buy unnecessary equipment. A **barrage** of words from a fast-talking salesperson is the last thing you need. We want you to find the computer that is right for you.

Vocabulary–Writing CONNECTION

When you go **online**, you can find a site on the Web for just about anything. What kind of site would you like to create? Take a few minutes to write down your ideas.

Cyber

by Nyla Ahmad

illustrated by
Martha Newbigging

Surfer

Logging on to the Internet is like entering a new world. On the Internet, you can talk to people from all over, send and receive e-mail, watch video clips, listen to music, and find a lot of great information at the click of a button! The Internet is constantly growing. Since this selection was written, even more advances to Internet technology have been made. The selection you are about to read will get you ready to explore this new world and become a cybersurfer!

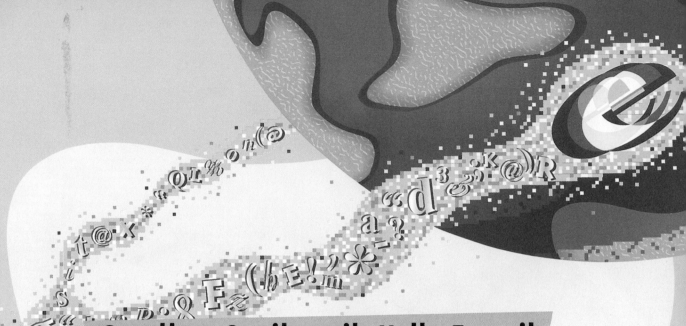

Goodbye Snail-mail, Hello E-mail

You've heard about "snail-mail," right? That's the usual way to send a letter—paper, pen, envelope, stamp. Why do cybersurfers call it snail-mail? Because it's s-o-o-o s-l-o-o-o-w! If you send snail-mail to your buddy in France, for example, you must write the letter, stuff it in an envelope, put your address and your buddy's on the front, and slap on a stamp. Then, you walk over to the closest mailbox, toss in your letter— THUMP!—and go home to wait. You could wait for days, maybe even weeks, before your pal gets your letter, reads it, and writes back.

Say "Goodbye snail-mail, hello e-mail." The fastest way to send a letter anywhere in the world is through the Net. With electronic mail, or e-mail for short, your modem can send messages around the Net in just a few seconds. Type a letter on your computer, zip it across the Net to the computer of the person you're trying to reach, and you can be sure that it gets there before you even have time to yawn.

E-mail is quick and lots of fun. In this section, you'll find out how to talk to cyberpals on the Net. There's a new language of symbols you should learn, a netiquette to follow, and some hot flames that you should be aware of. So read on, and get the message.

Who Are You?

In real life, there might be several people in the world with the same name as you—maybe even hundreds. But on the Net, no two users can have the same name. Each user is known by an e-mail address. An e-mail address is a lot like a telephone number—just as there's a different number for every telephone, there's a different e-mail address for every person on the Net.

At first an e-mail address looks like a bowl of alphabet soup. All the letters, numbers, dots, and symbols couldn't possibly make any sense, right? Well, believe it or not, they do. Just as the combination of area code and numbers tells you a lot about where a telephone is located, an e-mail address reveals a lot about who the user is and where the message is coming from. But beware—some people enjoy "spamming," or using your e-mail address to pull a Net prank on someone else! You wouldn't give your phone number to a stranger you meet on the street, and you should also be careful with your e-mail address when dealing with strangers on the Net— but more about that later.

Anatomy of an Address

Any time you see an Internet address—online, in a magazine, here, or in the "Yellow Pages" Directory—it will be a string of letters, numbers, symbols, and sometimes words. Type every character into your computer exactly as you see it. Keep the characters all on one line, even if the address runs over two lines on the page. And don't leave any spaces—Internet addresses never contain spaces.

Take a look at the e-mail address below. When you read it aloud, the address is pronounced: "newbie at cyberguide dot surfcity dot e-d-u." Sounds strange, doesn't it? But it's actually a lot like a regular address, with periods or "dots" separating the different elements. So let's take a look at what this address means—just so you know what you're seeing and saying.

newbie@cyberguide.surfcity.edu

At the beginning of the address is the user ID, the identity of the person sending or receiving the message. It can be a name written in letters, a series of numbers, or a combination of both. In this case, the person is identified as "newbie."

The "at" symbol is one of the most important symbols in an e-mail address. It separates the user ID to the left of it from the location to the right of it.

This tells you where the user is. It could be the name of a school, office, club, or organization. In this case, newbie is at "cyberguide."

In most cases, this part of the e-mail address is the geographic location, called the subdomain. In this example, cyberguide is located in a place called "surfcity."

This is the user's domain. It tells you what kind of user this is. In this case, "edu" means that cyberguide is an educational institution.

To: alan@rugby.com
From: lorraine@blossom.edu
Subject: Funny stuff
Attchmnt: http://www.joke.html

Hi, Alan! I found a bunch of knock-knock jokes I thought...

Anatomy of E-mail

You can send e-mail from your computer to anyone who has an e-mail address any place in the world. E-mail is faster than regular mail—it only takes a few seconds!—and electronic letters rarely get lost.

Once you've seen one piece of e-mail you've seen them all! All e-mail looks exactly the same, because it follows a standard format, or protocol, that all computers on the Net can understand. Here's how it all works:

1. Sending e-mail is very simple. All you do is type your message, fill in the complete e-mail address of the person you're sending the message to, and then click on "SEND." The Internet will take care of the rest.

2. The Internet breaks down your message into small packets of information that travel individually. Each packet contains the address of the destination of the whole message. In a process known as routing, the Internet chooses the best way to send your message to the destination.

3. Messages going a long distance may need to be amplified, or given a boost, to make sure they get to where they're going.

4. When your message arrives at the destination, its tiny packets are put back in the correct order. The Internet checks that all the packets have arrived, in the correct order, and lets you know by telling you "transmission was successful" or "message sent." Signed, sealed, and delivered!

The **To** line is the address of the person receiving the message. If the address on this line is incorrect, the message will be returned.

The **From** line contains the address of the person sending the message.

The **Subject** line tells you what the message is about in a few words.

Attachments are files that you add to your e-mail message. An attachment can be anything—a story, a picture, a game—you want to pass along on the Net.

The **Message** is the "letter" part of the e-mail. It can be as long as you like. But be nice on the Net, or you might get flamed!

Netiquette and Flames

When you speak to someone face to face or on the phone, it's usually easy to tell when they're joking and when they're not. But on the Net, where you communicate by messages on a computer screen, it's not so easy. And you might send a message to a person you've never met—so they may not understand the way you express yourself or your sense of humor. Getting along with others on the Net requires rules of netiquette. If you don't follow them you might get flamed—receive a barrage of negative responses to your rude behavior—and then it could get difficult to cool things down!

• On the Net, TYPING A SENTENCE IN CAPITAL LETTERS, LIKE THIS, IS LIKE SHOUTING, and it's considered very rude. Type in caps only if you are very angry, or only a word or two if you're expressing a very STRONG point.

• When you receive an e-mail message, try to answer it as soon as possible. Since the message only took a few seconds to get to you, why should it take weeks before you reply?

• Using **boldface** or <u>underlined</u> type is not a good idea. While these may look good on your screen, chances are the computer you're sending your message to will be unable to read them.

• E-mail makes it easy—too easy— to send a message you might regret later. Swearing, name-calling, and general rudeness are absolute no-no's on the Net. If you forget your manners, you'll get flamed back— you'll be bombarded with angry messages from unhappy people on the Net. So remember: "Sticks and stones may break your bones, but flames could really hurt you!"

Say It with a "Smiley" :-)

If you're being funny on the Net, or just want to have some fun, try an emoticon. Emoticons show your feelings on faces made up of symbols and letters from your keyboard. Here are a few to help *say* it with a smiley— just tilt your head to the left to *see* it with a smiley!

:-)	Smiley	:-#	My lips are sealed!
:-o	Wow!	I-{	Good grief!
:-I	Hmmm . . .	8-o	No way!
'-)	Wink	%-)	Bug-eyed
:^D	Great idea!	8-)	I wear glasses
:-*	Ooops!	3:)	My pet
:-(	Frown	I-I	Sleeping
:-,	Smirk	I-O	Yawning
:-V	Shout	:-S	I'm totally confused!
:-T	Keeping a straight face	:-()	Ouch!
:-D	Big smile	<:-D	It's my birthday!

Acronyms FYI—For Your Information

On the Net you may see abbreviations of common expressions or sayings. People use these just for fun, or to save time. Here's a list of some popular Net acronyms. So the next time someone says BBL, you know to say CYA!

BBL	Be back later	**NBD**	No big deal
BRB	Be right back	**NOYB**	None of your business
BTW	By the way	**OIC**	Oh, I see . . .
CYA	See ya!	**OTL**	Out to lunch
FYI	For your information	**ROFL**	Rolling on the floor laughing
IMHO	In my humble opinion	**TTFN**	Ta-ta for now
IOW	In other words	**TTYL**	Talk to you later
ITC	It's the coolest!	**YMBJ**	You must be joking!
LMHO	Laughing my head off	**WYSIWYG**	What you see is what you get
LOL	Laughing out loud		

Surfing the Net

Sending and receiving e-mail is one fun thing you can do on the Net, but surfing the Net is where it's really at. Surfing the Net means hopping onto the Internet's digital waves and riding the computer network to just about any place in the world. Surfers cruise between computers, databases, and forums around the globe, moving from site to site, in search of the perfect wave . . . er . . . file.

You can log on at the computer in your home, hook up to the Louvre Museum in Paris, jump over to the United Nations in New York, then check out the latest version of your favorite video game—all in the time it takes to suck a cough drop! Getting, sending, and receiving information from the Net can take only a few seconds, as long as you know how to surf.

Surfing the Net, or being able to find what you're looking for, takes a bit of practice. There's so much information on the Net, and so many places to go to get it, that you may not know where to start. Then there's the problem of knowing how to get to where you want to go, once you've decided what you're looking for! But have no fear, this section tells you all you need to know about surfing the Net—without ever getting wet. Surf's up, dude!

A Web of Waves

Once you start exploring the Net in search of cool things to see, download, and explore, it won't be long before you get caught in the WWW, or the World Wide Web. It's called the Web, for short, and it's the main reason surfing the Net has become so popular for millions of scientists, teachers, business people, adults, and kids around the world. It's a part of the Net that's great because it's easy to use. The Web uses graphics and hypertext, and these make all the difference when it comes to smooth surfing.

Grab Graphics and Hyper Surf

Web graphics are more than just pretty pictures that can move around or spin on your computer screen! The pictures, called icons, allow you to click with your mouse instead of typing in commands. Icons are a serious bonus when it comes to surfing the Net because you just point-and-click at certain commands without having to spell them out for your computer. If you can see the icons on your screen and can click your mouse, then you've got what it takes to surf the Web of waves.

Hypertext makes surfing the Net hyper-easy. With hypertext, certain words are underlined or appear in color on your computer screen. These words are linked automatically to related information somewhere else on the Web. To get to this information, you click on the hypertext words with your mouse and your computer jumps to a new site. Let's say you're on the Web reading about monk seals at a zoo Web site. You read: "Monk seals are protected in the Frigate Shoals off the coast of the Hawaiian Islands. . . ." If the words Frigate Shoals are hypertext, clicking on those words with your mouse will get you more information about where they are—and this information might be posted by a tourist office in Hawaii!

Web Text

Browser: special software that lets you surf or "browse" through the Net, and especially the Web, by letting you use your mouse to point-and-click at icons instead of typing in commands

Home Page: a page or screen that a site on the Web uses as its main base or home

Hypertext: text that appears underlined or in a different color on your screen. Clicking on hypertext will automatically link you to other documents, sites, and information on the Web that are related to that subject

Hypertext Markup Language, or HTML: a computer language used by programmers to design Web Home Pages

Hypertext Transfer Protocol, or HTTP: a special computer code used by programmers that makes it possible for users to get and see documents on the Web

Site: a place you visit on the Web, usually starting with the Home Page, that's filled with lots of things to check out

Uniform Resource Locator, or URL: the address for a site on the Web

Home Sweet Home...

When you get to a site on the Web, the first
thing you'll see is a Home Page. This is where you
start exploring a site. Some Home Pages have lots
of photos or graphics and others don't. Some have
a lot of hypertext areas and others don't. But the
one thing that every Home Page has in common is
that it says, "Welcome to our cyberhome!" Here's an
example of what a Home Page might look like.

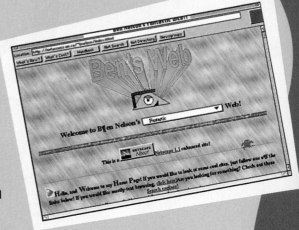

A Home Page can be as long as you want it to be.
Ben's takes up more than three screens as you scroll down. On the first screen, Ben
welcomes you and lets you choose a description of what you see: Fantastic, Incredible,
Beautiful, or Fantastically Well Made. (Humble, isn't he?) The second screen lets you visit
different sections of the site to do some cool stuff: send e-mail, play games, learn more
about Ben, chat in real time. It also tells you how many people have visited Ben's Home
Page before you—Ben makes a joke that the counter is wrong, and that a lot more
people than *that* have checked out his site.

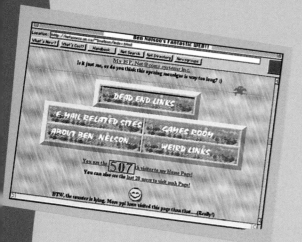

On the third screen, Ben suggests some of the
more popular things to do when you visit him at his
cyberhome. For example, you can play Hairball, a game
Ben invented, and chase a crazy cat through a large
hotel in Ben's home town. Ben ends up by inviting you
to e-mail your comments to him, if only to let him know
how many spelling mistakes or stray paragraphs you
can find. Ben's Fantastic Home Page is loads of
interactive fun, and has made him lots of cyberpals.

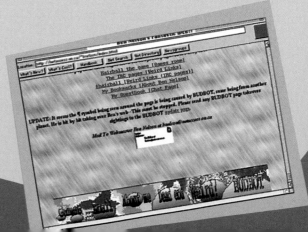

The Safety Net

Don't talk to strangers. Look both ways before you cross the street. Don't play with fire. Be careful. Do these safety rules sound familiar? They should, because you've probably heard them over and over again. All kids get the same warnings from parents, teachers, and other people who care. They're giving you one simple message: play it smart no matter what you do.

Wherever you are, being smart helps you to keep safe, and the Internet is no exception. The Internet isn't really a dangerous place. For the most part, it's lots of fun. On the Net, anything goes—that's why you'll find lots of wonderful stuff to see and do. But this freedom also has its flip side.

Just like dangers in the real world, problems on the Net include theft, intruders, nasty messages, hate literature, and people you want to avoid, who may be dishonest or dangerous or both. Because millions of computers on the Net are hooked up to each other, nasty messages from nasty people spread quickly across the Net. Computer illnesses, or viruses, are also very contagious. If you download a file that contains a virus, your computer can "catch" a virus from Japan, for example, and pass it on to a computer in Boston. In just a few seconds, thousands of computers around the world can become "sick."

Luckily, it's easy to have fun and be safe. From buying a virus checker, a program that spots bad bugs, to being careful about the information you share, there are ways for you and your computer to be safe on the Net.

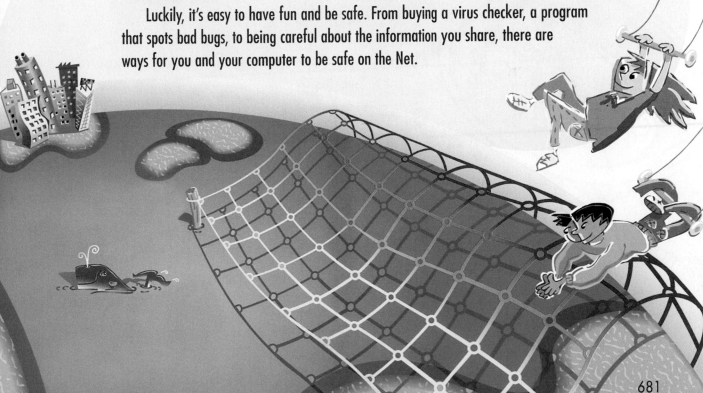

Be a Street-smart Surfer

Be cool, not cruel

Play it cool—not cruel—and you'll make more friends than enemies on the Net. Don't be mean to cyberpals and stay away from those who say mean things to you.

Mum is always the word

It's cool to talk to strangers on the Net, but it's not cool to tell them certain things: your home address or phone number; where you go to school; where your parents work or what they do; or anything else about your family or friends. After all, they're still strangers and they could really hurt you.

Go for the good, steer clear of the bad

Most kids go on the Net for the same reason you do—to have fun, make friends, and find cool stuff. But there are bad guys on the Net, too. These people fill the Net with nasty messages, horrible pictures, and dangerous information. You'll know what the bad stuff is when you see it, so you should know that it's better to stay away. Stay out of trouble, go for the good, and you'll be a street-smart surfer.

Think and Respond

1. How do cybersurfers use the Internet to explore new "worlds"?

2. Why do you think cartoon illustrations were used in this selection instead of realistic pictures?

3. How do you think the author feels about the **interactive** world of the Internet? Explain your answer.

4. Do you think the author's informal style is appropriate to the topic and audience? Why or why not?

5. Explain a reading strategy that helped you understand this selection.

Meet the Author
Nyla Ahmad

To: readers@yourschool.edu
From: cybersurfer@cyberspace.com
Subject: Meet an adventurous writer!

Hi! Have you ever read *OWL* or *Chickadee*? Nyla Ahmad has edited both of these magazines for young readers for more than twenty years. In 1996 she launched an Internet site called OWLkids Online. It was named a Canadian Cool Website of the Day. Ahmad doesn't just work at her computer, though. She's visited more than sixteen countries and she likes hiking, cycling, and sea kayaking. Nyla Ahmad loves adventure!

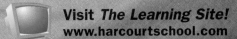

Visit *The Learning Site!*
www.harcourtschool.com

Your heart will beat nearly three times.

The planet Earth will orbit 56 miles around the sun.

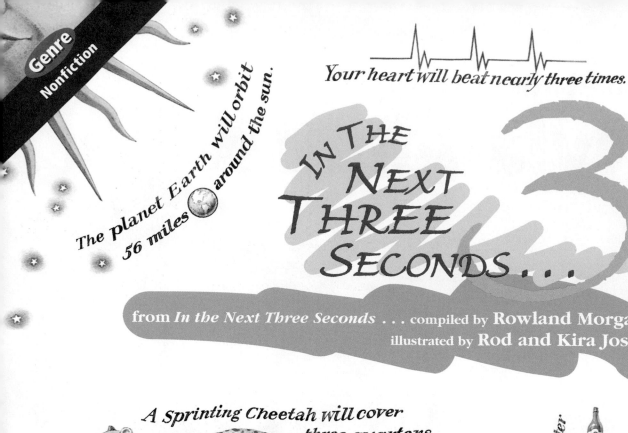

IN THE NEXT THREE SECONDS . . .

from *In the Next Three Seconds . . .* compiled by **Rowland Morgan**
illustrated by **Rod and Kira Josey**

A Sprinting Cheetah will cover three-quarters... the length of a soccer field.

The human population

will increase by NINE.

Motor Vehicles

will use three tanker

trucks of gasoline.

Italians will DRINK a stack of cases of mineral water as HIGH as the Statue of Liberty.

AMERICANS will eat
6, eggs.

95 AIRLINERS WILL TAKE OFF.

IN THE NEXT THREE HOURS...

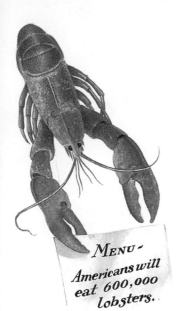

MENU—
Americans will eat 600,000 lobsters.

Americans will use paper that requires 375,000 trees to make.

More than 500 baby rabbits will be adopted as family pets.

Certain types of bamboo will grow 9.0 in. when exposed to the sun.

It's for you–hoo!

Americans will buy one STACK of telephones four times as high as Toronto's CN communications tower.

Nine OIL tankers will dock in British ports.

A butterfly will transform from a pupa into a beautiful, fluttering adult.

Americans will buy 4,500 pairs of jeans.

Americans will throw away 99 miles of plastic pens.

Meteosat, the weather satellite, will take six complete pictures of the clouds over Europe, Africa, and the Atlantic Ocean.

More than 2,000 products will be trade-marked in the U.S.A.

A blue shark in a hurry could travel 1,600 miles, or from Africa . . . . to India.

IN THE NEXT THREE DAYS . . .

FRENCH pet dogs will eat the weight of a herd of 700 African elephants in pet food.

WOOF

More than 2,000 people OR half-mile bumper-to-bumper busloads of people will move to Florida.

TALLAHASSEE   JACKSONVILLE
WELCOME TO
ORLANDO
TAMPA
FLORIDA
MIAMI
THE SUNSHINE STATE

MEMO

Enough paper to cover one tennis court will be used per office worker.

Signed

JOURNEY INTO SPACE

Enough writing will move on the computer Internet to make a stack of THICK paperback books reaching into outer space (37 miles).

A ton of wood in a forest will release a ton of oxygen.

O₂

DOCTOR'S NOTE:

Your cold virus will multiply itself 10,000 million times before causing your first sneeze.

More than

1,0,0

new bicycles will be wheeled out of factories.

686

345 pop-songs will be released as singles in the U.K.

132,000 people will visit the Tower of London.

200 square m (9) solar furnaces in the Sahara Desert working at 10% efficiency could supply all the world's electricity.

France will spend the value of 725 Mona Lisas subsidizing Art & Culture.

.073

The leaning tower of PISA will move another 0.0028 inch off vertical.

6,575 sightseers will take a flight over the Grand Canyon.

The young herb Puya Raimondii will move one-thirteen-hundredth nearer the flowering of its only panicle in at least 80 years' time.

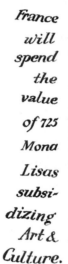

Americans will eat 80 pizzas as BIG as the White House grounds.

Think and Respond

Which piece of information did you find most interesting? Why?

Making Connections

Compare Texts

1 Do you think "CyberSurfer" belongs in the theme Expanding Worlds? Explain.

2 How is "CyberSurfer" different from a manual that tells how to use a computer or another product?

3 How do you think the author of "CyberSurfer" feels about time? How about the author of "In the Next Three Seconds"?

4 Compare your purposes for reading "CyberSurfer" and "In the Next Three Seconds."

5 What questions do you still have about using the Internet to find information and to communicate?

Write an E-Mail

To:

From:

Subject:

[Body of Message]

Your Name

Write an imaginary e-mail to a friend or family member. In your message, describe what you like about the selection "CyberSurfer." Be sure to follow the rules of netiquette!

Writing CONNECTION

Conduct a Poll

With a partner, conduct a poll of your classmates to find out how many times a week they use the Internet. First, develop your questions. Then interpret students' answers, and express your findings in percentages. Record the information in a chart.

Math CONNECTION

Student Internet Use		
Number of Times a Week	Number of Students	Percentage of Students
Less than 1		
1		
2		
3		
4		
More than 4		

Surf the Net

Do research on the Internet to find information about life in ancient civilizations. Make up two questions about the geography and culture of one of these early civilizations: Egypt, Rome, Mesopotamia, Greece, India. Then use the Internet to find the answers to your questions. Write the information you found, as well as the websites you used, on a piece of paper. Discuss your findings with small groups of students.

Social Studies CONNECTION

▲ CyberSurfer

Fact and Opinion

You have learned that a **fact** is something that can be proved to be true, but an **opinion** is what someone thinks or feels. You cannot prove an opinion to be true or false, but you *can* support an opinion with facts and reasons.

The author of "CyberSurfer" expresses her opinions about the information she presents. Read the following passage from the selection. What is the author's opinion? What facts support the author's opinion?

> **Hypertext makes surfing the Net hyper-easy. With hypertext, certain words are underlined or appear in color on your computer screen. These words are linked automatically to related information somewhere else on the Web. To get to this information, you click on the hypertext words with your mouse and your computer jumps to a new site.**

Fact	**Fact**	**Fact**	**Opinion**
With hypertext, certain words are underlined or appear in color on your computer screen.	These words are linked automatically to related information somewhere else on the Web.	To get to this information, you click on the hypertext words with your mouse and your computer jumps to a new site.	Hypertext makes surfing the Net hyper-easy.

Visit *The Learning Site!*
www.harcourtschool.com

See *Skills* and *Activities*

Test Prep

Fact and Opinion

▶ **Read the passage. Then answer the questions.**

> Everyone with a computer should have Internet service. With a few clicks of the mouse, you can find information on any subject, from outer space to your school's lunch menu. Many Internet sites are very entertaining, with sound and video. You can use the Internet to find out what is going on almost anywhere and to communicate with people all over the world. For information, entertainment, and communication, there's nothing like the Internet.

1. **Which statement is an *opinion* from the passage?**

   A You need to be careful when using the Internet.

   B Everyone with a computer should have Internet service.

   C Many Internet sites have sound and video.

   D You can use the Internet to communicate with people around the world.

Tip

Some of the choices state facts, and some state opinions. Be sure to choose the opinion that is from the passage.

2. **According to the passage, the Internet is valuable because—**

   F it is inexpensive

   G you can trust the information you find

   H it provides information, entertainment, and communication

   J you can use it to shop

Tip

Look at the entire paragraph. Which choice sums up the main idea?

▲ The Case of the
Shining Blue Planet

Vocabulary Power

Einstein Anderson uses his brain and his scientific knowledge to solve mysteries. Can you solve these silly mysteries?

enrolls

cosmonaut

formulas

dejectedly

disregarded

satellite

breakthrough

altimeter

①After a student is accepted at a space school and **enrolls** there, he or she must train for several years. This Russian **cosmonaut** is on his first mission, working many miles above Earth. First, he uses scientific **formulas** to figure out his craft's position. Then it is time for lunch. When he tries to pick up his spoon, it slips out of his hand. He stares **dejectedly** at the food on his tray. Unhappily, he tries to grab the spoon again. Why does it keep floating in the air?

(2) The space scientists were so busy on launch day that they **disregarded** the time. They didn't even check their own watches. This 6 A.M. launch would prove that their new type of rocket could carry a **satellite** into orbit. After years of planning, they hoped its design would be a scientific **breakthrough**. They checked the **altimeter** to see how high the craft was flying. Zero miles! How could this be possible?

Where is it?

Vocabulary–Writing CONNECTION

Learning can seem like a series of mysteries—from how to ride a bike to how to do multiplication. Write a paragraph about a time when you had a **breakthrough** and learned to do something.

Award-Winning
Author

Genre

Short Story

A short story is a fictional narrative that is not part of a novel.

In this selection, look for

- A main character who learns something

- One problem and main event

THE CASE BLUE

by Seymour Simon
illustrations by Leo Espinosa

OF THE SHINING PLANET

December
31

"I think this is my breakthrough science discovery, Einstein," Stanley Roberts said. The teenage science buff impatiently pushed back his long black hair, which was forever falling over his eyes. "I know this is the New Year's weekend, but I'm glad you came over to my laboratory. Now take a look at my computer. I just found this incredible website. You won't believe the opportunities to make science explorations that I found on the Internet."

"You mean like the backward space alien," Einstein said innocently. He liked the older boy but enjoyed kidding him. "Or the photograph of the biggest animal ever seen? You thought those people were going to send you a dinosaur photograph taken by a time machine. And when you paid them twenty-five dollars, they sent you a photo of a blue whale, which really is the biggest animal that ever lived."

"Never mind about that," said Stanley impatiently. "Those are small failures in the life of a scientist. This will be a great success. I'm sure of it!"

Einstein walked slowly through Stanley's "laboratory." The attic room was overflowing with electronic gear, computers, a humanoid figure that looked like a half-finished robot, plastic containers, rocks and minerals, and all kinds of test tubes and beakers. It was even more cluttered than the last time Einstein was there.

"Stanley," Einstein said, "I think you should remember that if at first you don't succeed, try reading the directions."

"Is that so, Einstein?" Stanley said. "Then just tell me what you think about this. Look at the photograph on the computer monitor."

Einstein looked at the screen. It showed a picture of a beautiful blue-and-white globe. Einstein knew that it was a photo of Earth taken from space. He knew that the blue and white were caused by Earth's atmosphere, its clouds, and its oceans. Underneath the photo was a caption that said the picture had been taken recently from a space satellite by astronauts as their spacecraft orbited Earth.

"This website is all about sending up a space satellite for communications and research," said Stanley. "The person in charge of the project was a cosmonaut from the former Soviet Union. His name is Dr. Kronkheit. He told me that he and several other cosmonauts had never been publicized because they had been doing spy research."

"I thought spies buy their equipment at a snooper-market," said Einstein. "What does Dr. Kronkheit want you to do?"

Stanley disregarded Einstein's joke. "Dr. K. wants me to send him fifty dollars. That money enrolls me in the satellite program and allows me to perform one experiment in space. For every additional fifty dollars, I can perform one more experiment. Would you like to join, too?"

"It sounds very strange to me," said Einstein. "Sending up a space satellite costs a lot of money."

"That's what I thought, too," replied Stanley. "But Dr. K. sent me a lot of detailed pages of mathematical formulas that explain how he can send up a satellite for a lot less

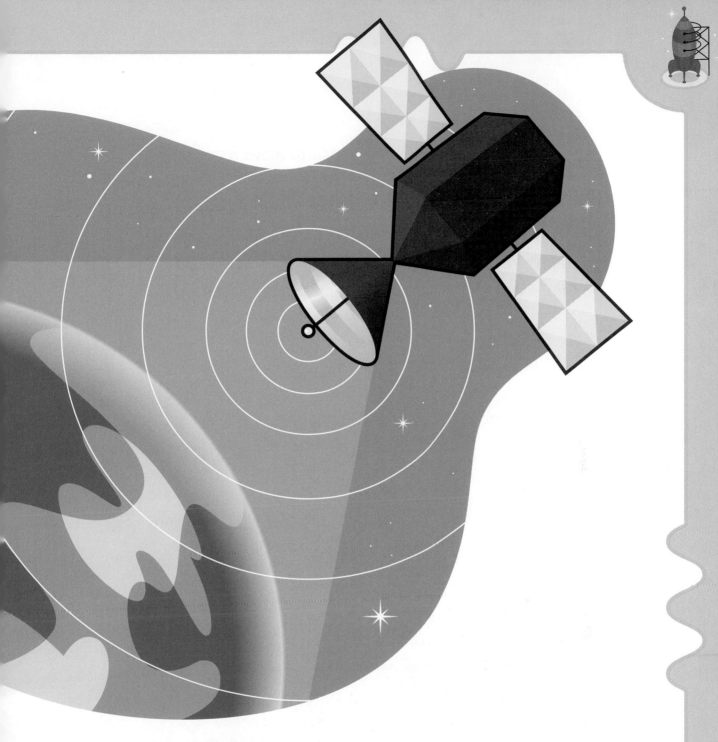

money than you think."

"Do you understand the formulas?" asked Einstein.

"No," admitted Stanley. "But just read Dr. K.'s description of blasting off from Earth. Here it is on his website. Let me go to that link."

Stanley used his computer mouse to move a pointer over a blue line at the bottom of the page that read: *Click here for a description of Kronkheit's first space launch.* Stanley clicked twice with the button on his mouse, and a page of text appeared on the screen. "Read this," Stanley said.

Einstein looked at the screen and began to read:

Starting in the 1950s, experimental rocket planes have taken photographs of Earth from the edge of space. But the most spectacular photographs of our shining blue-and-white planet have been taken by the spaceships that the Soviet Union and the United States sent into space from the 1960s until the present day.

No one who has ever been in a spaceship will ever be able to forget the thrill of first seeing our planet from space. I'll never forget my first liftoff in a rocket ship in the early 1960s. It was a winter day, with blue skies and white clouds. When the rocket ship blasted off, we passed quickly through the clouds and could see their tops below us. The altimeter read one hundred miles, and we were going up fast. All around us the blue sky spread out as far as you could see. Above us, the moon and the stars twinkled in the blue. It was the most beautiful sight I have ever seen.

Einstein pushed back his glasses, which were slipping off the end of his nose. "I don't think the so-called Dr. Kronkheit has ever been a cosmonaut," he said. "And I wouldn't send him any money if I were you, Stanley," he added.

Can you solve the mystery: What made Einstein realize that Dr. Kronkheit was a phony cosmonaut?

"Why?" asked Stanley. "The Earth does look blue and white from space."

"Our planet does look like a blue globe from space," Einstein agreed. "But it's surrounded by darkness. The blue sky, the white clouds, and most of the other colors we see in the sky come from light being reflected in different directions when the light collides with air and water molecules. But as you go higher than twelve miles above the surface, the sky begins turning dark around you, because there are fewer molecules of air and water."

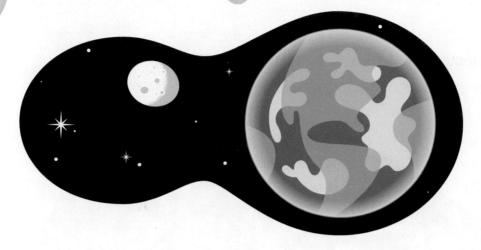

"But the Earth still looks blue and white from space," said Stanley.

"Yes," said Einstein. "If you look down from a spaceship, the planet still looks blue and white. But darkness is all around you, and the moon and the stars are set against a black sky, not a blue one."

"Oh," said Stanley dejectedly. "I guess I shouldn't listen to so-called experts without making sure of their facts."

Think and Respond

❶ Why is Stanley lucky that Einstein has a good understanding of science?

❷ When do you think this story was written, and how can you tell? In your answer, think about the important **breakthroughs** referred to in this story.

❸ Do you think it was a good idea for the author to tell you to stop and solve the mystery? Explain your answer.

❹ Does this story make you aware of any problems with visiting unfamiliar websites? Explain your answer.

❺ What strategies did you use to help you understand this mystery? How did they help you?

Meet the Author
Seymour Simon

Before becoming a full-time children's author, Seymour Simon taught science and creative writing to middle-school students. Although Simon was the teacher, he learned a lot from his students. They taught him that children want to explore the world by discovering it firsthand. Creating the *Einstein Anderson* fiction series was Simon's way of providing children with the opportunity to become young scientists.

Simon has authored more than 100 titles, many of them award-winning. Whether he is writing about Earth or outer space, he tries to capture the imagination of his readers and encourage them to look, learn, and discover. As Simon explains, "A book about nature or science has to be more than just an answer book."

705

Making Connections

Compare Texts

1 Why is "The Case of the Shining Blue Planet" in a theme titled Expanding Worlds?

2 How does Stanley's attitude toward information he finds on the Internet change by the end of the story?

3 Compare "The Case of the Shining Blue Planet" to another short story you have read.

4 How would the selection change if it were not told as a mystery?

5 Would you like to read more stories about Einstein Anderson? Why or why not?

Write a Mystery

Einstein solves a mystery and helps his friend avoid making a costly mistake. Write your own mystery in which you help someone by using science. Plan your story before beginning to write.

Writing CONNECTION

Title: _____

Characters: _____

Problem: _____

Events in story: _____

_____

Solution: _____

Make a Time Line

Einstein solves the mystery because of his knowledge of the solar system. People have been observing the planets for thousands of years. Do research to find out how the ancient Egyptians contributed to the study of astronomy. Record your information on a time line.

```
            3000 B.C.
    ————————|————————————
         Egyptians develop
          solar calendar
```

Role-Play an Interview

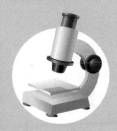

Work with a partner to find information about the first moon landing, on July 20, 1969. Role-play an interview between a television news reporter and U.S. astronaut Neil Armstrong, commander of *Apollo 11*, who became the first person to set foot on the moon. Present your role-plays in class.

▲ The Case of the
Shining Blue Planet

Draw Conclusions

When you **draw conclusions**, you use clues found in the text, along with personal knowledge. Sometimes you must identify conclusions made by a story character or an author and then evaluate them. To evaluate a conclusion, ask yourself:

- What evidence did the character or author use to support the conclusion?

- Is the character's or author's conclusion valid or invalid? Why?

In "The Case of the Shining Blue Planet," Dr. Kronkheit said he saw a blue sky as he traveled higher in space. Reread pages 702–703. What conclusion does Einstein draw? What information does he use to support his conclusion? Is his conclusion valid?

Conclusion	Story Evidence	Evaluate Conclusion	Reason
Dr. Kronkheit wasn't a cosmonaut.	The planet does look like a blue globe from space, but the sky around you begins turning dark at 12 miles up because there are fewer molecules of air and water.	Valid	Einstein is using scientific facts to prove that Dr. Kronkheit couldn't have seen a blue sky as he traveled higher in space.

Test Prep
Draw Conclusions

▶ **Read the passage. Then answer the questions.**

> Leo and Sam spent the afternoon setting up Sam's new computer. When Sam had bought the computer, the salesperson had told him that it was the newest model available. "I couldn't pass up such a great deal," Sam said to Leo. But Leo just shook his head. He was convinced that Sam should return the computer to the store.
>
> Leo explained that Sam's computer did not come with a modem, a CD-ROM drive, or a printer, as the salesperson had said it did. "Also, this isn't the newest model available. The date in the manual is three years ago," Leo added.

1. **What conclusion does Leo draw?**

   A The computer is a great bargain.

   B The computer is a new model.

   C Sam did not get a good deal.

   D The salesperson knew a lot about computers.

Tip

You may choose the wrong answer if you confuse the characters. What does *Leo* think about the computer?

2. **What evidence does Leo use to support his conclusion?**

   F The computer modem doesn't work.

   G The computer doesn't include all the equipment that was promised.

   H The computer was expensive.

   J The computer was manufactured three months ago.

Tip

You can quickly eliminate some of the answers because they contradict facts in the passage.

Writer's Handbook

Contents

Planning Your Writing

Purposes for Writing 712

The Writing Process 714

How to Get Ideas 716

Using References and Resources: Reading Functional Texts

Internet 718

Technology Resources 720

Periodicals 722

Organizing Information

Taking Notes 724

Citing Sources 725

Making Outlines 726

Polishing Your Writing

Traits of Good Writing 728

Using a Rubric 730

Peer Conferences 731

Presenting Your Writing

Formatting Documents 732

Using a Word Processor 733

Planning Your Writing

Purposes for Writing

To write well, you should know why you are writing and to whom you are addressing your ideas. In other words, know your **purpose** and your **audience.** Each main type of written composition has a specific purpose. However, sometimes you may write for more than one purpose.

Expository Writing

The purpose of expository writing is to present information or explain ideas. Some of the kinds of expository writing are instructions, process explanations, cause-and-effect explanations, comparison-and-contrast essays, summaries, responses to literature, news reports, and research reports.

Sample prompt: *Write an essay for an audience of fifth-graders explaining what sixth grade is like. Tell how sixth grade is similar to and different from fifth grade.*

Tips for Expository Writing

- State the main idea at or near the beginning.

- Develop a paragraph around each main point. Include details, such as facts and examples, to explain each point.

- Put the main points in a clear, logical order.

- In a conclusion, restate and reflect on the main idea.

Expressive Writing

The purpose of expressive writing is to entertain or to express thoughts and feelings. Expressive writing includes stories, personal narratives, poetry, plays, friendly letters, and diaries.

Sample prompt: *Think of a time when you were in a difficult or frightening situation. Write a personal narrative about the experience.*

Tips for Expressive Writing

- Introduce yourself or your characters.

- Introduce the problem or conflict.

- Give details about the events in time order. Use vivid, specific words to make the events come alive for your reader.

- Tell what you learned from the experience or how the conflict was resolved.

Persuasive Writing

The purpose of persuasive writing is to persuade the reader to think a certain way about something or to take a certain action. Persuasive writing may take the form of essays, letters, reviews, or advertisements.

Sample prompt: *Do you think the students in your school should or should not be required to wear uniforms? Write an essay on the subject for your school newspaper.*

Tips for Persuasive Writing

- Begin by getting your audience's attention and stating your opinion.

- Give several reasons to support your opinion.

- Develop each reason with details, such as facts and examples.

- Pay attention to the connotations, or emotional meanings, of the words you choose.

- Write a conclusion that restates your opinion and calls readers to take action.

Try This

Look in a newspaper or magazine (or both) to find an example of expository writing and an example of persuasive writing.

The Writing Process

When you look at a published piece of writing, you do not see the process the writer used to create it. A plan for a book or story might have changed considerably by the time the piece is in print. Authors usually rewrite their works many times.

The writing process is generally divided into five stages. Most writers go back and forth through these stages.

Prewriting

In this stage, you plan what you are going to write. You choose a topic, identify your audience and purpose, collect ideas, and organize information. Here are some prewriting strategies you may use:

- **Brainstorm** your topic, either by yourself or in a group. Write down words and ideas that come to mind. In brainstorming, one idea grows out of another.

- Create a **web,** or a connected cluster, of ideas. Write and circle a brief statement of your topic in the middle of a sheet of paper. Around the middle circle, write other ideas and words associated with your topic. Draw lines to show the connections between ideas.

- List ideas in a **chart** or a **diagram.**

- Make an **outline** showing main ideas and important details.

Drafting

In this stage, you write your composition, expressing your ideas in sentences and paragraphs. The first version of your composition should follow your prewriting plan. You can follow these steps to draft your composition.

- In the **introduction,** get your audience's attention, state your topic, and identify your purpose.

- In the **body** of the composition, organize main ideas and details logically in paragraphs. Give clear reasons or examples to support your topic.

- In the **conclusion,** restate your topic and sum up your most important points.

Revising

In this stage, you begin editing your work. You may work by yourself, with a partner, or even in a group. You reread your writing to make sure it fulfills its purpose. You may make broad changes that will improve your overall composition.

To revise, ask yourself questions such as these:

- How well have I focused on my purpose and audience?

- Can I improve the organization of ideas?

- Do all the details support the topic? Should I add or delete anything?

- How varied are my sentences? Do I keep repeating the same words and phrases?

- How well does my conclusion summarize my main points?

Proofreading

In this stage, you finish the editing process. You work on the details and check for errors in grammar, spelling, capitalization, and punctuation. After you have proofread, you make a final copy of your composition.

Publishing

Finally, you are ready to choose a way to present your work to an audience. You may decide to add illustrations, make a video, or combine your work with the work of others. You may publish your work orally or in writing.

Try This

Think of two topics that interest you, and write each on a separate sheet of paper. For each one, identify a different purpose and audience. Write down the kinds of information and ideas you would include. Then list ways you could publish the work to reach the audience you specified.

How to Get Ideas

Have you ever read an interesting story and wondered how the writer came up with the ideas for it? Just as artists often look at their surroundings for visual images, writers examine their own environments to get ideas for writing. Writers are keen observers of the people and places around them as well as explorers of their own thoughts, feelings, and experiences. Even writers of science fiction stories, set in the distant future, use ideas from their immediate surroundings.

Like all people, writers have a wealth of experiences. However, it is difficult to remember everything that happens. Therefore, writers use various techniques to ensure that they can use the experiences they have today in stories that they may write years later. Writers also have techniques for generating fresh ideas. Here are some you may want to try.

Keep a Journal

Many writers keep a journal to record their experiences and observations. They may record details about an interesting place or person, or describe feelings they had during the day. They may write down an interesting fact or quotation.

Talk and Listen to People

Another great source of ideas for writers is other people. Listen to the stories of others, and conduct your own interviews. For example, if you have a grandparent who fought in a war, you could interview him or her about the experience. Later, you might write an article based solely on the interview or write a report on how wars affect people's lives. By talking to other people, writers increase the size of their idea banks.

Ask Questions

Writers go beyond simply observing things; they analyze them by asking questions such as *Why?* and *How?* By asking yourself these questions, you may discover that topics you once thought of as ordinary are actually interesting subjects for writing. For instance, you may think that a composition about what you and your best friend do on the weekends would be a somewhat ordinary story. However, when you begin to ask yourself questions such as *How did we become friends?* or *Why is this person my best friend?* you have the start of a composition on friendship that people will relate to and want to read.

Surf the Internet

Writers who are looking for fresh ideas often use outside sources of information, such as the Internet. The Internet is a great tool for generating ideas because it allows you to explore a wide range of subjects with ease. You can start by looking up things you are interested in and would like to know more about. Along the way you may stumble upon topics you never would have thought to write about otherwise.

Read

One of the most useful techniques for generating ideas, as well as for becoming a good writer, is simply reading. By reading other people's creative works you gain an understanding of what makes a story interesting. By reading newspaper or magazine articles, you learn about what is going on in the world today. Both recreational and informational reading help writers generate ideas.

Try This

On a separate sheet of paper, write a journal entry about what you have experienced and observed in the last 24 hours. Include details about your interactions with people and how you traveled from place to place. Afterwards, review what you have written and identify two ideas for writing that you get from your journal entry.

Internet

You probably hear the term every day, but what exactly is the Internet? The **Internet,** often called the Net, is the largest computer network in the world. A network is a group of computers hooked together. The Internet is a "network of networks"— groups of networks hooked together. Each day, millions of people use this network.

Web pages

A **browser** is a software program that lets you view documents on the World Wide Web (WWW or the Web). The Web is a part of the Internet that contains documents called **Web pages.** Web pages are created with their own coded language, and each Web page has its own address, or URL (uniform resource locator). A Web page URL usually begins with **http://www.**

Internet searches

You can use the Internet in various ways to locate information on a wide variety of topics. To search the Net, you need to use a **search engine,** which allows you to navigate through the network of information. There are many search engines on the Internet.

Search engines find websites about a particular topic. A website is a collection of Web pages linked together, sharing a common focus. A search engine finds websites by using keywords that you type in a search box. A **keyword** is an important word or phrase about the topic. Choose one or more keywords that sum up what you are looking for, and type them in the search box. The search engine will look for websites that match them. When you find information you want to keep, you can download it, or copy it onto your computer.

Bulletin boards

Bulletin boards are also called BBS, or bulletin board systems. A computer bulletin board is usually part of a website. Interested people can read and post messages about the subject on the bulletin board. You can connect to a bulletin board by typing the website address or by using keywords. Once you reach the website, click the icon or button labeled "bulletin board," "messages," "further discussion," or something similar.

Databases

Computerized collections of data, or information, are called **databases.** The information in databases can be found and read quickly. Databases can be constructed for any kind of information. The telephone company may have a database with the names of all its customers. You can search a database on the Internet by doing keyword searches.

E-mail

Electronic mail, or **e-mail,** is a way of using the Internet to communicate quickly with others. Internet servers—computers that provide information to subscribers—issue an e-mail address to each subscriber. This address allows you to receive e-mail and to send e-mail to others. E-mail addresses have several parts:

The first part of the address is called the **mailbox.** It is often your personal or **user** name.

The second part of the address is called the **domain.** It is usually the name of your Internet server.

A period, or "dot," separates the domain from the last part of the address.

sherlock@detectives.com

This symbol means "at." It is used to separate the mailbox from the second part of the address.

The last part of the address is called the **top-level domain.** It is usually three letters and often tells you what kind of site you are visiting. The most common are as follows: .com—a commercial company; .nct—a networking company; .edu—an educational institution; .org—a nonprofit organization; .gov—a government department or organization

You would read the address above like this: "Sherlock at detectives dot com."

Try This

Use the Internet to find a bulletin board that focuses on a topic you would like to know more about. Search the bulletin board for three new things you didn't know about the topic. If you have questions or know something others might like to know about the topic, try posting a message. Remember not to give any personal information.

Technology Resources

Library Databases

Library indexes are tools for finding sources of information. An index to periodicals, for example, allows you to search by author, title, and subject for information on articles published in various periodicals. Many library indexes are now available as computer databases, which can be updated constantly and searched quickly.

Encyclopedias and **dictionaries** are available as CD-ROM databases. Most encyclopedia and dictionary databases, whether on CD-ROM or the Internet, allow you to find information by using a keyword search. Some encyclopedia databases offer specialized searches that allow you to move directly to an author or topic index.

CD-ROM

Intended for use on personal computers, a **CD-ROM** (compact disc read only memory) is a compact disc that holds large amounts of information. Many databases are stored on CD-ROMs. Libraries often use CD-ROMs to give people direct access to these databases. Although sometimes you will need a librarian's help to use a database or CD-ROM, most CD-ROMs are set up to be user-friendly so that anyone can find information on them.

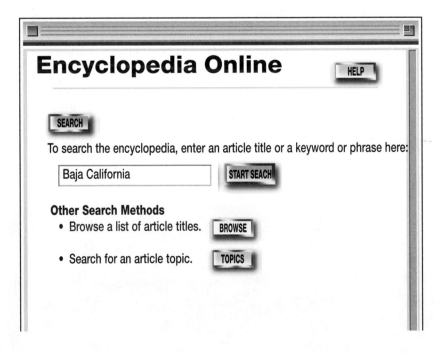

Automated library catalog

Computerized library catalogs have replaced traditional card catalogs in many libraries. An **automated library catalog** allows you to search online for books by title, author, or subject. Some automated catalogs can also search for articles in a periodical.

Decide on how you want to search for information: by **author's name,** by **title keyword,** or by **subject keyword.** Here is what a title keyword search for "California Gold Rush" might look like:

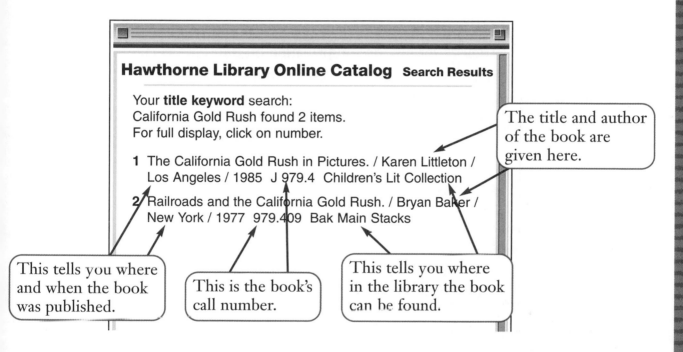

Hawthorne Library Online Catalog Search Results

Your **title keyword** search:
California Gold Rush found 2 items.
For full display, click on number.

1 The California Gold Rush in Pictures. / Karen Littleton / Los Angeles / 1985 J 979.4 Children's Lit Collection

2 Railroads and the California Gold Rush. / Bryan Baker / New York / 1977 979.409 Bak Main Stacks

The title and author of the book are given here.

This tells you where and when the book was published.

This is the book's call number.

This tells you where in the library the book can be found.

Try This

Go to a school or public library that has an automated catalog. Try three ways to search for information on a topic that interests you. Make a list of the information that the catalog provides. Find some of those sources in the places indicated. Use a search engine to find an online encyclopedia. Type in a keyword for a topic, and read the information you find.

Periodicals

A **periodical** is a work that is published at regular times. **Magazines** and **newspapers** are two kinds of periodicals. A periodical may come out every day, once a week, or once a month. Others appear four times a year, or quarterly. Each publication of a periodical is a new **issue.** A monthly magazine, for example, has a June issue, a July issue, and so on.

Magazines

Pieces of nonfiction writing in a magazine are called **articles.** Writers usually present facts in articles—for instance, information on the world's biggest roller coasters. Sometimes, however, a writer's purpose in an article is to entertain readers or to state an opinion about a topic. The main parts of a magazine are shown below.

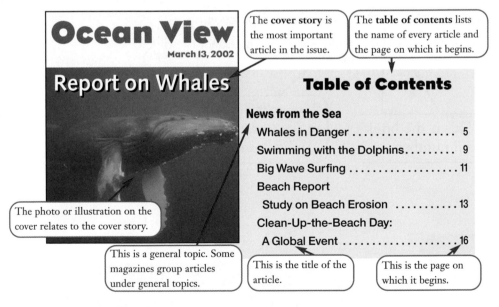

The **cover story** is the most important article in the issue.

The **table of contents** lists the name of every article and the page on which it begins.

Ocean View
March 13, 2002

Report on Whales

The photo or illustration on the cover relates to the cover story.

This is a general topic. Some magazines group articles under general topics.

Table of Contents

News from the Sea

Whales in Danger 5
Swimming with the Dolphins 9
Big Wave Surfing 11

Beach Report

Study on Beach Erosion 13

Clean-Up-the-Beach Day:

A Global Event 16

This is the title of the article.

This is the page on which it begins.

Periodicals are often more up-to-date than books are, so when you are writing a report, you may want to use magazines. You can find information about articles in the *Readers' Guide to Periodical Literature,* a reference book. Topics are in alphabetical order. The titles of the articles and the magazines in which they appear are listed under topics. Many libraries now have guides like this online.

Newspapers

Most newspapers are printed every day. In general, they tell about, or report on, events that have just happened. They usually cover local, national, and global stories.

The most important articles are on the **front page.** They may be continued on pages inside the paper. The **editorial page** contains **editorials** about important topics in the news. An editorial tries to convince readers to support an opinion. Readers, too, can state their opinions by writing letters to the editor. Those letters are usually printed together on the editorial page or on a page next to it.

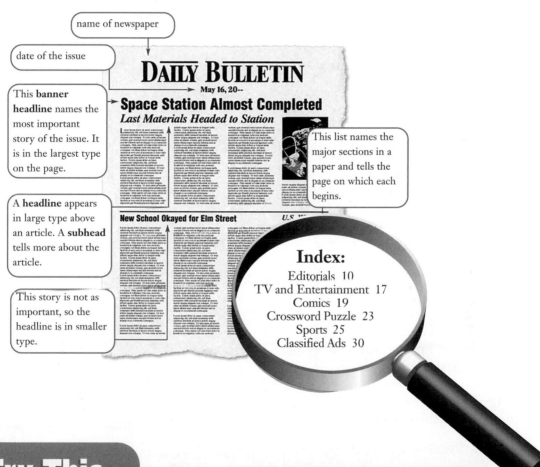

name of newspaper

date of the issue

This **banner headline** names the most important story of the issue. It is in the largest type on the page.

A **headline** appears in large type above an article. A **subhead** tells more about the article.

This story is not as important, so the headline is in smaller type.

This list names the major sections in a paper and tells the page on which each begins.

DAILY BULLETIN
May 16, 20--

Space Station Almost Completed
Last Materials Headed to Station

New School Okayed for Elm Street

U.S

Index:
Editorials 10
TV and Entertainment 17
Comics 19
Crossword Puzzle 23
Sports 25
Classified Ads 30

Try This

Find out how your library organizes its periodicals, and practice finding articles on topics that interest you. If you need help, ask a librarian.

Organizing Information

Taking Notes

Taking notes is a way of keeping information for later use. You can take notes on index cards. When you have decided to use a certain source, write down on one card all the source information you will need for a bibliography entry (see page 725). Then take notes on other cards. Use a separate card for each topic from the source. You should usually **paraphrase** information, or restate it in your own words. When you copy directly from source material, put the words in quotation marks.

This page shows a passage from a source and the notes a student might take for a report.

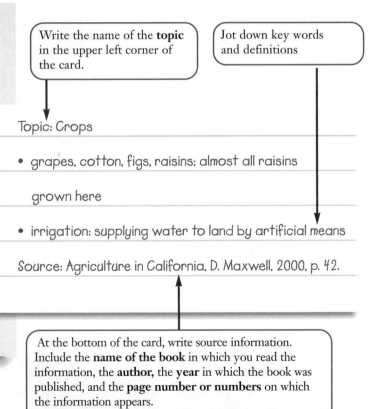

The San Joaquin Valley

The San Joaquin Valley lies in central California. It is a center of agricultural production. Fresno is the primary farming and financial city in the region. Irrigation, or the bringing of water artificially to dry land, has made the San Joaquin Valley a key growing area for many crops, such as grapes and cotton. Almost all of the country's raisins are grown in the Fresno area, and the country's largest fig orchards are there. Processing, packing, and shipping all of these agricultural products are Fresno's chief industries.

Write the name of the **topic** in the upper left corner of the card.

Jot down key words and definitions

Topic: Crops

• grapes, cotton, figs, raisins; almost all raisins grown here

• irrigation: supplying water to land by artificial means

Source: Agriculture in California, D. Maxwell, 2000, p. 42.

At the bottom of the card, write source information. Include the **name of the book** in which you read the information, the **author,** the **year** in which the book was published, and the **page number or numbers** on which the information appears.

Citing Sources

A research report ends with a **bibliography,** a list of sources used by the writer. It shows how much research the writer did and what kinds of sources were used. The items in a bibliography are alphabetized by the author's last name. Follow these examples for writing a bibliographic citation:

Book

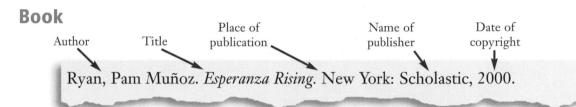

Author   Title   Place of publication   Name of publisher   Date of copyright

Ryan, Pam Muñoz. *Esperanza Rising.* New York: Scholastic, 2000.

Newspaper or Magazine Article

Author   Title of article   Newspaper or magazine

Klinkenborg, Verlyn. "Green Winter in Sonoran Desert." *The New York Times.* 24 Feb. 2001: A24.

Date of publication   Page number

Encyclopedia Article

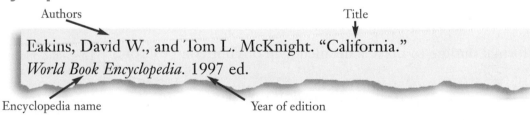

Authors   Title

Eakins, David W., and Tom L. McKnight. "California." *World Book Encyclopedia.* 1997 ed.

Encyclopedia name   Year of edition

Website

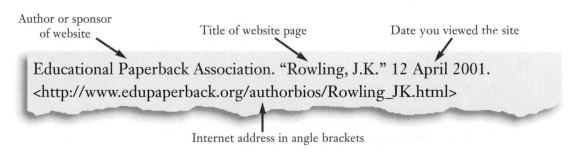

Author or sponsor of website   Title of website page   Date you viewed the site

Educational Paperback Association. "Rowling, J.K." 12 April 2001. <http://www.edupaperback.org/authorbios/Rowling_JK.html>

Internet address in angle brackets

Making Outlines

An **outline** helps a writer organize ideas. It is like a framework on which a writer can build a composition.

Informal outline

When you are researching a topic, you may want to use an informal outline to organize your information. After you have started to read and take notes on your sources, stop and use a graphic organizer like the one below. It will let you know if you are focused on your topic.

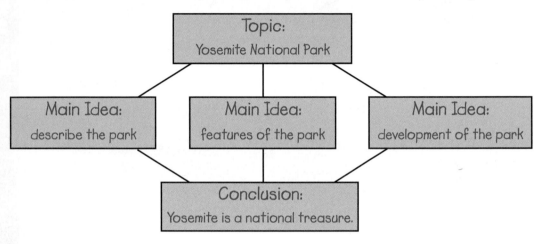

Topic:
Yosemite National Park

Main Idea:
describe the park

Main Idea:
features of the park

Main Idea:
development of the park

Conclusion:
Yosemite is a national treasure.

Formal outline

Use a formal outline to make a detailed map of your composition.

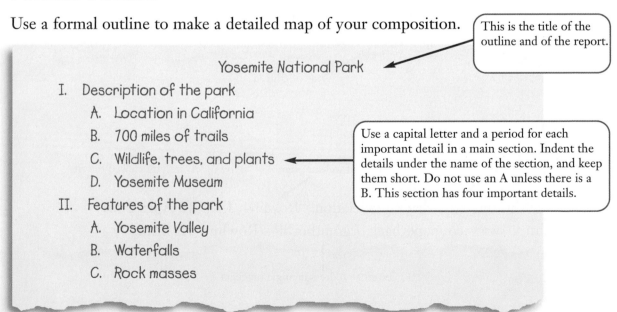

This is the title of the outline and of the report.

Yosemite National Park

I.   Description of the park
  A. Location in California
  B. 700 miles of trails
  C. Wildlife, trees, and plants
  D. Yosemite Museum
II. Features of the park
  A. Yosemite Valley
  B. Waterfalls
  C. Rock masses

Use a capital letter and a period for each important detail in a main section. Indent the details under the name of the section, and keep them short. Do not use an A unless there is a B. This section has four important details.

III. Development of Yosemite
   A. Yosemite tribe of Native Americans
   B. Valley given to California in 1864
   C. National park created in 1890

Use a Roman numeral for each main section, and write a period after the number. Keep the name of a main section short. Do not use I unless there is a II. This outline has three main sections.

This is the first paragraph of the report outlined on page 726.

The first paragraph goes with the first Roman numeral on the outline.

Yosemite National Park

Detail A

Detail B

Yosemite National Park is one of the country's best-known wilderness areas. The park lies in central California, about 200 miles east of San Francisco in the Sierra Nevada Mountains. Yosemite contains about 700 miles of trails, many of which lead to the lakes, streams, and mountains of the High Sierra. The park is home to more than 60 kinds of animals and more than 200 varieties of birds. There are also more than 1,300 kinds of plants and more than 30 types of trees, including the giant sequoia. The Yosemite Museum, which is in the park, has collections about the wildlife found there and about Native Americans.

etail C

Detail D

Try This

Think of a national landmark about which you would like to know more. It could be the Washington Monument, Mount Rushmore, a national park, the giant sequoias, Old Faithful, Death Valley, or any natural wonder or famous place. Create an informal outline that names the landmark as your topic. List three main ideas and a conclusion you could use in a report.

Traits of Good Writing

Although there are many different writing forms, all good writing shows similar characteristics. By using this list of traits as a checklist for your work, you will be sure to improve the quality of your writing. The notes below explain how the essay on page 729 shows these traits.

1 **FOCUS/IDEAS** The main focus of the composition is stated clearly, and the writer includes interesting information.

2 **ORGANIZATION** The writing is organized in a logical manner. It has a clear beginning, middle, and ending.

3 **EFFECTIVE PARAGRAPHS** The opening paragraph gives background information and makes the reader wonder what will happen. The writer starts a new paragraph for each main part of the story.

4 **DEVELOPMENT** The writer provides details about the events and about her feelings.

5 **VOICE** The voice is personal and strong. The tone is lively and appropriately informal.

6 **WORD CHOICE** The writer uses precise language that makes a clear picture in the reader's mind.

7 **EFFECTIVE SENTENCES** Variation in sentence length makes the writing interesting.

8 **CONVENTIONS** The writer has proofread the composition and corrected any errors in spelling, grammar, and punctuation.

The Championship Challenge

Yesterday was the championship softball game between our team and Central's. Many of our team members were home with the flu, so everyone but me was out on the field. It would take a miracle for me to get in the game, though. This game was so important, and I was the worst player on the team. The season was ending today, and I had yet to get a hit or catch a fly ball!

Our chance for winning looked good until our left-fielder fell while running on the wet grass. It looked as if her ankle really hurt! The trainer put some ice on her leg and wrapped it tightly, but I would have to take her place. Everyone looked nervous, especially me!

The game continued, but nothing came my way. In fact, I was hoping that nothing would, because I didn't want to lose the game for my team. I was OK so far, just a walk when I was up at bat. I just hoped no one would hit anything past the shortstop.

Before I knew it, it was the bottom half of the last inning, and our team was ahead by one run. Suddenly, it was Central's last turn at bat. The batter hit a fly ball. It was headed to left field — and coming right at me! I ran for all I was worth, reached out as far as I could, and felt the ball land in my glove.

I had made the final out! Everyone cheered and ran over to pat me on the back. We had won the championship, and I was part of it.

Using a Rubric

You can use a rubric to help you polish your writing. A **rubric** is a list of rules or guidelines against which you can measure your composition. Here is how you can use the rubric below:

Before writing   Look at the checklist to set your writing goals.

During writing   Check your draft against the list to see how you can make your writing better.

After writing   Check your finished work against the list to see if it shows all the traits of the best writing.

Your Best Score

 The composition stays focused on the task, purpose, and audience.

 The composition has a clear beginning that introduces the topic, a middle that develops ideas, and an ending that is logical. Transition words and phrases help the reader understand how the ideas are related.

 The composition uses the writer's personal voice. The viewpoint is clear, and the expression is original or thoughtful.

 The composition has useful, interesting descriptions or details.

 The composition has interesting words and phrases, such as specific nouns, vivid verbs, and figurative language.

 The composition uses a variety of sentence structures.

 The composition has few, if any, errors in spelling, grammar, or punctuation.

Peer Conferences

In a **peer conference,** two or more writers work together. The writers may read their compositions aloud or exchange papers and read each other's silently. Then they offer suggestions for improvement. A peer conference works best after the drafting stage of the writing process.

Below are some suggestions for helping your classmates in peer conferences.

- First, listen or read carefully, with an open mind. Try to understand what the author is saying.

- Next, tell the author what you understood from the writing. For example, tell what steps of a process you understood or what a story meant to you. Then let the author tell you whether your understanding is accurate.

- Finally, ask the author questions about things that were not clear. Tell the author where you think the writing needs to be clearer or more effective. You do not need to tell the author exactly what to do. Of course, you should tell what you think is effective about the writing, too!

- Throughout a peer conference, be polite to the author and constructive in your comments. Make your suggestions in a way that encourages the author.

Try This

Practice using the rubric on page 730 as a checklist with writing samples that you find at home or in the library. If the writing does not meet a certain guideline, think of specific ways the writer could improve the work.

Formatting Documents

Use these formatting guidelines if you are typing your composition on a computer. Many of these features can be performed automatically by a computer, but you still need to know specific information to set up the automatic function.

Margins Leave margins of 1 inch at the top and bottom and on both sides of your paper. A word processor will allow you to set margins through the Format function or on a ruler that appears on the screen.

Spacing Most compositions should be double-spaced throughout. The bibliography of a research report should also be double-spaced. For some kinds of compositions, however, you might want to experiment with line spacing.

Columns You might use double columns to make your writing easier to read. Columns might be particularly appropriate if you are writing a news story, since newspapers present text in columns. You might also use columns to organize information in a chart or table.

Tabs Tabs are used to indent text. You can set multiple tabs on a word processor by using the mouse pointer and the ruler, or you can type decimal measurements for tabs by using the Format function. Set a tab at ½ inch (about five spaces) to indent your paragraphs.

Page orientation Your paper should be positioned vertically for printing regular text, but you may need to turn your paper horizontally to accommodate graphics, illustrations, or drawings.

Using a Word Processor

You can use a word processor to format and print your compositions. Follow these steps.

Step 1 Start a word processing program. Open a new document file. Save the new file. Give it a name that you can easily find again.

Step 2 Type your document. Let the computer decide where to end one line and begin the next. Press the ENTER or RETURN key to start a new paragraph. Remember to save your work often.

Step 3 Use the spelling checker feature when you proofread your composition the first time. However, you must always check the composition yourself for misspellings, because the computer does not recognize every error. If you mistakenly use the word *there* instead of *their*, for example, the computer will not catch the error since no misspelling has occurred.

Step 4 You can use the Format function to choose a font, or style of type, and a type size. You also have options for making certain words stand out. For example, you can use **boldface** for the title of the work you are composing and *italics* for the titles of books.

Step 5 Print your finished document. Check it carefully on paper. Type any changes or corrections, and print it again. You can repeat this step until you are satisfied. **Always save your work.**

Try This

Practice adjusting the margins, spacing, tabs, and other settings on a word processor. Type a title, and experiment with its font and size.

Using the Glossary

Like a dictionary, this glossary lists words in alphabetical order. To find a word, look it up by its first letter or letters.

To save time, use the **guide words** at the top of each page. These show you the first and last words on the page. Look at the guide words to see if your word falls between them alphabetically.

Here is an example of a glossary entry:

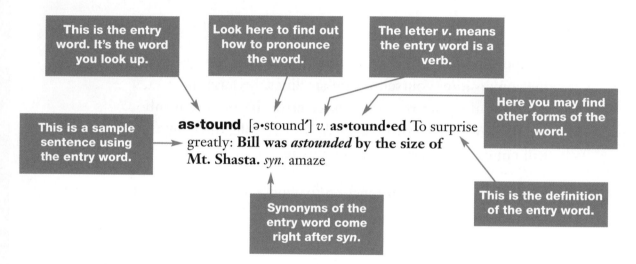

This is the entry word. It's the word you look up.

Look here to find out how to pronounce the word.

The letter *v.* means the entry word is a verb.

Here you may find other forms of the word.

This is a sample sentence using the entry word.

as·tound [ə·stound′] *v.* **as·tound·ed** To surprise greatly: **Bill was *astounded* by the size of Mt. Shasta.** *syn.* amaze

Synonyms of the entry word come right after *syn.*

This is the definition of the entry word.

Word Origins

Throughout the glossary, you will find notes about word origins, or how words got started and changed. Words often have interesting backgrounds that can help you remember what they mean.

Here is an example of a word-origin note:

> **endurance** The word *endurance* has as its root the Latin word *durus*, meaning "hard." The word *durable*, meaning "long-lasting," also has this root. The meanings of both these words fit with the idea of something tough or hard.

Pronunciation

The pronunciation in brackets is a respelling that shows how the word is pronounced.

The **pronunciation key** explains what the symbols in a respelling mean. A shortened pronunciation key appears on every other page of the glossary.

PRONUNCIATION KEY*

a	add, map	m	move, seem	u	up, done
ā	ace, rate	n	nice, tin	û(r)	burn, term
â(r)	care, air	ng	ring, song	yōo	fuse, few
ä	palm, father	o	odd, hot	v	vain, eve
b	bat, rub	ō	open, so	w	win, away
ch	check, catch	ô	order, jaw	y	yet, yearn
d	dog, rod	oi	oil, boy	z	zest, muse
e	end, pet	ou	pout, now	zh	vision, pleasure
ē	equal, tree	ŏŏ	took, full	ə	the schwa, an
f	fit, half	ōō	pool, food		unstressed vowel
g	go, log	p	pit, stop		representing the
h	hope, hate	r	run, poor		sound spelled
i	it, give	s	see, pass		*a* in *above*
ī	ice, write	sh	sure, rush		*e* in *sicken*
j	joy, ledge	t	talk, sit		*i* in *possible*
k	cool, take	th	thin, both		*o* in *melon*
l	look, rule	th	this, bathe		*u* in *circus*

Other symbols
- • separates words into syllables
- ′ indicates heavier stress on a syllable
- ′ indicates light stress on a syllable

Abbreviations: *adj.* adjective, *adv.* adverb, *conj.* conjunction, *interj.* interjection, *n.* noun, *prep.* preposition, *pron.* pronoun, *syn.* synonym, *v.* verb

a·bound [ə·bound′] *v.* **a·bound·ed** To be in plentiful supply: **The students learned about places on Earth where dinosaurs once *abounded*.**

ac·knowl·edge [ak·nol′ij] *v.* **ac·knowl·edged** To admit the truth of: **The judge *acknowledged* the professor as an expert.**

a·cous·tic [ə·kōōs′tik] *adj.* Of or having to do with sound or hearing: **That animal's *acoustic* organs are like human ears.**

ad·min·is·tra·tive [əd·min′is·trā′tiv] *adj.* Having to do with how something is run or managed: **John's *administrative* duties include hiring new employees.** *syn.* organizational

a·gen·da [ə·jen′də] *n.* A list of things to accomplish: **The first item on the *agenda* is reading the minutes of our last meeting.** *syn.* program, schedule

al·tim·e·ter [al·tim′ə·tər] *n.* An instrument used to measure how high an aircraft is flying: **The pilot checked the *altimeter* to ensure that he was making a smooth landing.**

an·guish [ang′gwish] *n.* Great pain or suffering: **Sue felt *anguish* when her grandmother passed away.** *syn.* torment, grief

ap·pre·ci·a·tive·ly [ə·prē′shē·ət·iv·lē] *adv.* In a way that shows enjoyment or valuing something: **The little girl stared at the ice cream man *appreciatively* as he handed her the ice cream cone.**

aq·ue·duct [ak′wə·dukt′] *n.* A large pipe or tunnel for supplying water, especially over long distances: **The *aqueduct* ensured that the city would have enough water.**

aqueduct

ar·cade [är·kād′] *n.* A covered passageway or street, often with an arched roof: **The guests walked through the *arcade* to get to the river.**

ar·chae·ol·o·gist [är·kē·äl′ə·jist] *n.* Someone who studies ancient civilizations: **An *archaeologist* studied the ruins of the ancient city.**

as·tound [ə·stound′] *v.* **as·tound·ed** To surprise greatly: **Bill was *astounded* by the size of Mt. Shasta.** *syn.* amaze

awe [ô] *v.* **awed** To overwhelm with greatness: **Dale was *awed* by the size of the cathedral.** *syn.* amaze

bail [bāl] *v.* **bailed** To scoop (water) out of a boat as with a pail or bucket: **I *bailed* water from the canoe as fast as I could to prevent it from sinking.**

bar·rage [bə·räj′] *n.* A physical or verbal onslaught: **Liana was not prepared for the *barrage* of phone calls that came in response to her sharp editorial.** *syn.* volley

bel·lig·er·ent·ly [bə·lij′ər·ənt·lē] *adv.* With a quarrelsome or hostile attitude: **The passenger spoke *belligerently* to the ticket clerk when she found that the airline had overbooked her flight.** *syn.* argumentatively

---

Word Origins

belligerently We often use the term *belligerently* to speak of people not getting along. The word is related to the Latin word *bellum*, meaning "war"—in this case a war of words.

bel·low·ing [bel′ō·ing] *n.* A loud, deep sound, like an animal's call: **The zoo was full of the animals'** *bellowing* **as feeding time grew near.** *syn.* roar

be·wil·dered [bi·wil′dərd] *adj.* Thoroughly confused: **The boy wore a** *bewildered* **expression when he first tried to solve the maze puzzle.** *syn.* mystified, puzzled

bom·bard [bäm·bärd′] *v.* **bom·bard·ed** To send a number of objects or a great deal of information at a very rapid pace: **The students** *bombarded* **the teacher with questions on the first day of school.**

break·through [brāk′throo′] *n.* An important discovery or advance: **The creation of the Internet was a** *breakthrough* **in technology.**

brute [broot] *n.* **brutes** A person who acts coarsely, like an animal: **The actors fought onstage like** *brutes*, **crashing into everything on the set.** *syn.* boor

buoy·an·cy [boi′ən·sē] *n.* The ability to keep afloat: **Using a life preserver gives you** *buoyancy* **in the water.**

bus·tle [bus′əl] *v.* **bus·tled** To be busy and active: **The train station** *bustled* **with people.**

cav·i·ty [kav′ə·tē] *n.* A hollow place in a solid thing: **A woodpecker made a** *cavity* **in the tree and moved in.** *syn.* hole

charge [chärj] *v.* **charg·ing** To run at something: **Soldiers on horseback were** *charging* **the fort.** *syn.* attack

civ·i·li·za·tion [siv′ə·lə·zā′shən] *n.* The culture and history of a group of people: **Roman** *civilization* **affected most of Europe.**

col·lide [kə·līd′] *v.* To come together or crash into violently: **The waves make a thunderous noise when they** *collide* **with the rocky coast.**

com·pli·ant [kəm·plī′ənt] *adj.* Yielding, giving in to others: **The flight attendant was** *compliant* **with our requests.** *syn.* agreeable, submissive

com·pli·ment [käm′plə·mənt] *n.* Praise for a job well done: **Kaitlyn received a** *compliment* **for the quilt she had made.** *syn.* tribute

com·pul·sion [kəm·pul′shən] *n.* A feeling that one must do something, whether one wants to or not: **His** *compulsion* **to eat chocolate made losing weight difficult.** *syn.* urge

con·sole [kən·sōl′] *v.* To give comfort: **The mother kissed the toddler to** *console* **him when he fell.** *syn.* soothe

con·vic·tion [kən·vik′shən] *n.* A firm belief in the rightness of something: **She spoke with such** *conviction* **that others agreed.** *syn.* fervor

cor·ral [kə·ral′] *v.* **cor·ralled** To drive animals into a fenced area: **The wranglers** *corralled* **the frightened ponies.** *syn.* herd

cos·mo·naut [koz′mə·nôt′] *n.* A Soviet or Russian astronaut: **Billy wondered what meals would be packed for a** *cosmonaut* **on a mission in space.**

Word Origins

cosmonaut *Cosmonaut* is the English version of the Russian word *kosmonavt*. It comes from the Greek words *kosmos*, meaning "universe," and *nautēs*, meaning "sailor." You might think of a cosmonaut as a "sailor of the universe."

crag·gy [krag′ē] *adj.* Bumpy and rugged, such as rocky land: **The ledges of the** *craggy* **cliffs were good nesting places for the puffins.** *syn.* jagged, rough

craggy

a	add	e	end	o	odd	oo	pool	oi	oil	th	this
ā	ace	ē	equal	ō	open	u	up	ou	pout	zh	vision
â	care	i	it	ô	order	û	burn	ng	ring		
ä	palm	ī	ice	oo	took	yoo	fuse	th	thin		

ə = { *a* in *above* / *e* in *sicken* / *i* in *possible* / *o* in *melon* / *u* in *circus* }

737

crest [krest] *v.* **crest·ed** To reach the highest point before going back down: **The waves** *crested* **close to shore.** *syn.* peak

cy·lin·der [sil′in·dər] *n.* A solid geometric figure bounded by two circles in parallel planes and all the parallel lines joining them: **The glossy** *cylinder* **I made in pottery class resembled the cookie jar I broke last year.**

de·hy·dra·tion [dē·hī·drā′shən] *n.* Lack of bodily fluids: **After gardening in the hot sun all day, the farmer felt dizzy from** *dehydration.*

de·jec·ted·ly [di·jek′tid·lē] *adv.* In a way that shows low spirits or unhappiness: **The puppy stared** *dejectedly* **at its owner when it wasn't offered any table scraps.**

dem·o·crat·ic [dem′ə·krat′ik] *adj.* According to the rules of a democracy: **In a** *democratic* **society, people vote to choose who will govern them.**

de·pen·dent [di·pen′dənt] *adj.* Affected by something else: **Our going to the picnic is** *dependent* **on whether or not it rains.** *syn.* determined

de·vise [di·vīz′] *v.* **de·vised** To work out an idea; to invent something: **Fran thought about the problem until she** *devised* **a solution.** *syn.* formulate

dis·be·lief [dis′bi·lēf′] *n.* Refusal to accept that something is true: **When Todd got the bad news, he stared in** *disbelief.*

dis·cour·ag·ing [dis·kûr′ij·ing] *adj.* Causing someone to lose hope or confidence in reaching a goal: **The news that Juan did not make the team was** *discouraging.* *syn.* daunting, dismaying

dis·dain·ful·ly [dis·dān′fəl·lē] *adv.* In a manner that shows scorn or contempt for something: **The haughty king spoke to his servant** *disdainfully.* *syn.* haughtily

dis·guise [dis·gīz′] *v.* **dis·guised** To hide something by making it look different: **The insect's camouflage** *disguised* **it from its predators.** *syn.* cloak

dis·re·gard [dis′ri·gärd′] *v.* **dis·re·gard·ed** To ignore or pay no attention to: **Louise** *disregarded* **my warning and almost got into an accident.**

dis·si·pate [dis′ə·pāt′] *v.* To break up and scatter or dissolve: **The dirt on the kitchen floor began to** *dissipate* **when I applied the cleaning solution.**

di·ver·sion [də·vûr′zhən] *n.* Something that takes one's attention from one thing and refocuses it on something else: **The performer creates a** *diversion* **so that you don't see how the trick is done.** *syn.* distraction

di·ver·si·ty [di·vûr′sə·tē] *n.* Variety: **The United States is known for the** *diversity* **of its population.**

dor·mi·tor·y [dôr′mə·tôr′ē] *n.* A building or part of a building where many people sleep; the place in an institution, such as a school, where on-campus students live: **Sal and Nick shared a room in the** *dormitory.*

dra·mat·i·cal·ly [drə·mat′ik·lē] *adv.* In a manner that shows a lot of feeling or action: **Rachel pounded** *dramatically* **on the table.** *syn.* theatrically

ed·i·ble [ed′ə·bəl] *adj.* Able to be eaten: **Not all plants are** *edible;* **some are poisonous.** *syn.* consumable

ef·fec·tive [ə·fek′tiv] *adj.* Producing the desired result: **Eating right is an** *effective* **way to stay healthy.** *syn.* practical, constructive

e·lab·or·ate [i·lab′ər·it] *adj.* Intricate, complex: **Nan made** *elaborate* **plans about what to plant in her garden.** *syn.* detailed

e·lec·tive [i·lek′tiv] *adj.* Optional; not required: **Aimee took two** *elective* **courses this year—Greek and gymnastics.** *syn.* voluntary

em·bar·rass·ment [im·bar′əs·mənt] *n.* A feeling of self-consciousness or shame: **Allowing the other team to score a goal caused him great** *embarrassment.* *syn.* shame

em·blem [em′bləm] *n.* A symbol, often with a motto, that stands for an institution or a place: **The fire department's uniform includes an** *emblem.* *syn.* symbol

en·gulf [in·gulf′] *v.* To swallow up; to make something disappear as if it fell into a gulf: **Rachel scoots under the big quilt and lets it** *engulf* **her.** *syn.* envelop, surround

en·roll [in·rōl′] *v.* **en·rolls** To join as a member: **As soon as Emily** *enrolls* **at the local gym, she'll start a workout program.**

en·ter·pris·ing [en′tər·prīz′ing] *adj.* Showing energy and a will to succeed: **The twins'** *enterprising* **efforts to earn money paid off.** *syn.* industrious, ambitious

ex·as·per·ate [ig·zas′pə·rāt′] *v.* **ex·as·per·at·ed** To annoy or push to the limits of one's patience: **The coach became** *exasperated* **as he argued with the referee's decision.** *syn.* irritate

ex·haus·tion [ig·zôs′chən] *n.* Extreme tiredness to the point of collapse: **The runner fainted from** *exhaustion* **at the end of the race.** *syn.* weariness

ex·panse [ik·spans′] *n.* A wide-open space: **The girls stood in the vast** *expanse* **of the empty gym.** *syn.* stretch

fa·cil·i·ty [fə·sil′ə·tē] *n.* **fa·cil·i·ties** An institution where a particular kind of task takes place: **A new eye care unit opened at one of the city's medical** *facilities*.

fam·ine [fam′ən] *n.* A serious shortage of food: **The people were starving due to the** *famine*.

fa·vor [fā′vər] *v.* **fa·vored** To prefer over others: **The star of the show was** *favored* **over the rest of the cast.** *syn.* preferred

flaw·less [flô′ləs] *adj.* Without blemish or mistake; perfect: **The violinist performed a** *flawless* **solo.** *syn.* impeccable

flex [fleks] *v.* **flexed** To bend, such as a body part: **The runner** *flexed* **her legs to warm up before the race.**

flood·plain [flud′plān′] *n.* A low, flat area on each side of a river that gets flooded if the river's level rises: **Because the** *floodplain* **is fertile, it is good for farming.**

flour·ish [flûr′ish] *n.* Showy display in doing anything: **The musician ended his act with a** *flourish*, **and the crowd applauded loudly.**

flus·ter [flus′tər] *n.* A state of being upset: **Rushing to the airport put Steve's parents into their usual** *fluster*. *syn.* tizzy

forge [fôrj] *n.* A place where metal is heated and worked into shapes: **The blacksmith heats iron until it is red-hot and shapes it into useful objects at his** *forge*. *syn.* smithy

forge

for·mu·la [fôr′myə·lə] *n.* **for·mu·las** An arrangement of symbols used for a mathematical statement or a chemical compound: **I had to memorize six math** *formulas* **for homework.**

foun·da·tion [foun·dā′shən] *n.* A base that supports a building: **The** *foundation* **of this house is cement, but the house itself is made of wood.** *syn.* groundwork

fran·tic [fran′tik] *adj.* Wild with anger or pain; furious: **The bees became** *frantic* **when the bear approached their hive.** *syn.* desperate

full-fledged [fŏŏl′-flejd′] *adj.* Fully developed and ready to operate at full capacity: **Karen practiced at the skating rink until she became a** *full-fledged* **figure skater.**

fume [fyŏŏm] *v.* **fumed** To feel anger or annoyance: **Don** *fumed* **when he found out that Lee had lost his favorite book.** *syn.* seethe

fund [fund] *v.* **fund·ing** To provide money for a worthy cause: **The city is** *funding* **a project to build more parks.** *syn.* sponsor

gauge [gāj] *n.* Any of various instruments used for measuring: **The** *gauge* **showed how much pressure was needed in the cockpit of the airplane.**

ges·ture [jes′chər] *v.* **ges·tured** To move the hands, head, or other part of the body to express a feeling or idea: **My mother** *gestured* **for me to stand next to her in line.**

glare [glâr] *v.* To stare angrily: **He whispered so the librarian would not** *glare*. *syn.* frown

grad·u·al·ly [graj′ŏŏ·wə·lē] *adv.* Step by step: **Tammy** *gradually* **increased the number of situps she did each day.**

gru·el·ing [grŏŏ′əl·ing] *adj.* Very tiring or exhausting: **Being on the plane for twelve** *grueling* **hours made me miss my warm bed back at home.**

high-tech [hī′-tek′] *adj.* Based on the most up-to-date technology: ***High-tech* appliances are soon made obsolete by other high-tech appliances.** *syn.* cutting-edge

a	add	e	end	o	odd	ōō	pool	oi	oil	th	this	*a* in *above*
ā	ace	ē	equal	ō	open	u	up	ou	pout	zh	vision	*e* in *sicken*
â	care	i	it	ô	order	û	burn	ng	ring			ə = *i* in *possible*
ä	palm	ī	ice	ŏŏ	took	yōō	fuse	th	thin			*o* in *melon*
												u in *circus*

hi·lar·i·ous [hi·lâr′ē·əs] *adj.* Very humorous: **I laughed so hard at my uncle's *hilarious* joke that I almost fell over.**

hy·giene [hī′jēn] *n.* The daily tasks and habits that preserve health: **Proper tooth care is an important part of *hygiene*.**

> **Word Origins**
> **hygiene** *Hygiene* comes from the name of the Greek goddess of health, Hygeia. The Greek word for *healthy* is *hygiēs*.

im·mune [i·myoon′] *adj.* Protected, such as from disease or damage: **This vaccine makes people *immune* to chicken pox.**

im·pass·a·ble [im·pas′ə·bəl] *adj.* Not able to be passed or traveled through: **Police cars filled the neighborhood, making it *impassable* for oncoming traffic.** *syn.* blocked

in·gen·i·ous [in·jēn′yəs] *adj.* Creative, inventive, and imaginative: **Jenna's *ingenious* plan for raising money worked.** *syn.* brilliant

in·ge·nu·i·ty [in′jə·noo′ə·tē] *n.* Skill or cleverness, as shown in inventing and solving things: **Rebecca demonstrated her *ingenuity* when she invented a game to teach her younger brother fractions.**

in·hab·it·ant [in·hab′ə·tənt] *n.* **in·hab·i·tants** People or animals that dwell in a certain place or environment: **Gorillas are *inhabitants* of the jungle.** *syn.* occupant

i·ni·tial [in·ish′əl] *adj.* Of or coming at the beginning; earliest; first: **The host's *initial* thought was to put the bread in the oven before his guests arrived, but he changed his mind.**

in·quir·y [in·kwīr′ē *or* in′kwər·ē] *n.* **in·quir·ies** An investigation of a public matter: **The reporter received many *inquiries* about the article he published in the newspaper.** *syn.* question

in·stall [in·stôl′] *v.* To put something in its proper place so it can be used: **A worker came to *install* the stove before we moved into our new home.**

in·stinct [in′stinkt] *n.* An ability to sense one's surroundings; a natural ability or impulse: **Her *instinct* told her that trouble was near.** *syn.* intuition

in·ter·ac·tive [in′tər·ak′tiv] *adj.* Having to do with two-way electronic communication, as when a computer prompts the user to give a response: **This *interactive* program asks what you want to know and then answers your questions.**

in·ven·tive [in·ven′tiv] *adj.* Able to plan and create new ideas: **She was so *inventive* that, by the age of 15, she was already creating new toys for a toy company.** *syn.* creative

ir·re·sist·i·ble [ir′i·zis′tə·bəl] *adj.* Causing so much emotional pull that something can't be avoided: **Some people find chocolate to be *irresistible*.** *syn.* overpowering

i·so·late [ī′sə·lāt] *v.* **i·so·lat·ed** To keep away from everything else: **The hospital *isolated* the patient with the disease to keep it from spreading to others.** *syn.* separate

is·sue [ish′oo] *n.* An important matter to be handled or discussed: **The *issue* between Philip and his parents was balancing his schoolwork with his outside activities.** *syn.* concern

leg·a·cy [leg′ə·sē] *n.* Something that has been handed down from one's ancestors or from the past: **The founders of the country gave us a *legacy* of democracy.** *syn.* heritage

lev·ee [lev′ē] *n.* **lev·ees** The side of a river that has been built up to prevent flooding: **During the rainstorm workers reinforced the *levees* with sandbags.**

lilt·ing [lilt′ing] *adj.* Having a light grace and rhythm: **The sound of the waltz was fast and *lilting*.**

lunge [lunj] *v.* **lung·ing** To suddenly surge forward, as if without control: **The two dogs were *lunging* toward each other, growling and barking, but their owners held them back.** *syn.* charge

man·eu·ver [mə·noo′vər] *v.* To move something skillfully: **Irita can *maneuver* the sailboat through strong winds and light winds.** *syn.* manipulate

me·lo·di·ous [mə·lō′dē·əs] *adj.* Having a pleasant tune: **Her *melodious* voice cheered up the whole house.** *syn.* tuneful, lyrical

me·men·to [mi·men′tō] *n.* An object for reminding oneself about a place or thing: **Judy brought home several beautiful shells as a *memento* of her trip.** *syn.* souvenir

mi·cro·scop·ic [mī′krə·skop′ik] *adj.* So small as to be visible only under a microscope: ***Microscopic* organisms are all around us, but we can't see them.**

mi·gra·tion [mī·grā′shən] *n.* A large group of the same type of animal making a seasonal journey to a specific place: **The southward *migration* of geese is a regular sight in the October skies.**

migration

mile·stone [mīl′stōn′] *n.* An important event or turning point in a lifetime: **The Wright brothers' first successful flight was a *milestone* in the history of transportation.**

min·i·a·ture [min′ē·ə·chər] *adj.* Very small; greatly reduced: **Dad's toy train set had *miniature* versions of everything you'd find in an old-time station.** *syn.* tiny

mis·sion [mish′ən] *n.* In space terminology, a specific flight and all the activities related to it: **It takes more than a year to prepare for a space *mission*.**

mo·dem [mō′dəm] *n.* An electronic device that translates a computer's data into electric impulses that can be sent and received along a telephone line: **The computer's *modem* allows you to connect to the Internet.** *syn.* interface

mo·sa·ic [mō·zā′ik] *n.* A decorative work made by cementing small bits of colored tile: **The builder discovered a very old *mosaic* in his grandmother's attic.**

mosaic

mus·ter [mus′tər] *v.* To collect or bring together; gather: **The firefighter had to *muster* all his courage in order to run into the burning building.**

mys·ti·fy [mis′tə·fī] *v.* **mys·ti·fied** To puzzle or baffle: **I was *mystified* when my little sister put pickles in her peanut butter sandwich.**

nav·i·ga·tion [nav′ə·gā′shən] *n.* The science of knowing how to plot a course for a ship, an aircraft, or a spacecraft: **Early methods of *navigation* were based on the stars' positions in the sky.** *syn.* piloting

new·fan·gled [noo′fan′gəld] *adj.* A slightly insulting term for a new, improved item or concept: **At first, people thought automobiles were *newfangled* contraptions that would never replace the horse.**

nour·ish·ing [nûr′ish·ing] *adj.* Including elements that produce health: **The juice of fresh vegetables is very *nourishing*.** *syn.* healthful

nov·el·ty [näv′əl·tē] *n.* The quality of being new or unusual: **The *novelty* of the new computer game soon wore off.** *syn.* newness

oc·cu·pa·tion [äk′yə·pā′shən] *n.* One country's presence in and military control over another country: **Latin spread throughout Europe because of the Roman *occupation* of many lands.** *syn.* foreign rule

on·line [än·līn′] *adj.* or *adv.* Connected to or available through a computer system: **You can access today's news on the *online* newspaper.**

or·di·nance [ôr′dən·əns] *n.* A rule for a city or town: **The town *ordinance* states that only residents may park at the town's beach.** *syn.* regulation

or·na·men·tal [ôr·nə·ment′əl] *adj.* Serving as a decoration: **An *ornamental* vase held the extravagant bouquet.** *syn.* decorative

or·ner·y [ôr′nər·ē] *adj.* Having a mean or disruptive attitude or nature: **The *ornery* dog was kept chained up.** *syn.* ill-tempered

a add	e end	o odd	o͞o pool	oi oil	th this		a in *above*
ā ace	ē equal	ō open	u up	ou pout	zh vision	ə =	e in *sicken*
â care	i it	ô order	û burn	ng ring			i in *possible*
ä palm	ī ice	o͝o took	yo͞o fuse	th thin			o in *melon*
							u in *circus*

pas·sage·way [pas′ij•wā] *n.* **pas·sage·ways** A narrow path, corridor, or tunnel: **Sleeping quarters on the ship opened onto various *passageways* below deck.**

peak [pēk] *adj.* The highest level of accomplishment: **The athlete displayed her *peak* performance in the Olympic event.**

per·il·ous [per′əl•əs] *adj.* Risky or dangerous: **The scientists went on a *perilous* journey through the jungle in search of a new animal species.**

per·me·ate [pûr′mē•āt] *v.* **per·me·ates** To fill every space with a substance: **When it rains, water *permeates* the soil and reaches roots deep underground.** *syn.* infiltrate

per·se·vere [pûr′sə•vir′] *v.* **per·se·vered** To continue working toward a goal regardless of difficulties or obstacles: **The scientists *persevered* in their search for a cure for the disease.** *syn.* persist

per·sis·tence [pər·sis′təns] *n.* The act of being firm or stubborn despite the pressure of obstacles: **Anne's hard work and *persistence* paid off when she won a gold medal for running the marathon.**

port·a·ble [pôr′tə•bəl] *adj.* Able to be carried: **The campers found it easy to travel with a *portable* stove.** *syn.* movable

post·pone [pōst•pōn′] *v.* To put off until later: **If it rains, they will *postpone* the parade.** *syn.* delay

pounce [pouns] *v.* **pounced** To spring out at something: **The cat crouched down, waited, and then *pounced* on a mouse.** *syn.* ambush

pre·ci·sion [pri•sizh′ən] *n.* The quality of doing something exactly as it should be done: **The clock keeps time with great *precision*.** *syn.* accuracy

pre·sen·ta·tion [prē′zen•tā′shən] *n.* Something that is performed: **Our rehearsal went more smoothly than the actual *presentation*.** *syn.* show

pre·serve [pri•zûrv′] *v.* **pre·served** To keep something in good condition: **Miri *preserved* an antique lace collar by wrapping it in tissue paper.**

pro·pel [prō•pel′] *v.* **pro·pelled** To use a force to push forward: **The jet engine *propelled* the plane down the runway.** *syn.* drive

prov·ince [präv′ins] *n.* **prov·in·ces** A territory that is far from the center of government: **When the Roman Empire controlled most of Europe, France was one of its *provinces*.** *syn.* district

qual·i·ty [kwäl′ə•tē] *n.* A characteristic or typical feature of someone or something: **Rocks have the *quality* of hardness.** *syn.* trait

quar·ry [kwôr′ē] *n.* **quar·ries** A place where stones are mined to be used as building material: **Vermont is famous for its granite *quarries*.**

quarry

ran·cid [ran′sid] *adj.* Having the bad taste or smell of spoiled fat or oil: **The meat had a *rancid* odor after being left out of the refrigerator for days.** *syn.* rotten, stale

re·al·is·tic [rē•ə•lis′tik] *adj.* Having the quality of looking real without being real: **The plastic flowers were so *realistic* that no one could tell the difference.** *syn.* lifelike

re·cog·ni·tion [rek′əg•nish′ən] *n.* Knowing something well enough to identify it after a previous encounter: **An expression of *recognition* lit up the old dog's face whenever its owner came home.**

re·con·struct [rē•kən•strukt′] *v.* To build again: **When the foundations of an old theater were discovered, scientists and architects were able to *reconstruct* it.** *syn.* rebuild

re·li·a·ble [ri•lī′ə•bəl] *adj.* Able to be depended upon: **This *reliable* old clock always tells the correct time.** *syn.* trustworthy

re·luc·tant·ly [ri•luk′tənt•lē] *adv.* With an unwilling attitude: **James left his best friend's party *reluctantly* and got back home later than he had planned.** *syn.* unwillingly

re·mote [ri•mōt′] *adj.* Faraway: **The explorers set up camp at a *remote* site, far from the main landing party.** *syn.* distant

re·pre·sent [rep′ri•zent′] *v.* To portray or exhibit in art: **He used cotton to *represent* clouds for his science project.** *syn.* depict

res·er·voir [rez′ər•vwär] *n.* **res·er·voirs** An artificial lake made to hold the water supply for all the people of a particular area: **The city's *reservoir* received runoff from melting ice and snow as well as rainwater.**

reservoir

re·source·ful [ri•sôrs′fəl] *adj.* Having good ideas; able to handle situations effectively and creatively: **The *resourceful* artist made a sculpture out of old rubber tires.** *syn.* ingenious

romp [rämp] *v.* **romp·ing** To run and leap in a playful way: **Baby lambs were *romping* in the grassy field.** *syn.* frolic

rouse [rouz] *v.* To cause someone or something to get up: **Julian was hard to *rouse* every morning, and he often missed the school bus.** *syn.* wake

rug·ged [rug′id] *adj.* Tough and rough as a result of use or exposure to wind, water, or heat: **The pioneers' *rugged* faces were no longer as soft as they had been when the pioneers first arrived on the Plains.** *syn.* coarse

rum·mage [rum′ij] *v.* **rum·maged** To look for something by digging energetically through a pile: **Searching for a pen, Mike *rummaged* through his backpack.** *syn.* search

sal·vage [sal′vij] *n.* The saving of a ship or its cargo from loss or destruction: **After the *salvage* of the sunken ship, parts of it were put on display.**

sat·el·lite [sat′ə•līt′] *n.* An object launched by means of a rocket into an orbit around the earth or other celestial body: **Sending a *satellite* into space requires hard work and preparation.**

scour [skour] *v.* **scour·ing** To search through a place: **Mandy continued *scouring* the field in search of her grandmother's lost pin.** *syn.* examine

scowl [skoul] *v.* To make a facial expression that shows displeasure: **The policeman continued to *scowl* at the driver of the speeding car.** *syn.* frown

seep [sēp] *v.* **seep·ing** To leak or ooze, as a liquid would: **Water began *seeping* through the crack in the ceiling.** *syn.* soak, trickle

sheep·ish·ly [shēp′ish•lē] *adv.* With feelings of shyness or embarrassment: **The child stood *sheepishly* in front of the audience when he forgot his lines.** *syn.* self-consciously

Fast Fact

sheepishly Sheep are characterized in many stories and images by their docility and fearfulness. The similarity between sheep and people also is reflected in the idea that if all the people in a group do the same thing, they are behaving as a flock of sheep might behave.

shrewd [shro͞od] *adj.* Clever, with a hint of cunning: **The manager made a *shrewd* deal that rocketed the business to first place in its field.** *syn.* calculating

sig·nif·i·cance [sig•nif′ə•kəns] *n.* Importance or meaning: **After reading the poem five times, I understood the *significance* of the author's words.**

a	add	e	end	o	odd	o͞o	pool	oi	oil	th	this	ə =	*a* in *above*
ā	ace	ē	equal	ō	open	u	up	ou	pout	zh	vision		*e* in *sicken*
â	care	i	it	ô	order	û	burn	ng	ring				*i* in *possible*
ä	palm	ī	ice	o͝o	took	yo͞o	fuse	th	thin				*o* in *melon*
													u in *circus*

sim·u·la·tion [sim′yoo·lā′shən] *n.* An artificial setup that imitates a real situation: **Scientists can use a computer *simulation* to understand how a change in a habitat would affect the living things there.** *syn.* fabrication

skew·er [skyoo′ər] *v.* To pierce with a thin, pointy stick before cooking: *Skewer* **the marshmallows before you toast them over the coals.**

so·cia·ble [sō′shə·bəl] *adj.* Friendly; able to get along with others: **Dolphins are *sociable* mammals that live in groups.** *syn.* outgoing

so·lemn·ly [säl′əm·lē] *adv.* With great seriousness: **The witness *solemnly* took the stand.** *syn.* gravely

sooth·ing·ly [sooth′ing·lē] *adv.* In a calm or comforting way: **The police officer spoke *soothingly* to the frightened child.** *syn.* comfortingly

spe·cial·ty [spesh′əl·tē] *n.* A famous, favorite thing that someone does: **Mike's hamburgers are the diner's *specialty*.** *syn.* trademark

styl·us [stī′ləs] *n.* A pointy tool used for writing in braille: **Nora held the *stylus* and began to write the braille alphabet.**

stylus

sub·lime [sə·blīm′] *adj.* Wonderful, awe-inspiring: **The music at the concert was *sublime*.** *syn.* majestic

sub·merge [səb·mûrj′] *v.* **sub·merged** To go underwater or cover with water: *Submerged* **icebergs are dangerous to ships.**

sulk·i·ness [sul′kē·nəs] *n.* The state of being in a gloomy or silent mood: **My little brother's *sulkiness***

became unbearable when his soccer team lost the championship game.

ten·ta·tive [ten′tə·tiv] *adj.* Hesitant; half-hearted: **The boy was *tentative* about jumping off the diving board into the deep water of the pool.**

ter·race [ter′əs] *n.* **ter·rac·es** A series of stepped parcels of land, such as used for farming: **The hilly farmland was covered in *terraces*.**

terrace

three-di·men·sion·al [thrē′də·men′shən·əl] *adj.* Having the three dimensions of height, width, and depth: **You can hold a *three-dimensional* box in your hand, but a picture of the same box is flat.**

tra·di·tion·al [trə·dish′ən·əl] *adj.* Of, handed down by, or following old customs or beliefs: **Having turkey on Thanksgiving is a *traditional* custom for us.** *syn.* inherited

tran·scribe [tran·skrīb′] *v.* **tran·scribed** To represent in a new but related way, especially with sounds or symbols: **The famous guitarist Andrés Segovia *transcribed* pieces for other instruments into music that could be played on the guitar.**

trans·mis·sion [tranz·mi′shən] *n.* A message that has been sent across a distance from one place to another: **The radio *transmission* started at the radio station and ended up in our dining room.** *syn.* message, signal

trans·par·ent [trans·pâr′ənt] *adj.* Clear or sheer enough to see through: **Mother decorated the dining room with white, nearly *transparent* curtains.**

transparent

trib·ute [trib′yōōt] *n.* **trib·utes** A present or a compliment in honor of something that someone has done: **Emily received *tributes* in the town paper for her caring volunteer work.** *syn.* praise

trot [trät] *v.* **trot·ted** To run with a jogging gait: **The horse *trotted* across the meadow.**

un·ac·com·pa·nied [un′ə·kum′pə·nēd] *adj.* Without other music: **After the orchestra left, the pianist played her *unaccompanied* piece so well that the audience cheered.** *syn.* alone

un·cer·tain·ly [un·sûrt′in·lē] *adv.* In a manner that shows a lack of confidence: **Sean answered *uncertainly* because he hadn't heard the question.** *syn.* doubtfully

un·wa·ver·ing [un·wāv′ər·ing] *adj.* Steady and unchanging: **She cast her *unwavering* gaze toward the horizon for sight of any ship.** *syn.* unfaltering

ven·dor [ven′dər] *n.* **ven·dors** A person who sells something, often out-of-doors: **After the show, the *vendors* packed up their carts and left.**

vi·o·la·tion [vī′ə·lā′shən] *n.* **vi·o·la·tions** The breaking of a law: **Exceeding the posted speed limit and driving without a license are *violations* of the traffic laws.** *syn.* infringement

vir·tue [vûr′chōō] *n.* **vir·tues** A positive character trait: **Honesty and steadfastness were among his many *virtues*.** *syn.* merit

vis·i·bil·i·ty [viz′ə·bil′ə·tē] *n.* The distance at which objects can be seen: ***Visibility* decreased as the fog grew thicker.**

wail [wāl] *v.* **wailed** To cry in grief or pain, or to make a sound such as the cry of grief or pain: **The child *wailed* when she stubbed her toe.** *syn.* weep

wa·ver [wā′vər] *v.* To become unsteady; to tremble: **Karen's voice began to *waver* as she described her lost cat.** *syn.* falter

yarn [yärn] *n.* **yarns** An exaggerated story: **The crew of the fishing boat told many *yarns* about "the ones that got away."** *syn.* tall tale

yearn [yûrn] *v.* **yearned** To feel a strong desire to do something: **After several weeks, the traveler *yearned* to return home.**

a	add	e	end	o	odd	o͞o	pool	oi	oil	th	this		a in *above*
ā	ace	ē	equal	ō	open	u	up	ou	pout	zh	vision		e in *sicken*
â	care	i	it	ô	order	û	burn	ng	ring			ə =	i in *possible*
ä	palm	ī	ice	o͝o	took	yo͞o	fuse	th	thin				o in *melon*
													u in *circus*

Index of Titles

Page numbers in color refer to biographical information.

Aesop's Fables, 366

Ahmad, Nyla, 668, 683

Ancient China, 284

Anderson, Joan, 578, 590

Anne of Green Gables, 550

Antarctica, 230

Armour, Richard, 79

Atlas in the Round, 602

Bernardo, Anilú, 440, 455

Best School Year Ever, The, 22

Boyd, Candy Dawson, 394, 406

Byars, Betsy, 162, 179

Campbell, Alastair, 602

Case of the Shining Blue Planet, The, 694

Catching the Fire: Philip Simmons, Blacksmith, 464

Cha, Dia, 522

Chinese Dynasties, The, 298

Clark, Margaret, 366

Collins, Carolyn Strom, 570

Courage, 124

Cowboys: Roundup on an American Ranch, 578

CyberSurfer, 668

Darnell Rock Reporting, 108

Dia's Story Cloth, 522

Direction, 125

Dive! My Adventures in the Deep Frontier, 628

Do-It-Yourself Project, A, 440

Earle, Sylvia A., 628, 637

Eriksson, Christina Wyss, 570

Fall Secrets, 394

Flood: Wrestling with the Mississippi, 238

Freedman, Russell, 532, 543

From the Autograph Album, 78

Frost, Robert, 478

George, Jean Craighead, 376, 387

Gipson, Fred, 186, 199

Girls Think of Everything, 416

Good Sportsmanship, 79

Grace, Catherine O'Neill, 646

Hicks, Peter, 328

I Want to Be an Astronaut, 646

In the Next Three Seconds, 684

It's Tiger Time!, 100

Johnson, Angela, 456

Kids Did It!, 408

Knots in My Yo-yo String, 66

Lauber, Patricia, 238, 253

Look Into the Past: The Greeks and the Romans, 328

Lopez, Alonzo, 125

Lowry, Lois, 134, 154

Lye, Keith, 602

Lyons, Mary E., 464, 477

Macdonald, Fiona, 262, 277

Marble Champ, The, 86

Maze, Stephanie, 646

McCurdy, Michael, 208, 229

Montgomery, Lucy Maud, 550, 569

Mora, Pat, 592

Morgan, Rowland, 684

Murray, Kirsty, 56

My Name Is San Ho, 508

My Side of the Mountain, 376

Myers, Walter Dean, 108, 123

Namioka, Lensey, 42, 55

Nicholson, Robert, 284

Nolan, Paul T., 352

Number the Stars, 134

Nye, Naomi Shihab, 124

Old Yeller, 186

Out of Darkness: The Story of Louis Braille, 532

Pettit, Jayne, 508, 520

Pint-Size Picasso, 56

Pope, Joyce, 230

Preface, 456

Puppies with a Purpose, 200

Pyramids, 306

Road Not Taken, The, 478

Robinson, Barbara, 22, 35

Seventh Grade, 488

Simon, Seymour, 694, 705

Skill of Pericles, The, 352

Some Like It Wet!, 638

Soto, Gary, 86, 98, 488, 501

Spinelli, Jerry, 66, 77

Stone Age News, The, 262

Strange Sled Race, A, 618

Summer of the Swans, The, 162

Tea Biscuits, 570

Thimmesh, Catherine, 416, 432

This Big Sky, 592

Thompson, Vivian L., 618

Trapped by the Ice!, 208

Turner, Jamie, 550

Watts, Claire, 284

What It's Like Up There, 658

Williams, A. Susan, 328

Yang the Eldest and His Odd Jobs, 42

Young, Karen Romano, 658

Acknowledgments

For permission to reprint copyrighted material, grateful acknowledgment is made to the following sources:

Arte Público Press – University of Houston: "A Do-It-Yourself Project" from *Fitting In* by Anilú Bernardo, cover illustration by Daniel Lechón. Text copyright © 1996 by Anilú Bernardo.

Candlewick Press Inc., Cambridge MA, on behalf of Walker Books Ltd., London: From *The Stone Age News* by Fiona MacDonald, cover illustration by Gino D'Achille. Text © 1998 by Fiona MacDonald; illustrations © 1998 by Walker Books Ltd.

Chelsea House Publishers, a division of Main Line Book Co.: From *Journey into Civilization: Ancient China* by Robert Nicholson and Claire Watts. Text copyright © 1994 by Two-Can Publishing Ltd.

Chicago Review Press Incorporated: "Pint-Size Picasso" from *Tough Stuff* by Kirsty Murray. Text © 2000 by Kirsty Murray.

Children's Better Health Institute, Indianapolis, IN: "It's Tiger Time!" from *Children's Digest* Magazine, September 1999. Text copyright © 1999 by Children's Better Health Institute, Benjamin Franklin Literary & Medical Society, Inc.

Children's Television Workshop, New York: "Some Like It Wet" from *Contact Kids* Magazine, July/August 1998. Text copyright 1998 by Children's Television Workshop.

Clarion Books, a Houghton Mifflin Company imprint: From *Out of Darkness: The Story of Louis Braille* by Russell Freedman, cover illustration by Kate Kiesler. Text copyright © 1997 by Russell Freedman; cover illustration © 1997 by Kate Kiesler.

Dutton Children's Books, a division of Penguin Putnam Inc.: From *My Side of the Mountain* by Jean Craighead George. Text copyright © 1959, renewed © 1988 by Jean Craighead George.

Michael Garland: Cover illustration by Michael Garland from *My Side of the Mountain* by Jean Craighead George. Published by Dutton Children's Books, a division of Penguin Putnam Inc.

Greey de Pencier Books Inc.: From *Cybersurfer* by Nyla Ahmad, Directory researched and written by Keltie Thomas, illustrated by Martha Newbigging, cover photo illustration by Bob Anderson. Text and directory compilation © 1996 by Owl Books; illustrations © 1996 by Martha Newbigging; cover photo illustration © 1996 by Bob Anderson.

Harcourt, Inc.: From *I Want To Be...An Astronaut* by Stephanie Maze. Text copyright © 1997 by Maze Productions. "Seventh Grade" and "The Marble Champ" from *Baseball in April and Other Stories* by Gary Soto. Text copyright © 1990 by Gary Soto.

HarperCollins Publishers: From *Old Yeller* by Fred Gipson, cover illustration by Carl Burger. Text and cover illustration copyright © 1956 by Fred Gipson; text and cover illustration copyright renewed. "Courage" from *Come With Me: Poems for a Journey* by Naomi Shihab Nye, illustrated by Dan Yaccarino. Text copyright © 2000 by Naomi Shihab Nye, illustrations copyright © 2000 by Dan Yaccarino. From *The Best School Year Ever* by Barbara Robinson, cover illustration by Michael Deas. Text copyright © 1994 by Barbara Robinson; cover illustration copyright © 1994 by Michael Deas. "The Case of the Shining Blue Planet" from *Einstein Anderson, Science Detective: The On-Line Spaceman and Other Cases* by Seymour Simon, cover illustration by S. D. Schindler. Text copyright © 1997 by Seymour Simon; cover illustration copyright © 1997 by S. D. Schindler.

John Hawkins & Associates, Inc.: "Good Sportsmanship" by Richard Armour. Text copyright © 1958 by Richard Armour. Published by McGraw-Hill.

Houghton Mifflin Company: From *Number the Stars* by Lois Lowry. Text and cover photograph copyright © 1989 by Lois Lowry. From *Catching the Fire: Philip Simmons, Blacksmith* by Mary E. Lyons. Text copyright © 1997 by Mary E. Lyons. From *Girls Think of Everything: Stories of Ingenious Inventions by Women* by Catherine Thimmesh, illustrated by Melissa Sweet. Text copyright © 2000 by Catherine Thimmesh; illustrations copyright © 2000 by Melissa Sweet.

International Publishers Inc.: "Direction" from *Voices from Wah'kon-Tah* by Alonzo Lopez.

The Ivy Press Limited: From *Atlas in the Round* by Keith Lye and Alastair Campbell. Copyright © 1999 by Ivy Press Ltd. and Alastair Campbell.

Kalmbach Publishing Co.: *Anne of Green Gables* by Lucy M. Montgomery, adapted by Jamie Turner from *Plays: The Drama Magazine for Young People*, March 1987. Text copyright © 1987 by Plays, Inc. This play is for reading purposes only; for permission to produce, write to Plays Magazine, 21027 Crossroads Cir., P.O. Box 1612, Waukesha, WI 53187-1612. *The Skill of Pericles* from *Folk Tale Plays Round the World* by Paul T. Nolan. Text and cover illustration copyright © 1982 by Paul T. Nolan. This play is for reading purposes only; for permission to produce, write to Plays Magazine, 21027 Crossroads Cir., P.O. Box 1612, Waukesha, WI 53187-1612.

Kids Discover: From "The Pyramids of Egypt" in *Kids Discover: Pyramids*. Text and cover © 1993 by Kids Discover. From *Kids Discover: Ancient China* (Retitled: "The Chinese Dynasties"). Text and cover © 1998 by Kids Discover.

Alfred A. Knopf Children's Books, a division of Random House, Inc.: From *Knots in My Yo-Yo String: The Autobiography of a Kid* by Jerry Spinelli, cover photograph by Penny Gentieu. Text and photographs copyright © 1998 by Jerry Spinelli; cover photograph copyright © 1998 by Penny Gentieu.

Lee & Low Books Inc., 95 Madison Avenue, New York, NY 10016: From *Dia's Story Cloth: The Hmong People's Journey of Freedom* by Dia Cha, stitched by Chue and Nhia Thao Cha. Copyright © 1996 by Denver Museum of Natural History.

Little, Brown and Company (Inc.): "The Fox and the Crow" and "The North Wind and the Sun" from *The Best of Aesop's Fables* by Margaret Clark, illustrated by Charlotte Voake. Text copyright © 1990 by Margaret Clark; illustrations copyright © 1990 by Charlotte Voake. From *Yang the Eldest and His Odd Jobs* by Lensey Namioka, illustrated by Kees de Kiefte. Text copyright © 2000 by Lensey Namioka; illustrations copyright © 2000 by Kees de Kiefte.

Lodestar Books, an affiliate of Dutton Children's Books, a division of Penguin Putnam Inc.: From *In the Next Three Seconds* by Rowland Morgan, illustrated by Rod and Kira Josey. Text copyright © 1997 by Rowland Morgan; illustrations copyright © 1997 by Rod and Kira Josey.

The Millbrook Press, Inc.: From "Antarctica" in *The Children's Atlas of Natural Wonders* by Joyce Pope. Text copyright © 1995 by Quarto Children's Books Ltd.

National Geographic Society, 1145 17th Street, N.W., Washington, DC 20036: "Keys to Success" by Laura Daily from "Kids Did It!" in *National Geographic WORLD* Magazine, August 1998. Text copyright © 1998 by National Geographic Society. From *Dive! My Adventures in the Deep Frontier* by Sylvia A. Earle. Copyright © 1999 by Sylvia A. Earle. From *Flood: Wrestling With the Mississippi* by Patricia Lauber. Text copyright © 1996 by Patricia Lauber; maps and illustrations copyright © 1996 by National Geographic Society. "Bridging Generations" by Judith E. Rinard from "Kids Did It!" in *National Geographic WORLD* Magazine, January 1999. Text copyright © 1999 by National Geographic Society. "Puppies with a Purpose" by Christina Wilsdon from *National Geographic WORLD* Magazine, March 1997. Text copyright © 1997 by National Geographic Society.

Penguin Books Canada Limited: "Tea Biscuits" and cover illustration from *The Anne of Green Gables Treasury* by Carolyn Strom Collins and Christina Wyss Eriksson. Text copyright © 1991 by Carolyn Strom Collins and Christina Wyss Eriksson; cover illustration copyright © 1991 by Pronk & Associates.

Puffin Books, a division of Penguin Putnam Inc.: Cover illustration by Lino Saffioti from *The Summer of the Swans* by Betsy Byars. Illustration copyright © 1991 by Lino Saffioti.

Quarto Children's Books Ltd.: From "Antarctica" in *The Children's Atlas of Natural Wonders* by Joyce Pope. Illustrations copyright © 1995 by Quarto Children's Books Ltd.

Random House Children's Books, a division of Random House, Inc.: From *Darnell Rock Reporting* by Walter Dean Myers, cover illustration by Mark Smollin. Text and cover illustration copyright © 1994 by Walter Dean Myers.

Marian Reiner: "From the autograph album" from *At the Crack of the Bat*, compiled by Lillian Morrison. Published by Hyperion Books for Children.

Barry Root: Cover illustration by Barry Root from *Baseball in April and Other Stories* by Gary Soto. Illustration copyright 1990 by Barry Root.

Scholastic Inc.: From *Cowboys: Roundup on an American Ranch* by Joan Anderson, photographs by George Ancona. Text copyright © 1996 by Joan Anderson; photographs copyright © 1996 by George Ancona. "Preface" from *The Other Side: Shorter Poems* by Angela Johnson. Text copyright © 1998 by Angela Johnson. Published by Orchard Books, an imprint of Scholastic Inc. "This Big Sky" from *This Big Sky* by Pat Mora, illustrated by Steve Jenkins. Text copyright © 1998 by Pat Mora, illustrations copyright © 1998 by Steve Jenkins. From *My Name Is San Ho* by Jayne Pettit. Text copyright © 1992 by Jayne Pettit.

Steck-Vaughn Company: From *Look Into the Past: The Romans* by Peter Hicks. Text copyright © 1993 by Wayland (Publishers) Ltd.; U.S. revision text copyright © 1994 by Thomson Learning. From *Look Into the Past: The Greeks* by Susan Williams. Text copyright © 1993 by Wayland (Publishers) Ltd.; U.S. revision text copyright © 1993 by Thomson Learning.

University of Hawaii Press: "A Strange Sled Race" from *Hawaiian Myths of Earth, Sea, and Sky* by Vivian L. Thompson. Text copyright © 1966 by Vivian L. Thompson.

Viking Penguin, a division of Penguin Putnam Inc.: From *Fall Secrets* by Candy Dawson Boyd, cover illustration by Jim Carroll. Text copyright © 1994 by Candy Dawson Boyd; cover illustration copyright © 1994 by Jim Carroll. From *The Summer of the Swans* by Betsy Byars. Text copyright © 1970 by Betsy Byars.

Walker and Company: From *Trapped by the Ice!* by Michael McCurdy. Copyright © 1997 by Michael McCurdy.

Karen Romano Young: Cover and text from "What It's Like Up There: An Interview With Astronaut Franklin Chang-Diaz" by Karen Romano Young from *Cricket* Magazine, October 1995. Copyright © 1995 by Karen R. Young.

Photo Credits

Key: (t)=top; (b)=bottom; (c)=center; (l)=left; (r)=right

Page 66-77, All baseball cards courtesy of Topps; 123(t), Christopher Myers; 160, AP / Wide World Photos; 161(t), Patti McConville / Dembinsky Photo Associates; 161(b), Arthur C. Smith III / Grant Heilman Photography; 236, Dan Dempster / Dembinsky Photo Associates; 237(t), Dominique Braud / Dembinsky Photo Associates; 237(b), Rafael Macia / Photo Researchers; 304, 305(t), (b), Archive Photos; 328(tr), (c), Michael Holford; 328(b), C.M. Dixon; 329, Michael Holford; 332, Michael Holford; 333, The British Museum; 333-334, The British Museum; 334, British Museum / Michael Holford; 335(t), Gerry Clyde / Michael Holford; 335(b), 336, The Mansell Collection / Time, Inc.; 337(t), 338, C.M. Dixon; 339, Robert Harding; 340-341(both), 340(bl), C.M. Dixon; 341(br), Focal Point; 342, Robert Harding; 343(t), Peter Hicks; 343(c), Robert Harding; 343(b), C.M. Dixon; 344, Peter Hicks; 345(t), The Mansell Collection / Time, Inc.; 345(b), F.H.C. Birch / Sonia Halliday; 348, Photowood / Corbis Stock Market; 349(t), Agence France Presse / Corbis; 349(b), Erich Lessing / Art Resource, Inc.; 455, Ron Kunzman; 462, Bob Talbot / Stone; 463, Pete Saloutos / Corbis Stock Market; 576, 577(t), The Granger Collection, New York; 577(b), Smithsonian American Art Museum, Washington, DC / Art Resource, Inc.; 600, Jeffrey L. Rotman / Peter Arnold, Inc.; 601, Adam G. Sylvester / Photo Researchers, Inc.; 623, Joseph Sohm / Corbis; 644, Superstock; 645(t), Culver Pictures; 645(b), Craig Schmittman / Stone.

Illustration Credits

Raul Colon, Cover Art; Cameron Clement, 4-5, 18-19; Karen Barbour, 6-7, 130-131; Raphael Lopez, 8-9, 258-259; Roger Chouinard, 10-11, 372-373; Andrew Powell, 12-13, 484-485; Chris Lensch, 14-15, 598-599; Ethan Long, 16-17, 37, 279, 481, 641, 689; Amy Young, 20-21; Tom Newson, 22-35; Polly Law, 40-41; Kees de Kiefte, 42-55; Larry Jones, 64-65; Gary Davis/Kather Lengyel, 66-77; Mike Gardner, 78-79; Terry Herman, 84-85; David Diaz, 86-99; Kathleen Newman, 106-107; James Ransome, 108-123; Dan Yaccarino, 124; Michael Luke, 125; Lise Rainville, 132-133; Russ Wilson, 134-155; Lori Lohstoeter, 162-179; Rick Allen, 184-185; David Moreno, 186-199; Val Paul Taylor, 206-207; Michael McCurdy, 208-229; Mary Ross, 260-261; Tom Boll, 282-283; Beata Szpura, 347, 389, 435, 527, 573; Gwen Connelly, 350-351; David Scott Meier, 352-365; Sean Kane, 374-375; Allen Garns, 376-387; Kelly Burke, 392-393; Floyd Cooper, 394-407; Tim Barnes, 414-415; Rick Peterson, 438-439; Karen Blessen, 440-455; Bethann Thornburgh, 486-487; Stephanie Garcia, 488-501; Elsa Myotte, 506-507; Amy Ning, 508-521; Gerard Dubois, 530-531; Glenn Harrington, 532-543; Sheila Alderidge, 548-549; Mitchell Heinze, 550-569; Leslie Wu, 618-619; Mylene Henry, 626-627; Michel Ribagliati, 666-667; Martha Newbigging, 668-683; Haydn Cornner, 692-693; Leo Espinosa, 694-705.